Using a Law Library

*A Guide for Students
and Lawyers in the
Common Law Provinces of Canada*

FOURTH EDITION

MARGARET A. BANKS

*Associate Professor and Law Librarian,
The University of Western Ontario*

1985
THE CARSWELL COMPANY LIMITED
Toronto, Canada

Canadian Cataloguing in Publication Data

Banks, Margaret A., 1928-
  Using a law library

Includes index.
Bibliography: p.
ISBN 0-459-37610-1 (bound)   0-459-37620-9 (pbk.)

1. Legal research – Canada.   2. Legal literature –
Canada.   I. Title

KE250.B37 1985   340'.07'2071   C85-098967-1

First edition, 1971
published by
The University of Western Ontario
School of Library and Information Science
London, Canada

Second edition, 1974, Third edition, 1980
published by
The Carswell Company Limited
Toronto, Canada

TO MY COLLEAGUES
IN THE LAW LIBRARY
THE UNIVERSITY OF
WESTERN ONTARIO

Foreword

It was with great pleasure that I accepted the opportunity to contribute a few words to the fourth edition of *Using a Law Library*. Glancing through the text, I was startled by the many changes that have taken place in the ten years since I last was making an attempt to explain the complexities of using a law library to novices. The fact that this fourth edition is more than six times the size of the original, written in 1969, reflects the phenomenal growth and increasing maturity of legal research in Canada over the past twenty years.

Students and researchers are greatly aided by having such a comprehensive guide to Canadian legal sources. We are fortunate that Margaret Banks did more than many of us who, in the late fifties and early sixties, bemoaned not only the dearth of good tools for accessing legal materials in Canada, but also the lack of a clear explanation of how to use what little was available. Each law librarian worked independently to prepare written and verbal explanations of how to access legal materials, and of the operations of his or her particular law library. Margaret, as we know, rose to the occasion and her first 1969 volume, intended for local use at the Faculty of Law, University of Western Ontario, has now grown into a standard text in use throughout the nation.

Readers will be pleased to have the chapter on Automated Legal Research, which appeared for the first time in the third edition. It provides an interesting historical note on the beginnings of automated legal research twenty-five years ago, and includes an up-to-date overview of the data bases now available, together with an introduction outlining what researchers may expect and how best to approach an automated search.

The fourth edition of *Using a Law Library* is the culmination of the author's effort, experience and know-how, consolidated during many years of using and assisting others to use a Canadian law library. I commend this important information resource to the reader, and trust that future readers will benefit from many subsequent editions.

Marianne Scott

Preface to the Fourth Edition

This book has had a rather chequered history. The idea of writing it came to me after several years of conducting tours for small groups of law students during their first week in law school. Though the tours were of some help, I realized that it was impossible for students, coming to a law library for the first time, to absorb all at once detailed information about the various types of law books and their use. Surely it would be better to put something in writing which students could read at their own speed and refer to from time to time as they needed specific information.

The first version of *Using a Law Library* was written in 1969 and included that year in a collection of *Supplementary Materials on Legal Method and Analysis,* edited by Professor G.J. Brandt for use in the first year legal method course in the Faculty of Law at The University of Western Ontario. Though designed primarily for first year law students, it also proved helpful to other persons learning to use a law library. It was used in courses on law librarianship by the School of Library and Information Science of The University of Western Ontario and by the Library School of the University of Toronto. I found it helpful in training new members of the law library staff at Western; so, I believe, did other law librarians who requested copies.

In view of the interest shown in the guide, it seemed worthwhile to revise and update it. At Professor Brandt's suggestion, I completely rewrote the chapter on legal encyclopedias and digests, adopting a more practical approach. The inclusion of copies of pages from the various types of law books to assist in explaining their use was also his idea. This revised and illustrated version of *Using a Law Library,* the first printed one, was published by the School of Library and Information Science of The University of Western Ontario in 1971. Unfortunately, the reproduction of sample pages from law books had presented problems; many of these illustrations were illegible and it was decided, a few weeks after the appearance of the book, to withdraw it and issue a replacement edition. Because of the difficulties encountered with the illustrations and the expense involved in including them, the replacement edition, also dated 1971, contains no illustrations. Though sometimes referred to as a revised or second edition, this is misleading as the text is almost the same as that of the illustrated one. Changes made in the text were mainly those necessitated by the removal of the illustrations. There is no indication on the cover, title page, or elsewhere that it is other than the first published edition.

The published version of *Using a Law Library* was generally well received. It was used in legal method courses in several Canadian law schools and in law clerk programs in some community colleges. Lawyers, as well as law students, apparently found it helpful, for sales to individual practitioners and to law firm libraries were encouraging. By the spring of 1973, it appeared that the book would soon be out of print. As the School of Library and

Information Science is permitted to publish only works which are not commercially feasible and the sale of *Using a Law Library* suggested that it did not belong to this category, I was advised to try to find a commercial publisher if I planned to prepare a new edition. The Carswell Company Limited agreed to publish it, and the second edition appeared in the summer of 1974.

A third edition was published by Carswell in 1980. Its main new feature was a chapter on automated legal research, suggested and financially supported by the Canadian Law Information Council (CLIC).

Between the dates of publication of the third and fourth editions of this book, there took place an event of considerable significance in Canadian history. This was the passage of the Canada Act 1982, a United Kingdom statute enacting for Canada the Constitution Act, 1982. The principal purposes of this legislation were to define and patriate the "Constitution of Canada" with the addition of an amending formula and an entrenched Charter of Rights and Freedoms. This development has led me to add to the chapter on statutes (now called "Statutes and Related Publications") a new section on the Constitution of Canada. Other references to the constitutional changes of 1982 and their effects occur elsewhere in the book.

This also seemed an appropriate time to make a change in the arrangement of the book that several people had suggested. In the first three editions, I dealt with English law reports and English statutes before discussing their Canadian counterparts. My reasoning was that much of Canadian law had its origins in England and historically it made sense to deal with the English first. However, since English cases and statutes play a less important role in the study and practice of law in Canada today than they did in the past, there is much to be said for dealing first with Canadian materials. Therefore, in Chapter 2 (Law Reports) and Chapter 3 (Statutes and Related Publications), I have reversed the order, dealing first with Canadian and then with English materials.

As with the second and third editions, much revision has been needed to bring the fourth up to date. I am grateful to the many people who answered my inquiries about various publications. In case I inadvertently omit anyone, I will not try to list all of them. However, I would like to say a special word of thanks to Jacques Prémont, Joelle Desjardins and Daniel Allaire of the Bibliothèque de l'Assemblée nationale and Guy Tanguay, law librarian at the Université de Sherbrooke, who, during my visit to Quebec City and Sherbrooke in September 1984, helped me to identify and understand numerous Quebec publications, some of which our law library at Western had had difficulty in obtaining.

During the summer of 1984, I had the help of a research assistant, Ian Shewan, with a long-term project on the Constitution of Canada on which I am working. Although his research did not relate directly to *Using a Law Library,* some of it has been helpful to me in adding information on the Constitution to this edition of the book. I am grateful to him for his thorough and painstaking work as well as to Western's Faculty of Law, which authorized his appointment, and the Law Foundation of Ontario, which provided the funds.

Since the third edition of this book was printed in 1980, QL Systems Limited has greatly expanded its coverage of law reports, statutes, and regulations. This, combined with the need to update computer searches, has led to many changes in the chapter on automated legal research. I am grateful to Carswell for providing funds to enable me to do extensive searching. I also want to thank Walter Zimmerman, Barry Taylor, and Judy Heinzen of The D.B. Weldon Library, The University of Western Ontario, for their help with my computer searches.

Members of the law library staff of The University of Western Ontario have again helped in many ways. In particular I wish to acknowledge my debt to Marianne Welch, with whom I have discussed various aspects of the revision and who has checked many references for me. Her knowledge of legal materials and expertise as a reference librarian make her advice especially valuable. As with earlier editions, Linda Aitkins has typed with care and efficiency everything that had to be typed. Eleanor Jones and Laurena Storey have given valued assistance, especially with proofreading. To all of them I extend my thanks.

For permission to reproduce pages from their publications, I wish to thank the following:

Butterworths, London (*The Digest, Halsbury's Laws of England, Halsbury's Statutes of England*)

Butterworths, Toronto (*Supreme Court of Canada Reports Service*)

Canada Law Book Limited (*All-Canada Weekly Summaries, Dominion Law Reports* and their finding aids, *Ontario Statute Citator,* and, on behalf of Western Legal Publications, *British Columbia Decisions – Civil Cases*)

CCH Canadian Limited (*Dominion Report Service*)

Her Majesty's Stationery Office, Publishing Division (Copyright), London (*Public General Acts* and *Index to the Statutes in Force*)

Maritime Law Book Ltd. (*New Brunswick Reports,* Second Series and *Nova Scotia Reports,* Second Series)

Queen's Printer, Manitoba (*Revised Statutes of Manitoba 1970* and *Continuing Consolidation Statutes of Manitoba*)

Queen's Printer for Ontario (*The Ontario Gazette, Revised Regulations of Ontario, 1980, Statutes of Ontario, 1983*)

Supply and Services Canada (*Revised Statutes of Canada, 1970*)

Finally, I would like to thank Barbro Stalbecker, Managing Editor, Carswell Legal Publications, and Jeff Mitchell, Senior Technical Editor at Carswell, for their work in preparing the fourth edition for publication. With a book that runs to multiple editions, there is always a challenge for both author and publisher to make each new one a little better than its predecessor. I was especially pleased with the editorial work on the third edition, and I appreciate Barbro and Jeff's efforts to make further improvements in the fourth. I am also grateful for Carswell's permission to add, as new appendices, amended versions of its internal "List of Preferred Citations" and the "Table of Periodical Abbreviations" in the *Index to Canadian Legal Literature.* Although similar lists are available in other publications, it is hoped that readers of

Using a Law Library will find it convenient to have this information at hand instead of having to look elsewhere for it.

Margaret A. Banks

London, Ontario
13 June 1985

Table of Contents

1

Introduction

It is reasonable to assume that students entering law school have had some experience in using a library; yet many of them, during their early weeks of legal study, express surprise and dismay at the differences between a law library and other types of libraries. They encounter books unlike those they have encountered in the past; they are faced with strange citations which they do not understand, and although some of them have seen volumes of statutes before, they have probably never heard of a statute citator or seen a law report, a legal encyclopedia or a digest.

The way in which books are arranged may also appear somewhat odd. Whereas most university libraries in Canada follow the Library of Congress classification scheme and many public libraries use the Dewey Decimal system, there is no uniform classification for law libraries. The provisions for law in the Dewey Decimal system are generally considered inadequate, and the Library of Congress has yet to provide a complete classification for law. So far it has published only the following schedules: Law [General] (K); Law of the United Kingdom and Ireland (KD); Law of Canada (KE), Law of the United States (KF), and Law of Germany (KK-KKC). Several other classification schemes for law books have been worked out in England and the United States, but none has found general acceptance.

The traditional way of arranging law books was very simple. Statutes, law reports, legal encyclopedias and digests were arranged by country, with some sort of chronological or alphabetical arrangement within each group. Journals were shelved alphabetically by title without regard to jurisdiction, and treatises (*i.e.* text books, monographs, *etc.*) were arranged alphabetically by author. Some law libraries in Canada and elsewhere still follow this general plan, but the alphabetical arrangement of treatises has been found unsatisfactory for law school libraries, where a subject arrangement is likely to be preferred. The first Library of Congress law schedule to appear was that for United States law (KF) in 1967. Because of the need for a subject classification of treatises, some Canadian Law school libraries began in 1968 to adapt the Library of Congress KF schedule for United States federal law to include as well law books from all common law jurisdictions within the Commonwealth.

It is not the intention of Canadian law school libraries using the adaptation to reclassify Commonwealth common law materials as the Library of Congress schedules for Commonwealth countries appear. Thus, they are not using the KD and KE schedules for treatises. It is generally felt that the jurisdictional approach of the Library of Congress Class K is unsatisfactory for the classification of treatises in Canadian law school libraries. Faculty and students in these schools generally prefer to have all common law treatises on a specific subject, such as contracts, torts, or criminal law, together, rather than having Canadian treatises on the subject in one place, English in another, Australian or American in another, and so on. However, a Canadian law library that is not using the KF adaptation may decide, if it begins a classification project, to follow without change the Library of Congress schedules – K, KD, KE, KF, *etc.*

The Library of Congress KF schedule provides for the classification not only of treatises, but also of law reports, statutes, journals, and other types of legal material. Canadian law school libraries participating in the adapted scheme are using different approaches regarding these other materials. Some are classifying them; others are not.[1]

If you want to learn to use your law library efficiently, a good first step is to find out how the books are arranged. Some sort of chart or list will probably be displayed in a prominent place in the library, and if there is anything you do not understand, a member of the library staff will no doubt be able to help you. It is also useful to browse around the library, becoming familiar with the location of books that will be used frequently. If you are a first year student, you should know especially where Canadian and English law reports, statutes, legal encyclopedias and digests are shelved; you should also find out whether journals are arranged alphabetically by title or if there is a division by country. With regard to treatises, it is probable that your library has adopted a subject classification, and you should find out what system is used.

---

1   The participating libraries use the regular Library of Congress schedules for non-legal materials, such as books on economics, political science, sociology, *etc.* At first, they used the Los Angeles County Law Library classification scheme for jurisprudence and foreign and comparative law, but this material has now been reclassified into the Library of Congress K classification for Law [General]. Some of the participating libraries classify journals in K 1-30. For the most part, this follows the traditional arrangement, as journals are classed in alphabetical order by title regardless of subject matter or jurisdiction. Some are classifying Canadian and English law reports, statutes, and related materials where a jurisdictional approach is desirable in KE and KD respectively. The law libraries at the University of Manitoba, York University, and the University of Windsor were the only ones to participate initially when work on the KF adaptation began in 1968, but many others – not only in law schools – have now adopted it.

The next step, after acquiring a general idea of the library's arrangement, is to learn something of the books you will be using. A good place to begin is with the primary source books of the law,[2] of which there are two main types – law reports, which contain case law or the law based on judicial decision, and statutes, which record the law made by the legislators.[3]

---

2   A Canadian treatise on legal writing and research defines primary sources of the law as "only those materials which state the law and which are formulated by those constitutionally vested with authority to declare law." See J. A. Yogis and I. M. Christie, *Legal Writing and Research Manual,* 2nd ed. (Toronto: Butterworths, 1974), p. 3.

3   There are other primary sources of the law as, for example, a country's constitution. In the third edition of this book, published in 1980, it was stated that "Britain has no written constitution and the constitution of Canada, in so far as it is written, consists of certain statutes of the British and Canadian Parliaments." Because certain "Acts and orders" have been given a special constitutional status by s. 52(2) of the Constitution Act, 1982 (being Schedule B to the Canada Act 1982, c. 11 U.K.), a new section dealing with the "Constitution of Canada" is being inserted into Chapter 3 of this edition of *Using a Law Library.* Regulations passed under the authority of statutes are also primary sources of the law. They too are dealt with in Chapter 3.

2

Law Reports

1. GENERAL

It is a principle of the common law that cases that are alike should be decided in the same way. Thus, it is important to have written reports of earlier cases to assist the courts in deciding new ones. The rule varies from one jurisdiction to another as to whether a court is bound by its own earlier decisions, but it is bound by decisions of higher courts in the same hierarchy. Even a decision that is not binding may influence a court's judgment. Thus, law reports play an important part in the legal process.

Generally, not all cases are included in the law reports; a routine case that raises no significant point of law is likely to be omitted.[1] Nor do the reports attempt to give a complete record of the litigation. The essential facts must be stated somewhere, but the arguments of counsel are seldom reported in full and are frequently completely omitted. The most important part of the report is the decision of the court and the reasons for it. Though there are variations in practice, it is customary to include at the beginning of the report of a case several catchwords, which indicate its subject matter, and a brief summary of the case, known as a headnote. Students should be made aware at the outset of their legal education that reading a headnote is no substitute for reading the complete report of a case.

It is important to lawyers and judges that reports of cases appear as soon as possible after they are decided by the courts. Therefore, most of them are first published in unbound form or advance sheets, as they are sometimes called. These unbound parts may appear as frequently as weekly; others are issued monthly or perhaps eight or ten times a year. The cases are arranged more or less chronologically and a list of the names of those reported is included in each part; usually an index to subject matter is also provided. The unbound parts or advance sheets are later replaced by a bound volume with a cumulative table of cases covering the whole volume. (Often there is also a table of cases cited – that is, referred to – in the volume; if you are checking to see whether a case is reported in a particular volume you must be sure that you are looking at the "cases reported" and not the "cases cited" – it is sometimes called the "cases judicially considered" – table.) There may be just one bound volume a year, but if advance sheets are published weekly, there are likely to be several volumes for each year. For some series of law reports, cumulative tables of cases and subject indexes covering several volumes in the set are

---

1   However, there is a trend towards reporting more and more cases decided by the superior courts. It is now the practice to report in the *Supreme Court Reports* all cases decided by the Supreme Court of Canada. See note 4 on p. 8.

published from time to time. In Canada in recent years, services that provide digests of cases very soon after they are decided and before they are reported have become available. More will be said of them in Chapter 4.

In addition to current sets of law reports your library will have many older ones that have ceased publication. Something will be said of specific series of law reports, both current and non-current, in the pages that follow.

2. CANADIAN LAW REPORTS

(a) Court System

There are both federal and provincial courts in Canada, but they do not constitute two separate systems as in the United States.[2] For instance, criminal law and divorce law are made by the Parliament of Canada, but they are administered mainly in provincial courts, because the Constitution Act, 1867, section 92(14), gives to each province the right to make laws in relation to "The Administration of Justice in the Province, including the Constitution, Maintenance, and Organization of Provincial Courts, both of Civil and of Criminal Jurisdiction . . . ." Thus, each province has its own hierarchy of courts, the structure and names varying somewhat from one province to another.

Section 101 of the Constitution Act, 1867, provides that Parliament may establish a general Court of Appeal for Canada and any additional courts considered necessary for the better administration of the laws of Canada. Under this section, two federal courts were established by an Act of 1875 – one a general Court of Appeal, called the Supreme Court of Canada, the other the Exchequer Court of Canada, which had jurisdiction in cases involving claims against the Crown. Later, the Exchequer Court was also given jurisdiction in certain other matters, such as copyrights, patents, and inter-provincial railways. (Other federal courts are the Court Martial Appeal Court, established in 1959, and the Tax Court of Canada – successor to the Tax Review Board – established in 1983.)

An important change in the federal court system took place on June 1, 1971 when the Federal Court Act of 1970 came into force.[3] It not only changed

---

2   It is not quite accurate to say that in the United States there is no overlapping between federal and state courts. On page 35 of the second edition of this book, I wrote that there are no appeals from state courts to the Supreme Court of the United States. Commenting on this statement in a letter dated January 9, 1975, Richard F. Breen, Jr., then Associate Law Librarian at the University of Maine, pointed out that in certain circumstances appeals are available. Under Title 28 of the U.S. Code §1257, final judgments of the highest court of a state may sometimes be reviewed by the Supreme Court when the validity of a treaty or of a federal or state statute is in question.

3   On page 15 of the second edition of this book, the in force date was given incorrectly as August 1, 1972. This resulted from the author's relying on a misleading, though technically correct, statement in the *Canada Statute Citator*. Under the title of the Act, the *Citator* gives its citation as "R.S.C. 1970, Chap. 10 (2nd Supp.)" and follows this with the statement "proclaimed in force August 1, 1972." The latter date is the one on which Acts in the second supplement to the *Revised Statutes of Canada, 1970* were collectively proclaimed in force. The Federal Court Act in its original form, S.C. 1970-71-72, c. 1, had, however, been proclaimed in force on June 1, 1971. See *Canada Gazette*, vol. 105, p. 1317.

the name of the Exchequer Court of Canada to the Federal Court of Canada, it also altered its structure and revised and extended its jurisdiction. The Federal Court, unlike the Exchequer Court, consists of two divisions – an Appeal Division (which may be referred to as the Court of Appeal or the Federal Court of Appeal) and a Trial Division. The principal area of new jurisdiction relates to cases arising out of decisions and orders of federal boards, commissions, and other tribunals. The right to hear and determine such cases is divided between the Trial and Appeal Divisions of the Federal Court. In some matters, the Federal Court (like the Exchequer Court before it) and the provincial courts have concurrent jurisdiction.

Appeals are allowed in some matters from the Federal Court of Appeal to the Supreme Court of Canada, which also hears appeals from the highest courts in the provinces.

(b) The Supreme Court Reports and The Federal (formerly Exchequer Court) Reports

Official reports of cases decided by the two federal courts from the time of their establishment in 1875 to the end of 1922 are contained in two series called the *Reports of the Supreme Court of Canada* and the *Reports of the Exchequer Court of Canada*. They are usually referred to as the *Supreme Court Reports* and the *Exchequer Court Reports* (the spines of the volumes are generally labelled in this way) and are cited S.C.R. and Ex. C.R. From 1923 to 1969 the two series are combined in a set called the *Canada Law Reports*; however, they are bound in separate volumes, one labelled *Canada Law Reports: Supreme Court,* the other *Canada Law Reports: Exchequer Court.* Actually, they are seldom referred to as the *Canada Law Reports* ; the letters S.C.R. and Ex. C.R. continue to be used in citing the volumes from 1923 to 1969, and it is customary to speak of them as the *Supreme Court Reports* and the *Exchequer Court Reports.* Before 1923, the volumes in each series are numbered consecutively, there being 64 volumes of the *Supreme Court Reports* and 21 volumes of *Exchequer Court Reports.* From 1923 to 1969, there is no consecutive numbering of the volumes, and citation is by year.

In 1970, a new format was adopted for both series. The name *Canada Law Reports* was dropped, and cases began to be printed in both languages, appearing in parallel columns on each page. (The format for the 1970 Exchequer Court volume is slightly different.) Before that date, cases were reported in the language in which the judgment was delivered, and no translation was provided. The new English titles of the series are *Canada: Supreme Court Reports* and until the change in the name of the court, *Canada: Exchequer Court Reports.* As in earlier years, they are cited S.C.R. and Ex. C.R. When the Federal Court Act came into force in 1971, the name of the Exchequer series was changed to *Canada: Federal Court Reports* (cited F.C.). When the last Exchequer Court volume was bound, there was a change back to the old title,

Canada Law Reports: Exchequer Court. Although the volume is dated 1970, it reports cases to the end of May 1971.

The firm of Butterworth & Co. (Canada) Ltd. in Toronto now publishes a *Supreme Court of Canada Reports Service,* which provides, in loose-leaf form, a cumulative index and case table covering all reports of Supreme Court cases since the establishment of the Court. If you know the name of a case, but not its date, you can look it up in the cumulative table of cases. (If you do not find the case listed in the main table, which covers the years 1876 to 1968, or if you know that the case is of more recent date, look it up in the supplemental case table, which precedes the main table. If the case is too recent to be included in the supplemental case table, you may find it in the "current service" volume.) The table gives you both the date and a page reference to the index. Find the reference in the index and it will give you the complete case citation. See Illustrations 1 and 2, which use the case of *Lehnert v. Stein* as an example. Sometimes (before 1975) a Supreme Court case was not reported in the *Supreme Court Reports,* but might be published in the *Dominion Law Reports.* This explains the D.L.R. citations in Illustration 2.[4] If you are not looking for a specific case, but rather for cases on a particular subject, your approach will be through the index in the *Supreme Court of Canada Reports Service,* rather than through the table of cases.

(c) The National Reporter

Maritime Law Book Ltd., which publishes several series of provincial reports that will be mentioned later, has also, since 1974, been publishing a federal series known as the *National Reporter.* Its original intent was to include, in two volumes a year, reports of all judgments of the Supreme Court of Canada and of the Federal Court of Appeal, together with selected judgments of the Trial Division of the Federal Court. Soon, however, this policy was somewhat changed; beginning with volume 2, the selected judgments of the Trial Division were dropped. From volume 4 on, the disposition of all motions for leave to appeal to the Supreme Court of Canada is also reported.[5] The number of volumes published each year varies, but is now always greater than the two originally planned and published in 1974. There are six in 1979, four in 1980, five in 1981, six in 1982, and five in 1983.

Although there is naturally much duplication between the *National Reporter* and the two official series (being official, the latter are preferred for

---

4   At the front of volumes of the *Supreme Court Reports,* there used to be published a list of unreported judgments. This list no longer appears because, since the beginning of 1975, all Supreme Court cases are reported in the official series. The change in reporting policy coincided with the passage at the end of 1974 of an amendment to the Supreme Court Act that ended the automatic right to appeal if the amount involved was more than $10,000. If the *Supreme Court of Canada Reports Service* now cites a series other than the official one, it is because a Supreme Court case was reported there first.

5   This is a change related to the amendment to the Supreme Court Act already mentioned in footnote 4, above.

ILLUSTRATION 1
Supreme Court of Canada Reports Service
(Volume 3)

CASE TABLE   1407
See also Supplemental Case Table on page 1251

Lefrançois, Morel v. [1906]...417, 532, 646

Lefrançois, R. v. [1908]...531, 609, 916, 1044

Lefrançois, Russell v. [1883]...99, 577, 740, 1199, 1205

Lefrenière, Dansereau v. [1926]... 314

Légaré, Ville de Chicoutimi v. [1897] ...37, 218, 311, 313, 340, 574

Legault v. Beauharnois [1930]...753

Legault v. Desève [1920]...550, 721, 1160

Leger v. Fournier [1887]...19, 202, 788, 1180

Leger, Fournier v. [1890]...51

Leger v. Poirier [1944]...896, 1206

Leger v. R. [1910]...380, 773, 1059

Leger, World Marine and General Insce. Co. Ltd. v. [1952]...594

Leggat v. Marsh [1899]...281, 855

Legislative Competence, Reference As to [1940]...809

Legislative Jurisdiction over Hours of Labour, *Reference Re* [1925]...§12

Le Havre Creamery Co. Ltd., Proctor & Gamble Co. of Canada Ltd. v. [1943]...1155

Lehnert v. Stein [1963]...1183

Leibovitch, Developpement Central Ville de l'Isle v. [1967]...208

Leighton v. Hall [1907]...97

Lemarre v. Prud'homme [1928]...631

Lemay, Gagnon v. [1918]...301, 991, 1179

Lemay v. Hardy [1922]...11, 544, 646, 873

Lemay, McRae v. [1890]...104

Lemay v. R. [1952]...88

Lemcke v. Newlove [1927]...3, 429, 845

Lemieux, Paradis v. [1955]...434

Lemieux v. R. [1967]...368

Lemire v. Nicol [1924]...609, 869, 1210

Lemiré v. Pelchat [1957]...983

Lemire, R. v. [1965]...370

Lemoine v. City of Montreal [1894] ...252

Lemoine, Trudel v. [1925]...240

Lennox Estate, *In re* [1949]...1204

Lennoxville, Village of v. County of Compton [1898]...6, 330, 334, 341, 346, 347

Lenoir v. Ritchie [1879]...60, 132, 385, 529, 642, 672, 791, 809, 870, 906, 1069

Leonard, Royal Electric Co. v. [1894] 16, 311, 1093

Leonard & Sons v. Kremer [1913]... 980A

Leonard & Sons, Williams v. [1896] ...73, 74, 197, 526, 855, 921

Leonard v. Wharton [1921]...668

Leong Ba Chai, R. v. [1954]...272, 551, 688

Lepage, C.N.R. v. [1927]...765

Le Page, Stewart v. [1916]...869, 1056, 1210

Lepine, University Hospital Bd. v. [1966]...777

Lepitre, Citizens' Light and Power Co. v. [1898]...746

Lerner, R. v. [1963].. 366

Le Roi Mining Co., McKelvey v. [1902]...90, 462, 748, 1115

Le Roi, No. 2., Hastings v. [1903]... 232, 1035, 1090

Le Roi, No. 2, Hosking v. [1903]... 232, 702, 1035

Leroux v. McIntosh [1915]...208, 217, 922, 955, 957, 1010, 1096, 1097

Leroux v. Parish of Ste. Justine [1906] ...88

Lesage, City of Montreal v. [1923]... 209, 755

Les Curé et Marguilliers de St. Gabriel de Brandon, Sarrazin v. [1935] ...147

Les Ecclésiastiques de St. Sulpice de Montreal v. City of Montreal [1889] ...64, 1084

Le Séminaire de Quebec v. La Cité de Lévis [1928]...113

Leslie v. Canadian Credit Corp. Ltd. [1928]...62

Leslie v. Canadian Press [1956]...626

Lespérance v. Goné [1905]...319, 446, 532, 820, 965

Les Petroles Inc. v. Tremblay [1963] ...651

Lessard v. Hull Electric Co. [1947]... 640, 766

Le Sueur, Morang & Co. v. [1911]... 134, 299, 678, 690

Letain v. Conwest Exploration Co. Ltd. [1961]...802

Letain, Conwest Exploration Co. Ltd. v. [1964]...309

Létang, Ottawa Electric Ry. Co. v. [1924]...619

Letellier, Kearney v. [1897]...878, 980A

ILLUSTRATION 2
Supreme Court of Canada Reports Service
(Volume 3)

VOLENTI NON FIT INJURIA

Application of maxim—Horses frightened by blasting operations—
Driver injured in endeavour to stop horses. *Town of Prescott* v.
Connell (1893), 22 S.C.R. 147.

Application of maxim—Employee killed during shunting operations—
Findings of jury—Deceased voluntarily accepted risks—Death due
to negligence in shunting. *Canada Atlantic Railway Co.* v. *Hurd-
man* (1895), 25 S.C.R. 205.

Application of maxim—Person visiting premises for own purposes and
without notice to occupants—Unsafe premises. *Rogers* v. *Toronto
Public School Board* (1897), 27 S.C.R. 448.

Application of maxim—Volunteer drowned—Attempt to prevent de-
struction of bridge by flood—Owner of bridge and volunteer both
to blame—Damages divided. *Price* v. *Roy* (1899), 29 S.C.R. 494.

Application of maxim—Injury to workman—Engaged in dangerous
occupation—Duty of giving necessary instructions and warning
delegated by employer to official—Incompetent foreman employed.
Canadian Northern Railway Co. v. *Anderson* (1911), 45 S.C.R.
355.

Application of maxim—Injured man acting under order which he was
bound to obey. *Grand Trunk Pacific Railway Co.* v. *Brulott* (1911),
46 S.C.R. 629.

Application of maxim—Employee injured trying to board moving train
—Regulation of Intercolonial Railway forbidding persons to get
aboard while train in motion. *Turgeon* v. *The King* (1915), 51
S.C.R. 588.

Application of maxim—To employee. *General Trust of Canada* v. *St.
Jacques*, [1931] 3 D.L.R. 654.

Application of maxim—Requires more than knowledge of danger.
Montreal Stockyards Co. v. *Paulin*, [1941] 3 D.L.R. 646.

Application of maxim—Drunken passenger injured in car driven by
drunken driver—Both setting out sober intending to drink. *Miller*
v. *Decker*, [1957] S.C.R. 624.

Application of maxim—Injury to passenger in motor vehicle driven by
intoxicated driver—Acceptance of physical, but not of legal, risk.
Lehnert v. *Stein*, [1963] S.C.R. 38.

Defence of—Action for personal injuries—Necessity for finding by
jury that person injured voluntarily incurred risk. *Canada Foundry
Co.* v. *Mitchell* (1904), 35 S.C.R. 452.

Defence of—Necessity to prove risk voluntarily incurred with full knowledge of danger of employment. *Montreal Park and Island Railway Co.* v. *McDougall* (1905), 36 S.C.R. 1.

Defence of—Whether necessary to submit to jury. *Grand Trunk Pacific
Railway Co.* v. *Brulott* (1911), 46 S.C.R. 629.

Defence of—Whether necessary to plead. *Grand Trunk Pacific Railway
Co.* v. *Brulott* (1911), 46 S.C.R. 629.

citation in court), using the *National Reporter* has certain advantages. Not only does it tend to report cases much more quickly than the official series, but it also provides better indexing. Its system is similar to that developed for American case law by the West Publishing Co. in St. Paul, Minnesota, in its well-established National Reporter System and key number digest system.

The system adopted by Maritime Law Book Ltd. assigns a name and topic number to each issue or topic in a report of a case. For instance, Criminal Law, Topic 1, is assigned to cases that define the words "criminal law"; Criminal Law, Topic 30, to those that discuss the topic "*mens rea*" and the meaning of the words "knowingly" or "wilfully". A key word index directs the reader to the appropriate topic and number. The system is designed to assist lawyers to locate quickly different cases dealing with the same issue. Consolidated digest and index volumes are published for every ten volumes of the series. There is now also a consolidated index of cases and motions reported in the first forty-seven volumes. The name "index" is perhaps misleading; it is not a subject index, but rather a consolidated table of cases. It does, however, contain "see" references, which are helpful in locating specific cases.

Maritime Law Book Ltd. uses the same indexing and digesting system for all of its report series. Illustrations of the system's use will be given when describing other Maritime Law Book series.

(d) The Dominion Law Reports

This set reports cases decided by both federal and provincial courts. Thus, many of the cases reported in the *Supreme Court Reports* and the *Exchequer* or *Federal Court Reports* also appear here. Numerous cases decided by the superior courts of the provinces are also included.

The *Dominion Law Reports* began publication in 1912; after volume 70 (1922), they ceased to be numbered consecutively and are cited by year to the end of 1955. Consecutive numbering of volumes resumed when the second series began in 1956; it was completed with volume 70 at the end of 1968. The third series began publication in 1969 and ended with volume 150 early in 1984. The fourth series began in 1984. As in the second and third series, volumes in the fourth series are being numbered consecutively. Illustrations 3 to 7 indicate these changes in numbering and citation. As the reports are published weekly, they run to several volumes a year. From 1979 to date, the number has varied from nine to fifteen.

The publisher of the *Dominion Law Reports,* Canada Law Book Ltd. in Toronto, issues a cumulative table of cases and a very useful annotation service. The purpose of the latter is to indicate the disposition of all appeals including applications for leave to appeal, and to show whether a case has been judicially considered in any subsequent reported case in any jurisdiction in Canada. It is vital for lawyers and judges to have ready access to this information, so that they will not cite as current law a decision that has either been reversed by a higher court or overruled, that is, held by a higher court in a

ILLUSTRATION 3

tort, but a claim (strictly limited in amount) for compensa-   Alta.
tion for the accident. The statute, therefore, does not make   App. Div.
the negligence of the fellow servant not justifiable by the
employer. There is no question in this case of criminal
liability.

For the above reasons, their Lordships will humbly advise
His Majesty that this appeal fails and should be dismissed
with costs.

Appeal dismissed.

BEGERT v. PARRY.

*Alberta Supreme Court, Appellate Division, Stuart, Beck and
Hyndman, JJ.A. November 11, 1922.*

New trial (§ II—6a)—Granting non-suit—Trial Judge in error
as to inference from evidence adduced—Sale of Goods
Ordinance C.O., 1915 (Alta.), ch. 39.

Where an Appellate Court is of opinion that the proper inference from the defendant's conduct and all the circumstances of
the case is that the parties intended the property in goods sold
to pass when the goods were shipped, and that the trial Judge
was in error in finding upon the evidence as far as it went that
the property had not passed, and in non-suiting the plaintiff
because he had not sued for damages for non-acceptance, the
Court will order a new trial.

APPEAL by plaintiff from the trial judgment granting a
non-suit in an action for the price of goods sold and delivered. New trial ordered.

I. B. Howatt, K.C., and *B. D. Howatt,* for appellant.
P. E. Graham, for respondent.

The judgment of the Court was delivered by

STUART, J.A.:—Plaintiff owned some baled hay piled on
his farm. Defendant came and bought all this specific pile
of hay so baled at $18 a ton. Plaintiff agreed to haul the
hay to Bentley and there weigh it on the town scales and
then deliver it to the railway company for shipment according to orders which defendant was to leave with the railway
company's agent. Nothing at all was said about the time
or manner of payment. Plaintiff hauled the hay, had it
weighed as agreed and shipped it as instructed. Then he
drew a draft on the defendant for the price, and attached
the bills of lading to it with instructions to the bank to
deliver the bills of lading on payment of the draft. By some
means, the defendant got access to the cars and, apparently,
found some defects in the hay, and refused to pay the draft.
Plaintiff sued for the price of goods sold and delivered.

At the close of the plaintiff's evidence, defendant asked

ILLUSTRATION 4

718   DOMINION LAW REPORTS. [[1955] 3 D.L.R.

concerning custody should there be any change in circumstances (*vide Willoughby* v. *Willoughby*, [1951] P. 184) and also concerning access should there be any difficulty.

I would also allow the wife the costs of the appeal and the interlocutory application to this Court.

Appeal allowed.

ZWICKER v. LEVY

Nova Scotia Supreme Court, Ilsley C.J.   June 6, 1955.

Mortgage I E, II—Mortgage on its face in defendant's favour—Assertion by plaintiffs of interest therein—Defendant's admission of plaintiffs' interest coupled with assertion of priority of own interest—Denial of priority by plaintiffs—Burden on plaintiffs—Failure to show interest greater than defendant admits.

ACTIONS for declarations as to plaintiffs' interests in a mortgage in favour of defendant.

E. F. Cragg, for plaintiffs.

C. R. Coughlan, Q.C., for defendant.

ILSLEY C.J.:—These two actions were by consent tried together. The plaintiff, William H. S. Zwicker, is a real estate agent doing business, not very actively, at Mahone Bay. The other plaintiff is his wife. The defendant was at all material times a solicitor practising in Lunenburg County.

By mortgage dated March 21, 1951, Georgie Mfg. Co. Ltd. mortgaged certain lands in Mahone Bay to the defendant in the sum of $14,000. This mortgage has been foreclosed. The defendant bought in the lands at Sheriff's sale and still has them and has secured a deficiency judgment against Georgie Mfg. Co. Ltd. for $8,494.58.

The plaintiffs claim declarations that the defendant held the mortgage and now holds the lands therein described and the deficiency judgment in trust for the plaintiffs and the defendant in the proportions of 65/140s to the plaintiff William H. S. Zwicker, 50/140s to the defendant and 25/140s to the plaintiff Mabel S. B. Zwicker without priority one over the other.

The defendant admits, as set out in the statements of claim, that he holds the lands and the deficiency judgment as trustee for himself and the two plaintiffs, but claims that he is preferred to the extent of $5,000 plus interest, taxes, insurance premiums and monies paid to the Workmen's Compensation Board in Nova Scotia and taxed costs. This was the position taken by the defendant at the trial and if it is the correct posi-

ILLUSTRATION 5

AAROE AND AAROE v. SEYMOUR et al.

Ontario Court of Appeal, Laidlaw, Gibson and Schroeder JJ.A.
April 3, 1957.

Covenants & Conditions III — Vendor & Purchaser I D — Short
Forms deed of conveyance containing usual covenants for
title — Covenant for quiet possession free of encumbrances
—Covenant that grantor had done no act to encumber—
Previous grant to municipality of sewer easement across
land — Purchaser's right to damages — Subsidence of house
owing to construction of sewer—

A landowner gave a sewer easement to a municipality across
land which he subsequently sold to purchasers under a Short
Forms Conveyance which contained covenants for (1) the right
to convey; (2) quiet possession free of encumbrances; and that
(3) the grantor had done no act to encumber the land. A house
erected on the land by the purchasers subsided because of a
sewer constructed by the municipality. *Held*, on appeal, the
grantor was liable under his covenant that he had done no act
to encumber the land, and on the pleadings and proceedings at
trial it was clear that this covenant was in issue in the action.
It was unnecessary to determine if the covenant for quiet possession free from encumbrance was a covenant for title or whether
it was applicable only to future acts and damages subsequent to
conveyance. Even if this be so, however, the existence of the
sewer was a continuing encumbrance and the subsequent col-
lapse of the house was a disturbance in fact of the purchaser's
possession.

While damages for breach of covenant for quiet possession are
measured on a different basis than for breach of a covenant that
there had been no act to encumber the land, the award in this
case should stand. The amount properly represented the de-
preciated market value of the land as damages for breach of
the latter covenant, and while the evidence established greater
damages under the first-mentioned covenant than what were
awarded, the lesser amount reflected that the purchasers had
some knowledge of the easement.

APPEAL from a judgment of LeBel J., 6 D.L.R. (2d) 100,
awarding damages to purchasers for breach of covenant in a
deed of conveyance. Affirmed.

W. B. Williston, Q.C., and *J. D. Taylor*, for appellants.
B. Grossberg, Q.C., for respondents.

The judgment of the Court was delivered by

LAIDLAW J.A. (orally) :—This is an appeal by the defendant
Brisson from a judgment pronounced by LeBel J. on July
31, 1956 [6 D.L.R. (2d) 100], after trial without a jury at St.
Catharines, and whereby the plaintiff was awarded damages in
the amount of $300 and costs on the Supreme Court scale.

The appellant Brisson was the owner of certain lands situate
in the City of St. Catharines. Several plans of subdivisions
have been registered against those lands and, under date of

ILLUSTRATION 6

accused added nothing which would preclude us from holding that the verdict would necessarily have been the same if this incident had not taken place.

For these reasons, we are all of the view that this appeal should be dismissed.

Appeal dismissed.

ALL-CANADIAN PEOPLES FINANCE LTD. v. MARCJAN

British Columbia Supreme Court, Gould, J.   *January 30, 1970.*

Consumer protection — Unconscionable transactions — Mortgagor of realty experienced real estate agent — Whether cost of borrowing excessive — Whether Court should reverse transaction — Consumer Protection Act (B.C.), s. 17.

The Courts are not empowered to relieve a man of the burden of a contract he has made while under no pressure and with his eyes open. Therefore, when an experienced real estate agent, as mortgagor, entered into three related short-term mortgages with effective annual rates varying from 74% to 60% depending upon when the loan was repaid, the Court could not say that the cost of borrowing was excessive under s. 17 of the *Consumer Protection Act*, 1967 (B.C.), c. 14. The mortgagor made no real effort to seek the best market but had entered into the transaction as part of a fast move in and out of the property market.

However, when the mortgagor sought a discharge of one of the mortgages because he had entered into a contract to sell the property, and the mortgagee refused to discharge that mortgage unless the remaining mortgages were rewritten with an additional bonus, it could not be said that the mortgagor had entered the subsequent rewritten mortgage transactions without pressure and with his eyes open. The second mortgage transaction should therefore be revised by the Court.

[*Miller et al. v. Lavoie et al.* (1966), 60 D.L.R. (2d) 495, 63 W.W.R. 359, refd to]

ACTION by the mortgagee on two mortgages of realty.

Niel M. Fleishman, for plaintiff.
J. Wood and *Wayne Powell,* for defendant.

GOULD, J.:— The plaintiff sues on the covenant of two first mortgages on realty, alternatively for foreclosure and the usual ancillary remedies. The defence is that the terms of each of the mortgages are such that ". . . the cost of borrowing is excessive and that the transaction is harsh and unconscionable . . ." (*Consumer Protection Act,* 1967 (B.C.), c. 14, s. 17). The defendant asks that the transaction be revised as provided for in s. 17 of the Act referred to above. The writ was issued February 20, 1968. On March 27, 1968, the

ILLUSTRATION 7

574   DOMINION LAW REPORTS   3 D.L.R. (4th)

For those reasons I would dismiss the appeal.

NEMETZ C.J.B.C. (orally):—I agree.

SEATON J.A. (orally):—I agree.

NEMETZ C.J.B.C. (orally):—The appeal is dismissed.

Appeal dismissed.

REGINA v. STARANCHUK

Saskatchewan Court of Appeal, Hall, Cameron and Tallis JJ.A.
September 26, 1983.

Constitutional law — Charter of Rights — Self-incrimination — Bankruptcy Act requiring bankrupt to provide sworn statement of affairs and to attend before official receiver for examination under oath as to conduct, causes of bankruptcy and disposition of property — Offence to refuse or neglect to answer fully and truthfully questions put to bankrupt at any examination — Whether statement of affairs and bankrupt's testimony before official receiver admissible against him on subsequent charges for such offence — Canadian Charter of Rights and Freedoms, s. 13 — Bankruptcy Act, R.S.C. 1970, c. B-3, ss. 129, 132, 169.

Section 13 of the *Canadian Charter of Rights and Freedoms* which provides that "a witness who testifies in any proceedings has the right not to have any incriminating evidence so given used to incriminate that witness in any other proceedings, except in a prosecution for perjury or for the giving of contradictory evidence" does not prevent the Crown from introducing a sworn statement of affairs and the transcript of an examination before the official receiver by a bankrupt on the bankrupt's trial of charges contrary to s. 169 of the *Bankruptcy Act*, R.S.C. 1970, c. B-3, for refusing to answer fully and truthfully in such statement of affairs and at the examination. A distinction must be drawn between those occasions where a person in the course of providing evidence under oath is required, when answering truthfully, to disclose the commission by him, previously, of an offence (in which event, generally speaking, that evidence cannot subsequently be used against him) and those occasions where a person makes false statements while under oath as the result of which he is charged with giving false evidence. In the latter case, as in charges under s. 169 of the *Bankruptcy Act*, the very essence of the offence and its *actus reus* is the giving of the false testimony. Further, even if on the occasions of the taking of his statements and evidence in the course of the bankruptcy proceedings it could be said that the accused bankrupt gave incriminating evidence within the meaning of s. 13, that section is of no application because the accused's allegedly false evidence forms the very substance of the offence with which he is then charged.

Statutes referred to

Bankruptcy Act, R.S.C. 1970, c. B-3, ss. 129, 132, 169
Canadian Charter of Rights and Freedoms, s. 13

EDITORIAL NOTE: The ruling of Grotsky J. which formed the basis for an appeal by the Crown is reported at 3 C.C.C. (3d) 138, [1983] 2 W.W.R. 145, 45 C.B.R. (N.S.) 200, 4 C.R.R. 243.

APPEAL by the Crown from a judgment of Grotsky J., acquitting the accused on charges contrary to s. 169 of the *Bankruptcy Act* (Can.).

later case to have been wrongly decided.[6] A permanent bound Consolidated Table of Cases covers the entire second series (1955 to 1968 inclusive). A temporary volume, which is updated and replaced annually, annotates cases reported in the second series and provides a cumulative table of cases and an annotation service to the third series. The completion of the third series and the commencement of the fourth will no doubt lead to the preparation of a permanent consolidated table of cases contained in the former and to the addition of annotations to the latter in the volume that is replaced annually.

To show you how to use the table of cases and the annotation service, let us again take the case of *Lehnert v. Stein* as an example. Suppose you have the *Supreme Court Reports* citation, but the volume is not available at the moment, so you decide to see whether the case is included in the *Dominion Law Reports.* Look it up in the Consolidated Table of Cases to the second series; you will find it listed on page 138 (see Illustration 8). From this you will learn that it is reported in volume 36 of the second series at page 159. You find the report of the case (see Illustration 9), read it, and decide it is relevant to your problem. As it is a judgment of the Supreme Court of Canada, decided after the abolition of appeals to the Judicial Committee of the Privy Council, it cannot have been appealed to a higher court.[7] However, it may have been judicially considered. To see if it has, you find the volume and page number – 36 D.L.R. (2d) 159 – in the annotations service (see Illustration 10). It tells you that the case has been applied, referred to, followed, considered and distinguished on numerous occasions. If a full citation is not given, the reference is to the *Dominion Law Reports.* Notice that under page 159 some references are to the *Dominion Law Reports,* but there are also several to other series. *Lehnert v. Stein* is a good example of a case that is frequently cited in later cases. In the 1970 edition of the annotation service, only twelve judicial considerations were listed; by 1973 the number had increased to twenty-nine; by 1979, to thirty-nine, and by 1984 to forty-nine.

(e) Provincial and Regional Law Reports

In the British North American provinces before Confederation, there were several different series of law reports. The courts in existence in the provinces at Confederation continued to function afterwards, and the same is true of some of the series of reports. For instance, the *Upper Canada Queen's Bench, Common Pleas,* and *Chancery Reports* (three separate sets) continued until shortly after the passage of the Judicature Act of 1881. In general, this Act did to the Ontario court system what the English Judicature Act of 1873 had done to the courts in England. It set up a Supreme Court of Judicature for

---

6   Pages vi-vii of the *Dominion Law Reports Annotation Service* contain a helpful list of abbreviations and definitions regarding appeals and judicial considerations. This volume is replaced annually, but each new one to date has included this list on the same pages in the "Introduction".

7   In 1949 the judgment of the Supreme Court of Canada was declared to be final. Criminal appeals had been abolished earlier – in 1933.

ILLUSTRATION 8
Consolidated Table of Cases

Leb - Lem DOMINION LAW REPORTS (SECOND SERIES)

Lebrun v. High-Low Foods Ltd.
(B.C.S.C.) 69/433
(B.C.S.C.) 70/718
Lecavalier, Gagnon v. *See* Gagnon
Lechman, Franco v. *See* Franco
Lechter, M.N.R. v. *See* M.N.R.
Leckie, M.N.R. v. *See* M.N.R.
LeClair and Dugas, Dugas v. *See* Dugas
Leclair and Leclair, Mitts v. *See* Mitts
Leclerc v. Leclerc (Man.Q.B.) 45/770
Leddy v. Sask. Gov't Ins. Office (Sask.C.A.) 45/445
Leduc, Re (Sask.C.A.) 25/680
Lee, Re (Ont.C.A.) 1/48
Lee, Re (Ont.H.C.J.) 24/363
Lee v. R.M. of Arthur
(Man.Q.B.) 46/448
(Man.C.A.) 52/263
Lee v. Darling Co. of Canada Ltd. (Ont.H.C.J.) 19/268
Lee and School Dist. of Green Valley No. 1358, Re (Man.Q.B.) 44/561
Leew, Altilio v.; Rewenko, Third Party *See* Altilio
Lefeaux, Re (B.C.S.C.) 37/235
Lefebvre v. Dowdall and McLean (Ont.H.C.J.) 46/426
Lefebvre, MacDonald v. *See* MacDonald
Lefolii v. Gouzenko (S.C.C.) 70/337
Lefolii, Gouzenko v. *See* Gouzenko
Leforte, R. v. *See* R.
Leftrook and Mid-West Truck Lines Ltd., Keystone Fisheries Ltd. v. *See* Keystone
Legal & Gen'l Assce Society Ltd., B.C. Hardwood & Millwork Ltd. v. *See* B.C. Hardwood
Legal & General Assce Society Ltd., Sturk v. *See* Sturk
Legal Professions Act, Re; Ex p. Tayler (B.C.S.C.) 18/369
Legault v. Compagnie d'Assce Generale de Commerce (Que.Q.B.) .. 65/230
Leger v. Royal Ins. Co. Ltd.; Leger v. Home Ins. Co. (N.B.S.C.) 70/344
Legere v. Caissie and Caissie (N.B.C.A.) 15/424
Leggett v. Taylor (B.C.S.C.) 50/516
Legion Oils Ltd. v. Barron (Alta.S.C.) 2/505
Lehnert v. Stein (S.C.C.) 36/159
Lehnert, Stein v. *See* Stein
Leier v. Shumiatcher and Luboff (Sask.C.A.) 32/584
Leighton v. Leighton and Swanson (B.C.C.A.) 41/166
Leighton v. Muir (N.S.S.C.) 31/383
Leighton v. Muir and Windsor Supply Co. Ltd. (N.S.S.C.) 34/332
Le Goff Re, Dheilly v. Trudel (Man.C.A.) 36/434
Lelievre, Association Internationale des Debardeurs, Loc. 375 v. *See* Association
Lelievre, R. v. *See* R.
LeMaster, Wenger v. *See* Wenger
Lemieux v. Twp. of Hallam (Ont.C.A.) 67/54
Lemieux v. The Queen (S.C.C.) 63/75
Lemieux and Lemieux v. Bedard, Re (Ont.H.C.J.) 6/49
Lemire, The Queen v. *See* Queen

138

ILLUSTRATION 9
Dominion Law Reports (Second Series), Volume 36

defendant against a third party which the defendant might enforce before he was damnified, and whether he was damnified or not was not a right to "relief over" within the Ontario Rules.

It is therefore held that the right to indemnity which the defendant, Godfrey, claims in the third party proceedings issued by him cannot be the subject of third party proceedings and accordingly the motion should be allowed, allowing the appeal from the order of the Master and directing that the third party proceedings should be struck out and setting aside the service thereof.

As against the third parties, Carrier Corp. and Carrier Engineering Ltd., the costs of the motion to the applicants and to Trion Inc. and Trion (Can.) Ltd. should be paid by the defendant, Godfrey.

Appeal allowed; application granted.

LEHNERT v. STEIN

Supreme Court of Canada, Kerwin, C.J.C., Cartwright, Martland, Judson and Ritchie, JJ. November 30, 1962.

Negligence — Volenti non fit injuria — Passenger aware that driver under influence of liquor — Contributory negligence.

Where a driver of a motor vehicle invokes the maxim *volenti non fit injuria* as a defence to an action for damages for injuries caused by his negligence to a passenger, the burden lies upon the defendant of proving that the plaintiff, expressly or by necessary implication, agreed to exempt him from liability for any damage suffered by the plaintiff occasioned by that negligence. It is not enough that the plaintiff was apprehensive that the defendant would drive negligently and that an accident might result but nevertheless decided to take a chance and go with him and thereby incur the risk of physical injury. To constitute the defence of *volenti non fit injuria* there must be an express or implied bargain between the parties whereby the plaintiff gave up his right of action for negligence, and where no such waiver of action has been made or can be inferred, the conduct of the plaintiff in going with the defendant and taking the chance of defendant's negligence only amounts to contributory negligence on his part.

In the instant case the plaintiff, a young woman, accepted defendant's invitation to drive out to a suburban night club. They remained there two hours during which time plaintiff had one drink while defendant was served with and consumed ten ounces of whiskey and became "noisy". Although plaintiff initially thought of going home by taxi, she eventually decided to return with the defendant as a result of his urging, and because she lacked the resolution to refuse him even though she was aware that he was under the influence of liquor to such an

ILLUSTRATION 10
D.L.R. Annotation Service   (Second and Third Series) 1984

ANNOTATIONS TO SECOND SERIES   36 D.L.R. (2d)

VOLUME 35 – Cont'd

Page 666
Refd to 41 (2d) 395
Apld 62 W.W.R. 735
Apld 14 (3d) 564
Refd to [1974] 6 W.W.R. 36

Page 672
Distd 39 (2d) 327
Refd to 46 (3d) 380
Apld 8 N.S.R. (2d) 672
Distd [1965-69] 1 N.S.R. 137
Apld [1965-69] N.S.R. 96

Page 680
Refd to [1972] 4 W.W.R. 1
Consd 112 (3d) 443

Page 684
Apld 59 (2d) 6
Aprvd [1972] 3 O.R. 712
Disaprvd 43 (3d) 393

Page 688
Apld 73 W.W.R. 424
Apld 12 R.F.L. 48

Page 690
Refd to 30 R.F.L. (2d) 277

Page 694
Folld 49 W.W.R. 375
Apld 49 W.W.R. 671
Apld 47 (2d) 374
Distd 51 (2d) 72
Refd to 54 (2d) 516
Apld 56 (2d) 193
Apld 57 (2d) 295
Apld 17 (3d) 302
Folld [1971] 5 W.W.R. 251
Refd to 42 (3d) 91
Apld [1975] 1 W.W.R. 222
Folld 84 (3d) 710
Refd to 87 (3d) 33
Refd to 87 (3d) 144
Distd 102 (3d) 117
Refd to 102 (3d) 288
Folld 102 (3d) 547
Distd 112 (3d) 443
Refd to 126 (3d) 364
Refd to 140 (3d) 685

Page 723
Apld 37 (2d) 409

Page 732
Apld 37 (2d) 409
Not folld 28 (3d) 730
Consd 103 (3d) 556

Page 742
Refd to 10 (3d) 384

Page 746
Refd to 142 (3d) 678

Page 775
Apld 75 W.W.R. 624
Refd to 4 C.P.C. 107

VOLUME 36

Page 4
Refd to 48 (2d) 581
Folld 55 (2d) 481
Apld 69 (2d) 629
Apld 16 (3d) 433
Folld [1975] W.W.D. 120
Not folld 69 (3d) 695

Page 17
Folld 21 R.F.L. 175

Page 45
Distd 48 (2d) 608
Distd [1965] 1 C.C.C. 343
Disaprvd 16 (3d) 609
Distd 22 C.R.N.S. 1
Distd 60 (3d) 690
Not folld 89 (3d) 731
Refd to 50 C.C.C. (2d) 564
Overd 117 (3d) 517

Page 51
Apld 42 W.W.R. 509
Refd to [1973] 5 W.W.R. 170

Page 58
Revd 39 (2d) 365
Refd to 44 (2d) 306
Distd 1 N. & P.E.I.R. 223
Apld 11 N.S.R. (2d) 665
Folld 13 N.S.R. (2d) 151

Page 81
Folld 39 (2d) 536
Refd to 57 (2d) 141

Page 97
Revd 42 (2d) 492
Refd to [1964] C.T.C. 219

Page 112
Refd to 2 L.C.R. 206
Refd to [1973] 4 W.W.R. 219

Page 122
Affd 39 (2d) 244

Page 126
Affd 50 (2d) 69
Refd to 6 L.C.R. 189
Refd to 9 L.C.R. 174
Refd to 146 (3d) 533

Page 138
Distd 66 W.W.R. 228

Page 145
Refd to 43 (3d) 222
Distd 66 (3d) 72
Refd to 133 (3d) 284
Apld 139 (3d) 136

Page 156
Not folld 58 (2d) 711
Folld [1966] 1 O.R. 1

Page 159
Apld 39 (2d) 761
Refd to 40 (2d) 444
Folld 43 (2d) 341
Apld 44 (2d) 629
Refd to 52 (2d) 272
Refd to 54 (2d) 133
Apld 58 (2d) 662
Refd to 63 (2d) 450
Refd to 52 M.P.R. 218
Refd to 68 (2d) 261
Refd to 68 (2d) 658
Refd to 5 (3d) 561
Refd to 73 W.W.R. 608
Apld 74 W.W.R. 594
Apld 75 W.W.R. 107
Apld 19 (3d) 589
Refd to [1971] 5 W.W.R. 212
Refd to 3 N.B.R. (2d) 603
Refd to 22 (3d) 386
Refd to 24 (3d) 26
Refd to 24 (3d) 561
Refd to 25 (3d) 218
Distd 25 (3d) 249
Refd to 25 (3d) 354
Refd to 26 (3d) 201
Refd to 28 (3d) 553
Refd to 29 (3d) 673
Refd to [1972] 1 W.W.R. 180
Apld 3 N. & P.E.I.R. 119

ILLUSTRATION 10 (cont'd.)

36 D.L.R. (2d)

D.L.R. ANNOTATION SERVICE

VOLUME 36—Cont'd

Refd to 35 (3d) 486
Refd to 6 N.B.R. (2d) 587
Refd to 42 (3d) 688
Distd [1974] 1 F.C. 465
Refd to 6 N. & P.E.I.R. 253
Refd to 12 N.S.R. (2d) 646
Refd to 7 N. & P.E.I.R. 402
Distd 12 N.B.R. (2d) 221
Consd 13 N.B.R. (2d) 679
Refd to 81 (3d) 302
Folld 94 (3d) 505
Folld 96 (3d) 611
Consd [1980] 3 W.W.R. 544
Consd [1980] 6 W.W.R. 298
Refd to 112 (3d) 106
Consd 28 N. & P.E.I.R. 113
Folld 131 (3d) 585
Refd to 35 O.R. (2d) 55
Apld 36 N. & P.E.I.R. 17
Folld 145 (3d) 247

Page 166

Revd in part 40 (2d) 243
Apld 43 W.W.R. 367
Consd 41 (2d) 652
Refd to 43 (2d) 461
Refd to 10 (3d) 47
Consd [1974] 4 W.W.R. 205
Refd to 2 Alta.L.R. (2d) 369
Refd to 119 (3d) 173
Distd [1981] 1 W.W.R. 552
Consd [1983] 6 W.W.R. 565

Page 177

Refd to 40 (2d) 120
Refd to 59 (2d) 45
Refd to 23 R.F.L. (2d) 448
Refd to [1981] 6 W.W.R. 385
Refd to 31 R.F.L. (2d) 135

Page 184

Refd to [1972] 3 W.W.R. 23

Page 197

Folld 2 N.S.R. (2d) 697
Not folld 82 (3d) 553

Page 199

Apld 67 (2d) 135
Distd 6 (3d) 120
Consd 70 W.W.R. 561
Apld 25 (3d) 692
Distd 52 (3d) 161
Refd to 76 (3d) 332

Page 218

Apld 10 (3d) 339

Page 223

Refd to 51 W.W.R. 757
Refd to 5 C.R. N.S. 395,
Refd to [1969] 2 O.R. 819
Consd 37 C.C.C. (2d) 352

Page 228

Refd to 52 (2d) 374
Refd to 54 (2d) 364

Page 245

Folld 52 (2d) 189
Apld 57 (2d) 188
Distd 60 (2d) 680
Consd 65 (2d) 346
Refd to 11 (3d) 722
Refd to 20 (3d) 496
Folld 3 N.B.R. (2d) 640
Refd to [1965-69] 4 N.S.R. 85
Refd to 54 (3d) 329
Refd to 64 (3d) 293
Refd to 78 (3d) 206
Refd to 96 (3d) 94
Refd to 105 (3d) 270
Refd to 116 (3d) 71
Refd to 121 (3d) 435
Not apld 127 (3d) 740
Folld 132 (3d) 126

Page 266

Affd 41 (2d) 125
Refd to 39 (2d) 408

Page 277

Refd to 9 N.S.R. (2d) 80

Page 289

Folld 2 L.C.R. 56
Refd to 5 L.C.R. 154
Refd to 27 L.C.R. 240

Page 295

Supplementary reasons 39 (2d) 227
Varied 41 (2d) 98
App Ct Affd 49 (2d) 1

Page 309

Apld [1970] 2 C.C.C. 273
Refd to 24 C.C.C. (2d) 36
Refd to 59 C.P.R. (2d) 99

Page 313

Refd to 53 W.W.R. 439

Refd to 53 (2d) 284
Apld [1983] 6 W.W.R. 380

Page 319

Refd to 31 N. & P.E.I.R. 90

Page 328

Distd 46 (2d) 12
Aprvd 64 (2d) 538
Refd to 1 (3d) 309
Apld 68 W.W.R. 440
Refd to 15 (3d) 112
Folld 3 R.F.L. 118
Apld [1972] 1 W.W.R. 759
Refd to 5 R.F.L. 12
Refd to 10 R.F.L. 285
Apld 10 R.F.L. 336
Apld 12 R.F.L. 100
Discd 48 (3d) 527
Refd to 17 R.F.L. 170
Refd to 18 R.F.L. 196
Refd to [1977] 5 W.W.R. 572
Refd to 26 R.F.L. 393
Refd to 27 R.F.L. 159
Apld 28 R.F.L. 230
Consd 30 R.F.L. 25
Apld 2 R.F.L. (2d) 220
Refd to 89 (3d) 660
Refd to [1979] 1 W.W.R. 496
Folld 5 R.F.L. (2d) 315
Apld 7 R.F.L. (2d) 152
Consd 25 R.F.L. (2d) 420
Consd 29 R.F.L. (2d) 113
Refd to 32 R.F.L. (2d) 38

Page 363

Apld [1974] 6 W.W.R. 564

Page 388

Refd to 40 O.R. (2d) 463

Page 391

Consd 1 (3d) 132
Refd to [1979] 2 S.C.R. 298
Refd to 99 (3d) 251

Page 398

Folld 8 C.C.C. (2d) 546
Refd to [1972] 4 W.W.R. 262
Refd to 19 C.C.C. (2d) 210
Refd to 37 C.C.C. (2d) 554
Apld [1978] 4 W.W.R. 124
Refd to 103 (3d) 193
Consd [1980] 5 W.W.R. 289
Folld [1982] 6 W.W.R. 517
Refd to 141 (3d) 138

Ontario, consisting of a Court of Appeal and a High Court of Justice, the latter being made up of Queen's Bench, Common Pleas, and Chancery Divisions (an Exchequer Division was added in 1903, but six years later the Divisions of Ontario's High Court were abolished.)[8] In 1882, the *Ontario Reports* replaced the *Upper Canada Queen's Bench, Common Pleas,* and *Chancery Reports.*[9] Cases decided by the Court of Appeal were until 1900 reported in a series known as the *Ontario Appeal Reports,* which had begun publication in 1876. From 1901 on they are included in the *Ontario Law Reports,* the successor to the *Ontario Reports.* The name, *Ontario Law Reports,* was used from 1901 to 1931. In the latter year the name was changed back to *Ontario Reports.* This name continues to be used and in 1974 a second series began.

Volumes in the current series are being numbered consecutively, altering the practice followed from 1931 to 1973. Therefore, citation is by volume number rather than by year. Thus, whereas the third volume for 1973 is cited [1973] 3 O.R., the first volume of the current series is cited 1 O.R. (2d). As is customary when volumes are numbered consecutively throughout a series, the date of the decision may be included in the citation in round brackets after the name of the case and before the volume number. A two-volume Consolidated Index to volumes 1 to 40 of the second series has recently been published.[10]

The *Ontario Weekly Notes,* 1909-62, which published notes of judgments of the Ontario courts, were incorporated into the *Ontario Reports* in 1963.

In 1984, Maritime Law Book Ltd. began to publish *Ontario Appeal Cases,* "a series of law reports for the publishing of judgments of the Ontario Court of Appeal and the Ontario Divisional Court." Obviously, there is considerable duplication between this series and the *Ontario Reports,* although the coverage of the two is by no means identical. Both include cases decided by the Court of Appeal and the Divisional Court (a division of the High Court that, since its establishment in 1972, hears certain types of appeals). However, Maritime Law Book, in announcing the commencement of the new series, claimed that only 35 per cent of the judgments of the Ontario Court of Appeal were being published in the *Ontario Reports* and that *Ontario Appeal Cases* will report all of them. The *Ontario Reports,* in addition to reporting appeal cases, publish decisions of the High Court (that is, the trial division or branch of the Supreme Court of Ontario) and occasional cases from other Ontario courts, such as county and surrogate courts. (Under the Courts of Justice Act, 1984, the county courts and certain other courts are being amalgamated to form a new District Court of Ontario.)

---

8   For further details regarding changes to the English court system, see pp. 41-42.
9   Volume 1 (1882) of the *Ontario Reports* includes only cases decided by the Queen's Bench and Chancery Divisions of the High Court. Reports of cases decided by the Common Pleas Division are incorporated into volume 2 (1882-83).
10   This index, "consolidated under the authority of the Law Society of Upper Canada," was published by Butterworths in 1984. This may seem odd because Canada Law Book publishes the *Ontario Reports,* also authorized by the Law Society. However, for a short period in 1982-83 (2d series, v. 34 to 41) the *Ontario Reports* were published by Butterworths.

A good way to become familiar with the various series of provincial reports, both before and after Confederation, is to look at the lists under each Canadian province in volume 3 of Sweet and Maxwell's *Legal Bibliography of the British Commonwealth*. (The lists go up only to 1955, so you cannot depend on them for changes that have taken place or new series that have begun since that date.) You will probably find, at least occasionally, that you want to refer to a case in an early series of reports, especially in your own province.

In the present century, at least until the late 1960's, there was a trend away from publication of separate reports for each province. From 1905 to 1916, the *Western Law Reporter* was published and in 1912, another series, the *Western Weekly Reports,* published by The Carswell Company Ltd., began reporting cases from November, 1911. Both these sets contained reports of cases decided by the courts of Manitoba, Saskatchewan, Alberta, British Columbia, and the Yukon Territory. The *Western Law Reporter* also included cases determined by the Supreme Court of Canada on appeal from the western provinces. The advent of these publications did not at once lead the law societies of the western provinces to stop publishing reports. Indeed, Saskatchewan and Alberta, which achieved provincial status in 1905, the year the *Western Law Reporter* appeared, began to publish their own law reports in 1907 and 1909 respectively. The *Saskatchewan Law Reports* continued until 1931, the *Alberta Law Reports* to 1933, the *British Columbia Reports* to 1947, and the *Manitoba Reports* to 1963.

The first ten volumes of the *Western Weekly Reports* were numbered consecutively. Then from 1917 to the end of 1950, they were cited by year. In 1951, a new series began in which volumes were again numbered consecutively. This new series ended with volume 75 at the close of 1970. Beginning in 1971, citation is once more by year.

In 1924, a *Synoptic Digest of Cases* reported in the *Western Weekly Reports* was published, covering cases from its inception to the end of 1923. This is a comprehensive digest of over 7500 cases reported in the 31 volumes covered, classified and sub-classified under traditional subject headings. Less ambitious, but nevertheless very useful, is the *Western Weekly Reports Table of Cases* covering all cases from the first volume (1911-12) of the first series to (1961-62) 36 W.W.R. inclusive (144 volumes in all). This volume was published in 1962. In 1972, an *Index to Volumes 1 to 75* was published, covering the years 1951 to 1970. There is now also an Index covering the volumes of the current series from 1971 to 1980 inclusive, and a Cumulative Index from 1981 on is published annually. The contents of these index volumes have gradually become more comprehensive. The 1971-80 Index contains a table of cases reported, an index to subject matter, and tables of statutes and of words and phrases judicially considered, whereas the current Cumulative Index lists the following:

Cases Reported
Digest of Cases
Cases Considered

Statutes Considered
Rules Considered
Regulations Considered
Forms Considered
Tariffs Considered
Authorities Considered
Words and Phrases Considered
The Canadian Abridgment (2d) Research Guide (by classification number)

This latter type of indexing is used in other Carswell report series, notably its topical law reports.

The coming into force of most of the provisions of the Canadian Charter of Rights and Freedoms in 1982[11] led Carswell to add a new feature to the *Western Weekly Reports.* Because of the large number of cases arising under the Charter, it has been possible, in this series, to provide full-text reporting of only a few of them. However, at the front of the weekly parts of *Western Weekly Reports* appears the *Western Charter Digest,* which digests Charter cases originating in the Western provinces. The *Western Charter Digest* is not included in the bound volumes of *Western Weekly Reports,* but is published annually in a separate volume, the first being *Western Charter Digest 1983.*

Late in 1976, The Carswell Company Ltd. and Maritime Law Book Ltd. each began to publish a separate series of Alberta reports. The Maritime series is called *Alberta Reports;* the Carswell series, *Alberta Law Reports,* Second Series (to distinguish it from the earlier series of *Alberta Law Reports,* also published by Carswell). A note at the front of each volume of *Alberta Reports* states that the series contains all judgments of the Alberta Court of Appeal, selected judgments from other Alberta courts, and judgments of the Supreme Court of Canada in cases originating in Alberta. The *Alberta Law Reports,* Second Series, are said to contain "Reports of Selected Cases from the Courts of Alberta and Appeals". Obviously, there is some duplication between these two series, and between them and the *Western Weekly Reports.* However, the two series devoted exclusively to Alberta appear, as would be expected, to give better coverage to cases decided by the courts of that province.[12]

In addition to the *Alberta Law Reports,* Second Series, Carswell now publishes a similar series for another western province. Called *British Columbia Law Reports,* it contains, according to its title pages, "Reports of Selected Cases from the Courts of British Columbia and Appeals".

---

11   Section 15 – the "equality rights" section – came into force on April 17, 1985. See s. 32(2) of the Charter. Section 23(1)(a) dealing with minority language educational rights is to come into force in Quebec by proclamation, but such a proclamation will not be issued until authorized by the legislative assembly or government of Quebec. This provision is easily overlooked, being contained in s. 59 of the Constitution Act, 1982, which is outside the Charter.

12   For a comparison of the early paper parts of the two Alberta series, see Gail Starr, *Review of Alberta Reports* (Fredericton: Maritime Law Book Ltd., 1976-   ) and *Alberta Law Reports,* 2d series (Toronto: Carswell Co. Ltd. 1976-   ), *Canadian Association of Law Libraries Newsletter* (hereafter cited *CALL Newsletter*) 1976-1977 (Nov.-Feb.), pp. 65-68.

The decision to publish its two new series of western reports led Carswell, at the beginning of 1977, to discontinue its shortlived *Western Weekly Digests*. They had been instituted in 1975 "as a preliminary step in dealing with the increasing number of judgments handed down by the Courts in Western Canada".[13] The ultimate goal was to provide increased full judgment coverage. As it was felt that this had been largely realized by the introduction of the two new provincial series, the digest service was discontinued.

In 1979, Maritime Law Book Ltd. began to publish two new series for the other two western provinces, *Manitoba Reports*, Second Series, and *Saskatchewan Reports*.

The *Northwest Territories Reports*, a new Carswell series, began to appear in 1983. The inauguration of this series, published under the authority of the Law Society of the Northwest Territories, which was created in 1978 under legislation similar to that of the provinces, is an indication of the growing maturity of the legal and judicial systems of the Northwest Territories.

For the maritime provinces, a series similar to the *Western Law Reporter* was published between 1906 and 1914. Entitled the *Eastern Law Reporter*, it contained reports of cases from New Brunswick, Nova Scotia, and Prince Edward Island. Some of the early volumes also included Quebec cases of general interest, while the later volumes contained a selection of decisions of the Supreme and Exchequer Courts of Canada and the Judicial Committee of the Privy Council in cases arising in the maritime provinces. Nova Scotia and New Brunswick continued to publish their own reports during this period. Prince Edward Island had no regular series of law reports; collections of cases had been published but the latest date covered was 1882. In 1929, the *Nova Scotia Reports* and the *New Brunswick Reports* were replaced by the *Maritime Provinces Reports*, which contained cases from New Brunswick, Nova Scotia, and Prince Edward Island and were sponsored by the law societies of the provinces concerned. From 1949, when Newfoundland became Canada's tenth province, cases decided by its courts were included in the *Maritime Provinces Reports*. The last few volumes of the set also report cases in the Supreme Court of Canada, on appeal from courts of the maritime provinces.

When the *Maritime Provinces Reports* ceased publication with volume 53 (1967-68) it appeared that the *Dominion Law Reports* and the various sets of subject reports would be the only sources for reports of cases from these provinces. However, there began in 1969 a second series of *New Brunswick Reports* and, in 1970, a second series of *Nova Scotia Reports*. In January 1971, the first issue of a new series reporting cases from the remaining two maritime provinces was published. Its title is the *Newfoundland & Prince Edward Island Reports*. These three series are published by Maritime Law Book Ltd., publisher of the *National Reporter*. Its key word and key number system, already mentioned in relation to it, has been in use in these series since the spring of 1973.

---

13   *Western Weekly Digests*, 1976, Preface.

After the publication of the second series of *Nova Scotia Reports* began, the Nova Scotia Barristers' Society approached Maritime Law Book Ltd. regarding the possibility of publishing judgments of the Nova Scotia courts for the years 1965-69. As a result, a five-volume set entitled *Nova Scotia Reports, 1965-69,* appeared between 1973 and 1975. The later cases were reported first; practically all those reported in the first two volumes were decided in 1968 or 1969. Thus, most of them belong to the period that was missed by both the *Maritime Provinces Reports* and the *Nova Scotia Reports,* Second Series.

There is now another Maritime Law Book series called *Atlantic Provinces Reports,* which duplicates material in the *New Brunswick Reports,* Second Series, *Nova Scotia Reports,* Second Series, and *Newfoundland & Prince Edward Island Reports.* No advance parts to this series are issued. It is suitable for subscribers who require some coverage of Atlantic province cases, but who do not need the advance part service. Some law school libraries that subscribe to the three separate series also purchase the *Atlantic Provinces Reports* to provide an extra copy of cases from the four Atlantic provinces.

Consolidated Digest and Index volumes comparable to those accompanying the *National Reporter* are published by Maritime Law Book Ltd. for each of its provincial series. As with the *National Reporter,* they generally cover every ten volumes. However, for the *Atlantic Provinces Reports,* the first four Digest and Index volumes cover volumes 1 to 20, 21 to 40, 41 to 60, and 61 to 100 of the series. The first Nova Scotia Digest and Index volume covers not only volumes 1-10 of the *Nova Scotia Reports,* Second Series, but also the five volumes of *Nova Scotia Reports, 1965-69.* There are also consolidated indexes of cases (comparable to the *National Reporter* equivalent) for volumes 1-49 of the *New Brunswick Reports,* Second Series, and volumes 1-58 of the *Nova Scotia Reports,* Second Series; the latter also lists cases in the *Nova Scotia Reports, 1965-69.*

An illustration will show you how to use Maritime Law Book's key word and key number system. Suppose you are looking for recent Nova Scotia cases relating to whether failure to use a seatbelt constitutes contributory negligence if injuries are sustained by a passenger in an automobile accident. Unless you know the word and number used for this topic, begin by looking up "seatbelt" in the key word index in the most recent *Nova Scotia Reports* Digest and Index volume; at the time of writing it is the one that covers volumes 51 to 60. There you will find "Seatbelt, failure to use, contributory negligence" listed, the key word and number being "TORTS 346" (see Illustration 11). Next, look up "TORTS – TOPIC 346" in the topical index. There you will find brief digests of cases that considered whether, in a motor vehicle accident, a passenger's failure to wear a seatbelt constituted contributory negligence, together with a citation to the report of each case in the *Nova Scotia Reports,* Second Series (see Illustration 12). Note that the citations include references to paragraph numbers. Since the mid-1970's, Maritime Law Book has been numbering the paragraphs in its report of each case. This is a useful feature and makes the finding of a specific reference much easier. Using the first case under "TORTS

ILLUSTRATION 11

Salary, employees – see Master and servant, remuneration above.

Sale and foreclosure, mortgages – see Mortgages, mortgage actions, foreclosure above.

Sale, and partition – see Partition and sale above.

Sale and seizure, chattel mortgages and bills of sale – see Chattel mortgages and bills of sale, seizure above.

Sale, bills of – see Chattel mortgages and bills of sale above.

Sale, distress, landlord and tenant – see Landlord and tenant, distress above.

Sale, mortgages – see Mortgages above.

Sale of goods, actions by seller, evidence, burden of proof – SALE OF GOODS 8506.

Sale of goods, actions by seller, identity of purchaser, estoppel – ESTOPPEL 1164.

Sale of goods, breach, remedies of buyer, rescission, substantial breach – SALE OF GOODS 6509.

Sale of goods, conditions and warranties, implied terms, general, respecting price – SALE OF GOODS 4188.

Sale of goods, damages – see Damages, contracts, sale of goods above.

Sale of goods, general, scope of Sale of Goods Act, sale distinguished from contract for work and material – SALE OF GOODS 69.

Sale of land, completion, conditions and conditions precedent, condition respecting financing to be arranged – SALE OF LAND 6038.

Sale of land, completion, seller's duties, general, respecting quiet enjoyment – SALE OF LAND 6210.

Sale of land, completion, seller's duties, respecting title, marketable title, what constitutes – SALE OF LAND 6231.

Sale of land, completion, time, time of the essence, general – SALE OF LAND 6061.

Sale of land, completion, time, time of the essence, waiver of – SALE OF LAND 6062.

Sale of land, contract, consensus, validity of the contract, uncertainty, general – SALE OF LAND 2010.

Sale of land, contract, discharge rescission or annulment, grounds, non est factum – SALE OF LAND 3761.

Sale of land, contract, implied terms, respecting payment – SALE OF LAND 1830.

Sale of land, contract, necessity for writing, part performance in lieu of writing, part performance, what constitutes – SALE OF LAND 1351.

Sale of land, general, validity, effect of lack of deed – SALE OF LAND 46.

Sale of land, mortgage sale, purchase by mortgagee, calculation of deficiency – MORTGAGES 5553.

Sale of land, remedies of purchaser, damages, bars, waiver – SALE OF LAND 8766.

Sale of land, remedies of purchaser, specific performance, bars, laches – SALE OF LAND 8568.

Sale of liquor, illegal – see Liquor control, offences and penalties above.

Sale of property – see Receivers, property above.

Sale, of security, discharge of guarantor, duties of creditor – GUARANTEE AND INDEMNITY 2767.

Sale of security, s. 178 bank loans – see Banks and banking, loans, secured loans, s. 178 (s. 88) loans above.

Sale price, actual cash value, meaning of – REAL PROPERTY 3504.

Sale, tax sale – see Real property tax above.

Sales and service taxes, business tax, priorities, municipality v. secured creditor – SALES AND SERVICE TAXES 3210.

Sales and service taxes, sales tax, credits, trade-in on account of purchase price – SALES AND SERVICE TAXES 986.

Sales and service taxes, sales tax, exemptions, manufacture or production of goods – SALES AND SERVICE TAXES 543.

Sales and service taxes, theatre and amusement tax, places liable, place of amusement, what constitutes – SALES AND SERVICE TAXES 3646.

Sales, conditional – see Conditional sales above.

Sales tax – see Sales and service taxes above.

Sales, tax sales for delinquent taxes – see Real property tax, tax sales for delinquent taxes above.

Salesman, failure to meet production quotas, dismissal, grounds – MASTER AND SERVANT 7573.

Salesman, licensing, residency requirement, validity – CIVIL RIGHTS 503.

Salesman, route – see Route salesman above.

Same class – see Of the same class above.

Sanderson or Bullock order, costs, where success divided among plaintiffs and defendants – PRACTICE 7155.

Scales, accuracy of, charge of excess weight, evidence and proof – MOTOR VEHICLES 3210.

Scales, prima facie accuracy of, presumption of innocence, reverse onus provisions – CIVIL RIGHTS 4945.

Search and seizure, civil rights – see Civil rights above.

Search and seizure, liquor control – see Liquor control above.

Search, fish and game – see Fish and game, enforcement above.

Search, title, negligence, lawyers – BARRISTERS AND SOLICITORS 2593.

Search warrants – see Criminal law above.

Searching title, barristers and solicitors, relationship with client – BARRISTERS AND SOLICITORS 1705.

Seatbelt, failure to use, contributory negligence – TORTS 346.

Section 178 bank loans – see Banks and banking, loans, secured loans above.

Secured bank loans – see Banks and banking, loans above.

Secured creditor, business tax, priority over municipality – SALES AND SERVICE TAXES 3210.

Secured creditor, priority, statutory liens – RECEIVERS 3585.

Secured creditors – see Bankruptcy above.

Security, conduct of sale of, guarantee and indemnity – see Guarantee and indemnity, discharge and other defences of surety above.

Security, curing of defects in realization of, chattel mortgages – CHATTEL MORTGAGES AND BILLS OF SALE 6150.

Security for costs – see Practice, costs above.

Security, for loan advances, failure to acquire, lawyers, negligence – BARRISTERS AND SOLICITORS 2588.

Security instruments, registration of – see Company law, borrowing, registration above.

Security of the person – see Civil rights above.

Security, sale of, s. 178 bank loans – see Banks and banking, loans, secured loans, s. 178 (s. 88) loans, sale above.

Security, sufficiency of, order vacating mechanics' lien – MECHANICS' LIENS 7008.

Seizure and sale, chattel mortgages and bills of sale – see Chattel mortgages and bills of sale above.

Seizure and search, civil rights – see Civil rights above.

Seizure and search, liquor control – see Liquor control, search and seizure above.

Seizure, fish and game – see Fish and game, offences, seizure above.

Seizure, of motor vehicles, when authorized – MOTOR VEHICLES 3345.

Seizure, power of – see Criminal law, seizure above.

Seizure, property – see Civil rights, property, search and seizure above.

Self-defence, assault, defences – CRIMINAL LAW 1420.

Self-incrimination, protection against – see Civil rights, protection against self-incrimination above.

Self-interest, lawyers, conflict of interest – BARRISTERS AND SOLICITORS 1609.

ILLUSTRATION 12

748   Nova Scotia Reports (2d) - Digest - Volumes 51 to 60

Torts - Topical Index (cont'd)

NEGLIGENCE
(1 - 999)
(cont'd)

TORTS - TOPIC 328
- Negligence - Motor vehicle - Gratuitous passengers - Gross negligence -
What constitutes - The defendant was
driving during the early morning, after
driving through the night approximately
300 km. - She was probably tired -
Driving a new vehicle with an unfamili-
ar front-wheel drive, she failed to
slow down or take evasive action respecting gravel on her side of the
highway - The Nova Scotia Supreme
Court, Trial Division, held that the
defendant driver was grossly negligent
in overreacting and failing to keep
the vehicle under control - See paragraphs 6 to 23 - Perry et al. v. Acker
et al., 58 N.S.R.(2d) 206; 123 A.P.R.
206.

TORTS - TOPIC 329
- Negligence - Motor vehicle - Gratuitous passenger - Gross negligence defined - The Nova Scotia Supreme Court,
Trial Division, stated that gross negligence is proved when it is shown on a
balance of probabilities that the car
was operated in a manner which was a
"very marked departure from the standard by which responsible and competent
people in charge of cars habitually
govern themselves" - See paragraph 2 -
Taylor v. Stone, 52 N.S.R.(2d) 259;
106 A.P.R. 259.

TORTS - TOPIC 346
- Negligence - Motor vehicle - Passengers - Contributory negligence of passengers - Failure to use safety equipment - Seatbelts - The Nova Scotia
Court of Appeal stated that failure to
use a seatbelt was not negligence per
se and because there was no mandatory
seatbelt legislation in Nova Scotia, a
defendant had to prove that a plaintiff,
who did not wear a seatbelt, was at common law, contributorily negligent for
failing to take precautions to minimize
his injuries - The court affirmed a
trial judge's decision that the plaintiffs were 10% at fault for failing to
wear their seatbelts - See paragraphs
19 to 39 - Shaw Estate v. Roemer et al.,
51 N.S.R.(2d) 229; 102 A.P.R. 229.

TORTS - TOPIC 346
- Negligence - Motor vehicle - Passengers - Contributory negligence of -
Failure to use safety equipment - Seat
belts - The Nova Scotia Court of Appeal
affirmed a decision holding the plaintiff passenger contributorily negligent

and 10% liable for her injuries, because she did not use a seat belt; although she knew the road was slippery -
See paragraph 35 - Sibbins v. Atkins
et al., 52 N.S.R.(2d) 112; 106 A.P.R.
112.

TORTS - TOPIC 346
- Negligence - Motor vehicle - Passengers - Contributory negligence of passengers - Failure to use safety equipment - The Nova Scotia Supreme Court,
Trial Division, refused to find the
occupants of a motor vehicle, which was
struck by an oncoming vehicle, contributorily negligent in failing to use
their seat belts, where it was not
proved that the use of the seat belts
would have reduced their injuries - See
paragraphs 26, 32, 44 - Bannister v.
MacDougall's Estate, 53 N.S.R.(2d) 201;
109 A.P.R. 201.

TORTS - TOPIC 346
- Negligence - Motor vehicle - Passengers
- General - Contributory negligence of
passenger - Failure to use safety equipment - Motor vehicle accident - The Nova
Scotia Supreme Court, Trial Division,
held that passengers who failed to wear
their seat belts were contributorily
negligent and accordingly, reduced their
entitlement to damages by 10% - See
paragraph 18 - Nyiti and Nyiti v. LeBlanc
and LeBlanc, 53 N.S.R.(2d) 520; 109
A.P.R. 520.

TORTS - TOPIC 346
- Negligence - Motor vehicle - Passengers - General - Contributory negligence of passenger - Failure to use
safety equipment - A passenger was not
wearing a seat belt at the time of a
motor vehicle accident - The Nova Scotia
Supreme Court, Trial Division, held
that the driver could not rely on this
defence, because he failed to establish
that the wearing of a seatbelt would
have resulted in less severe injuries
to the passenger - See paragraphs 61
to 65 - MacEachern v. MacKenzie, 54
N.S.R.(2d) 459; 112 A.P.R. 459.

TORTS - TOPIC 346
- Motor vehicle - Passengers - General
- Contributory negligence of passenger
- Failure to use safety equipment -
A passenger in a motor vehicle was injured as a result of an accident caused
by the negligence of the driver of the
other vehicle - The passenger was not
wearing a seat belt at the time of the
accident - The Nova Scotia Supreme
Court, Trial Division, held that the
passenger was contributorily negligent
and 10% at fault for her injuries - See

– TOPIC 346" in Illustration 12 as an example, see paragraphs 19 and 20 in Illustration 13. If you want to find later Nova Scotia cases dealing with the same question, look up "TORTS – TOPIC 346" in the topical indexes from volume 61 on. Should you be looking for similar cases in other jurisdictions covered by Maritime Law Book reports, look up "TORTS – TOPIC 346" in the appropriate topical indexes.

Note at the top of Illustration 13 the double citation to 51 N.S.R. (2d) and 102 A.P.R. This double citation is used in all the Atlantic province series to enable users to find the case in either the *Atlantic Provinces Reports* or in the appropriate provincial series; the page numbers are the same in both. Since the *New Brunswick Reports*, Second Series, became bilingual with volume 45 (1983), the French citation is also included for New Brunswick cases – see Illustration 14.[14]

In 1974, the Prince Edward Island Department of Justice began to publish on an experimental basis a series entitled *Prince Edward Island Supreme Court Reports*. The first volume, covering the year 1971, is the only one published to date. It is said that subsequent volumes are still being planned, but there is no indication of when they will appear.[15]

Although you will probably refer only occasionally to Quebec law reports, you should be aware of the principal set, *Recueils de jurisprudence du Québec,* now published in three series by the Société québécoise d'information juridique (SOQUIJ) for the Editieur officiel du Québec. The current parts are filed in three loose-leaf binders, one for the Cour d'Appel, one for the Cour Supérieure, and the third for other courts including the Cour provinciale, Cour des sessions de la paix, and Tribunal de la jeunesse, previously named Cour du bien-être social. Up to 1975, there were only two series of Recueils – Cour Supérieure and Cour d'Appel, the latter formerly called Cour du banc de la reine. The earlier name for the *Recueils de jurisprudence du Québec* (from 1892 to 1966) was *Rapports judiciaires de Québec.* The reports of each court in the third series are paged and cited separately, but are generally bound together since they are indexed together. The cases are reported in the language in which the proceedings are held; thus, most are in French with a few in English. Two other series of Quebec law reports to which most law school libraries in the common law provinces subscribe are the *Revue légale* and the *Revue de droit judiciaire,* successor to the *Rapports de Pratique de Québec.*

(f) Subject Reports

In addition to law reports covering a specific court, jurisdiction, or region, there are various series that bring together cases of a particular type or dealing with a particular subject. This, of course, leads to considerable du-

---

14   The title of the series is now given in both languages, the French title being *Recueil du Nouveau-Brunswick.* Cases are reported in both languages, but notes, indexing, *etc.* continue to be in English only.

15   Douglass T. MacEllven, *Legal Research Handbook* (Toronto: Butterworths, 1983), p. 21.

ILLUSTRATION 13

240   51 N.S.R.(2d)   and   102 A.P.R.

lights were on a vehicle in the other lane. They argue that
the actions of the truck driver were negligent acts which
caused or contributed to the accident. They say he should
have warned the Shaw vehicle of the danger on the highway by
extinguishing all the lights except the emergency flashers so
that the obstruction could be seen by approaching traffic.

16   The trial judge reached the conclusion, however, that
the efforts of the truck driver were made during the agony
of collision and there was not in fact time to give adequate
warning of the peril. He found that Mr. Roemer was not negligent in taking the action that he did, but that Mr. Shaw was
to a limited extent responsible for the injuries received by
the persons in his vehicle as he could perhaps have done
something more that might have reduced the effect of the
respondents' negligence.

17   The respondents argue that the trial judge should have
found a much higher degree of negligence on the part of the
driver of the Shaw vehicle. They say that Mr. Shaw was proceeding at a very high rate of speed and failed to heed the
warnings of peril emanating from the truck's lights and from
the two ladies in his vehicle, who had suggested that someone
was trying to get them to stop. They claim that 10% does
not properly reflect the degree to which Mr. Shaw's negligence
contributed to the accident.

18   In my opinion there was some evidence to support the
extreme positions taken by each of the parties to this appeal but there was also evidence to support the findings of
the trial judge. I would therefore not disturb his finding
that Mr. Shaw was guilty of negligence which contributed to
the injuries caused by the accident, nor would I disturb
his assessment of that contributory negligence at 10%.

19   Mr. Justice Richard also found as a fact that none of
the persons in the Shaw vehicle was wearing a <u>seatbelt</u> at the
time of the collision, and, in the case of Mr. Shaw, Mrs.
Shaw and Mrs. Brooks, accepted medical evidence to the effect
that their injuries would have been less severe had they
been wearing the apparatus provided in the vehicle to restrain
their movement during the course of collision. He made no
such finding concerning Mr. Brooks who was relatively unin-
jured and walked away from the crash.

20   The appellants argue that there is evidence upon which
it could have been determined that Mr. Shaw did in fact have
his <u>seatbelt</u> attached at the time of the accident, but there

ILLUSTRATION 14

accepted, a principal actor in the third count but merely an aider or an abettor with respect to the first two counts.

preuve apportée par la Couronne est acceptée, il semble, selon celle-ci, que l'appelant était un des auteurs principaux de l'infraction visée par le troisième chef, mais qu'il n'a qu'aidé ou encouragé les autres des infractions visées par les deux premiers chefs.

[20] In **R. v. Chlow (1982)**, 41 N.B.R. (2d) 179; 107 A.P.R. 179, I indicated the significance and my understanding of the use in an indictment of the words "acting together with" which were used in the indictment in the present case. It is my view that the use of those words indicates that the prosecution relies on s. 21(1)(a) and thereby excludes the assistance which it may receive by the other subsections of s. 21.

[20] Dans l'arrêt **R. c. Chlow** (1982), 41 N.B.R.(2d) 187; 107 A.P.R. 179, j'ai indiqué la signification des mots "en agissant conjointement" et l'interprétation que je donne à leur utilisation dans un acte d'accusation comme c'est le cas en l'espèce. Je suis d'avis que l'utilisation de ces mots montre que la Couronne se fonde sur l'al. 21(1)a) et qu'elle renonce à l'aide que peuvent lui apporter les autres alinéas de l'art. 21.

[21] In those circumstances it may be that the appellant cannot be found guilty of the first two counts as worded. However, that question need not be answered here, since I have come to the conclusion for other reasons that a new trial should be ordered, at which time the indictment could be worded differently.

[21] Dans ces circonstances, il se peut que l'appelant ne puisse être déclaré coupable des deux premiers chefs tels qu'ils sont rédigés. Cependant, il n'est pas nécessaire de répondre à cette question en l'espèce car, pour d'autres motifs, je suis arrivé à la conclusion qu'un nouveau procès doit être ordonné; l'acte d'accusation pourra alors être rédigé différemment.

CONCLUSION

[22] Having considered the nature and cumulative effect of the errors which occurred in this case in the light of the whole of the evidence, I do not think that the curative provisions of s. 613(1)(b)(iii) of the **Criminal Code** should be relied upon.

CONCLUSION

[22] Compte tenu de la nature et des effets cumulés des erreurs commises en l'espèce, je ne crois pas, à la lumière de l'ensemble de la preuve, que les dispositions curatives du s.-al. 613 (1)b)(iii) du **Code criminel** devraient être appliquées.

[23] For these reasons, I would allow the appeal, quash the conviction and order a new trial.

[23] Pour ces motifs, j'accueille l'appel, j'annule la déclaration de culpabilité et j'ordonne un nouveau procès.

Appeal allowed.

Appel accueilli.

Editor: David C.R. Olmstead
cmn

Arrêtiste: David C.R. Olmstead
cmn

plication; you may find a criminal case reported in the *Criminal Reports* –
until 1967, called the *Criminal Reports (Canada)* – in *Canadian Criminal
Cases*,[16] and in one or more of the general sets as well. Some of the subject
reports do, however, have features not found in the general series. For
instance, *The Canadian National Topical Law Reporting System,* published
by Carswell and consisting of fifteen titles, contains articles and case comments as well as reports of cases. Some of these topical law reports also include
decisions of lower courts and administrative boards not reported elsewhere.
The following is a list of the reports comprising this system:

Administrative Law Reports,
vol. 1, 1983-
Business Law Reports,
vol. 1, 1977-
Canadian Bankruptcy Reports, New Series,
vol. 1, 1960/61-
(The earlier series consists of 38 volumes covering the years
1920-1959/60.)
Canadian Cases on Employment Law,
vol. 1, 1983-
Canadian Cases on the Law of Insurance,
vol. 1, 1983-
Canadian Cases on the Law of Torts,
vol. 1, 1976/77-
Canadian Intellectual Property Reports,
vol. 1, 1984-
Carswell's Practice Cases,
vol. 1, 1976/77-
Construction Law Reports,
vol. 1, 1983/84-
Criminal Reports, Third Series,
vol. 1, 1978-
(The original series consists of 50 volumes
covering the years 1946-1967. This is
followed by the new series, comprising
40 volumes, 1967-1978.)
Estates and Trusts Reports,
vol. 1, 1978/79-
Motor Vehicle Reports,
vol. 1, 1979-
Municipal and Planning Law Reports,
vol. 1, 1976/77-

---

16   There is now an annotation service to *Canadian Criminal Cases* similar to the *D.L.R.
Annotation Service.* The volume issued in 1983 is, however, a permanent one containing a
complete table of cases for the second series, which ended with volume 70. A softcover
volume issued in 1984 updates the annotations in the 1983 volume and begins a table of
cases and annotation service for the third series. It will be replaced annually.

Real Property Reports,
vol. 1, 1977-
Reports of Family Law, Second Series,
vol. 1, 1978-
(The earlier series consists of Vols. 1-30,
1971-78.)

The indexing of these topical law reports is comparable to that described for the current series of *Western Weekly Reports*, the various finding aids being consolidated regularly into booklets and/or bound volumes.[17]

The *Criminal Law Digest* and *Family Law Digests*, companion volumes to the report series on these subjects, reprint material in Carswell's general digest, *The Canadian Abridgment*, Second Edition, about which more will be said in the fourth chapter of this book.

Subject reporting in Canada has developed, to some extent, along American lines. In fields such as labour and taxation, for instance, reports include or consist of loose-leaf volumes that are updated frequently, sometimes at two-week intervals. Loose-leaf publications are not uncommon in England. Some legal reference books are published in this form and, as we shall see in the next chapter, an edition of statutes in force is being issued in loose-leaf binders. However, in the field of law reporting loose-leaf services have been adopted to a much greater extent in the United States.

In Canada, as in the United States, loose-leaf services sometimes contain more than reports of cases. Many include statutes and regulations relevant to the subject area with which they deal. It is also quite common for them to give summaries of the law on various aspects of the subject indicating, if it is one wholly or partly under provincial jurisdiction, variations from one province to another. Loose-leaf services of this type are really a combination of primary and secondary sources, and Innis Christie, in the first edition of his *Legal Writing and Research Manual*, included them in his chapter on secondary legal materials.[18] They do not fit neatly into any one category. In the titles of some of them, the word "Service" or "Manual" is used, but others of the same class are called "Reporters".

An example of this type of loose-leaf service is the *Canadian Labour Law Reporter*, published by CCH Canadian Limited. At the beginning of the first volume, you will find instruction sheets entitled "How to Use this Reporter". They tell you that the general topical index leads you to editorial comment on the law in the topical outline divisions. The topical outline gives a summary of the law under specialized headings within the field of labour law, such as trade unions, collective bargaining, and worker's compensation. After a general explanation, it points out the particular provisions for each jurisdiction – federal and provincial. The topical outline is cross-referenced to paragraphs

---

17   See above, pp. 23-24.
18   Innis Christie, ed., *Legal Writing and Research Manual* (Toronto: Butterworths, 1970), c. 3, at p. 32. The section on loose-leaf services is not included in the second edition by Yogis and Christie (1974).

in the law division where the relevant statutes and regulations are reproduced under tabs for each of the various jurisdictions. The cumulative index is described as "a final check for new cases and new developments that interpret or amend the law." After finding the relevant paragraph in the topical outline, you should turn to the same paragraph number in the cumulative index where pertinent new items are listed with references to the complete report in the "New Matters" section.

The reports of court and labour board decisions in the "New Matters" section were previously replaced automatically by bound volumes entitled *Canadian Labour Law Cases.* You will probably find that your law library has at least four bound volumes of these cases covering the years 1944 to 1969. For later years you may, depending on your library's acquisitions policy, find either transfer binders or bound volumes. Because of the expense involved, CCH Canadian Limited no longer supplies bound volumes as part of the subscription to the loose-leaf service. Instead, it provides soft binders with instructions to transfer reports in the "New Matters" section to them. These transfer binders have the title *Canadian Labour Law Reports* on the cover and title page, but the cases continue to be cited C.L.L.C. (see headings on pages in the "New Matters" section in the loose-leaf *Canadian Labour Law Reporter* and in the transfer binders if your library uses them). The bound volumes of *Canadian Labour Law Cases* continue to be published, and law libraries in which labour cases are heavily used are likely to purchase them.

Note that the bound volumes and transfer binders consist entirely of reports of cases. Unlike the current loose-leaf service, they are not combined primary and secondary sources. The early bound volumes and transfer binders covered more than one year. Beginning with 1976, there is one bound volume or transfer binder for each calendar year. If your library uses the transfer binder, the case table for that year is transferred from the current service to it. If the bound volume is purchased, the case table, like the cases for that year in the current service, will be discarded since it is contained in the bound volume. The main case table in the current service, which is filed at the end of the "New Matters" section, is cumulative and indexes cases in the bound volumes and transfer binders. The supplemental case tables, while in the current service, refer to cases in the "New Matters" section.

Loose-leaf services generally include adequate instruction on their use, and the *Canadian Labour Law Reporter* has been described in some detail simply as an illustration of this type of publication. It should be noted that there are other loose-leaf publications that limit themselves to reporting cases. An example is *Canada Tax Cases*, New Series, which began in 1973 and supersedes the earlier *Canada Tax Cases* and the *Tax Appeal Board Cases.* Bound volumes are a part of this series, as they were of the two earlier ones. Richard De Boo Ltd., the publisher of these tax series, also issues loose-leaf publications of the "service" or "manual" type.

With so many cases arising under the Canadian Charter of Rights and Freedoms, it is not surprising that there are now reporting services devoted exclusively to them. The *Canadian Rights Reporter*, a Butterworths publication, began with volume 1 (1982). *Charter of Rights Decisions*, published by Western Legal Publications, also began in 1982 and is a digesting and indexing service. The latter, unlike the former, is published in loose-leaf format.

(g) Administrative Board Decisions

There are in Canada many administrative boards, some created federally, others provincially. Many of these boards have judicial as well as administrative powers. The decisions of some of them are published, whereas those of others are not. A very useful survey of the availability of such decisions was made by Alice H. Janisch and published by the Canadian Association of Law Libraries in 1972. Entitled *Publication of Administrative Board Decisions in Canada: A Report*, it gives the name and address of each board, how it was created, its status (independent body, part of a government department, *etc.*), whether its decisions are published and, if so, where. If not published, some indication is given as to whether reports of specific decisions are available on request.

In some cases, administrative board decisions are not published by the board itself, but are forwarded for inclusion in a series of reports dealing with the subject with which the board is concerned. The series may also include reports of relevant court cases and of decisions of other administrative boards. For example, the decisions of the Newfoundland Labour Relations Board are issued as press releases and are also sent to CCH Canadian Limited for inclusion in the *Canadian Labour Law Reporter*. CCH Canadian Limited also receives reports of decisions from similar boards in other provinces and makes selections for publication. For instance, Mrs. Janisch notes that the *Canadian Labour Law Reporter* publishes only those decisions of the Ontario Labour Relations Board that are considered to set an important precedent.

Of course, there have been new developments relating to administrative board decisions since Mrs. Janisch's report was published. For instance, in the area of labour relations, which we have been using as an example, Butterworths (Canada) began in 1974 to publish a series entitled *Canadian Labour Relations Boards Reports*, which covers decisions of such boards across Canada; a new series commenced in 1982. Butterworths notes that chairmen of the various boards co-operate to ensure that all key decisions are reported. Series that publish decisions of individual labour relations boards are also increasing in number.

Some decisions of administrative boards are published in law report series. For instance, as we have seen, some of Carswell's topical law reports include administrative board decisions; the *Municipal and Planning Law Reports* are an example. The *Administrative Law Reports*, however, report court cases that review decisions of administrative tribunals. A Butterworths series, *Canadian Customs and Excise Reports*, which began in 1980, reports decisions of the Tariff Board and the Anti-Dumping Tribunal, as well as appeals from these bodies to the Federal Court of Appeal. *Land Compensation Reports*, published by Canada Law Book and beginning with volume 1

(1971-72) is another example of a series that contains both administrative board and court decisions.

3. ENGLISH LAW REPORTS

Some English cases are binding on Canadian courts because there are "in force" dates as of which English law – both statutory and judge-made – was formally received in the various common law provinces of Canada.[19] This law could, of course, be changed by local legislation or modified by local judicial decision, but the fact remains that English law has had a unique role to play in the development of Canadian law. Moreover, until the middle of the twentieth century, the court of final appeal for Canada was not the Supreme Court of Canada, but the Judicial Committee of the Privy Council in England.[20] With the development of Canadian case law and the abolition of appeals to the Judicial Committee of the Privy Council, it is undoubtedly true that reports of English cases are not as important to Canadian lawyers and judges as they used to be. Nevertheless, Canadian law students should still become familiar with the basic sets of English law reports, for they will sometimes want to refer to them.

Law reporting in England, before 1865, was carried out mainly by private reporters. For a time there was no regular publication of these reports and, indeed, some of them were little more than notes made for the reporters' own use. Not all were published at the time they were written; some appeared after their authors' deaths. Regular publication became more common in the years following 1785, and certain reports came to be authorized for exclusive citation in court. Altogether, hundreds of series of reports were published between the end of the fifteenth century and 1865; many of them have now been reprinted in a 178-volume set known as the *English Reports*.

(a) The English Reports

You may want to find a case in the *English Reports*, but you know only the citation to the original report, which your library may not have. Perhaps, for instance, you are looking for the case of *Shrewsbury v. Blount*, which is reported in 2 Man. & G. 475. Since you know the name of the case, you can go directly to the index in the last two volumes of the *English Reports*. Look up *Shrewsbury v. Blount* and you will find that it is reprinted in volume 133 of the *English Reports* at page 836 (see Illustration 15). Suppose, however, that you are not sure of the name of the case; all you have is the citation 2 Man. & G. 475. You want to find out what the letters Man. & G. stand for and whether the volume in question has been reprinted in the *English Reports*. The best

---

19   For further information on the reception of English law in the common law provinces of Canada, see p. 83, below. A more detailed study of the subject is found in Bora Laskin, *The British Tradition in Canadian Law* (London: Stevens, 1969), pp. 3-10.

20   See note 7, on page 17, above.

ILLUSTRATION 15
English Reports, Volume 178

place to find this information is in the abbreviations listed at the end of a little volume called *Where to Look for Your Law*. The same list, with amendments, is printed at the back of *Osborn's Concise Law Dictionary*.[21] If you look up Man. & G., you will find that it is the abbreviation for Manning & Granger, a seven-volume set of Common Pleas reports covering the years 1840-1844. The column at the extreme right-hand side of the page tells you that these reports are reprinted in volumes 133-5 of the *English Reports* (see Illustration 16). If you then go to volume 133, you will find, by looking at the spine, that it contains volume 6 of Bingham, N.C. [Bingham, New Cases, another series of Common Pleas reports] and volumes 1-3 of Manning & Granger. Since the case you are looking for is reported in volume 2 of Manning & Granger, it must be found somewhere in volume 133 of the *English Reports*, probably towards the back since two other volumes precede it, and only one follows it. The page references to the original reports are printed at the top of the pages (in most volumes at the centre as the book lies open); thus, you can turn to page 475 of volume 2 of Manning & Granger, which you will find on page 836 of volume 133 of the *English Reports* (see Illustration 17). If it happens that neither *Where to Look for Your Law* nor *Osborn's Concise Law Dictionary* is available, much the same information can be obtained from the chart of the *English Reports*. Your library may hang this chart on the wall near the reports; if not, you will probably find it bound in a thin volume and shelved at the end of the set. The chart, however, is not so complete as the other lists, for it indexes each set of reports under only one title, whereas many were known by various titles or abbreviations. Moreover, if the volume you want happens to be reprinted in the *Revised Reports*, rather than the *English Reports*, this is indicated in *Where to Look for Your Law* and *Osborn* by enclosing the number in the extreme right hand column in square brackets (see Illustration 16, listing immediately following Man. & G.). The *Revised Reports*, another reprint, cover the years 1785-1866, but are less frequently used than the *English Reports*.

(b) The Law Journal Reports

The named reporters usually dealt with cases decided by one court, but in the nineteenth century, several major sets that reported cases from various courts began publication. Finding cases in the *Law Journal Reports*, which appeared first in 1823, presents some problems, mainly because of the manner of numbering and paging the volumes. After volume 9 (1831), a new series begins with volume 1 (1832). From new series volume 5 (1836) to volume 44

---

21   The information regarding early English reports is the same on both lists. However, the list in both volumes notes abbreviations for law reports other than those reprinted in the *English Reports*. Indeed, abbreviations for some Canadian series and those published in other Commonwealth countries are included. *Where to Look for Your Law* has not been updated since 1962, whereas the seventh edition of *Osborn's Concise Law Dictionary* was published in 1983. The list in *Osborn* has been updated with regard to English law reports, but not Canadian ones. For instance, the *Maritime Provinces Reports* are listed as current although they ceased publication with volume 53 (1967-68).

ILLUSTRATION 16
Where to Look for Your law

Law Reports

ABBR.	REPORTS	SERIES	VOLS.	PERIOD	E.R. [R.R.]
Mac.P.C.	.. Macrory	Pat.Cas.	1	1852–1860	—
MacCarthy	MacCarthy's Irish Land Cases ..	..		1887–1892	
Maccl.	.. Modern Cases, temp. Macclesfield (10 Modern Reports)..	K.B. ..	1	1710–1725	88
MacDev.	.. MacDevitt's Irish Land Cases ..	..		1882–1884	
Macl.Rem. Cas.	.. Maclaurin's Remark Cases (Scotland)..	..		1670–1773	
M'Cle. (McCl.)	M'Cleland	Ex. ..	1	1824	148
M'Cle. & Yo.	M'Cleland & Younge	Ex. ..	1	1824–1825	148
Macph.	.. Session Cases, 3rd Series [Macpherson] (Sc.)	C.S. ..	11	1862–1873	—
Macq.	.. Macqueen (Sc.) ..	H.L. ..	4	1851–1865	—
Macr.	.. Macrory	Pat.Cas.	1	1852–1860	—
Macr. & H..	. Macrae & Hertslet ..	Bky. ..	2	1847–1852	—
Macr.P.Cas.	Macrory	Pat.Cas.	1	1847–1860	—
Mad. & Gel.	Maddock & Geldart	V.C. ..	1	1819–1822	56
Madd.	.. Maddock	V.C. ..	6	1815–1822	56
Madd. & G.	Maddock & Geldart	V.C. ..	1	1821–1822	56
Mag. Cas.	.. Magistrates Cases. See " Law Journal."				
Man.	.. Manning's Revision Cases	..		1832–1835	
Man. & G. ..	. Manning & Granger	C.P. ..	7	1840–1844	133–5
Man. & Ry.	Manning & Ryland ..	K.B. ..	5	1827–1830	[31–4]
Man. & Ry. M.C.	.. Manning & Ryland ..	M.C. ..	3	1827–1830	—
Man. & Sc. ..	. Manning, Granger & Scott, Common Bench Reports ..	C.P. ..	19	1845–1856	135–9
Man.Gr. & S.	Manning, Granger & Scott, Common Bench Reports ..	C.P. ..	19	1845–1856	135–9
Man.L.J.	.. Manitoba Law Journal				
Man.L.R.	.. Manitoba Law Reports	All ..	★	1884–date	—
Manson	.. Manson	Bky. ..	21	1894–1914	—
Mar.	.. March	K.B. ..	1	1639–1642	82
Mar.L.C. (Mar.L.R.)	Maritime Law Cases (Crockford)	... Adm.	3	1860–1870	—
Mar.L.C.,N.S.	See "Aspinall."				
March [N.C.]	March's Translation of Brook's New Cases	K.B. ..	1	1515–1558	73[1]
March N.C.	March's New Cases ..	K.B. ..	1	1639–1642	82
Marr.	.. Marriott	Adm...	1	1776–1779	165

[1] See note [2] on p. 178.

216

ILLUSTRATION 17
English Reports, Volume 133

836　　　　　　　　　SHREWSBURY *v.* BLOUNT　　　　2 MAN. & G. 475.

[475]　SHREWSBURY *v.* BLOUNT AND OTHERS.　Jan. 15, Feb. 1, 1841.

[S. C. 2 Scott, N. R. 588.]

In an action by A. against B. C. and D. for false representations alleged to have been made by them, acting as directors of a joint stock company, conversations between B. and C., and conversations between C. and E. a former agent of the company, are admissible in evidence to shew the bona fides of the defendants in making such representations.—Books in the hand writing of E. sent by him after he had ceased to be such agent, to the secretary of the company, are not admissible in evidence for the plaintiff, unless it be shewn that the books were kept by E. as agent.—An action does not lie for a false representation whereby the plaintiff, being induced to purchase the subject matter of the representation from a third party, has sustained damage,—the representations appearing to have been made bona fide under a reasonable and well grounded belief that the same were true (*a*).

Case. The declaration stated, that before the time of the committing of the grievances by the defendants, the defendants, one Joseph Malachy and Thomas May, one James Husband and Thomas Husband, and divers other persons, had formed themselves into a company, by the name or style of "The Wheal Brothers Copper, Tin, Lead, and Silver Mining Company," for the working and exploring of a certain copper tin lead and silver mine, called and known by the name of "The Wheal Brothers Mine," situate in the parish of Calstock (*b*), in the county of Cornwall; which company, before and at the time of the committing of the said grievances, after and before and at the time of the purchase by the plaintiff of divers shares in the said company, as thereinafter next mentioned, had been and was an existing company for the purposes aforesaid; and that also before and at the time of the committing, &c. the defendants Blount, Harrison, and Heathorn, had [476] become and were the trustees of the funds and property of the said company; and as such trustees the said Blount, Harrison,

---

of the city aforesaid, to wit, I. G. and W. W., return, that at the county court of the city of Y., holden there on Monday, to wit, the 17th day of September, in the thirty-second year of the reign of the lord the now king, and so at four county courts next preceding, the said E. was demanded, and did not appear; and because he appeared at none of the said county courts, he was outlawed; as I. I. and I. W., late sheriffs of the city aforesaid, the last predecessors of the said now sheriffs, have, on the back of the said writ of exigent, to them the now sheriffs, delivered; and that afterwards a writ of supersedeas of the execution of the said writ of exigent was delivered to the now sheriffs by their said predecessors, containing therein that by His other writ to His justices of the bench directed, He had recorded that the said E. is one of the barons of His kingdom coming to His parliaments, and that he willed that if he should be impleaded before them at the suit of any one by action personal, they should cause to be made such process, and not other, against him, in such action, as against lords, magnates, earls, or barons of His kingdom of England, who ought to come to His parliaments, or against any of them, according to the law and custom of His kingdom of England, ought to be made.

And, because this was recorded before the justices of the lord the king here, a long time before the promulgation of the outlawry aforesaid; as by the said writ thereof, amongst the records without day affiled, sufficiently appears; and no process against any of them by attachment of their bodies, or by writs of exigent, ought to be made, but rather they, by summons, attachment, and distress (but see 1 Rot. Parl. 61 b.) by their lands and chattels, in the court of the lord the king, ought, in such pleas, to be brought to answer: therefore let the said outlawry be annulled," &c. Rastall's Entries, 313.

(*a*) As to the necessity of the existence of a reasonable ground of belief where there is bona fides, see *Haycraft* v. *Creasy*, 2 East, 92; *Tapp* v. *Lee*, 3 Bos. & Pull. 367. *Hamar* v. *Alexander*, 2 N. R. 241, 244; *Scott* v. *Lara*, Peake, N. P. C. 226; *Ames* v. *Millward*, 2 B. Moore, 714; *Ashlin* v. *White*, Holt, N. P. C. 387.

(*b*) As to the assessionable manor of Calstock, its tenure and its minerals, see 3 Mann. & Ryl. 140, 141, 142, 155, 188, 190, 230, 231, 243, 461, 464, 467, 477. As to its tin-bounds in 1559, see Mann. Exch. Pract. 380, n.; post, 507.

(1875), each volume is bound in two parts, one labelled "Common Law," the other "Equity". Thus, there are really two volumes bearing the same number. Sometimes additional information is included on the labels, for one or both volumes often report some cases decided by courts that cannot be strictly classified as of either common law or equitable jurisdiction. Whatever is listed on the labels, more complete information as to the contents of the volume is included on the title page. From volume 45 (1876) on, the labelling is different, as a result of changes in the structure of the courts, which will be explained later, but the practice of having two volumes with the same number continues throughout most of the set. It should also be noted that, except in the last three volumes (volumes 116-118, 1947-49), reports of cases in different courts are paged separately. This, together with the mode of citation, adds to the difficulty of finding the case you want. For instance, one of the citations for the case of *Long v. Champion* is 9 L.J.O.S.K.B. 248; when you go to volume 9 of the old series, you must be sure to find page 248 of the section reporting King's Bench cases. When citing cases reported in the new series, it is not customary to include the letters "N.S." (even in the volumes up to 9 where there might be confusion), so you will find the case of *Hunter v. Caldwell*, reported in volume 16 of the new series, cited as 16 L.J.Q.B. 274. Here you must remember that there are two volumes numbered 16 and that Queen's Bench is a common law court, not a court of equity. Having found the common law volume 16, you must, as in the earlier example, see that you are in the right section of the book; it is easy to forget this and turn perhaps to page 274 of the Common Pleas.

(c) The Law Times Reports

Another important nineteenth century set, which continued into the twentieth century, is the *Law Times Reports*. At first these reports appeared in the *Law Times* magazine, which began publication in 1843. For the first eighteen years, the reports are not paged separately; this means that when the issues are bound, the reports are scattered throughout the volume. Beginning with volume 17 (1851) the reports are paged separately and bound at the end of the volume. After volume 34 (1859-60), the *Law Times* and the *Law Times Reports* ceased to appear as a joint publication. From volume 35 on the *Law Times* continued on its own, while there commenced a new series of *Law Times Reports*. If your library shelves law reports by country, and journals alphabetically by title, you will probably find that the old series and the new series of the *Law Times Reports* are shelved in different sections of the library. Being part of a magazine, the old series will be shelved with journals; if your citation is to the L.T.O.S., you will know to look there.

(d) The Law Reports

In 1865, the Incorporated Council of Law Reporting began to publish its *Law Reports*. At that time, the English judicial system was much more complex than it is today, and for the first ten years of their existence the *Law Reports* appeared in eleven series. The Judicature Act of 1873, which came into effect in 1875, simplified the judicial system by bringing together in one Supreme Court of Judicature the administration of common law and equity; probate, divorce, and admiralty, which did not really belong to either system, were also included. The different branches of the law were not merged completely, for the Supreme Court of Judicature consisted of a Court of Appeal and a High Court of Justice, the latter being made up of five divisions – Queen's Bench, Common Pleas, Exchequer (the successors to the three superior courts of common law), Chancery (the successor to the Court of Chancery, which had administered equity) and finally, combined in one division, Probate, Divorce, and Admiralty. In 1881, the Common Pleas and Exchequer Divisions merged with the Queen's Bench, thus reducing the number of divisions comprising the High Court to three. These changes in the judicial structure had the effect of simplifying the arrangement of the *Law Reports*. In 1875, the number of series was reduced from eleven to six; in 1881, it was further reduced to four. From the latter date to the present, the *Law Reports* have appeared in four main series: Appeal Cases, Queen's Bench, Chancery, and until the end of 1971, Probate (short for Probate, Divorce, and Admiralty).

Since January 1, 1972, the Probate Division has been called the Family Division. This is not simply a name change, for the Administration of Justice Act 1970 provided for a redistribution of business among the divisions of the High Court. Probate, Divorce, and Admiralty had, in the words of Glanville Williams, been "lumped together for no better reason than that they were all founded (to some extent) on Roman and canon law."[22] The 1970 Act changed this by transferring jurisdiction in Admiralty cases to the Queen's Bench Division, and in contentious probate business to the Chancery Division. Non-contentious probate remains with the Family Division, which is assigned jurisdiction in a wide variety of matrimonial and related matters.

Several features of the *Law Reports* are confusing. In the first place, the manner of shelving is rather difficult to follow. The various series are arranged by court and date; in some libraries, the reports of the highest courts (the House of Lords and the Judicial Committee of the Privy Council) are shelved at the beginning of the set, while in others they will be found at the end. The latter arrangement seems to be preferred in Canada, so it will be followed in the list given below. In the list, the citation appears in parentheses after the name of the series; more will be said about this later.

Chancery Appeal Cases	(L.R. .... Ch. or Ch. App.)	1865-75	v. 1-10
Equity Cases	(L.R. .... Eq.)	1865-75	v. 1-20
Chancery Division	(... Ch.D.)	1875-90	v. 1-45
Chancery Division	([ ] Ch.)	1891-date	by year

---

22   Glanville Williams, *Learning the Law*, 11th ed. (London: Stevens, 1982), p. 5.

Common Pleas Cases	(L.R. . . . C.P.)	1865-75	v. 1-10
Common Pleas Division	(. . . C.P.D.)	1875-80	v. 1-5
Exchequer Cases	(L.R. . . . Ex.)	1865-75	v. 1-10
Exchequer Division	(. . . Ex.D.)	1875-80	v. 1-5
Queen's Bench Cases	(L.R. . . . Q.B.)	1865-75	v. 1-10
Queen's Bench Division	(. . . Q.B.D.)	1875-90	v. 1-25
Queen's Bench Division	([ ] Q.B.)	1891-1900	by year
King's Bench Division	([ ] K.B.)	1901-1952	by year
Queen's Bench Division	([ ] Q.B.)	1952-date	by year
Probate & Divorce Cases	(L.R. . . . P. & D.)	1865-75	v. 1-3
Admiralty & Ecclesiastical Cases	(L.R. . . . A. & E.)	1865-75	v. 1-4
Probate Division	(. . . P.D.)	1875-90	v. 1-15
Probate Division	([ ] P.)	1891-1971	by year
Family Division	([ ] Fam.)	1972-date	by year
Crown Cases Reserved	(L.R. . . . C.C. or C.C.R.)	1865-76	v. 1, 2
English & Irish Appeals	(L.R. . . . H.L.)	1866-75	v. 1-7
Scotch & Divorce Appeals	(L.R. . . . H.L.Sc. or L.R. . . . H.L.Sc. and Div.)	1865-75	v. 1-2
Privy Council Appeals	(L.R. . . . P.C.)	1865-75	v. 1-6
Appeal Cases	(. . . App. Cas.)	1875-90	v. 1-15
Appeal Cases	([ ] A.C.)	1891-date	by year

The manner of numbering and citing the volumes may also give rise to difficulties. Up to 1875, the letters L.R. traditionally appear in the citation; from that date on, only the abbreviation for the series is used. At first, the volumes of each series were numbered, but from 1891 on, there is no consecutive numbering of volumes; they are cited instead by year. If there is more than one volume a year in a series, the year is followed by a number. Thus, [1967] 2 Q.B. means the second volume of the reports of the Queen's Bench Division for 1967. In the above table, dots (. . .) indicate the place where the volume number would appear in the citation; square brackets indicate where the year would appear.[23]

A few other peculiarities may be noted. In the list above, you will see a series called *English and Irish Appeals*. Its full title is *English and Irish Appeal Cases and Claims of Peerage before the House of Lords*. Although the title used on the spine of the volume is *The Law Reports: English and Irish Appeals* (or *E. & I. App.*) the series is cited L.R. . . . H.L. Thus, if you are looking for the case of *Bain v. Fothergill*, reported in L.R. 7 H.L. 158, you will find it in the volume lettered *The Law Reports: English and Irish Appeals*, (or *E. & I. App.*) vol. 7.

It would be reasonable to expect cases decided by the Court of Appeal to be reported in the series called *Appeal Cases*. This, however, is not where you

---

23   Williams, p. 39.

find most of them. Instead, they appear in the other three series, depending on the origin of the case. Cases decided by the House of Lords and the Judicial Committee of the Privy Council are reported in *Appeal Cases*.[24] In the period before Canada abolished appeals to the Privy Council, many Canadian appeal cases, decided by the Judicial Committee, were reported in this series.

If you look through the Queen's Bench volumes, you may notice that some of them include reports of cases decided by the Court of Criminal Appeal. This may appear somewhat odd, unless you know that the court in question was presided over by the Lord Chief Justice, who is also President of the Queen's Bench Division of the High Court, and that the other judges of the Court of Criminal Appeal were also judges of the Queen's Bench Division. The Court of Criminal Appeal, established by an Act of 1907, was abolished in 1966, its place being taken by a newly established Criminal Division of the Court of Appeal. This division, like the earlier Court, is presided over by the Lord Chief Justice, who may request the attendance of any judge of the Queen's Bench Division. The Lords Justices of Appeal, who are "ordinary" (as opposed to "ex- officio") judges of the Court of Appeal are also members of the Criminal Division. Reports of cases decided by the Court of Appeal, Criminal Division, are, like those of the Court it replaces, published in the Queen's Bench series of the *Law Reports*. An unofficial set, the *Criminal Appeal Reports*, also publishes cases decided by the Court of Criminal Appeal and its successor, the Court of Appeal, Criminal Division.

(e) Continuation of Unofficial Law Reporting

The advent of the *Law Reports* in 1865 did not bring an end to private or unofficial law reporting. Both the *Law Journal Reports* and the *Law Times Reports* continued to the middle of the twentieth century, and yet another set, the *Times Law Reports* began publication in 1884. The first volume of the *All England Law Reports* appeared in 1936. It is the only privately owned general set that remains current. The *Law Times Reports* merged with the *All England Law Reports* at the beginning of 1948. Two years later, the *Law Journal Reports* followed the same course. In 1952, the *Times Law Reports* ceased publication.

(f) The Weekly Law Reports

Since 1953, the Incorporated Council of Law Reporting has been publishing the *Weekly Law Reports*, the main purpose of which is to provide reports of cases much more promptly than do the *Law Reports*. This had also been the object of the *Times Law Reports* and it was the announcement of the beginning of the new series that led to the decision to discontinue their publication.

---

24   Dealing with this subject in the eleventh edition of his book *Learning the Law*, Glanville Williams has added a footnote on page 37 stating: "Sometimes the Appeal Cases contain a report of the decision in the C.A. as well as the H.L."

The *Weekly Law Reports* are bound each year in three volumes. The cases reported in volume 1 are not repeated in the *Law Reports*, but the reports of cases in volumes 2 and 3 are expected to be superseded by the *Law Reports* version, which may appear as long as a year or two later.[25] Before 1953, the Incorporated Council had published the *Weekly Notes*, which, as the name implies, had contained brief notes rather than detailed reports of recent cases.

(g) Subject and Other Specialized Reports

In addition to the general series of reports, there are some that bring together cases on a particular subject. Examples are the *Criminal Appeal Reports* (mentioned above), *Reports of Tax Cases*, and *Reports of Patent, Design, Trademark, and Other Cases*. The last two are government publications. Many of the cases in these volumes duplicate those reported in the *Law Reports* and the *All England Law Reports*, but their publication is a convenience for those engaged in specialized practice or study. In some of the subject report series, one volume covers several years.

There are also reports of courts of special jurisdiction that for the most part do not duplicate material in the *Law Reports*. In fact, the *Reports of Restrictive Practices Cases*, 1957-72, were published by the Incorporated Council of Law Reporting and, although not generally listed with the main series of *Law Reports*, are regarded as part of them. Indeed, they are cited L.R. ... R.P., a form not used for the main series since 1875. They reported cases heard in the Restrictive Practices Court and on appeal therefrom, as well as other cases arising under the Restrictive Trade Practices Act 1956 in England, Scotland, and Northern Ireland. The later volumes also included reports of cases arising under the Resale Prices Act 1964. In 1973, the *Reports of Restrictive Practices Cases* were incorporated into a new series, the *Industrial Court Reports*, also published by the Incorporated Council of Law Reporting, but not regarded as part of the *Law Reports*. In addition to reporting restrictive practices cases, this series published reports of cases heard in the National Industrial Relations Court (created by the Industrial Relations Act 1971), appeals therefrom, and decisions of the High Court of Justice relating to industrial relations. This series, like the National Industrial Relations Court, was short-lived. It ceased publication when the Court was abolished in 1974. The current series, *Industrial Cases Reports*, which began in 1975, reports decisions of a new Employment Appeal Tribunal, as well as those of the High Court, Court of Appeal, and House of Lords dealing with industrial relations. Like its predecessor, this series incorporates *Reports of Restrictive Practices Cases*.

---

25   Glanville Williams notes that sometimes, as it turns out, they are not included in the Law Reports after all. See *Learning the Law*, 11th ed., p. 38.

(h) European Court Reports and Common Market Law Reports

Many changes in the structure of the courts have taken place during recent years. Only those that have affected law reporting are noted here. One interesting fact is that the House of Lords is no longer Britain's highest court. Since that country's entry into the European Economic Community on January 1, 1973, the decisions of the European Court of Justice, sitting in Luxembourg, are binding on British courts.[26] Thus, it is appropriate to close this section on English law reports with references to the *European Court Reports*, which publish in the procedural language of the case the official reports of proceedings before that court, and the unofficial *Common Market Law Reports*, which have been published in English since 1962. This latter series reports cases decided by the European Court, as well as judgments of the national courts of the Common Market nations that relate to matters within the framework of the European Economic Community.

---

26   Williams, p. 16.

3

Statutes and Related Publications

1. GENERAL

The reports of which we have been speaking record case law, that is, the law based on judicial decision. We now turn to enacted or statute law, the law made by the legislators.

Statutes are passed to codify areas of case law that require clarification, to change or reform case law, or to deal with problems that it does not touch.[1] If case law is altered by statute, the former ceases to be law. For instance, in an action for injuries arising from negligence, it was a defence at common law if the defendant proved that the plaintiff, by some negligence on his part, directly contributed to the injury. However, both the United Kingdom Parliament and the Legislatures of most Canadian provinces have enacted statutes changing this rule. Now, if the plaintiff's negligence contributed to his injury, his claim is not automatically defeated, but the damages recoverable are reduced, the extent depending on his share of responsibility for the injury. Ontario's first Contributory Negligence Act was passed in 1924. The name has since been changed to the Negligence Act. Thus, in deciding an Ontario case involving contributory negligence, a judge clearly would not cite without explanation a decision on the subject made in that province at an earlier date when the common law rule was still in effect. As we have seen, case law can be altered by a legislature, but the courts have no authority to change statute law. One judge may, however, interpret it differently from another. In some jurisdictions, a court may find a particular statute invalid if the legislature that passed it had no authority to do so, but that is a different matter.

The United Kingdom is a unitary state without a written constitution. Acts or statutes in that country are passed by a sovereign Parliament; their validity cannot be questioned by the courts. There are other bodies that have law making powers – municipal corporations, for instance – but they derive their powers from Parliament, and the legislation that they pass is subordinate in nature.

In Canada the situation is different. Both Parliament and the provincial legislatures derive their powers from the Constitution Act, 1867, enacted as The British North America Act, 1867, by the Parliament at Westminster.[2]

---

1   J.A. Yogis and I.M. Christie, *Legal Writing and Research Manual*, 2nd ed. (Toronto: Butterworths, 1974), p. 52.
2   The name was changed to Constitution Act, 1867, by the Constitution Act, 1982 [enacted by the Canada Act 1982 (U.K.), c. 11, Sched. B), s. 53(2) in conjunction with the Schedule, Item 1. As the Constitution Act, 1982, which makes the name change, was enacted for and has the force of law *in Canada*, the 1867 Act is still correctly called the British North America Act in *Statutes in Force*, the official loose-leaf edition of U.K. statutes.

Canada's Parliament has the right to legislate in certain areas, the provincial legislatures in others. If either enacts legislation that appears to encroach on the authority of the other, the courts can be called upon to determine its validity. Within their own jurisdictions, Parliament and the provincial legislatures can delegate to other bodies authority to enact subordinate legislation.

An Act or statute begins as a bill and it must pass through three "readings" and certain other stages in both Houses of Parliament and receive the royal assent before it becomes an Act of Parliament. In Canada's provincial legislatures there are fewer steps to the process since each now consists of only one house. An Act of the United Kingdom or the Canadian Parliament comes into effect as soon as it receives the royal assent, unless the Act itself specifies a different date or states that it (or certain of its sections) will not come into force until proclaimed. The law regarding the effective date of statutes varies from one province to another; in Ontario, for instance, in the absence of express provision in a statute, it comes into force "on the sixtieth day after the prorogation of the session of the Legislature at which it was passed or on the sixtieth day after the day of signification, whichever is the later date."[3] When a bill is introduced into a legislative body it is given a number. For instance, Bill C-15 would be the fifteenth bill – or fifteenth government bill – introduced in the Canadian House of Commons during a particular session. If the bill had originated in the Senate, the prefix would have been "S" instead of "C". Sometimes private members' bills are numbered in a separate sequence from government bills. Private bills may also be numbered in a different sequence from public bills (both government and private members'). Usually a bill is printed after first reading and often at a later stage as well. The exact practice varies from one jurisdiction to another. When a bill becomes an Act its "clauses" become "sections" and the bill number is replaced by a chapter number; there is no relationship between these two numbers. In Britain, a paper copy of an Act usually appears a few days after it receives the royal assent. Acts of the Canadian Parliament are also published in this form. They also appear in Part III of the *Canada Gazette*. In all jurisdictions, the statutes, or at least the public general statutes, for a calendar year or a session are eventually published in a bound volume. Practice varies as to how local and private Acts, that is, those that apply only to a certain locality, individual, or institution, are published. In Britain, for instance, they are printed individually, but not in collected form.

---

3   Statutes Act, R.S.O. 1980, c. 483, s. 5(1). In the absence of a statutory provision such as this within a jurisdiction, the common law rule is that an Act is considered to have come into effect on the first day of the session in which it was passed unless provision is made within the Act for a later commencement. This rather strange rule was changed in Britain by the Acts of Parliament (Commencement) Act 1793 (33 Geo. 3, c. 13), which stipulates that, unless otherwise provided in its text, a statute comes into effect when it receives the royal assent.

2. THE CONSTITUTION OF CANADA

Although the British North America Act and certain other British and Canadian enactments were always regarded as the written part of Canada's constitution – there are also many unwritten conventions – it was not until the passage of the Canada Act 1982, enacting for Canada the Constitution Act, 1982, that specific statutes and orders were given a special constitutional status. In many countries, the United States of America being an example, the constitution is a single document, quite separate from its statutes. In Canada, this is not the case. Nevertheless, there is now a "Constitution of Canada", which is said to be "the supreme law of Canada".[4] It is, therefore, desirable to devote a section of this chapter to explaining what the Constitution is.

At the time of patriation in 1982, it was often said that Canada was getting a new constitution. This is not correct. Usually, when people talk about the new constitution, they are thinking of the Canadian Charter of Rights and Freedoms, which is Part I of the Constitution Act, 1982. Calling the Charter the Constitution is, however, comparable to confusing the main body of the U.S. Constitution with its first ten amendments, the Bill of Rights. The Charter is part of the "Constitution of Canada" – a part that is attracting a great deal of attention because of the number of cases arising under it – but it is not the only or even the most important part.

According to s. 52(2) of the Constitution Act, 1982, the Constitution of Canada includes:

(a) the Canada Act 1982, including this Act [that is, the Constitution Act, 1982];

(b) the Acts and orders referred to in the schedule; and

(c) any amendment to any Act or order referred to in paragraph (a) or (b).

Thirty items (Acts or orders) are listed in the schedule, but of these six are repealed. Therefore, only twenty-four "continue as law in Canada".[5]

There is disagreement among constitutional authorities as to whether the Acts and orders listed in s. 52(2) and the schedule are the only ones included in the Constitution of Canada. For instance, some of the provisions for amending the Constitution refer to the Supreme Court of Canada, and this raises the question of whether the Supreme Court Act, though not listed, is part of the Constitution. In legislative enactments, the use of the word "includes," instead of the word "means," usually indicates that the definition is not exhaustive.[6] If this is the case, we are left without a clear definition of the "Constitution of Canada". Should a problem arise as to the proper method of amending a specific statutory provision that may or may not be part of the Constitution, a judicial ruling will no doubt be sought.

---

4   Constitution Act, 1982, s. 52(1).
5   Constitution Act, 1982, s. 53(1).
6   For differing views on the matter, see Stephen A. Scott, "Pussycat, Pussycat or Patriation and the New Constitutional Amendment Processes" (1982), 20 U.W.O. Law Review, 247 at 250 and Peter W. Hogg, *Canada Act 1982 Annotated* (Toronto: The Carswell Company Limited, 1982), pp. 92-94 and 105.

The Canada Act 1982, a statute of the Parliament at Westminster, enacted for Canada the Constitution Act, 1982, and provided that thereafter no
Act of the Parliament of the United Kingdom was to extend to Canada as part
of its law. The Constitution Act, 1982, includes the Canadian Charter of
Rights and Freedoms, some provisions relating to the rights of the aboriginal
people of Canada and to equalization and regional disparities, procedures for
amending the Constitution of Canada, provisions for the holding of constitutional conferences, a definition of the Constitution of Canada (already noted),
and amendments to the British North America Act, 1867, and other constitutional documents, including the name change from British North America
Acts to Constitution Acts.

Under its new name, the Constitution Act, 1867, remains Canada's
principal constitutional statute. Many of the other twenty-three documents
listed in the schedule and still in force are Acts amending it directly or
indirectly or Acts or orders admitting new provinces to Confederation.[7]

The parts of the Constitution of Canada most frequently consulted by
law students and lawyers are the Constitution Act, 1867, and the Canadian
Charter of Rights and Freedoms. If you are studying or practising law in a
province that entered Confederation later than 1867, the Act or order admitting your province will also be of interest to you. Constitutional documents
are printed in many places, but care must be exercised in using them because
many of the printed versions are not up to date. The best source to use for the
Constitution Acts is *A Consolidation of the Constitution Acts 1867 to 1982*,
published by the federal Department of Justice in 1983. It updates the earlier
work of Elmer A. Driedger, which takes into account not only direct amendments, but also indirect amendments and spent provisions,[8] by adding the
text of the Constitution Act, 1982, and incorporating into the 1867 Act those of
the former's provisions that directly amended it. It also prints in a footnote on
page 61 the text of the Canada Act 1982. An excellent annotated edition of the
Canada Act 1982 (including the Constitution Act, 1982) has been prepared by
Peter Hogg.[9]

For the text of other constitutional documents, one has to look elsewhere.
The appendices volume to the *Revised Statutes of Canada, 1970* contains the
original texts of most of them, but with little and generally no updating. Some

---

7   New provinces or territories were admitted to Canada by British orders in council.
     However, if a province was being created out of territory that was part of Canada, this was
     done by an Act of the Canadian Parliament. The Manitoba Act, 1870, was passed on the
     assumption that "Rupert's Land and the North-Western Territory" would be admitted
     "into the Union or Dominion of Canada, before the next Session of the Parliament of
     Canada". Manitoba was created out of "part of the said Territories". (Preamble to the
     Manitoba Act, 1870.) The procedure followed for admitting Newfoundland was somewhat
     different, the terms of union between Canada and Newfoundland being confirmed and
     given effect by an Act of the Parliament at Westminster.

8   The Driedger consolidation, entitled *A Consolidation of The British North America Acts,
     1867 to 1975*, was published by the Department of Justice in 1976. Its foreword, which is
     reprinted with the necessary changes in the 1983 consolidation, explains the differences
     between direct amendments, indirect amendments, and spent provisions, and indicates
     how each is dealt with in the consolidation.

9   See above, note 6.

of the provinces print constitutional documents along with their revised statutes, but practice varies from one province to another. The version of the Manitoba Act, 1870, printed in the *Revised Statutes of Manitoba, 1970*'s appendix volume is much more useful than the one in the *Revised Statutes of Canada, 1970* because the former indicates sections that have been repealed or amended either directly or indirectly. Similarly, in printing the text of the British North America Act, 1867, in the appendix volume to the *Revised Statutes of Ontario, 1980*, changes affecting Ontario are noted in square brackets at the end of the relevant sections. A complicating factor, and one of the reasons why it is difficult to keep the texts of these enactments up to date, is that some of the provisions in the Constitution Act, 1867, and in the Acts and orders admitting new provinces are regarded not only as part of the Constitution of Canada, but also as part of the constitutions of the provinces. With certain exceptions, those constituting the latter can be changed by provincial legislation.[10]

The first amendments to the Constitution of Canada under one of the new amending procedures were made by proclamation, as prescribed by the Constitution Act, 1982, on June 21, 1984. The proclamation is published in an extra issue of the *Canada Gazette*, Part I.[11] Unfortunately, the format is confusing, the text of the amendments being contained in a schedule that is itself described as a proclamation and includes a directive to cite it as follows: "Constitution Amendment Proclamation, 1983". It appears that confusion has arisen between a proclamation bringing a statute into force and this new type of proclamation that *makes* the amendments. The legislative resolutions on which the proclamation is based are neither statutes nor proclamations, and it is not their date that should be used in citing the proclamation or the amendments made by it. In my opinion the correct citation is "Constitution Amendment Proclamation, 1984," but since it is necessary to follow the directive in the proclamation, I suggest the following citation: "Constitution Amendment Proclamation, 1983 [*i.e.* 1984]". I hope that the wording of future Constitution Amendment Proclamations will more accurately reflect the new amending procedures. It would be better if the resolutions proposing amendments left the date in the citation blank, to be filled in when the proclamation is issued.

Under s. 52(2)(c) of the Constitution Act, 1982, the amendments made by the 1984 proclamation become part of the Constitution of Canada.

---

10   Section 92(1) of the British North America Act, 1867, authorized the Legislature of a province to amend the constitution of the province "except as regards the office of Lieutenant Governor". This provision was repealed by the Constitution Act, 1982, s. 53(1) and the Schedule, item 1(4). The right of a provincial Legislature to amend the constitution of the province is now dealt with by s. 45 of the Constitution Act, 1982, subject to restrictions contained in s. 41.

11   *The Canada Gazette*, Part I, Vol. 118, EXTRA No. 35, June 21, 1984. Under the general procedure described in s. 38(1) of the Constitution Act, 1982, the proclamation makes six amendments to that Act. All were authorized by a resolution adopted by "the Senate, the House of Commons and the legislative assemblies of at least two-thirds of the provinces that have, in the aggregate, according to the latest general census, at least fifty per cent of the population of all the provinces".

3. CANADIAN STATUTES AND STATUTORY INSTRUMENTS

(a) Sessional or Annual and Revised Statutes – Canada

Canadian statutes, both federal and provincial, appear in either sessional or annual volumes and are also consolidated from time to time in volumes called revised statutes.

Traditionally, the statutes of one session were published together, and this is still the case in most Canadian provinces. In 1977, however, Ontario adopted the modern United Kingdom practice of numbering consecutively and printing together all the statutes that received royal assent in a calendar year. Newfoundland, after some confusion in the mid-1970s, has also adopted this practice. Such a system avoids the complications that occur when a session continues through more than one calendar year or conversely when there are two sessions in one calendar year.

The disadvantages of publishing statutes by session became especially apparent when federal parliamentary sessions began to extend into more than two calendar years. The worst example was the session of 1980 to 1983 (four calendar years). Its statutes did not become available in bound permanent form until late in 1984. For a record of that session's legislation before the publication of these sessional volumes, one was dependent on Part III of the *Canada Gazette.* By s. 62 of the Miscellaneous Statute Law Amendment Act, 1984, provision has now been made for the future publication of federal statutes by calendar year.

Early English statutes were always cited by regnal rather than calendar year, and this practice continued in the United Kingdom until 1962. This made it necessary, when looking for a statute, to know not only the year, but also the exact date, of a monarch's accession to the throne. In 1962, the Acts of Parliament Numbering and Citation Act provided for citation by calendar year from the beginning of 1963. If you look at any volume of United Kingdom statutes after 1962, you will see that the only place the regnal year appears is in a note at the beginning of the volume; the calendar year alone appears at the top of the individual pages.

Canada, at least at the federal level, has continued officially to use regnal year citation to the present day. In federal statutes, both regnal and calendar year appear on the title page and throughout the volume. With the change from sessional to annual volumes of statutes, there will probably also be some modification of the policy relating to inclusion of the regnal year. Practice in the provinces varies, some using only the calendar year in their sessional or annual statutes, others retaining both. Teachers of legal method in Canadian law schools generally favour citation by calendar year.

Statutes are frequently amended or repealed or through passage of time cease to be in effect. This means that a statute in a sessional or an annual volume may no longer be in force or, if it is, its text may be out of date. Thus, there is a need for periodic updating, and this is why revised statutes are published.

Traditionally, the preparation of a new revision was authorized by an Act, either of Parliament or of a Provincial Legislature, that established a Statute Revision Commission to examine and consolidate the previous edition of revised statutes and the subsequent volumes of sessional statutes. With the trend towards continuing consolidations of statutes, this practice has now been modified in some Canadian jurisdictions. For instance, under an Act passed by the Canadian Parliament in 1974, a permanent Statute Revision Commission was established. Similarly, a 1977 Newfoundland statute authorizes the preparation from time to time of a draft consolidation and revision of the statutes of that province. Such legislation removes the need for a separate Act authorizing each new revision.

Acts or parts of Acts that have been repealed or have otherwise ceased to be in force are omitted from the revision. Moreover, since it is sometimes difficult to determine with certainty whether an Act is still in force, and the Commission is generally given considerable discretion in deciding which Acts to include, some are omitted from the revision, but not expressly repealed by it. It is, therefore, usual to include, with the revised statutes, tables showing the history and disposal of Acts in the previous consolidation and in the sessional or annual volumes published in the years between the two consolidations. These tables show, in one form or another, Acts consolidated in and superseded by the new revision and where within it each provision is found, Acts omitted from the new revision because of their repeal by legislation, Acts omitted from but not expressly repealed by the new revision, and Acts omitted from it and repealed by it.

When the work of revision is complete, the new edition of revised statutes is generally brought into force by proclamation. The statutes included in the new revision then supersede the corresponding ones in the previous revision and subsequent sessional or annual volumes; when referring to such a statute, you should cite the version in the latest revision. Thus, Ontario's Family Law Reform Act is no longer cited S.O. 1978, c. 2, but R.S.O. 1980, c. 152.

It may occasionally be necessary to cite the sessional or annual version of a statute if, for instance, you are comparing the provisions of an Act in its original form with one that amended it. If you are referring to new Acts or to amendments that have been passed since the latest revision, you will generally cite the sessional or annual volumes. Now, however, some jurisdictions issue loose-leaf editions of statutes, in which amendments and new Acts are incorporated into the latest revision. More will be said later about these continuing consolidations and the problems related to citing them.

It used to be customary, in revised statutes, to group Acts together by subject; for instance, all Acts dealing with the structure of the courts might be found together. Now the usual practice is to arrange and number the statutes alphabetically by short title.[12] For example, Acts in the *Revised Statutes of*

---

12   There are variations from one jurisdiction to another regarding the location of the short title. In some it is given in the first section of an Act, in others, in the last. Even within a jurisdiction, the practice may be different in revised and sessional or annual volumes. There is now a trend towards not having a long title at all and using the short title in the heading. In this situation there is no need to provide for a short title in the text of the Act.

Ontario, 1937 are arranged by subject, whereas in the *Revised Statutes of Ontario, 1950* they are arranged alphabetically by title. The same is true of the *Revised Statutes of Ontario, 1960, 1970* and *1980;* in the last mentioned, the Abandoned Orchards Act is Chapter 1, the Absconding Debtors Act, Chapter 2, the Absentees Act, Chapter 3, and so on. The change from a subject arrangement to an alphabetical arrangement has been accompanied in some jurisdictions by the adoption of an alphanumeric numbering system. This has been adopted in the latest revision of federal statutes and in those of all provinces except British Columbia, Newfoundland, and Ontario.

The frequency of issuing revised statutes varies considerably. Since Confederation consolidations of the federal statutes have been issued only five times; they are dated 1886, 1906, 1927, 1952, and 1970. A new revision is expected to be published in 1986. Some of the provinces have attempted to consolidate their statutes at about ten year intervals, but there has not been much consistency. The dates of the latest revisions of provincial statutes are as follows:

Alberta, 1980
British Columbia, 1979
Manitoba, 1970
New Brunswick, 1973
Newfoundland, 1970
Nova Scotia, 1967
Ontario, 1980
Prince Edward Island, 1974
Quebec, 1977
Saskatchewan, 1978

Because the revised statutes for the most part replace the sessional or annual volumes, you will probably find that unless you are tracing the history of an enactment you will have little need to consult the sessional or annual statutes before the latest revision. If you are interested in the history of a particular Act, or a particular provision in an Act, you will find very useful the notation at the end of each section of the Act in the revised statutes of most Canadian jurisdictions. It tells you where in the previous revision or a subsequent sessional volume you will find that specific provision. If the Act was passed many years ago, you can trace it back in this way, noting when and what amendments were made.

The Northwest Territories and the Yukon Territory, which do not have provincial status, are each governed by a federally appointed commissioner and an elected council. Ordinances passed by the Commissioner-in-Council are, like federal and provincial statutes, consolidated from time to time. The dates of the latest revised ordinances are:

Northwest Territories, 1974
Yukon Territory, 1971[13]

---

13   In the third edition of *Using a Law Library* (p. 64), it was stated incorrectly that there was a new revision of the ordinances of the Yukon Territory in 1976. Actually, the 1976 loose-leaf edition is an office consolidation rather than a revision.

Since 1982, the ordinances of the Yukon Territory have been called statutes and the Council is now referred to as the Legislative Assembly. This change was brought about by an ordinance of the Yukon Council, 1982 (1st), c. 4. The use of the new terminology is justified by defining "Act" as "an ordinance of the Territory enacted pursuant to the Yukon Act (Canada)," and "Legislative Assembly" as "the Council of the Yukon Territory constituted under section 9 of the Yukon Act (Canada)". Ordinances and revised ordinances, even those enacted before 1982, are now cited as statutes.

(b) Revised Statutes of Canada, 1970

Since the *Revised Statutes of Canada, 1970* differs in certain important respects from previous consolidations of federal statutes and from most provincial statutes published before that date, it is appropriate to deal with it in some detail.

This is the first time a revision of federal statutes has been published in a bilingual format; English and French versions of each statute are printed together, appearing in parallel columns on the same page. An alphanumeric system of numbering chapters has been adopted and an explanatory note at the beginning of the volume of appendices states that this type of designation "would facilitate the introduction of a permanent decimal system of numbering in any succeeding periodic revisions or in any future system of continuous current revision the government may adopt."

Volumes 1-7 of the *Revised Statutes of Canada, 1970* contain Chapters A-1 to Y-4, consolidated to December 31, 1969. The eighth volume is a first supplement, which contains amendments to Acts in the *Revised Statutes of Canada, 1970* and new Acts passed in 1970 during the second session of the 28th Parliament. The ninth volume is a second supplement. The summary table of contents, which appears at the beginning of each volume, states that it publishes "Amendments to Acts contained in the Revised Statutes of Canada, 1970, enacted during the Third Session of the Twenty-eighth of Parliament commencing on the 8th day of October 1970. . . ." However, some new Acts are included: for instance, the Federal Court Act becomes R.S.C. 1970, c. 10 (2nd Supp.). In the detailed table of contents in the volume itself, which was published in 1972, the second supplement is described as "Amendments and Additions". The second supplement also contains a table showing the history and disposal of Acts and a table of public statutes. Part I of the latter shows "all the chapters of the Revised Statutes of Canada, 1970, with amendments and new Acts from January 1, 1970," whereas Part II shows "certain public Acts in force before January 1, 1970 that were not consolidated in the Revised Statutes of Canada, 1927, 1952 or 1970." The English version of the table of public statutes is printed on yellow pages; the French version is printed on blue.

The tenth volume of the *Revised Statutes of Canada, 1970* contains appendices. Appendix I consists of a table showing the history and disposal of

Acts. It is important to note, however, that it has now been replaced by the table of the same name that is published in the second supplement, beginning at page 443. Appendix II contains constitutional Acts and documents, and Appendix III, the Canadian Bill of Rights. An index volume to the *Revised Statutes of Canada, 1970* was published late in 1973.

In this latest revision of federal statutes, changes have been made in the arrangement of some of the Acts. If the first word in the short title of an Act does not relate to its subject matter, another word in the title is generally used to determine the arrangement. For example, the Canada Evidence Act is listed as Evidence, Canada, and given the prefix E, rather than C. Its chapter number is E-10. However, this policy does not apply if the Act concerns a corporation, commission, or similar entity. In this case, entry is by name. Thus, the Canadian Film Development Corporation Act is given the prefix C, not F, its chapter number being C-8. The English title of an Act is used in determining its arrangement and citation; for instance, the French title of the Canada Evidence Act is "Loi sur la preuve au Canada," but it is cited E-10 in French as in English (see Illustration 18).

Because the Canada Elections Act now in force was passed in 1970 during the second session of the 28th Parliament, its text is not included in the main volumes, but in the first supplement. The alphanumeric system is not followed in the supplements, though the Acts are arranged in alphabetical order. The Canada Elections Act is listed as Elections, Canada, and is given the chapter number 14; it is cited R.S.C. 1970, c. 14 (1st Supp.).

The Criminal Code was not included in the *Revised Statutes of Canada, 1952* because a complete revision was underway at the time. It is contained in the *Revised Statutes of Canada, 1970.*

Although the Income Tax Act appears in the *Revised Statutes of Canada, 1970* as chapter I-5, it has not come into force in this form because of the following provision in the *Statutes of Canada,* 1970-71, c. 43, s. 1:

> Notwithstanding any deposit and proclamation of the printed Roll of the Revised Statutes of Canada, 1970, under *An Act respecting the Revised Statutes of Canada,* chapter 48 of the Statutes of Canada, 1964-65, that portion of the Roll containing the consolidation of the *Income Tax Act* shall not come into force or have effect as law and the *Income Tax Act,* chapter 148 of the Revised Statutes of Canada, 1952, as amended, shall continue to be in force and have effect as law after such deposit and proclamation.

In effect, therefore, the Income Tax Act must be regarded as omitted from the *Revised Statutes of Canada, 1970.*

There is no official loose-leaf edition of the *Revised Statutes of Canada, 1970,* but a commercial publisher, Formules Municipales Ltée/Municipal Forms Ltd. ("F.M.") in Farnham, Quebec (now owned by CCH Canadian Limited) has issued such an edition. It is different from the provincial loose-leaf editions, which will be described later, because it incorporates into the *Revised Statutes of Canada, 1970,* only amendments to Acts contained in it. New Acts passed since the latest revision are not included. Instead, F.M. issues them in separate sessional loose-leaf volumes and incorporates amend-

ILLUSTRATION 18
Revised Statutes of Canada, 1970
Reproduced by permission of the Minister of Supply and Services Canada

CHAPTER E-10	CHAPITRE E-10
An Act respecting witnesses and evidence	Loi concernant les témoins et la preuve

SHORT TITLE	TITRE ABRÉGÉ

Short title **1.** This Act may be cited as the *Canada Evidence Act*. R.S., c. 307, s. 1.

1. La présente loi peut être citée sous le titre: *Loi sur la preuve au Canada*. S.R., c. 307, art. 1. Titre ab

PART I
Application

Application **2.** This Part applies to all criminal proceedings, and to all civil proceedings and other matters whatever respecting which the Parliament of Canada has jurisdiction in this behalf. R.S., c. 307, s. 2.

PARTIE I
Application

2. La présente Partie s'applique à toutes les procédures criminelles et à toutes les procédures civiles, ainsi qu'à toutes les autres matières de la compétence du Parlement du Canada. S.R., c. 307, art. 2. Applicati.

Witnesses

Interest or crime **3.** A person is not incompetent to give evidence by reason of interest or crime. R.S., c. 307, s. 3.

Témoins

3. Nul n'est inhabile à rendre témoignage pour cause d'intérêt ou de crime. S.R., c. 307, art. 3. Intérêt ou .

Accused and spouse **4.** (1) Every person charged with an offence, and, except as otherwise provided in this section, the wife or husband, as the case may be, of the person so charged, is a competent witness for the defence, whether the person so charged is charged solely or jointly with any other person.

4. (1) Toute personne accusée d'infraction, ainsi que, sauf dispositions contraires du présent article, la femme ou le mari, selon le cas, de la personne accusée, sont habiles à rendre témoignage pour la défense, que la personne ainsi accusée le soit seule ou conjointement avec quelque autre personne. Accusé et conjoint

Idem (2) The wife or husband of a person charged with an offence against section 33 or 34 of the *Juvenile Delinquents Act* or with an offence against any of sections 143 to 146, 148, 150 to 155, 157, 166 to 169, 175, 195, 197, 200, 248 to 250, 255 to 258, 289, paragraph 423(1)(c) or an attempt to commit an offence under section 146 or 155 of the *Criminal Code*, is a competent and compellable witness for the prosecution without the consent of the person

(2) La femme ou le mari d'une personne accusée d'infraction à l'article 33 ou 34 de la *Loi sur les jeunes délinquants*, ou à l'un des articles 143 à 146, 148, 150 à 155, 157, 166 à 169, 175, 195, 197, 200, 248 à 250, 255 à 258, 289, à l'alinéa 423(1)c), ou d'une tentative de commettre une infraction visée à l'article 146 ou 155 du *Code criminel*, est un témoin compétent et contraignable pour la poursuite sans le consentement de la personne accusée. Idem

ments into them. Acts that have been repealed are removed from the appropriate loose-leaf volumes. If you consult the loose-leaf edition and are citing a federal statute, you should check the official text to ensure accuracy.

The new revision of federal statutes, scheduled for publication in 1986, is expected to be similar in format to the *Revised Statutes of Canada, 1970*. The cut-off date for legislation to be included in the main volumes is July 1, 1984. Supplementary volumes will contain legislation passed between that date and 1986. There is likely to be a loose-leaf edition in addition to the traditional bound volumes, but a definite decision on this matter has not been reached at the time of writing.

(c) Revised Statutes of Manitoba, 1970

In its statutory consolidation of 1970, the Province of Manitoba began an experiment with a new numbering and updating system. In some ways, this revision resembles the *Revised Statutes of Canada, 1970*, but it also has features peculiar to itself. The *Revised Statutes of Manitoba, 1970*, are published in bound volumes and in a loose-leaf edition. In both, the chapters, instead of being numbered consecutively, are given an alphanumeric notation beginning with the first letter of the first word (other than "the") of the Act. Generally only every tenth number is used; thus the Agricultural Credit Corporation Act is A10; the Agricultural Productivity Council Act is A20, the Agricultural Societies Act, A30 and so on. This leaves the numbers in between to be used for new Acts passed before the next consolidation. There is no continuous numbering of pages in either bound volumes or loose-leaf service, each Act being paged separately. When an Act is amended or a new one passed, replacement or new pages are supplied for the loose-leaf edition. For instance, when s. 15 of The Noxious Weeds Act (c. N110) was amended in 1978, a replacement sheet for pages 7-8, dated September 1978, was issued. The only changes are, of course, in s. 15, which appears on page 7. Compare the page in the bound volume (Illustration 19) with the replacement page in the loose-leaf edition (Illustration 20). An example of a new Act that has been inserted in the loose-leaf edition is the Age of Majority Act, which, coming alphabetically before the first act (A10) in the consolidation, has been numbered "Cap. A7".[14] Sessional bound volumes continue to be issued so that there will be a complete record of legislation, but the advantage of the loose-leaf service is not only that it provides much prompter updating, but also that it keeps the consolidation current, something that the sessional bound volumes cannot do.

The inauguration of a continuing consolidation of Manitoba Statutes created problems regarding the citation of Acts passed subsequent to the *Revised Statutes of Manitoba, 1970*. Such Acts have a year and chapter number in the sessional volumes and a continuing consolidation number in

---

14   *Revised Statutes of Manitoba, 1970* consolidated statutes in force at the end of 1969. The Age of Majority Act was passed in 1970.

ILLUSTRATION 19
Revised Statutes of Manitoba, 1970, Bound Volume 3

NOXIOUS WEEDS   Cap. N110

Additional inspectors as minister may require.

14(5) Where, in the opinion of the minister, it is impossible or impracticable for one inspector to perform the inspectoral work in any municipality, he may, at his discretion, require of the council the appointment and employment of such additional inspectors or sub-inspectors as to him seems necessary; and in case of neglect or failure on part of council to comply with the requirement of the minister, he may appoint, employ, and provide remuneration for such persons as he deems necessary under the conditions and terms similar to those outlined in subsection (1).

Temporary assumption of duties by minister.

14(6) In case of failure to keep noxious weeds under control as required within the municipality by this Act, the minister may, at his discretion, employ for that purpose such persons as may seem to him fit, and any expenditures shall be paid out of the funds of the municipality.

S.M., 1968, c. 46, s. 14.

Action on default of municipality.

15   Where a municipal council neglects or refuses to make a payment as is required by section 14, it may be made by the Minister of Urban Development and Municipal Affairs on the recommendation of the minister, and included by him in his next annual levies under The Department of Urban Development and Municipal Affairs Act against the municipality so in default.

S.M., 1968, c. 46, s. 15.

Unorganized territory.

16   In unorganized territory the Lieutenant Governor in Council may appoint and fix the remuneration of inspectors to be known as "district noxious weeds inspectors"; and they have authority to the same extent as municipal noxious weeds inspectors over such territory as defined by the Lieutenant Governor in Council.

S.M., 1968, c. 46, s. 16; am.

Duties of inspector.

17(1) Every inspector or sub-inspector shall, with all diligence, proceed to examine the lands in the area over which his jurisdiction extends for the purpose of ascertaining that the provisions of the Act and regulations are complied with.

Service of notice.

17(2) Where he finds noxious weeds on any lands, he may serve notices upon the persons as are responsible under this Act in respect of the lands.

Contents of notice.

17(3) The notice may require the noxious weeds to be destroyed within a certain time to be prescribed and set forth in the notice, not exceeding fifteen days.

Service of notice.

17(4) The notice may be served as provided in subsection (4) of section 9.

S.M., 1968, c. 46, s. 17.

7

ILLUSTRATION 20
Continuing Consolidation of the Statutes of Manitoba (Loose-leaf)

NOXIOUS WEEDS

Cap. N110

Additional inspectors as minister may require.

14(5)   Where, in the opinion of the minister, it is impossible or impracticable for one inspector to perform the inspectoral work in any municipality, he may, at his discretion, require of the council the appointment and employment of such additional inspectors or sub-inspectors as to him seems necessary; and in case of neglect or failure on part of council to comply with the requirement of the minister, he may appoint, employ, and provide remuneration for such persons as he deems necessary under the conditions and terms similar to those outlined in subsection (1).

Temporary assumption of duties by minister.

14(6)   In case of failure to keep noxious weeds under control as required within the municipality by this Act, the minister may, at his discretion, employ for that purpose such persons as may seem to him fit, and any expenditures shall be paid out of the funds of the municipality.

S.M., 1968, c. 46, s. 14.

Action on default of municipality.

15   Where a municipal council neglects or refuses to make a payment as is required by section 14, it may be made by the Minister of Municipal Affairs on the recommendation of the minister, and included by him in his next annual levies under The Municipal Affairs Administration Act against the municipality so in default.

S.M., 1968, c. 46, s. 15.
Am. S.M. 1978, c. 49, s. 74.

Unorganized territory.

16   In unorganized territory the Lieutenant Governor in Council may appoint and fix the remuneration of inspectors to be known as "district noxious weeds inspectors"; and they have authority to the same extent as municipal noxious weeds inspectors over such territory as defined by the Lieutenant Governor in Council.

S.M., 1968, c. 46, s. 16; am.

Duties of inspector.

17(1)   Every inspector or sub-inspector shall, with all diligence, proceed to examine the lands in the area over which his jurisdiction extends for the purpose of ascertaining that the provisions of the Act and regulations are complied with.

Service of notice.

17(2)   Where he finds noxious weeds on any lands, he may serve notices upon the persons as are responsible under this Act in respect of the lands.

Contents of notice.

17(3)   The notice may require the noxious weeds to be destroyed within a certain time to be prescribed and set forth in the notice, not exceeding fifteen days.

Service of notice.

17(4)   The notice may be served as provided in subsection (4) of section 9.

S.M., 1968, c. 46, s. 17.

the loose-leaf service. For instance, the Age of Majority Act, as we have seen, is numbered A7 in the continuing consolidation. In the 1970 sessional volume it is c. 91, though "Cap A7" appears after this number at the top of each page of text. Since some institutions subscribe to the sessional volumes and not to the continuing consolidation and *vice versa*, it is desirable that a citation be used from which the Act can be found in either. For a completely new Act, passed since the 1970 revision, the following form is recommended: The Age of Majority Act, S.M. 1970, c. 91 (A7). Note the difference between this and the citation for an Act that was in the 1970 revision: The Agricultural Credit Corporation Act, R.S.M. 1970, c. A10. In the case of an Act that amends one in the 1970 revision, there is no need to assign a number in the continuing consolidation as it will take the number of the Act into which it is incorporated. In this situation, the following form of citation is recommended: The Noxious Weeds Act, R.S.M. 1970, c. N110, as amended S.M. 1978, c. 49, s. 74. There is now, however, a trend towards using the citation C.C.S.M. Thus, the Noxious Weeds Act can also be more simply cited C.C.S.M., c. N110.

Although the arrangement of Acts in the *Revised Statutes of Manitoba, 1970* and the continuing consolidation is, for the most part, alphabetical by short title, there are a few exceptions which may cause confusion. For instance, all Acts relating to the courts are grouped together under the letter "C". Thus, the County Courts Act is cited c. C260 and the Queen's Bench Act, c. C280. Still more confusing is the citation, c. A180, for the Manitoba Public Insurance Act. It appears that this Act was originally called the Automobile Insurance Act and that its name, but not its number, was changed. The Act continues to be filed with the A's rather than the M's. In spite of its number, this Act was not included in the *Revised Statutes of Manitoba, 1970*. It was passed in 1970, and its sessional volume citation was the Automobile Insurance Act, S.M. 1970, c. 102. Coming alphabetically after the Attorney-General's Act, R.S.M. 1970, c. A170, the last A-lettered Act in that edition, it did not have to be placed between other Acts with short titles beginning with the letter A. It was therefore given the number A180 in the Continuing Consolidation.

The three-volume index to the Continuing Consolidation has not been kept up to date; it is simply an index to the *Revised Statutes of Manitoba, 1970*. The tables of contents to individual volumes are updated, though they are not always current.

(d) Loose-leaf Editions of Statutes of Provinces other than Manitoba

Several other provinces have followed Manitoba's lead in issuing loose-leaf editions of their statutes; Ontario and Newfoundland are the only exceptions. Most provinces have done so in conjunction with the publication of a new revision of the statutes, but British Columbia and Nova Scotia began by issuing loose-leaf consolidations as a step towards new revisions. British Columbia's interim edition has now been replaced by the loose-leaf version of the *Revised Statutes of British Columbia, 1979*, but Nova Scotia's loose-leaf consolidation of the *Revised Statutes of Nova Scotia, 1967* and subsequent sessional volumes has still to be superseded by a new revision of Nova Scotia statutes.

There are loose-leaf editions of the *Revised Statutes of New Brunswick, 1973* and the *Revised Statutes of Prince Edward Island, 1974*. The numbering system used in both the bound-volume and loose-leaf editions is an alpha-numeric one. However, instead of using every tenth number, as in Manitoba, a decimal system has been adopted to allow for an unlimited number of insertions. In addition, New Brunswick has adopted a new system of number-ing statutes in its sessional volumes so that they can easily be fitted into the continuing consolidation. New Acts are grouped together at the beginning of the sessional volumes and given alphanumeric notations. Amending Acts are also grouped together, but they are numbered 1, 2, 3, *etc*. An example of a new Act, passed in 1977, is the Metric Conversion Act. It is cited S.N.B. 1977, c. M-11.1, and it is inserted into the loose-leaf edition with the same number.

An example of an amending Act passed the same year is An Act to Amend the Liquor Control Act. It is cited S.N.B. 1977, c. 31, but is now incorporated into the Liquor Control Act, which is c. L-10 in the continuing consolidation. This Act is a good example of one that is frequently amended. At the time of writing in 1984, some pages in the loose-leaf version of the Liquor Control Act are dated as recently as September 1983 and March 1984.

New Brunswick, which is officially bilingual, now publishes its statutes in both English and French in the same volume. In the *Revised Statutes of New Brunswick, 1973*, the format is similar to that used in the *Revised Statutes of Canada, 1970*.

On the cover of the loose-leaf edition of Prince Edward Island statutes, the title *Statutes of Prince Edward Island* is used. The title page reads: *The Revised Statutes of Prince Edward Island (1982 up-date)*. The year of the up-date changes as each new one is issued. If an Act in the *Revised Statutes of Prince Edward Island, 1974* has been repealed, it is still listed in the index with the word "Repealed" entered in brackets after it: *e.g.*, C-21 Co-operative Associations Act (Repealed) 387. If you turn to page 387, you will find the chapter number and short title listed followed by the statement: "Repealed by Stats. P.E.I. 1976, c. 7". In this case, the repealed Act was replaced by one of the same name. It is numbered C-21.1. On page 389 of the continuing consol-idation where the text begins, a footnote states: "Also being Stats. P.E.I. 1976, c. 7".

An example of a repealed Act that has been replaced by one of a different title is the Floral Emblem Act, chapter F-11. It is stated in the continuing consolidation that it was repealed by Stats. P.E.I. 1977, c. 33, s. 3. If you have the bound-volume edition, you can look it up and see that 1977, c. 33 is the Provincial Emblems Act. However, the citation is not very helpful if you have access only to the loose-leaf edition. The Provincial Emblems Act is num-bered P-24.1 in the continuing consolidation. As with the Co-operative Asso-ciations Act, a footnote states: "Also being Stats. P.E.I. 1977, c. 33".

The Condominium Act may be used as an example of a completely new Act incorporated into the continuing consolidation. It is numbered C-16.1, following the Conditional Sales Act, which is chapter C-16. The Condominium Act is chapter 6 in the 1977 sessional volume, but curiously this is not noted on the appropriate updated page in the continuing consolidation.

The French and English versions of the the *Revised Statutes of Quebec, 1977* are published in separate volumes, this being a different format from that used in the *Revised Statutes of Canada, 1970* and the *Revised Statutes of New Brunswick, 1973*. There are bound volumes and a loose-leaf edition in both languages. An alphabetical arrangement and an alphanumeric numbering system are used. Whereas in the federal and New Brunswick revisions the English title is used in assigning the letter in the alphanumeric notation, in the Quebec revision the French title is used. Thus, the Loi sur les enfants immigrants, L.R.Q. 1977, c. E-7 is cited, in English, Immigrant Children Act, R.S.Q. 1977, c. E-7. An example of an Act passed since the 1977 revision is the Loi sur la santé et la securité du travail; An Act Respecting Occupational Health and Safety. In the 1979 sessional volumes it is chapter 63, whereas in the loose-leaf editions, both French and English, it is chapter S-2.1.

The *Revised Statutes of Saskatchewan, 1978* are available in bound volumes and in a loose-leaf format. An alphanumeric system, with no numbers being left out, has been adopted; decimals are used in numbering new Acts in the continuing consolidation.

Although the *Revised Statutes of British Columbia, 1979* are also available in both bound and loose-leaf formats, the alphanumeric notation system is not used. Acts are arranged alphabetically by title and numbered in the traditional manner – 1, 2, 3, *etc.* The same system of numbering is used in subsequent sessional volumes. In the loose-leaf edition, amendments are incorporated into the appropriate Acts. If an Act is repealed, it is removed from the continuing consolidation and a sheet noting its repeal inserted. If the repealed Act has been replaced by a new one with a different name, the new name is noted so that you will be able to find it. If a completely new Act is passed, it is inserted into the loose-leaf edition in its correct alphabetical position. In addition to its chapter number in the sessional volume, a new or replacement Act is given an appropriate number – a decimal system is used – in the loose-leaf edition. Thus, in the *Revised Statutes* there is a Wildlife Act, which is cited R.S.B.C. 1979, c. 433. It, however, has now been repealed and replaced by a new Wildlife Act, S.B.C. 1982, c. 57. This citation appears in both the 1982 sessional volume and in the loose-leaf edition, but in the latter, the following notation is added: "Index Chap. 433.1". The Waste Management Act, S.B.C. 1982, c. 41, is given the "index chapter" number 428.5 in the continuing consolidation, placing it between the Warehouse Receipt Act, c. 428, and the Water Act, c. 429.

The most recent revisions of provincial statutes are the *Revised Statutes of Alberta, 1980* and the *Revised Statutes of Ontario, 1980*. Whereas Ontario has maintained the traditional numbering system and published only bound volumes, Alberta has adopted an alphanumeric system and issued both bound volumes and a loose-leaf edition. Its numbering system resembles most closely that of New Brunswick, the alphanumeric system being used as well for new public Acts in its sessional volumes.

As noted earlier, the loose-leaf consolidation of the *Statutes of Nova Scotia* differs from those of the other seven provinces that publish such an edition.[15] The Nova Scotia consolidation is a step towards a new revision of the statutes. An alphanumeric system is used with the intention, no doubt, of officially adopting it in the next revision, but the reader is told to cite the Acts to the 1967 revision or, where appropriate, to a subsequent sessional volume. Thus, the Social Workers Act is given the chapter number S-23 in the loose-leaf consolidation, but it is still cited R.S.N.S. 1967, c. 285. Similarly, a more recent statute, the Municipal Board Act, is numbered M-25 in the consolidation, but is cited S.N.S. 1981, c. 9.

The loose-leaf edition of the ordinances – now called statutes – of the Yukon Territory is similar to that of Nova Scotia in that it is a consolidation rather than a new revision. In citation, however, it seems to be acceptable to use either the alphanumeric chapter number in the consolidation or the number in the 1971 revision or, where appropriate, in a sessional or annual volume. (Since 1982, Yukon statutes have been published by calendar year rather than by session.) The table of statutes in the annual volumes lists the alphanumeric citation in one column and the more traditional citation, including amendments, in another column headed "History".

(e) Status of Loose-Leaf Editions of Statutes

It is important to know that the status of loose-leaf editions or continuing consolidations of statutes is not the same in all provinces that maintain them. There is statutory authority for both the Manitoba and the Quebec loose-leaf editions. Manitoba's continuing consolidation is said to have official status in an indirect way, though it is not the official record of the Legislative Assembly. In the introduction to the *Revised Statutes of Quebec, 1977,* it is said that both bound and loose-leaf editions are equally authentic; this applies to both the French and English versions. As noted earlier, it is acceptable to cite Manitoba's loose-leaf edition as C.C.S.M. without a date.[16] Quebec's loose-leaf editions are cited L.R.Q. in French and R.S.Q. in English without a date. The status of the loose-leaf editions of New Brunswick, Prince Edward Island, and British Columbia statutes appears to be similar to that of Manitoba's continuing consolidation, though there are variations, and no uniform mode of citing these editions has been adopted. For instance, it appears to be acceptable in Prince Edward Island to use the date of the latest revision (1974) in citing a statute in the continuing consolidation even if it was passed later. In Alberta and Saskatchewan, the situation is different. At the beginning of each a note appears stating that it has no legislative sanction and that the original

---

15   See above, at p. 62.
16   See above, at p. 61.

Acts should be consulted for all purposes of interpreting and applying the law.[17] This creates problems with regard to Saskatchewan because sessional volumes since the latest revision are very difficult to obtain (presumably an insufficient number have been published) and some Canadian law school libraries do not have them.

(f) Future of Revised Statutes

It is not yet clear what effect technological change and the advent of loose-leaf editions of statutes will have on future revisions of federal and provincial statutes. Complete revisions at frequent intervals will probably become unnecessary. Indeed, it seems likely that keeping statutes up to date on a continuing basis will become the norm and that revised statutes in the traditional format will become obsolete. If that happens, it will be more difficult to trace the history of a statute, though it will still be possible through use of the sessional or annual volumes.

(g) Bilingual Statutes

It is required by s. 18(2) of the Canadian Charter of Rights and Freedoms (which is also s. 18(2) of the Constitution Act, 1982) that federal statutes be published in both English and French. This is not new; s. 133 of the British North America Act, 1867 (now in Canada called the Constitution Act, 1867) contains the same requirement, and federal statutes, revised and sessional, have always been published in both languages. The current practice, which began with the session of 1968/69, is to print both versions in the same volume in parallel columns on the same page. We have seen that this practice was adopted as well in the 1970 revision of federal statutes.[18] Formerly, English and French versions of federal statutes were published in separate volumes.

New Brunswick is the only province that has agreed to entrench in the Charter – s. 16(2) – a declaration that English and French are its official languages. The requirement that its statutes be published in both languages is contained in s. 18(2). We have seen that the format used in printing New Brunswick statutes is similar to the federal one.[19]

Although other provinces are not mentioned in the "Official Languages of Canada" sections (16-22) of the Charter, there are requirements elsewhere

---

17   The status of loose-leaf editions of statutes and the manner of citing them are complex questions with which I dealt in more detail in a paper entitled "Problems in Statutory Citation" at the annual conference of the Canadian Association of Law Libraries in London, Ontario in May 1984. For the text of the paper see *CALL Newsletter,* NS 10, No. 1 (Jan.-Feb. 1985) pp. 3-6.

18   See above, at p. 55.

19   See above, at p. 62.

in the Constitution of Canada that the statutes of Quebec and Manitoba be published in both French and English. The provision relating to Quebec is contained in s. 133 of the Constitution Act, 1867; for Manitoba it is found in s. 23 of the Manitoba Act, 1870. Until recently, there was doubt as to whether these provisions formed part of the "Constitution of the Province," in which case they would have been amendable by provincial legislation, but the Supreme Court of Canada, in separate judgments relating to each province, has ruled that this is not the case.[20] Section 41(c) of the Constitution Act, 1982, confirms that amendments to the Constitution of Canada relating to the use of the English or the French language cannot be made unilaterally by a province.

As required by s. 133 of the Constitution Act, 1867, Quebec has always published its statutes in both French and English. However, with the passage of the Charter of the French Language in 1977,[21] an attempt was made to enact statutes only in French (ss. 8 and 9), though an English version was to be provided by the civil administration (s. 10). Affirming the decisions of Quebec courts, the Supreme Court of Canada held these sections of the Charter of the French Language to be in conflict with s. 133, which was said to cover "enactment by implication". "What is required to be printed and published in French and in English is described as 'Acts' and texts do not become 'Acts' without enactment."[22] Therefore Quebec statutes continue to be enacted and published in both French and English.

In spite of s. 23 of the Manitoba Act, 1870, which was assumed to be part of the constitution of the province, the Legislative Assembly of Manitoba in 1890 passed legislation providing, among other things, that its statutes need be published only in English. Although there were protests at the time, the constitutionality of the 1890 Act was not challenged in the courts until the 1970s; it was held by the Supreme Court of Canada in 1979 to be *ultra vires* the Legislative Assembly of Manitoba. The constitutionality of all the Acts passed since 1890 because they are in English only is still in doubt and the task of translating those still in force is a monumental one. Although the 1890 Act has now been repealed and "official language" defined as "the English language or the French language", provisions for translating even those Acts passed since the 1979 court ruling do not appear to be very satisfactory.[23] French versions of some, but by no means all, Acts appear in the sessional volumes.

There is no constitutional requirement that Ontario publish its statutes in French and they are enacted only in English. The provincial government has, however, instituted a program making certain statutes and regulations available in French. The first translations were issued in pamphlet form in

---

20   *Attorney General of Quebec v. Blaikie*, [1979] 2 S.C.R. 1016, 49 C.C.C. (2d) 359, 30 N.R. 225, 101 D.L.R. (3d) 394; *Attorney General of Manitoba v. Forest*, [1979] 2 S.C.R. 1032, [1980] 2 W.W.R. 758, 2 Man. R. (2d) 109, 49 C.C.C. (2d) 353, 30 N.R. 213, 101 D.L.R. (3d) 385.

21   Still popularly called by its bill number in the 1977 session – 101 – the Charter is c. 5 of the statutes of that session. In the *Revised Statutes of Quebec, 1977*, its chapter number is C-11.

22   *Attorney General of Quebec v. Blaikie*, [1979] 2 S.C.R. 1016 at 1017.

23   An Act Respecting the Operation of Section 23 of the Manitoba Act in Regard to Statutes, S.M. 1980, c. 3.

1979. An asterisk before the name of an Act in the table of public statutes in the annual volumes now indicates that an official French translation is available in office consolidation form. (See Illustration 18.)

A government bill (C-26) amending the Northwest Territories Act and the Yukon Act to make English and French the official languages of these territories was introduced in the Canadian House of Commons on March 21, 1984. The bill, which did not proceed beyond first reading, would have provided that, in order to remain in force, ordinances, regulations, *etc.* would have to be published in both official languages by January 1, 1988. The government of the Northwest Territories, preferring to prepare its own legislation, rather than have it imposed from Ottawa, has now (1984) passed an ordinance establishing English and French as the official languages of the Northwest Territories, as well as giving more limited official recognition to the aboriginal languages of the Territories.

(h) Tables of Public Statutes and Statute Citators

If you are looking for a statute and know its name, but not the date it was passed, there are different ways to find it. You can go to the table of public statutes at the back of the latest sessional or annual volume. (Federal and all provincial statutes have such a table, although Saskatchewan's is no longer included in the sessional or annual volumes, but is published in a separate loose-leaf volume entitled *Tables of the Statutes of Saskatchewan and Saskatchewan Regulations*. For federal statutes, you may find a more up-to-date table in the *Canada Gazette*, Part III, where it is also published from time to time. Quebec's table is called Tableau des modifications/Table of Amendments.) There you will find its chapter number in the revised statutes if it was in force at the time of the latest revision; the date and chapter number of amending Acts since this revision will also be listed in the table. (Using Ontario's Highway Traffic Act as an example, see Illustration 21.) If the Act was passed after the revised statutes came into force, there will be no entry in the revised statutes column, but the date and chapter number of the Act will be given, so that you can find it in the appropriate sessional or annual volume. (See the entry for the Health Protection and Promotion Act in Illustration 21. The Act was passed in 1983.) Another way to find the statute, if it is a federal, Ontario, or British Columbia one, is to look it up in the *Canada, Ontario,* or *British Columbia Statute Citator.* These are not government publications, but privately published loose-leaf services. The advantage that the *Canada* and *Ontario Statute Citators* have over the tables of public statutes is that they print the text of all amendments (exceptions may be made if the amendments are very voluminous[24]), arranging them according to the section numbers of

---

24   For instance, the text of amendments to the Criminal Code and to the Income Tax Act is not
      included in the *Canada Statute Citator*. If you look up the Criminal Code in the *Citator* it
      directs you to the current edition of *Martin's Annual Criminal Code* "for a complete, fully
      annotated text of the Code with all amendments to date . . . ." For the text of the Income Tax
      Act "as amended to date" and a complete treatment of the decided cases relevant to it, the
      Citator refers you to "the special text and services available." Both CCH Canadian Limited
      and Richard De Boo Limited provide such services. The former is called *Canadian Income
      Tax Act*; the latter's, *Income Tax Act Annotated*, edited by H.H. Stikeman.

ILLUSTRATION 21
Statutes of Ontario, 1983
(*Asterisk indicates official translation into French
is available in office consolidation form.)

TABLE OF PUBLIC STATUTES		857
Title of Act	R.S.O. 1980 Chap.	Amendments in 1981, 1982, 1983
Gas and Oil Leases Act	184	
*Gasoline Handling Act	185	
Gasoline Tax Act	186	1981, c. 11.
General Sessions Act	187	
*General Welfare Assistance Act	188	
George R. Gardiner Museum of Ceramic Art Act	...	1981, c. 64.
Gold Clauses Act	189	
Government Contracts Hours and Wages Act	190	
*Grain Elevator Storage Act	191	1983, c. 40, sup.
Guarantee Companies Securities Act	192	
H		
*Habeas Corpus Act	193	
Haliburton Act	194	1982, c. 57, s. 5, rep.
(See now Haliburton (County of) Act)		
Haliburton (County of) Act	...	1982, c. 57.
Healing Arts Radiation Protection Act	195	
*Health Disciplines Act	196	1983, c. 59.
*Health Facilities Special Orders Act	...	1983, c. 43.
*Health Insurance Act	197	
*Health Protection and Promotion Act	...	1983, c. 10.
*Highway Traffic Act	198	1981, c. 48, c. 54 and c. 72; 1982, c. 15 and c. 28; 1983, c. 63.
Historical Parks Act	199	
*Homemakers and Nurses Services Act	200	
*Homes for Retarded Persons Act	201	
*Homes for Special Care Act	202	
Homes for the Aged and Rest Homes Act	203	
Horticultural Societies Act	204	1982, c. 52.
*Hospital Labour Disputes Arbitration Act	205	
Hospitals and Charitable Institutions Inquiries Act	206	
Hotel Fire Safety Act	207	
Hotel Registration of Guests Act	208	
Housing Development Act	209	
*Human Rights Code	...	1981, c. 53.
*Human Tissue Gift Act	210	
Hunter Damage Compensation Act	211	
Hypnosis Act	212	
I		
IDEA Corporation Act	...	1981, c. 34.
*Immunization of School Pupils Act	...	1982, c. 41; 1983, c. 76.
Income Tax Act	213	1981, c. 13 and c. 46; 1983, c. 37.
Indian Welfare Services Act	214	
Industrial and Mining Lands Compensation Act	215	
*Industrial Standards Act	216	
Inflation Restraint Act	...	1982, c. 55.
*Innkeepers Act	217	
*Insurance Act	218	
International Bridges Municipal Payments Act	...	1981, c. 60.
*Interpretation Act	219	
Interprovincial Subpoenas Act	220	
Investment Contracts Act	221	

the original Act. Thus, to ascertain the present text of a statute, one does not have to look at all the amending ones, but simply at the version in the latest revision (or in a sessional or annual volume if the Act was passed after the latest revision) in conjunction with the statute citator. The *British Columbia Statute Citator* does not, however, print the text of amendments. It notes the citation and directs you to the appropriate sessional volume. Of course, for federal and Ontario statutes, when accuracy is important, you should check the official text in the appropriate sessional or annual volumes. Citators also provide information with regard to the judicial interpretation of statutes; cases involving such interpretation are cited in the appropriate places.

Suppose your sister and her eighteen-month old son, who live in another province, are planning to visit you. They will be passengers in your car, and you are not sure of the Ontario law relating to seat belts or other restraints for small children. You know that you, as the driver of the car, are responsible for seeing that passengers under the age of sixteen wear seat belts, but you think there is an exemption for children under the age of two. Now assume you have found the statement of this exemption in s. 90(6) of the Highway Traffic Act, R.S.O. 1980, and you are now checking to see whether this sub-section has been amended. If you look up the title of the Act in the table of public statutes in the latest annual volume of the *Statutes of Ontario* (see again Illustration 21) you will see that the Act has been amended several times. However, you cannot tell from the table of public statutes whether any of the amendments relates to the provision in which you are interested. On checking you will find that the exemption relating to passengers under the age of two was removed by the 1982 amending Act. If you go instead to the *Ontario Statute Citator* and look for references to s. 90 of the Highway Traffic Act, you will immediately find the text of the amendment to sub-section 6, together with the citation to the amending Act (see Illustration 22). (For the different type of restraint system to be used by small children, you will have to look at the regulations made under s. 90 of the Act.) The tables of public statutes in sessional or annual volumes of most provinces do indicate what sections of an Act are affected by subsequent amending ones. Ontario and Manitoba are the exceptions.

It should be noted that in the *Canada Statute Citator* the new method of arranging Acts in the *Revised Statutes of Canada, 1970* has not been adopted. Thus the Canada Evidence Act is found under "Canada," not under "Evidence" in both the *Revised Statutes of Canada, 1952* and the *Revised Statutes of Canada, 1970* editions of the *Canada Statute Citator*.

The *Canada, Ontario,* and *British Columbia Statute Citators* are published by Canada Law Book Limited.

A service similar to a citator entitled *Statutes Judicially Considered* is published by Carswell for the four western provinces (one service for each province). Thus, British Columbia has a citator and a statutes judicially considered service. Judicial considerations of rules of court are also noted in the Carswell services.

ILLUSTRATION 22
Ontario Statute Citator

HIGHWAY TRAFFIC ACT—*Continued*

Section 88

Subsec. (1) repealed and the following subsecs. (1) and (1a) substituted 1983, c. 63, s. 19:

(1) No person shall ride on or operate a motorcycle or motor assisted bicycle on a highway unless he is wearing a helmet that complies with the regulations and the chin strap of the helmet is securely fastened under the chin.

(1a) No person shall carry a passenger who is under sixteen years of age on a motorcycle on a highway unless the passenger is wearing a helmet that complies with the regulations and the chin strap of the helmet is securely fastened under the chin.

Section 90

Subsec. (2) repealed and the following substituted 1982, c. 28, s. 3(1) (proclaimed in force November 1, 1982):

(2) No person shall drive on a highway a motor vehicle in which a seat belt assembly required under the provisions of the *Motor Vehicle Safety Act* (Canada) at the time that the vehicle was manufactured or imported into Canada has been removed, rendered partly or wholly inoperative, modified so as to reduce its effectiveness or is not operating properly through lack of maintenance.

Subsec. (6) amended 1982, c. 28, s. 3(2) (proclaimed in force November 1, 1982) by striking out "has attained the age of two years and" in the second and third lines.

Subsec. (7)(c) repealed and the following substituted 1982, c. 28, s. 3(3) (proclaimed in force November 1, 1982):

(c) is secured in the manner prescribed by the regulations.

Subsec. (8)(b) repealed and the following substituted 1982, c. 28, s. 3(4) (proclaimed in force November 1, 1982):

(b) governing the use of different child seating and restraint systems based on the birth date, age, height or weight of a child or the relationship of a child to the driver or owner of the motor vehicle and prescribing, or adopting by reference manufacturer's recommendations concerning, the manner in which a child is to be secured therein;

(c) prescribing classes of motor vehicles, drivers and passengers;

(d) adopting by reference, in part or in whole, any code, standards or specifications concerning child restraint systems;

(e) exempting from any of the provisions of this section or the regulations made under this section,
(i) any class of motor vehicle,
(ii) any class of driver or passenger, or
(iii) drivers carrying any prescribed class of passenger,
and prescribing conditions for any such exemption.

Section 92

Subsec. (6) amended 1982, c. 28, s. 4(1); repealed and the following subsecs. (6) to (6c) substituted 1984, c. 21, s. 7:

(6) Subject to section 93, no vehicle, other than a fire apparatus, a semi-trailer or a bus, including load, shall exceed the length of 12.5 metres while on a highway.

In *Statutes of Manitoba Judicially Considered,* Acts are listed in the main section only if they have been judicially considered. A complete listing, with amendments noted, is contained in a table of public statutes, which is published as an appendix. The text of amendments is not given. The Manitoba format used to be followed in the services for the other three western provinces, but changes have been made in the new editions relating to the *Revised Statutes of Saskatchewan, 1978,* the *Revised Statutes of British Columbia, 1979,* and the *Revised Statutes of Alberta, 1980.* In the British Columbia and Alberta services, there is now a table of Acts, which lists only their names. Amendments and repeals are noted in what is called the casematter section, that is, in the same section as judicial considerations. This new arrangement makes the British Columbia and Alberta services more similar to Canada Law Book's citators, especially the *British Columbia Statute Citator* since the text of amendments is not included. *Statutes of Saskatchewan Judicially Considered* now does not list amendments at all; it deals exclusively with judicial considerations. This is probably because information on amendments is now provided by a new service called *Tables of the Statutes of Saskatchewan and Saskatchewan Regulations,* published by the Saskatchewan government.

(i) Statute Indexing

If you are looking for a statute but do not know its name and have only an idea of its subject matter, your task may be more difficult. Traditionally, indexes to statutes were arranged by Act, not by subject, but fortunately this is gradually changing.

Law librarians in Canada have long felt the need for proper subject indexes to statutes, and since the early 1960's, when it was founded, the Canadian Association of Law Libraries has been trying to persuade the appropriate government officials to have them produced. An important step towards the achievement of this goal was taken by the Canadian Law Information Council (CLIC) in sponsoring a pilot project on indexing the *Revised Statutes of Newfoundland, 1970.* A detailed subject index was published. The story of how the index was produced has been told in an interesting report on the project by Alice Janisch, under whose direction it was carried out.[25] CLIC's indexing committee conducted a limited test among various groups of users to determine whether the index was satisfactory. It concluded that it was seen by most users as an improvement over other statutory indexes. The report on the test, published by CLIC, made suggestions to help further improve future indexes.[26]

---

25 Alice Janisch, *Report of Pilot Project on Indexing Revised Statutes of Newfoundland (1970),* Ottawa, Canadian Law Information Council [1979?]
26 *Report on the Test of the Index to the Revised Statutes of Newfoundland (1970),* Indexing Committee, Canadian Law Information Council, June, 1978 (Cover title: "Working Paper: Indexing"). Text in English and French.

The Newfoundland statutes index was the first of several to be produced by CLIC. Since the completion of that pilot project, CLIC has prepared indexes to the *Revised Statutes of British Columbia, 1979,* the *Revised Statutes of Ontario, 1980,* and most recently an index to the statutes of Alberta, which covers not only the *Revised Statutes of Alberta, 1980,* but also subsequent sessional statutes up to and including the spring sitting of 1983. All are comprehensive subject indexes, not indexes to individual Acts. CLIC will also be preparing an English subject matter index to the new revision of federal statutes. The Société québecoise d'information juridique (SOQUIJ) will prepare the French index on contract with CLIC. The index to the *Revised Statutes of Canada, 1970* is better than most of the statute indexes of its day since it contains cross references from subject headings to Acts. However, a comprehensive subject index to the new revision will greatly facilitate research into federal statutes.

Indexes in sessional or annual volumes of statutes were generally unsatisfactory, being arranged by Act rather than by subject, and several provinces have now stopped publishing indexes in these volumes. In the case of provinces for which indexes have been prepared by CLIC, this is presumably because there is an intent to update the indexes on a continuing basis, using computer facilities. For instance, in the "Guide Notes to Index, R.S.B.C. 1979," it is stated that the index will be revised at regular intervals to include later material and exclude repealed material.

(j) Local and Private Acts

When we speak of statutes, we generally mean public general statutes. Local and private Acts, relating to specific towns, cities, counties, institutions, individuals, *etc.,* are generally published at the end of the sessional or annual volumes. Chapter numbering is usually consecutive. If the last public Act is chapter 93, the first local or private one will be chapter 94. This varies, however, from one jurisdiction to another. The table of contents at the beginning of a volume usually indicates at what number the local and private Acts begin.[27]

---

27   In some jurisdictions, public general statutes are designated Part I, and local and private Acts, Part II. In others, there are three divisions, with local Acts being separated from private ones. For instance, in the 1983 sessional volume of *Nova Scotia Statutes,* chapters 1-67 are public Acts, chapters 68-84 are local, and chapters 85-100, private. In Ontario, there is now separate numbering for private Acts. Thus, in the annual volume for 1983, chapters 1-89 are public Acts and chapters Pr. 1-Pr. 45 are private. In numbering its private and local Acts, British Columbia includes them alphabetically in the same sequence as its public Acts, but prints them at the end of the volume. Thus, the Northwest Baptist Theological College Amendment Act, 1982, is chapter 51 of the 1982 *Statutes of British Columbia,* but it is printed immediately after chapter 78, the last public Act for that session. The arrangement in some volumes of the *Statutes of Canada* is rather confusing. From 1875 to 1925, there were two volumes a session, volume 1 containing public general Acts and volume II, local and private Acts. (You will sometimes find the two volumes bound together.) In 1926, there was a change in terminology from volumes to parts. By 1947 the number of private Acts granting divorce had become very large and it was decided to exclude them from Part II. From that date to 1963, when a change in parliamentary divorce procedure brought an end to private divorce Acts, Part I (public general Acts) and Part II (local and private Acts, excluding divorce Acts) were bound together with "Vol. 1" lettered on the spine. Volume II,

Local and private Acts are not included in the revised statutes of Canada, 1970 or its provinces, but British Columbia, Manitoba, Nova Scotia and Ontario do include in their latest revised statutes tables of local and private Acts, indicating dates and chapter numbers.[28] Nova Scotia, Manitoba and Ontario update these tables in their sessional or annual volumes, whereas British Columbia, in its sessional volumes, now incorporates the names of local and private Acts into the same table as its public general statutes. Newfoundland's list of private Acts in its annual volumes goes back to 1834, one hundred and fifteen years before it became Canada's tenth province. Alberta publishes a table of private Acts in its sessional volumes and Saskatchewan includes such a table in its loose-leaf *Tables to the Statutes of Saskatchewan and Saskatchewan Regulations.* Quebec's Bibliothèque de la legislature (now Bibliothèque de l'Assemblée nationale du Québec published in 1976 an "Index des lois à caractère privé du Québec, 1867-1975". It is updated by "Addenda à l'index des projets de loi d'intérêt privé" in "Les projets de loi d'intérêt publies 1963-1980," also published by the Bibliothèque. In 1983, a *Table of Local and Private Acts, Statutes of Canada, 1867 to 1979* was published. It is described as an "historical index showing all local and private Acts of Canada other than those Acts that deal with divorces, that have been enacted since 1867 and that appear in the Statutes of Canada 1867 to 1978-79". Each Act is listed alphabetically under one of several broad subject headings. Supplements are planned; the first, covering the period March 27, 1979 to November 4, 1984, has just become available at the time of writing. Maritime Law Book Ltd. now issues in loose-leaf form a subject-matter index to both public and private statutes of New Brunswick. Arranged by year, it consists of chapter indexes and a key word index.

(k) Bills and Their Finding Aids

Tables of public statutes and statute citators keep you reasonably current about Acts that have been passed. Often, however, students and lawyers want to know about legislation that is before the Canadian Parliament or a provincial legislature. Therefore, most law school libraries subscribe to federal bills and the bills of their own provincial legislature; some subscribe to the bills of the legislatures of other provinces as well. The bills are usually arranged in numerical order, but in some jurisdictions there are separate sequences for government bills, private members' public bills, and private bills.

---

containing divorce Acts, could be purchased separately, but many libraries do not have the second volume for these years.

28   The *Revised Statutes of Nova Scotia, 1967* has several tables of local and private Acts, one covering the period up to 1900, the others, 1901-23, 1924-54, and 1955-67. The *Revised Statutes of Manitoba, 1970* has two separate tables, one of municipal Acts, the other of private Acts. *Revised Statutes of British Columbia, 1979*'s table lists not only local and private Acts, but also in the same sequence unconsolidated public Acts. Ontario's Table of Private Acts, 1867-1980, lists private Acts that "may still have effect". It is divided into "Municipal Private Acts" and "Other Private Acts", the latter having numerous subdivisions.

There is now a companion volume to the *Ontario Statute Citator* called *Current Bills Service.* It provides the text of the third reading of Ontario bills that have been passed, thus giving an interim service until they appear as Acts in the *Statutes of Ontario.* Bills in this service are filed alphabetically by short title. Part II of the Summary of Legislation at the front shows the chapter number that has been assigned to each newly passed Act, replacing the bill number. Quebec's *Répertoire legislatif de l'Assemblée nationale* lists bills that have received royal assent (lois sanctionnés). The bill number is followed by the newly assigned chapter number and the dates of each reading, royal assent, and coming into force are noted. There is also an indication of whether the new Act amends any earlier ones.

The Library of Parliament prepares on a regular basis for the use of Members of Parliament a *Status of Bills Report* showing the stage each bill has reached. Bills are listed in numerical order, Commons bills in one section, Senate bills in another. The Canadian Law Information Council makes this service available to the public, and you may find that your law school library subscribes to it. Provincial legislative libraries also produce status of bills reports for the use of members of their respective legislatures, but their availability to the public varies. That compiled by the Legislative Library of Ontario is distributed bi-weekly when the Legislature is in session to selected libraries. York University Law Library, which receives it, makes it available to other law school libraries in Ontario that wish to subscribe to it. As with the federal *Status of Bills Report,* the bills are listed in numerical order. The need for access to this type of service is less than it used to be because the same information is now available in an increasing number of published sources.

Canadian Current Law, a monthly Carswell publication, of which more will be said in the fourth chapter of this book, includes information on the status of federal, provincial and territorial bills in its "Progress of Bills" section.

Another source of information on the progress of federal bills is the *Ottawa Letter,* a loose-leaf service published by CCH Canadian Limited. Basically it is a newsletter published weekly throughout the year, giving information about new legislation and related matters. When Parliament is sitting, it includes a section called "Progress of Bills through Parliament". When Parliament is not in session or has been dissolved, its news relates to such matters as cases interpreting legislation and the progress of the election campaign. At the end of a session, all bills are listed in numerical order within their various categories – government bills, private members' public bills, bills introduced in the Senate, *etc.* The list shows what happened to each bill – whether it passed and, if not, how far it progressed.

CCH Canadian Limited also publishes another loose-leaf service called *Provincial Pulse,* which gives similar information regarding provincial and territorial legislation. Published twice a month, its most useful feature is the legislative record on green pages at the back of the volume. This is a progress of bills report for all the provinces and territories. Bills are listed in numerical order within the province or territory, and it does not take long to scan the list and find the bill you want.

Dealing with only one province, the *Ontario Legislative Digest Service – Carswell* is able to give more information about Ontario legislation than does *Provincial Pulse*. Highlights of the throne and budget speeches are included, and, in addition to noting the status of bills, there is a brief summary of the main provisions of each.

In November 1984 Carswell commenced publishing a similar service relating to federal legislation, entitled *Canadian Parliamentary Digest*. When Parliament is in session, this weekly, bilingual service provides summaries of all government public bills introduced into the House of Commons and all public bills introduced into the Senate.

(l) Proclamations

As noted earlier, the date on which a statute comes into effect, if no express provision is made in its text, varies from one jurisdiction to another.[29] Sometimes, however, provision is made in the statute itself for its not coming into force until proclaimed by the Governor General-in-Council (or the Lieutenant Governor-in-Council if it is a provincial statute). It may be, too, that part of an Act comes into effect immediately, but certain sections are delayed until proclaimed. The proclamation is published in the *Canada Gazette*, Part I or official Gazette of the province concerned. In the sessional or annual volumes of statutes of some of the provinces, there is included a table of public statutes requiring proclamation, which tells whether such Acts or sections of Acts have been proclaimed and, if so, the date they came into force. Information on the proclamation of statutes is also included in the statute citators, the Ontario *Current Bills Service,* and for federal statutes, the statutes of all provinces, and the ordinances or statutes of the territories in the monthly parts of *Canadian Current Law.*

Proclamations can, of course, have purposes different from bringing an Act into force. One other type of proclamation should be mentioned here. Under the Constitution Act, 1982, certain types of amendments to the Constitution of Canada can be made only by proclamation issued by the Governor General under the Great Seal of Canada. These proclamations are to be issued only when authorized by certain legislative bodies; the exact requirements vary according to the type of amendment. As we have seen, the first such proclamation was issued by the Governor General on June 21, 1984, and published in an extra issue of the *Canada Gazette,* Part I.[30]

(m) Regulations

Sometimes Parliament or a provincial legislature delegates to the executive, to a particular Minister, or to a board or other authority the right to

---

29   See p. 48, above.
30   See p. 51, note 11.

make rules or regulations under a statute – the broader term "statutory instrument" may be used when speaking of these rules and regulations.[31] This relieves the bodies that enact statutes of the need to legislate on matters of detail, some of which require frequent change.

Regulations made under federal statutes are published in Part II of the *Canada Gazette*; those made under provincial Acts appear in the official Gazettes of the provinces. Some provinces follow the federal policy of publishing regulations in a separate part of the Gazette: Alberta, British Columbia, Newfoundland, Nova Scotia, Prince Edward Island, and Quebec now publish regulations in Part II of their official Gazettes. (Acts of the National Assembly are also published in Part II of the *Gazette officielle du Québec/ Quebec Official Gazette*.) Saskatchewan publishes its regulations in both Parts II and III of the *Saskatchewan Gazette*. A note at the beginning of each part explains the difference. Those printed in Part II are regulations or amendments to regulations included in the *Revised Regulations of Saskatchewan*, a loose-leaf service now in course of publication, which, when completed, is expected to consist of four or five volumes. Amendments to existing regulations that have not yet been revised are printed in Part III. Ontario regulations are printed at the back of each issue of the *Ontario Gazette*. Double pagination is used, so all regulations for a year can be separated from the issues of the *Gazette* and bound together if desired. Manitoba publishes its regulations on sheets that are part of the *Manitoba Gazette*, but are paged separately from it. New Brunswick issues annual volumes of regulations, which are not part of the *New Brunswick Royal Gazette*.

The regulations of the Yukon Territory are published in Part II of the *Yukon Gazette*, but Parts I and II of each issue are contained in the same booklet and pagination is continuous. Part II of the *Northwest Territories Gazette* containing regulations is, on the other hand, paged separately.

There is much variation from one jurisdiction to another as to a policy of issuing revised or consolidated regulations.

Included in the *Consolidated Regulations of Canada, 1978* are all those regulations of general application that were in force on December 31, 1977. Consisting of 19 volumes, this consolidation came into force on August 15, 1979. A two-volume special issue of the *Canada Gazette*, Part II supplement-

---

31   The Statutory Instruments Act, S.C. 1970-71-72, c. 38, s. 2(1)(*b*) & (*d*) gives some useful definitions. In para. (*b*), "Regulations" is defined as "a statutory instrument (i) made in the exercise of a legislative power conferred by or under an Act of Parliament, or (ii) for the contravention of which a penalty, fine or imprisonment is prescribed by or under an Act of Parliament, and includes a rule, order or regulation governing the practice or procedure in any proceedings before a judicial or quasi-judicial body established by or under an Act of Parliament, and any instrument described as a regulation in any other Act of Parliament." In para. (*d*), "statutory instrument", a broader term, "means any rule, order, regulation, ordinance, direction, form, tariff of costs or fees, letters patent, commission, warrant, proclamation, by-law, resolution or other instrument issued, made or established (i) in the execution of a power conferred by or under an Act of Parliament, by or under which such instrument is expressly authorized to be issued, made or established otherwise than by the conferring on any person or body of powers or functions in relation to a matter to which such instrument relates, or (ii) by or under the authority of the Governor in Council, otherwise than in the execution of a power conferred by or under an Act of Parliament."

ing the consolidation contains amendments made in 1978 with appropriate references to regulations in the consolidation that are amended or repealed. An index of statutory instruments – the term used since the passage of the Statutory Instruments Act in 1971 – is issued as part of the *Canada Gazette*, Part II. Cumulating quarterly, it assists the user in finding regulations in both the consolidation and in the *Canada Gazette*, Part II, since the former was published.

Carswell now publishes in both English and French the *Canada Regulations Index/Index des Règlements du Canada*, which is composed of two elements: the Consolidated Index to the Regulations of Canada and monthly supplemental indexes. In a "How to Use" section at the beginning, it is stated that both these elements provide various features not found in the *Canada Gazette* indexes, including the following:

1. Where a regulation contains internal headings, these are reproduced in the index along with the titles of all schedules, tables and forms. In addition, the numbers of the regulation sections appearing under the individual headings are also reproduced. The reader is, therefore, provided with a better indication of the regulation's content. As headings, schedules, tables, *etc.* are amended, added to or deleted from the regulation, these changes will be indicated in the monthly indexes and incorporated into the following Consolidated Index.

2. Where a regulation is amended, the sections of that regulation that are affected by the amendment are indicated in the index. Similarly, where new provisions are added to an existing regulation, these additions are also indicated. In the case where an entire regulation has been revoked, the fact of the revocation is also noted.

Ontario has adopted the practice of consolidating its regulations and publishing them as companion volumes to its revised statutes. In the *Revised Regulations of Ontario, 1980*, as in the *Consolidated Regulations of Canada, 1978*, the texts of regulations are printed under the name of the appropriate Acts, the latter being arranged alphabetically by title. A supplement to the *Revised Regulations of Ontario, 1980* contains all regulations filed under the Regulations Act after December 31, 1980 and before November 16, 1981, the day the *Revised Regulations of Ontario, 1980* came into force. The annual volumes of the *Statutes of Ontario* contain at the back a table of regulations, indicating the number of the regulation (if contained in the main volumes of the *Revised Regulations of Ontario, 1980*) and the year and number, together with the date of the *Ontario Gazette* in which it is published, if the regulation was made later. Using as an example seatbelt regulations made under the Highway Traffic Act, Illustrations 23-25 show you the listing in the table of regulations, the regulation in the *Revised Regulations of Ontario, 1980*, and an amendment in the *Ontario Gazette, 1982*.

Carswell also provides an Ontario regulation service, subscribers to which are supplied with the pages of the *Ontario Gazette*, which contain regulations. An annual consolidated index is supplemented monthly. Illustra-

ILLUSTRATION 23
Statutes of Ontario, 1983

938   TABLE OF REGULATIONS

	R.R.O. 1980	O. Reg	Date of Gazette
[Highway Traffic Act, cont'd.]			
amended..................................		396/82	June 26/82
amended..................................		502/82	Aug. 7/82
amended..................................		644/82	Oct. 16/82
amended..................................		801/82	Dec. 25/82
amended..................................		31/83	Feb. 5/83
amended..................................		131/83	Mar. 26/83
amended..................................		189/83	Apr. 16/83
amended..................................		228/83	May 7/83
amended..................................		400/83	July 16/83
amended..................................		457/83	Aug. 6/83
amended..................................		661/83	Oct. 29/83
amended..................................		682/83	Nov. 12/83
Portable Lane Control Signal Systems........	478	-	
Reciprocal Suspension of Licences...........	479	-	
Restricted Use of Left Lanes by Commercial Motor Vehicles.............................	480	-	
amended..................................		535/81	Aug. 29/81
amended..................................		17/82	Feb. 6/82
amended..................................		804/83	Jan. 7/84
Restricted Use of the King's Highway........	481		
Safety Helmets..............................	482	-	
amended..................................		249/81	May 16/81
Safety Inspections..........................	483	-	
amended..................................		507/81	Aug. 15/81
amended..................................		800/81	Dec. 12/81
amended..................................		839/81	Jan. 2/82
amended..................................		59/82	Feb. 20/82
amended..................................		544/82	Aug. 21/82
amended..................................		596/82	Sept. 18/82
amended..................................		742/82	Nov. 27/82
School Buses................................	484	-	
amended..................................		277/81	May 23/81
amended..................................		598/82	Sept. 18/82
amended..................................		19/83	Jan. 29/83
amended..................................		336/83	June 18/83
Seat Belt Assemblies........................	485	-	
amended..................................		545/82	Aug. 21/82
amended..................................		629/83	Oct. 15/83
Security of Loads...........................		428/81	July 11/81
Signs.......................................	486	-	
amended..................................		372/81	June 20/81
amended..................................		802/81	Dec. 12/81

ILLUSTRATION 24
Revised Regulations of Ontario, 1980

REGULATION 485

under the Highway Traffic Act

SEAT BELT ASSEMBLIES

1. Correctional Service of Canada vehicles that are modified to facilitate the transportation of persons held in custody and police department vehicles are exempt from the requirement that,

(a) upper torso restraints;

(b) seat belt assemblies in the centre front seat seating position; and

(c) seat belt assemblies in the rear seat seating positions,

not be removed, rendered partly or wholly inoperative or modified so as to reduce their effectiveness.
O. Reg. 1087/80, s. 1.

2. A police officer, constable or peace officer who in the lawful performance of his duty is transporting a person in his custody is exempt from subsections 90 (3), (4) and (6) of the Act.   O. Reg. 1087/80, s. 2, *part*.

3. A person who is in the custody of a police officer, constable or peace officer is exempt from subsection 90 (4) of the Act.   O. Reg. 1087/80, s. 2, *part*.

4. An employee or agent of the Canada Post Office while engaged in rural mail delivery is exempt from subsection 90 (3) of the Act.   O. Reg. 34/76, s. 4.

5.—(1) In this Regulation "taxicab" means,

(a) a motor vehicle licensed as a cab by a municipality; or

(b) a motor vehicle designed for carrying less than ten passengers and operated under

the authority of an operating licence issued under the *Public Vehicles Act*.

(2) Taxicabs are exempt from the requirement that,

(a) upper torso restraints for drivers' seating positions; and

(b) seat belt assemblies in the centre front seat seating positions,

not be removed, rendered partly or wholly inoperative or modified so as to reduce their effectiveness.

(3) The driver of a taxicab while transporting for hire a passenger is exempt from subsection 90 (3) of the Act.   O. Reg. 192/76, s. 1, *part*.

6. The driver of a motor vehicle is exempt from the provisions of subsection 90 (6) of the Act in respect of a passenger under the age of five years or weighing less than 22.7 kilograms.   O. Reg. 192/76, s. 1, *part*; O. Reg. 571/78, s. 1.

7. Where a motor vehicle that was manufactured in or imported into Canada prior to the 1st day of January, 1974 is driven on a highway,

(a) the driver and passengers are exempt from the requirement to wear the upper torso restraint component of a seat belt assembly; and

(b) the driver is exempt from the provisions of subsection 90 (6) of the Act with respect to the requirement that passengers wear upper torso restraint components.   O. Reg. 192/76, s. 1, *part*.

ILLUSTRATION 25

3304   O. Reg. 543/82   THE ONTARIO GAZETTE   O. Reg. 545/82

HIGHWAY TRAFFIC ACT

O. Reg. 543/82.
Driver's Licences.
Made—July 29th, 1982.
Filed—August 5th, 1982.

REGULATION TO AMEND
REGULATION 462 OF
REVISED REGULATIONS OF ONTARIO, 1980
MADE UNDER THE
HIGHWAY TRAFFIC ACT

1. Subsection 2 (3) of Regulation 462 of Revised Regulations of Ontario, 1980 is revoked and the following substituted therefor:

(3) A Class D motor vehicle,

(a) owned or leased by a farmer and used for his personal transportation or the transportation, to or from a farm, of farm products, supplies or equipment where the transportation is not for compensation; and

(b) for which the amount of the fee paid for the permit for the vehicle was determined under subparagraph iii of paragraph 10 of subsection 5 (1) of Regulation 469 of Revised Regulations of Ontario, 1980,

shall be deemed to be a Class G motor vehicle. O. Reg. 543/82, s. 1.

2. This Regulation comes into force on the 15th day of September, 1982.

(1064)   34

HIGHWAY TRAFFIC ACT

O. Reg. 544/82.
Safety Inspections.
Made—July 29th, 1982.
Filed—August 5th, 1982.

REGULATION TO AMEND
REGULATION 483 OF
REVISED REGULATIONS OF ONTARIO, 1980
MADE UNDER THE
HIGHWAY TRAFFIC ACT

1. Subsection 5 (2) of Regulation 483 of Revised Regulations of Ontario, 1980 is revoked and the following substituted therefor:

(2) Subsection (1) does not apply to,

(a) an unladen dump vehicle;

(b) a dump vehicle for which a permit has been issued under the Act authorizing a gross weight of 5.500 kilograms or less; or

(c) a dump vehicle,

(i) owned or leased by a farmer and used for the transportation of his goods to his farm, and

(ii) for which the amount of the fee paid for the permit for the vehicle was determined under subparagraph iii of paragraph 10 of subsection 5 (1) of Regulation 469 of Revised Regulations of Ontario, 1980. O. Reg. 544/82, s. 1.

2. This Regulation comes into force on the 1st day of September, 1982.

(1065)   34

HIGHWAY TRAFFIC ACT

O. Reg. 545/82.
Seat Belt Assemblies.
Made—July 29th, 1982.
Filed—August 5th, 1982.

REGULATION TO AMEND
REGULATION 485 OF
REVISED REGULATIONS OF ONTARIO, 1980
MADE UNDER THE
HIGHWAY TRAFFIC ACT

1. Section 6 of Regulation 485 of Revised Regulations of Ontario, 1980 is revoked and the following substituted therefor:

6.—(1) The following classes of passengers are prescribed for the purposes of clause 90 (7) (c) of the Act:

1. Children weighing less than nine kilograms are classified as infants.

2. Children weighing nine kilograms or more but less than eighteen kilograms are classified as toddlers.

3. Children weighing eighteen kilograms or more but less than twenty-three kilograms are classified as pre-schoolers.

(2) For the purposes of clause 90 (7) (c) of the Act, an infant born after the 31st day of October, 1982, shall be secured in a rearward-facing child restraint system that,

(a) conforms to the requirements of Standard 213.1 under the *Motor Vehicle Safety Act* (Canada);

1174

ILLUSTRATION 26
Ontario Regulations Service – Annual Consolidated Index, 1983

HIGHWAY TRAFFIC ACT

Seat Belt Assemblies (R.R.O. 1980, Reg. 485) s. 6: am. O. Reg. 545/82.
S. 6(2)-(4), (7): am. O. Reg. 629/83.
Security of Loads: O. Reg. 428/81.
    Schedule A (Securement Requirements for Coiled Metal)
    Schedule B (Securement Requirements for Miscellaneous Metal Articles)
Signs (R.R.O. 1980, Reg. 486) s. 20a (new): am. O. Reg. 372/81.
    S. 24a (new): am. O. Reg. 802/81.
    Ss. 12-14, 29, 30, 33-40, 43(2), 48: am. O. Reg. 414/82.
    S. 1: am. O. Reg. 600/82.
    Speed Limit Signs (1-5)
    Stop Signs (6-11)
    Stopping Signs (12-14)
    Yield Right-of-Way Signs (15-17)
    Pedestrian Crossover (18)
    Symbol Pedestrian Control Signals (19)
    Turn Signals (20)
    No U Turn Sign (21)
    Parking Control Signs (22-24)
    School Bus Loading Zones (25-26)
    One-Way Sign (27)
    Do Not Enter Sign (28-30)
    Truck Sign (31)
    Lane Designation Signs (32)
    Figures 1-7)
    Do not Pass Sign (33-34)
    No Bicycles Sign (35-36)
    Pedestrian Prohibition Signs (37-40)
    Interdictory Symbol (41)
    Load Restriction Sign (42)
    Gross Weight on Bridges Sign (43)
    Figures (1-2)
    Construction Zone Sign (44)
    General (45-49)
Slow-Moving Vehicle Sign: R.R.O. 1980, Reg. 487.
    Schedule
Special Permits: R.R.O. 1980, Reg. 488.
Specifications and Standards for Trailer Couplings: R.R.O. 1980, Reg. 489.
    Interpretation
Speed Limits (R.R.O. 1980, Reg. 490) Sched. 14, Part 2, para. 16, paras. 31-32
(new); Part 5, paras. 19-20 (new); Sched. 30, Part 4, para. 8; Sched. 37, Part 3,
paras. 6, 7, 14; Part 4, para. 6 (new); Sched. 81, Part 2 (new); Part 3, para. 1; Part
5, para. 2 (new); Sched 232 (new): am. O. Reg. 67/81.
    Sched. 20, Part 5, para. 1; Sched. 233 (new): am. O. Reg. 109/81.
    Sched. 30, Part 3, para. 18; Sched. 53, Parts 5-6; Part 4, para. 4 (new); Sched.
58, Part 3, para. 4; Part 4, para. 1; Sched. 119, Part 5; Sched. 232, Part 4, para. 1:
am. O. Reg. 176/81.
    Sched. 2, Part 5, paras. 6, 18 (new); Part 6, para. 4 (new); Sched. 23, Part 2,
paras. 21, 42-43 (new); Part 4, para. 25 (new): am. O. Reg. 200/81.
    Sched. 1, Part 5, para. 41 (new); Sched. 50, Part 3, para. 2; Part 5, para. 1: am.
O. Reg. 338/81.
    Sched. 234 (new): am. O. Reg. 453/81.

tion 26 shows the entry in Carswell's Annual Consolidated Index, 1983, for "Seat Belt Assemblies" under "Highway Traffic Act". Comparing it with that in the table of regulations in Illustration 23, you will see that the former, unlike the latter, includes references to the section and sub-sections of Regulation 485 amended by later regulations. On the other hand, the Carswell index does not give the date of the *Ontario Gazette* in which the amending regulation is published. It is not really necessary for it to do so, as it is assumed the user will be looking it up in the regulation service.

The other provinces do not publish revised regulations as companion volumes to their revised statutes. There was, however, a consolidation of Nova Scotia regulations in 1942 and of New Brunswick regulations in 1963. A first consolidation of Manitoba regulations, the *Revised Regulations of Manitoba, 1971,* consisting of seven bound volumes, was published in 1974. It should also be noted that regulations made under the authority of selected statutes are printed on yellow sheets and filed with the appropriate Acts in the *Continuing Consolidation of Statutes of Manitoba.*

In 1972, Quebec published a ten-volume loose-leaf consolidation of its regulations, but it was updated only once. For a time, Formules Municipales, with the authority of the Official Publisher, issued a loose-leaf edition of Quebec regulations. It is no longer published because this authority was revoked when the *Règlements refondus du Québec, 1981,* consisting of eleven volumes was published. The English edition is called *Revised Regulations of Quebec, 1981.* There is no loose-leaf edition of either, but supplements are issued in both languages.

A loose-leaf consolidation of British Columbia regulations is in course of publication by the Ministry of the Attorney General. It is already available in part, but a note at the beginning states that not all British Columbia regulations are as yet included in the service. Users are advised to check the *Index of Current B.C. Regulations* to see what other regulations may exist. A two-volume loose-leaf revision of Prince Edward Island regulations has been published; updating appears to be rather slow.

The three-volume loose-leaf "consolidation and revision" of the *Orders and Regulations of the Northwest Territories,* dated 1979, has been replaced by one large bound volume called *Revised Regulations of the Northwest Territories, 1980.* There is a loose-leaf edition of *Yukon Regulations.*

Butterworth now publishes in loose-leaf format an *Alberta Regulations Service.* It contains selected regulations, that is, those made under what it describes as important and frequently used statutes.

Indexing of regulations varies considerably from one province to another. Reference has been made above to the cumulative *Index of Current B.C. Regulations,* filed under the Regulations Act since 1958 and published by the Registrar of Regulations, Ministry of the Attorney General. There is also a table of regulations at the back of the *British Columbia Statute Citator.* A cumulative Index of Regulations is issued as part of the *Alberta Gazette.* There is also a table of regulations at the back of the loose-leaf, *Statutes of Alberta Judicially Considered* and *Statutes of Manitoba Judicially Consid-*

ered. A table of Saskatchewan regulations is included in the volume, *Tables to the Statutes of Saskatchewan and Saskatchewan Regulations.* Western Legal Publications' *Saskatchewan Decisions Citator* also contains a table of regulations; its corresponding publications for the other three western provinces do not.

The *Ontario Gazette* publishes annually a cumulative table of regulations; the same table is printed at the back of the annual volumes of Ontario statutes, an excerpt of which is shown in Illustration 23. A similar table is published in the annual volumes of regulations of New Brunswick. There is an "Index cumulatif des textes réglementaires de 1867 au 31 décembre 1981" in the loose-leaf *Gazette officielle du Québec.* Information on more recent regulations is found in the "Index cumulatif des actes réglementaires/Cumulative Index of Regulatory Instruments, which accompanies the supplements to the *Règlements refondus.* An "Index of Subordinate Legislation filed pursuant to The Statutes and Subordinate Legislation Act" is now published annually as part of the *Newfoundland Gazette.* A cumulative index of Nova Scotia regulations was published in the 1970-71 sessional volume of statutes, and subsequent annual indexes have appeared, some in the sessional statutes, others in the *Royal Gazette,* Part II. There is a consolidated table of regulations in the loose-leaf *Revised Regulations of Prince Edward Island* and additional listings are included with the updates. The annual bound *Northwest Territories Gazette,* Part II includes a cumulative listing of regulations. There is also a table of regulations in force in the sessional volumes of ordinances. The Yukon Territory's loose-leaf regulation service includes an index of regulations in force.

Another source of information on regulations promulgated in all Canadian jurisdictions is *Canadian Current Law.* A table of regulations in each monthly part lists, by enabling statute, all new and amending regulations. Reference is made to instrument number, Gazette citation, and, for amendments, the sections of regulations affected.

4. ENGLISH STATUTES AND STATUTORY INSTRUMENTS

(a) General

As is the case with judicial decisions, English statutes[32] are important in the study and practice of Canadian law because some of them are still in force in Canada. For instance, the first statute enacted in 1792 (32 Geo. 3, c. 1) by the Legislature of the newly established province of Upper Canada introduced English civil law as it stood on October 15, 1792. The effect of this reception of

---

32   Sometimes I use the word "English" when "British" or "United Kingdom" might seem more appropriate. There is really no all-inclusive term that applies to every period of English history or to every edition of statutes. Law reports present fewer difficulties in this regard because English law reports do not normally include Scottish or Irish cases except those appealed to the House of Lords.

English law in Upper Canada can be seen by using as an example the Acts of Parliament (Commencement) Act 1793, referred to in the introduction to this chapter.[33] Had this Act been in force in Britain on October 15, 1792, it would have been the law of Upper Canada unless the Legislature of that province chose to alter it. However, since it was not passed until 1793, it had no effect in Upper Canada; the common law rule that provided that an Act came into force on the first day of the session in which it was passed unless provision was made in its text for a later commencement was still the law of Upper Canada. This common law rule was changed by the Legislature of Upper Canada in 1801 by an Act (41 Geo. 3, c. 11) almost identical in language with the Acts of Parliament (Commencement) Act 1793. Thus Upper Canadian statutes henceforth came into force on the date they received the royal assent unless provision was made in the text of an Act for a different time of commencement. As we have seen, the law relating to the effective date of Ontario statutes is now quite different.[34]

English statutes date back to the thirteenth century. The early volumes are somewhat difficult to use, partly because there are different editions and variations between them as to year and chapter number. The fact that the regnal year is printed in Latin may also cause difficulty. More recent statutes are easier to find, though until the change from sessional to annual publication there may be some confusion when a parliamentary session falls partly in one calendar or regnal year and partly in another. Moreover, if your citation is by regnal year and you are not familiar with the order and dates of English monarchs, you should know where to find a list of them. Perhaps the most convenient place to look is at the back of *Osborn's Concise Law Dictionary*. Hicks' *Materials and Methods of Legal Research* (Appendix I) also contains such a list. The same information can be found at the back of many textbooks on English history. Much has been done in the present century to simplify the citation of English statutes. Up to 1940, a bound volume contained the statutes passed during a particular parliamentary session. Since that date, however, each volume has included the statutes passed during a single calendar year. As we have seen, statutes continued until the end of 1962 to be officially cited by regnal year, but since the beginning of 1963, calendar year citation has been used.[35]

If you are looking for a particular English statute, there are several places where you can find it, especially if it is still in force. The most obvious one is in the annual (or in earlier years the sessional) volumes of *Public General Acts* – you will probably find that your library subscribes to either the official edition or to the one published as an extra section of the *Law Reports,* the two editions being identical. As they date from only the nineteenth century, your library is likely also to have one or more of the earlier editions or reprints of English statutes. Pickering's *Statutes at Large* (1225-1806), continued by the *Statutes of the United Kingdom* (1807-69) is perhaps the most common. However, the

---

33   See note 3 on p. 48.
34   See p. 48.
35   For complete details, see p. 52.

Statutes of the Realm, covering the years 1215-1714, is regarded as the best edition of early English statutes.

(b) Statutes in Force

In the foregoing sets you will find whatever statute you want, even if it has been repealed. Since there is greater need to consult those in force than those no longer in effect, revised editions of the statutes, including only those in force, have been prepared from time to time under the supervision of the Statute Law Committee. The *Statutes Revised,* as they were called, were simply a re-publication in chronological order of the statutes in force; there was no consolidation of amending Acts and no re-numbering of chapters. In Canada, as we have seen, the term "Revised Statutes" means something quite different. A law library could get along quite well without the latest revision of the English statutes if it had the annual volumes; the same is not true of the revised statutes of Canada and its provinces. And, as the following paragraphs will show, the manner of publishing revised statutes or statutes in force is now changing in England.

The third edition of the *Statutes Revised* was published in 1950. It began to be replaced in 1972 by a new official revised edition under a different title, *Statutes in Force.* This new edition is a different type of publication. "It breaks new ground," said the Lord Chancellor, Lord Hailsham, "by being designed as a self-renewing and thus permanent collection of the statutes."[36]

Each statute in force is being printed in a separate booklet perforated for storage in special loose-leaf binders. A subscriber may place the statutes in the binders in any order he chooses, but the recommended arrangement is by groups and sub-groups according to subject matter. Within a group or sub-group, Acts should be arranged in chronological order. Authorized by the Statute Law Committee, the work is being published in instalments. At the time of writing in 1984 it was still incomplete.

Statutes in Force is kept up to date by issuing booklets for newly enacted statutes, with instructions to remove any that have been repealed, revised booklets for statutes that have been so extensively amended as to require replacement, and annual cumulative supplements setting out amendments that have not yet been incorporated in the edition.

The complete edition of *Statutes in Force* will include not only Acts applying to the United Kingdom as a whole, but also those of more limited territorial application. It is possible to subscribe either to the complete edition or to a territorially limited one. A standing order may be limited to Acts that apply to England and Wales, to Scotland, or to Northern Ireland. Groups, sub-groups, and booklets may also be bought individually according to one's subject requirements.

Not all Canadian law school libraries subscribe to *Statutes in Force* and my impression is that those that do find that this edition is used only

---

36   "Message from the Lord Chancellor," in announcement of forthcoming publication of *Statutes in Force.*

occasionally. That has certainly been our experience at The University of Western Ontario. There is now a microfiche edition of *Statutes in Force* and because it is much less expensive to subscribe to the publication in this format, it may become available in more Canadian libraries. In view of its low use, some libraries that have been subscribing to the loose-leaf service may replace it with the microfiche edition.

(c) Finding Aids to Statutes

With *Statutes in Force* incomplete and rarely used, it is important to know how to find a statute in the sessional or annual volumes if you do not have a citation to it. There are two finding aids that will assist you. The *Index to the Statutes in Force* and the *Chronological Table of the Statutes* are intended to be published and to cumulate annually, but they sometimes fall behind schedule. The *Index* provides a subject listing of all public general statutes in force at the end of a given year. The *Table* lists all public general Acts from 1235 on in chronological order, and indicates whether they, or any sections of them, have been repealed or amended. An illustration may help you to use these finding aids.

We have referred briefly to the Ontario statute that deals with contributory negligence. Suppose you want to find the English statute relating to the same subject. If you look up "Contributory Negligence" in the *Index to the Statutes in Force*, you will find nothing, so you try "Negligence". Under this subject heading, you will see several sub-headings, but "Contributory Negligence" is not one of them. However, there is an entry which reads "Joint and several tortfeasors, see Damages, 3, 6" (see Illustration 27). Now you may have joint and several tortfeasors without contributory negligence being involved (two or more persons may have taken part in an act which caused injury to someone else), but the subjects are closely related and if you are familiar with the Ontario Act, you may remember that it deals with both. So look up "Damages" in the *Index*, concentrating on the entries under subheadings 3 and 6. In addition to references to joint and several tortfeasors, you will find near the end of subheading 6, the following entry: "Contributory negligence, apportionment of liability: 1945 c. 28 ss. 1(1)(2)(5)(6), 4; E & W 1976 c. 30 ss. 5, 6(2), sch. 2; E & W 1978 c. 47 s. 9(2), sch. 2; E & W 1982 c. 53 ss. 3(2), 75(1), sch. 9, Pt. I." (See Illustration 28 and note that the *Index to the Statutes in Force* now cites even pre-1963 statutes by calendar year.) If you then look up 1945, c. 28, in the statutes, you will find that you are reading the Law Reform (Contributory Negligence) Act (see Illustration 29). If you check the 1976 and 1978 citations you will find that they refer to the Fatal Accidents Act 1976 and the Civil Liability (Contribution) Act 1978, both of which contain provisions relating to "contributory negligence, apportionment of liability" and both of which make minor amendments to the Law Reform (Contributory Negligence) Act. The 1982 citation refers you to amendments to the Fatal Accidents Act 1976. "E & W" indicates that the 1976, 1978, and 1982 Acts extend only to England and Wales, not to Scotland or Northern Ireland.

ILLUSTRATION 27
Index to the Statutes, 1235-1982, Volume 2
Crown copyright – reproduced with permission of HMSO

NAVY *cont.*

5 Miscellaneous *cont.*

Incitement to disaffection: illegal posssession of documents: search warrant (High Ct., E&W and NI, sheriff ct., S): punishment: prosecution: 1934 c.56

Aliens inciting to sedition or disaffection: 1919 c.92 s.3(1)

Forfeiture of and disqualification for office on conviction for treason:
E&W NI 1870 c.23 s.2
1967 c.58 s.10,sch.3,Pt.III

Bringing contempt on naval uniform: 1894 c.45 ss.3,4
1967 c.80 ss.92,106(2),(3),sch.3,Pts.I,IV
1981 c.55 s.20,sch.3,para.5

Dredging for stores near HM's ships, etc.   *See* STORES, PUBLIC, 1

Fraudulent representation on entering navy   *See* 2 *above*

Trafficking in commns.   *See* PUBLIC OFFICE, 2

(c) POWERS IN RELATION TO PERSONS UNDER INCAPACITY

Temporary removal to and detention in service hospitals abroad of servicemen and others suffering mental disorders: 1981 c.55 s.13

Temporary removal to and detention in place of safety abroad of children of service families in need of care and control: 1981 c.55 s.14

(d) OTHER PROVISIONS

Abolition of office of Treasurer, and trans. of duties to Paymaster-General   *See* PAYMASTER-GENERAL

Abolition of office of Accountant General of the Navy; transfer of functions to Secy. of State: 1981 c.55 s.24(1)

Agriculture or other work of national importance, employment of naval personnel in *(temp.)   See* Defence (Armed Forces) Regs., 6: as set out in Pt. C of sch. 2 of Emergency Laws (Repeal) Act 1959 c.19 and made permanent by Emergency Powers Act: 1964 c.38 s.2

Billeting and requisitioning: 1971 c.33 s.67
    offences   *See* 3*(a)*(xii) *above*

Births and deaths at sea, registration of   *See* REGISTRATION OF BIRTHS, ETC., 5*(c)*

Navy accounts and accounts of manufacturing establishments, etc., preparation and audit of   *See* PUBLIC ACCOUNTS

Naval stores   *See* 3*(a)*(xi)*(c)*(ii) *above: and* STORES, PUBLIC

Supplies for naval services   *See* APPROPRIATION

Coastguard   *See* COASTGUARD

Housing for armed forces, loans for provisions of   *See* PUBLIC LOAN AND GUARANTEE

Exemption of Govt, factories, magazines, etc., and HM's ships. from Explosives Act 1875   *See* EXPLOSIVE SUBSTANCE, 4

Marriage in naval chapels   *See* MARRIAGE, 5

Enforcement by officers of Conventions with France as to fishing, or of Whaling Industry (Regulation) Act   *See* FISHERIES UNDER INTERNATIONAL CONVENTIONS, 2*(b)*(*c*),4

Naval defence, colonial   *See* 2 *above:* COLONIAL LEGISLATURE

Naval Medical Compassionate Fund   *See* NAVAL MEDICAL COMPASSIONATE FUND

Naval reserves   *See* RESERVE AND AUXILIARY FORCES, 1*(a)*, 2, 3

Naval savings banks, abolition of   *See* SAVINGS BANK, 2

Road transport, lighting of   *See* ROAD TRAFFIC AND VEHICLES, 4*(c)*

Smuggling, powers for prevention, etc., of: rewards, protection, etc.   *See* CUSTOMS AND EXCISE MANAGEMENT, 6*(d)*,11*(a)*

See also DEFENCE

NEGLIGENCE

Causing injury to aircraft or danger to life   *See* AIR FORCE, 4*(a)*: ARMY, 4*(a)*: NAVY, 3*(a)*(vii)

Building society director's liability for   *See* BUILDING SOCIETIES, 6*(c)*(*f*)

Common employment, abolition of doctrine of   *See* MASTER AND SERVANT, 3

Company director's liability for   *See* COMPANY, 4*(d)*(xiii)

Contractual exclusion of   *See* CONTRACT, 4*(a)*(i)

In performance of ecclesiastical duties   *See* ECCLESIASTICAL JURISDICTION, E, 2

Factories Act accident, etc., due to   *See* FACTORIES, 5

Joint and several tortfeasors   *See* DAMAGES, 3,6

Occupier's liability to visitors   *See* OCCUPIERS' AND LANDLORDS' LIABILITY

Reckless or dangerous driving   *See* ROAD TRAFFIC AND VEHICLES, 3*(a)*

See also HEALTH, SAFETY AND WELFARE AT WORK

ILLUSTRATION 28
Index to the Statutes, 1235-1982, Volume 1
Crown copyright – reproduced with permission of HMSO

(a) Collective title (the Interest on Damages (Scotland) Acts 1958 and 1971) given by 1971 c.31 s.2(2)

ILLUSTRATION 29
Public General Acts, 1945
Crown copyright – reproduced with permission of HMSO

1945.   *Welsh Church*   CH. 27, 28.   221
                  (Burial Grounds) Act, 1945.

(3) Where a burial in any such burial ground is conducted otherwise than in accordance with the rites of the Church in Wales, the following enactments shall apply as if the burial were a burial in pursuance of a notice given under the Burial Laws Amendment Act, 1880, that is to say—

    (*a*) section ten of that Act (which relates to the registration of burials) ;

    (*b*) sections one to three of the Births and Deaths Regis- 16 & 17 Geo. 5. tration Act, 1926 (which prohibit the disposal of a body c. 48. except on a registrar's certificate or coroner's order and provide for matters connected therewith).

    5. In this Act the following expressions have the meanings Interpreta-hereby respectively assigned to them—   tion.

    " appointed day " means such day as the Secretary of State, after consultation with the Welsh Commissioners and the representative body, may by order appoint ;

    " representative body " means the representative body established under subsection (2) of section thirteen of the principal Act.

    6.—(1) This Act may be cited as the Welsh Church (Burial Short title, Grounds) Act, 1945, and this Act and the Welsh Church Acts, citation and 1914 to 1938, may be cited together as the Welsh Church Acts, repeal. 1914 to 1945.

    (2) Paragraph (*b*) of subsection (1) of section eight of the principal Act is hereby repealed.

CHAPTER 28. ✓

An Act to amend the law relating to contributory negligence and for purposes connected therewith.

                                                 [15th June 1945.]

BE it enacted by the King's most Excellent Majesty, by and with the advice and consent of the Lords Spiritual and Temporal, and Commons, in this present Parliament assembled, and by the authority of the same, as follows :—

    1.—(1) Where any person suffers damage as the result partly Apportion-of his own fault and partly of the fault of any other person or ment of persons, a claim in respect of that damage shall not be defeated liability in by reason of the fault of the person suffering the damage, but the case of contributory damages recoverable in respect thereof shall be reduced to such negligence. extent as the court thinks just and equitable having regard to the claimant's share in the responsibility for the damage :

You should also check the Law Reform (Contributory Negligence) Act in the Chronological Table under 8 & 9 Geo. 6, c. 28. The Table gives more information than the *Index* on the effect of the passage of other Acts on this one. To find out if there have been recent amendments, not yet noted in the *Index* or Table, you may check the paper copies of Acts if your library subscribes to them. However, not all Canadian law libraries do so, and you may have to be satisfied with checking a less current source, such as the lists of statutes in the unbound parts of the Statutes series of the *Law Reports.* Another possible source is the loose-leaf service to *Current Law Statutes,* a part of the Current Law Service, of which more will be said later in this chapter as well as in the next. Still another is the current statutes service to *Halsbury's Statutes of England,* a set to which we will now turn.

(d) Halsbury's Statutes of England

A very good place to look up an English statute in force, especially if you want to know something of its history, is in *Halsbury's Statutes of England.* In this set statutes are grouped together alphabetically by subject, an arrangement similar to that adopted in the official edition of *Statutes in Force.* *Halsbury,* however, is not a self-renewing and permanent collection of the statutes; it is updated, but new editions are also published from time to time. Moreover, *Halsbury* does not include Acts or parts of Acts affecting only Scotland, though there are annotations concerning the application of Acts to Northern Ireland.

The third edition of *Halsbury's Statutes,* which was current at the time of writing (a fourth, to begin publication in April 1985, has been announced), consists of 39 main volumes, which are updated by continuation volumes, an annual cumulative supplement, and a current statutes service in loose-leaf form. There is also a volume entitled "Tables of Statutes and Index for Volumes 1-50". It contains a summary of titles, an alphabetical list of statutes, a chronological list of statutes, a general index, and an index of words and phrases. Volume 50 (in two parts) being a continuation volume for 1980, the tables and index thus cover the period to the end of that year. The first continuation volume, volume 40, covered the years 1968-70; later continuation volumes to date cover just one year. As noted above, there are really two volumes for 1980, but they are numbered 50(1) and 50(2). There is also a volume numbered 42A entitled "European Continuation Volume 1, 1952-72". Since at the beginning of 1973 community law became part of English law, the aim of this volume is to make the former accessible to English lawyers. Volume 42A is updated at the end of the cumulative supplement (at the time of writing this part of the supplement occupied almost half the second volume) and on buff-coloured pages in the Current Statutes Service. This service publishes Acts passed since the latest continuation volume was issued; it also contains a "noter-up", which updates the cumulative supplement. New Acts are printed on white pages; the "noter-up" on blue. Further updating is contained in the "Unannotated Acts" section on green pages at the end of the current service.

An illustration may assist you in the use of *Halsbury's Statutes*. Let us take the same example as we did with the *Index to the Statutes in Force* and see how to go about finding the statutory provisions regarding contributory negligence in *Halsbury's Statutes*. Forget that you already know the title of the Act and begin, as you did with the *Index*, by adopting the subject approach.

When you looked up "Contributory Negligence" in the *Index to the Statutes in Force*, you found nothing. If you look it up in the Index contained in the Table of Statutes and Index volume of *Halsbury's Statutes*, you will find it listed, but it refers you to "Negligence" (see Illustration 30), which *Halsbury* also uses as a main subject heading. Under "Negligence" there is a subheading "contributory" with numerous subdivisions under it. (See Illustration 31 and compare it with Illustration 27; you will probably agree that *Halsbury's* indexing is better than that in the *Index to the Statutes in Force*.) The most helpful entries, from your point of view, are "apportionment of liability" and "damages, apportionment"; for the former you are directed to volume 23, pages 789-791, for the latter to the same volume, page 789. If you look up volume 23, page 789, you will find the beginning of the text of the Law Reform (Contributory Negligence) Act 1945; it is published under the general title "Negligence" (see Illustration 32). Section 1 deals with "Apportionment of liability in case of contributory negligence". The Act continues on pages 790, 791, and 792. If you look at these pages you will see that more than the text is given; there are also notes or annotations. If words or phrases in the Act have been defined by statute or have been judicially considered, a summary of the interpretation, together with the statute or case citation is given. If sections of the Act have been amended or repealed up to the time the volume was published this too is indicated.

To determine whether there have been later amendments or judicial considerations, go to the cumulative supplement. Refer to volume 23, page 789 (see Illustration 33). When using the cumulative supplement, you must be careful to look under the correct title because the references to a particular title are dealt with together. Thus, the example that we are using is found under the title "Negligence". The next title in volume 23 is "Northern Ireland," but before updating it, the cumulative supplement deals with references to negligence in the continuation volumes.

To check developments since the publication of the current cumulative supplement, which is replaced annually, refer to volume 23, page 789 in the noter-up section of the loose-leaf current statutes service. At the time of writing there was no entry for that page or the pages immediately following relating to the Law Reform (Contributory Negligence) Act (see Illustration 34).

If you know the name of the Act for which you are looking, it is unnecessary to use the subject approach; you can locate it quickly through the alphabetical list of statutes in the Table of Statutes and Index volume, or in the cumulative supplement if it was passed later than 1980. Thus, if you had known that the Act dealing with contributory negligence was called the Law Reform (Contributory Negligence) Act, you could have found from the

ILLUSTRATION 30
Halsbury's Statutes of England (3rd ed.), Index to Volumes 1-50

ILLUSTRATION 31
Halsbury's Statutes of England (3rd ed.), Index to Volumes 1-50

ILLUSTRATION 32
Halsbury's Statutes of England (3rd ed.), Volume 23

THE LAW REFORM (CONTRIBUTORY NEGLIGENCE) ACT 1945

(8 & 9 Geo. 6 c. 28)

ARRANGEMENT OF SECTIONS

An Act to amend the law relating to contributory negligence and for purposes connected therewith   [15th June 1945]

Application to the Crown. This Act binds the Crown; see the Crown Proceedings Act 1947, s. 4 (3), Vol. 8, p. 848. For the liability of the Crown in tort, see s. 2 of that Act, Vol. 8, p. 846.

Northern Ireland. This Act does not apply; see s. 6 (2), *post.*

1. Apportionment of liability in case of contributory negligence

(1) Where any person suffers damage as the result partly of his own fault and partly of the fault of any other person or persons, a claim in respect of that damage shall not be defeated by reason of the fault of the person suffering the damage, but the damages recoverable in respect thereof shall be reduced to such extent as the court thinks just and equitable having regard to the claimant's share in the responsibility for the damage:

Provided that—

(a) this subsection shall not operate to defeat any defence arising under a contract;

(b) where any contract or enactment providing for the limitation of liability is applicable to the claim, the amount of damages recoverable by the claimant by virtue of this subsection shall not exceed the maximum limit so applicable.

(2) Where damages are recoverable by any person by virtue of the foregoing subsection subject to such reduction as is therein mentioned, the court shall find and record the total damages which would have been recoverable if the claimant had not been at fault.

(3) Section six of the Law Reform (Married Women and Tortfeasors) Act, 1935 (which relates to proceedings against, and contribution between, joint and several tortfeasors), shall apply in any case where two or more persons are liable or would, if they had all been sued, be liable by virtue of subsection (1) of this section in respect of the damage suffered by any person.

(4) Where any person dies as the result partly of his own fault and partly of the fault of any other person or persons, and accordingly if an action were brought for the benefit of the estate under the Law Reform (Miscellaneous Provisions) Act, 1934, the damages recoverable would be reduced under subsection (1) of this section, any damages recoverable in an action brought for the benefit of the dependants of that person under the Fatal Accidents Acts, 1846 to 1908, shall be reduced to a proportionate extent.

(5) Where, in any case to which subsection (1) of this section applies, one of the persons at fault avoids liability to any other such person or his personal representative by pleading the Limitation Act, 1939, or any other enactment

ILLUSTRATION 33
Halsbury's Statutes of England (3rd ed.), Cumulative Supplement, 1984

Vol. 23	NEGLIGENCE

PAGE

Law Reform (Miscellaneous Provisions) Act 1934 (c. 41)

788 For the purposes of this Act, any damage for which a person is liable under ss. 2 to 4 of the Animals Act 1971, is to be treated as due to his fault; see s. 10 of the 1971 Act, Vol. 41, p. 94.

A scheme under the Industrial Injuries and Diseases (Old Cases) Act 1975, s. 5, Vol. 45, p. 1327, must not provide for the payment of benefit to which that section applies, if sums are recoverable under this Act; see s. 6 (1) (d) of that Act, Vol. 45, p. 1329.

" **Section 2**
Repealed by the Fatal Accidents Act 1976, s. 6 (2), Sch. 2, Vol. 46, pp. 1124, 1125, and replaced as noted in the destination table to that Act, ibid., p. 1126.

Law Reform (Contributory Negligence) Act 1945 (c. 28)

789 For the purposes of this Act, any damage for which a person is liable under ss. 2 to 4 of the Animals Act 1971, is to be treated as due to his fault; see s. 10 of the 1971 Act, Vol. 41, p. 94.

This Act applied with a modification in relation to liability for oil pollution by the Merchant Shipping (Oil Pollution) Act 1971, s. 1 (5), Vol. 41 p. 1346.

Any damage for which a person is liable by virtue of the Deposit of Poisonous Waste Act 1972, s. 2 (1), Vol. 42, p. 1545, is to be treated for the purposes of this Act, as due to his fault; see s. 2 (4) of the Act of 1972, ibid.

For the purposes of this Act, any damage for which a person is liable under s. 88 (1) of the Control of Pollution Act 1974 is to be treated as due to his fault; see ibid., s. 88 (4), Vol. 44, p. 1269.

This Act is applied in relation to the law of the court referred to in the Merchant Shipping Act 1979, Sch 3, Article 6; see ibid, s 51(2), Sch 3, Part II,.para 3, Vol 49, pp 1234, 1252.

By the Water Act 1981, s 6(4), Vol 51, p 203, this Act applies in relation to any loss or damage for which statutory water undertakers (as defined in the Water Act 1973, s 11(6), Vol 43, p 1834), are liable under s 6 of the 1981 Act, but which is not due to their fault, as if it were due to their fault.

789– **Section 1**
790 Sub-s. (3) and in sub-s. (5), the words "or contributions" are repealed by the Civil Liability (Contribution).Act 1978, s. 9 (2); Sch. 2, Vol. 48, pp. 366, 368.

Sub-s. (4) is repealed by the Fatal Accidents Act 1976, s. 6 (2), Sch. 2, Vol. 46, pp. 1124, 1125, and replaced as noted in the destination table to that Act, ibid., p. 1126.

790 n. Partly of his own fault. When a car passenger fails to wear a fitted seat belt and is injured, he may be guilty of contributory negligence, and the driver of negligence; see Pasternack v. Poulton, [1973] 2 All E.R. 74, not followed in Smith v. Blackburn (1974), 124 N.L.Jo. 524.

Pasternack v. Poulton, cited above, approved, and Smith v. Blackburn, cited above, disapproved, in Froom v. Butcher, [1975] 3 All E.R. 520, C.A. (test is not what was cause of accident, but what was cause of damage).

790– Apportionment of liability. See also Ashton v Turner, [1980] 3 All ER 870, [1980]
791n 3 WLR 736 (duty of care owed by criminal to fellow participant in crime); Marshall v Osmond [1983] QB 1034, [1983] 2 All ER 225, CA (although police officer entitled to use such force as is reasonable in arresting suspected criminal, in all other respects the duty owed by officer is standard duty of care owed to anyone else—to exercise such care and skill as is reasonable in all the circumstances).

791– **Section 4**
792 The definition of "dependant" is repealed by the Fatal Accidents Act 1976, s. 6 (2), Vol. 2, Sch. 2, Vol. 46, pp. 1124, 1125, and replaced as noted in the destination table to that Act, ibid., p. 1126.

Meaning of "fault" applied by the Animals Act 1971, s. 11, Vol. 41, p. 95, by the Deposit of Poisonous Waste Act 1972, s. 2 (3) (b), Vol. 42, p. 1545, by the Control of Pollution Act 1974, s. 88 (3), Vol. 44, p. 1269, and by the Water Act 1981, s. 6 (7) (d), Vol 51, p 2203.

ILLUSTRATION 34
Halsbury's Statutes of England (3rd ed.)
Current Statutes Service – Noter-Up

Vol 23   NEGLIGENCE

NEGLIGENCE

VOLUME 23
PAGE

Preliminary Note

779   *Occupiers' Liability Act 1984.* The Occupiers' Liability Act 1984, 1984 Statutes, replaces with statutory rules the rules of the common law governing the duty of an occupier as to the safety of persons who are outside the scope of the Occupiers' Liability Act 1957, Vol 23, p 792, that is to say, persons who are on his land without his permission, either with lawful authority or without. Section 2 of the Act redraws the boundaries of "business liability" for the purposes of the Unfair Contract Terms Act 1977, Part I, Vol 47, p 86. It enables the occupier of business premises, who permits visits for recreational or educational purposes, to include terms in the permission which restrict or exclude his liability to such visitors in respect of the dangerous state of the premises.

Law Reform (Contributory Negligence) Act 1945 (c 28)
Section 1

790n   *Partly of his own fault.* See also *Basildon District Council v J E Lesser (Properties) Ltd* [1984] 3 WLR 812 (this section only applies to actions brought in tort—there is no defence of contributory negligence either at common law or under this section to a claim in contract).

Section 4

792n   *Fault.* See also *Basildon District Council v J E Lesser (Properties) Ltd* [1984] 3 WLR 812, noted to p 790, ante.

Occupiers' Liability Act 1957 (c 31)
Section 1

793–   *General Note.* For the liability of an occupier to persons on his land who are
794n   outside the scope of this Act, see the Occupiers' Liability Act 1984, SI 1984 Statutes.

Section 2

795n   *Sub-s (1): Occupier; visitors.* Any person who owes in relation to premises the duty referred to in this section and those who are his visitors for the purposes of that duty, are the persons who are to be treated respectively as an occupier of any premises and as his visitors, for the purposes of the Occupiers' Liability Act 1984, s 1; see sub-s (2) thereof, 1984 Statutes.

795–   *Duty to take such care as ... is reasonable, etc.* See also *Salmon v Seafarer Restaurants*
796n   *Ltd (British Gas Corp, third party)* [1983] 3 All ER 729 (occupier owes same duty of care to firemen extinguishing fire on his premises as he owes to other visitors under this section—defendants liable since fire on their premises caused by employee's negligence and resulting explosion injuring fireman was reasonably foreseeable); *Titchener v British Railways Board* [1983] 3 All ER 770, [1983] 1 WLR 1427, HL (boundary fence along railway line containing unrepaired gaps— occupiers showing reasonable care to entrant in view of her age and intelligence and circumstances of the case). See also note "sub-s (5): Risks willingly accepted", below.

796n   *Sub-s (5): Risks willingly accepted.* See also *Titchener v British Railways Board* [1983] 3 All ER 770, [1983] 1 WLR 1427, HL (plaintiff volens risk in crossing railway line because of her age, intelligence and circumstances of case, and, since train which hit her not driven negligently, the risk of being hit was one accepted by plaintiff).

alphabetical list of statutes that it was printed under the title "Negligence" in Volume 23, beginning at page 789.

If you know the year (regnal before 1963, calendar from that date on) in which an Act was passed, and its chapter number but not its title, you can locate it by using the chronological list of statutes.

(e) Current Law Statute Citator

Perhaps you are making a detailed study of the Law Reform (Contributory Negligence) Act and want to be sure that you have found all relevant references to it. A good place for you to check is the *Current Law Statute Citator*, which forms part of the Current Law Service. There is now a bound volume covering the years 1947-71. This does not mean that it relates only to statutes passed from 1947; statutes from 1235 are listed, but cases in which they are cited and articles that discuss them are noted only from 1947, the year the Current Law Service began. The *Current Law Statute Citator*, 1947-71, is updated by the statute citator at the back of the *Current Law Citator*, a temporary volume, which also includes a case citator and which cumulates and is replaced annually. There is further updating of the statute citator in the loose-leaf service to *Current Law Statutes*.

To find information concerning the Law Reform (Contributory Negligence) Act, look up the regnal year citation, 8 & 9 Geo. 6, c. 28 in the *Current Law Statute Citator*, 1947-71. (Remember that if the Act in which you are interested was passed in 1963 or later, citation will be by calendar year.) Illustration 35 shows you the information you will find. First you are told what sections of the Act have been repealed, next that an article on the Act was published in volume 13 of the *Conveyancer* (the full title of this journal is *Conveyancer and Property Lawyer*), beginning at page 414. Then references are given to digests of cases in which the Law Reform (Contributory Negligence) Act was cited. These references are to paragraphs in the *Current Law Consolidation*, 1947-51, or the *Current Law Year Books* for subsequent years. For instance, 4512 refers to the paragraph of that number in the *Current Law Consolidation*, whereas 71/641 directs you to paragraph 641 in the *Current Law Year Book*, 1971. See Illustrations 36 and 37, and note that paragraph 4512 in Illustration 36 digests an Alberta case that cited that province's Contributory Negligence Act; it is stated that it corresponds to the Law Reform (Contributory Negligence) Act 1945. This shows that cases citing a statute from another jurisdiction may be helpful if the statutory provisions of the two jurisdictions are the same. In the *Current Law Statute Citator* entry (Illustration 35), note that references are made first to cases in which the Act as a whole was considered; these are followed by references to cases in which a particular section of the Act was cited. Thus, if you are interested in a particular section of the Act, you will look especially at the paragraphs in the *Current Law Consolidation* and the *Current Law Year Books* that relate to it. Some of the information in the *Current Law* volumes may have been found in

ILLUSTRATION 35
Current Law Statute Citator 1947-71

STATUTE CITATOR 1947–71   **1945**

CAP.

8 & 9 Geo. 6—cont.

17. Wages Councils Act, 1945—cont.
3169; 56/3202, 10608; 57/1296, 3967; 58/1230, 3767; 59/1193; cases 3659; 54/1219.
s. 11, cases 54/1218; 61/10026.
s. 15, regs. 3658.
s. 16 (1), case 54/1219.
s. 20, orders 3658; 48/4262; 49/4611; 50/4788; 52/1278; 55/1002.
ss. 21, 23, regs. 3658.
s. 23 (1), case 54/1219.

18. Local Authorities Loans Act, 1945.
Repeals:
ss. 1, 2 (part), 3, 4 (part), 5, 6, 8 (part), 9 (1) (part) (3), 12 (2), repealed: 14G.6,c.34,sch.13,I; S.L.R. 1950; S.L.R. 1953; 5–6E.2,c.56,sch.11; S.L.R. 1963; 1963,c.33,sch.18; 1964,c. 9,sch.3; 1968,c.13,sch.6.
applied, restricted, etc.: 10–1G.6,c.22,s.3; 11–2G.6,c.32,s.11; 1968,c.13,s.1.
s. 1 (1), regs. 5299.
s. 2, regs. 5791; 61/5092; 64/2158; 67/ 2329.
s. 8, regs. 52/4219; applied: 6–7E.2,c.55, s.55(2).
s. 10, minutes 61/5086; 62/1779.

19. Ministry of Fuel and Power Act, 1945.
applied, restricted, etc.: 1964,c.39,s.1.
order 57/545.
s. 1, repealed in part: S.L.R. 1966; amended: 1964,c.29,s.1(6); S.I.1969, No.1498.
ss. 2, 3, repealed: S.I.1969,No.1498.
s. 4, repealed: 5–6E.2,c.20,sch.4,I.
s. 5, repealed: S.I.1969,No.1498.
s. 7, repealed in part: S.L.R. 1950; 1953; 1965,c.58,sch.2.
sch. 2, repealed: 1965,c.58,sch.2.
sch. 3, repealed: S.L.R. 1950.

20. Colonial Development and Welfare Act, 1945.
repealed: 7–8E.2,c.71,sch.

21. Ministry of Civil Aviation Act, 1945.
repealed: 12–4G.6,c.91,sch.3.

22. Army and Air Force (Annual) Act, 1945.
repealed: 3–4E.2,c.20,s.5(1).

23. National Loans Act 1945.
repealed: 1968,c.13,sch.6.

24. Finance Act, 1945.
Repeals:
ss. 1–4, 6, repealed: 12–4G.6,c.47,sch. 1; 15–6G.6&1E.2,c.10,sch.25; 1968,c. 13,sch.6.

25. Appropriation Act, 1945.
repealed: S.L.R. 1950.

27. Welsh Church (Burial Grounds) Act, 1945.
article: 119 J.P.J. 248.
s. 4, applied: 1–2E.2,c.20.s.24(6).
s. 6 (2), repealed: S.L.R. 1950.

CAP.

8 & 9 Geo. 6—cont.

28. Law Reform (Contributory Negligence) Act, 1945.
Repeals:
ss. 1 (part), 6 (part), repealed: 9–10 E.2,c.27,sch.2.
article: 13 Conv. 414.
applied: 10–1G.6,c.44,s.4(3).
cases 4512, 7561, 9531; 52/2351; 55/ 5981; 71/641.
s. 1, cases 3982; 48/4292–4294, 4699; 52/4362; 54/862; 55/1934; 56/903; 66/ 3452.
s. 1 (1), cases 1923, 3998, 4511, 6637, 6653; 52/368, 2352, 2356; 55/1069; 56/5865; 58/2219.
s. 1 (2), case 1923.
s. 1 (4), case 52/368.
s. 4, cases 6637; 52/368; 55/1934; 56/ 903.

29. Liabilities (War-Time Adjustment) (Scotland) Act 1945.
repealed: 1971,c.52,sch.
expired: S.I.1950,No.1467.

30. Government of Burma (Temporary Provisions) Act, 1945.
repealed: 11–2G.6,c.3.sch.2.I.

31. Emergency Powers (Defence) Act 1945.
repealed: 1971,c.52,sch.

32. Income Tax Act, 1945.
repealed: 15–6G.6&1E.2,c.10,sch.25,I.
s. 2, case 1608.
s. 2 (1), case 50/4928.
s. 7 (3), case 52/1611.
s. 8, cases 4715; 50/4928; 52/1609.
s. 8 (3), case 57/1648.
s. 14 (1) (b), case 52/1608.
s. 15 (1), cases 52/1613, 4125.
s. 17, cases 52/1612; 54/1527; 57/1651; 59/1485.
s. 17 (1), cases 50/4929; 53/1665; 55/ 1256, 1257.
s. 17 (3), case 55/1257.
s. 22, case 52/1612.
s. 33, case 53/1662, 4272.
s. 55 (3), case 52/1612.
s. 59, cases 53/1669; 54/1528.
s. 60 (1), case 53/1665.
s. 314, cases 62/1460, 3466.

33. Town and Country Planning (Scotland) Act 1945.
repealed as applied by the New Towns Act 1946: 1968,c.16,sch.11.
s. 22, regs. 48/4920; 55/1183; 63/4301.
s. 27, regs. 48/4910.

34. Hydro-Electric Undertakings (Valuation for Rating) (Scotland) Act, 1945.
repealed: 11–2G.6,c.26,sch.2.

35. Forestry Act, 1945.
repealed: 1967,c.10,sch.7.
order 4149.
s. 4, order 61/3651.
s. 10, orders 52/1453; 53/82; 54/74; 58/ 63; 59/54; 61/3652.
sch. 1, rules 7844.

ILLUSTRATION 36
Current Law Consolidation, 1947-51

1 C.L.C. *HUSBAND AND WIFE*

to him, however, that by s. 1 of the Act of 1935, the legislature reaffirmed as respects the husband the provision that except as therein provided no husband or wife should be entitled to sue the other for a tort. [*Reported by J. A. Griffiths, Esq., Barrister-at-Law.*] See also [1952] 1 C. L. 149, 181.

4511. —— **by husband and wife for injury to wife—contributory negligence.** (Law Reform (Contributory Negligence) Act, 1945 (8 & 9 Geo. 6, c. 28), s. 1 (1).) From the earliest times a husband's cause of action for a wrong done to him by reason of a tort done to his wife *per quod consortium amisit* has been separate from that of his wife, because the husband did not derive his cause of action from his wife, but from his marriage. Consequently, a husband's cause of action is unaffected by the contributory negligence of the wife and he recovers his damages in full, because the husband making his own claim for the damage which he has sustained is not a person claiming in respect of damage which is "the result partly of his own fault" within the meaning of s. 1 (1) of the Law Reform (Contributory Negligence) Act, 1945: MALLETT *v.* DUNN, [1949] 2 K. B. 180; [1949] L. J. R. 1650, Hilbery, J. (applying *Hyde v. Seyssor* (1619), Cro. Jac. 538; disagreeing with *Young and Young v. Otto*, § 4512). [*Note:*—Dicta in this case were not followed in *Baylis v. Blackwall*, § 4510.]

4512. —— —— ——. [Can.] In YOUNG AND YOUNG *v.* OTTO, [1948] 1 D. L. R. 285, the Supreme Court of Alberta held that the effect of the Contributory Negligence Act, R. S. A., 1942, c. 116 (which corresponds to the Law Reform (Contributory Negligence) Act, 1945) is that a husband's or a father's claim for loss of service abates by the same fraction as that of the wife or child where contributory negligence on the part of the wife or child is found by the Court, the true purport of the Act being "a limitation as to responsibility". [*Note:*—Cf. *Mallett v. Dunn*, § 4511.]

4513. —— —— ——. See also DRINKWATER *v.* KIMBER, § 6665.

4514. —— —— **against husband—injunction.** See SCOTT *v.* SCOTT, § 3041; [Eire.] O'MALLEY *v.* O'MALLEY, § 4556.

4515. —— —— —— **personal injuries.** (Married Women's Property Act, 1882 (45 & 46 Vict. c. 75), ss. 2, 12, 24.) The definition of property in s. 24 of the Married Women's Property Act, 1882, makes it clear beyond doubt that a wife's personal property (which forms part of her separate property) includes her things in action. Under s. 12 of the Act the right of suing which is given to a married woman extends, so far as concerns what may be the subject-matter of the action, to all her property. The limitation which is imposed by that section is not on the kind of property which may be the subject of an action by her, but only on the purpose for which the action may be brought; it must be for the protection or security of her property. It follows, that a married woman is entitled to maintain an action claiming damages for personal injuries, which she has sustained in a motor car accident, against her husband to whom she has been married after the beginning of the action: CURTIS *v.* WILCOX, [1948] 2 K. B. 474; [1948] 2 All E. R. 573, C. A. (applying *Re Park Gate Waggon Works Co.* (1881), 17 Ch. 234; overruling *Gottliffe v. Edelston*, [1930] 2 K. B. 378).

4516. —— —— **claim for contribution against husband.** [Cty. Ct.] See DRIBBELL *v.* ROBINSON, § 6668.

4517. **Agency—of necessity—payments made by third party to provide necessaries.** It is settled law that a person who has advanced money to a married woman deserted by her husband for the purpose of, and which has been actually applied towards, her support, is entitled in equity to recover such sums from the husband. In order to be able to recover any such advances from the husband, the person who has made the advances must prove that the advances were not only intended for the support of the wife but were in fact needed for her support: WEINGARTEN *v.* ENGEL, [1947] 1 All E. R. 425, Humphreys, J. (applying *Deare v. Soutten* (1869), L. R. 9 Eq. 151).

4518. —— —— **security for costs of appeal.** See BRIGHTSTEIN *v.* BRIGHTSTEIN, § 2804.

ILLUSTRATION 37
Current Law Year Book, 1971

BILLS OF EXCHANGE   [1971]

the contravention of such suspension order an offence; s. 3 extends the provisions of ss. 14 and 92 of the Bills of Exchange Act 1882; ss. 4, 5 are consequential and supplementary.

The Act received the Royal Assent on December 16, 1971, and came into force on that day with the exception of s. 3 which came into force on January 16, 1972.

640. Bona fide holder for value—illegal intention of earlier parties

[Bills of Exchange Act 1882 (c. 61), s. 30 (2). R.S.C., Ord. 14, rr. 1, 3 (1).]

A holder in due course of a bill of exchange is entitled to summary judgment if he gave value bona fide subsequent to any fraud or illegality at the earlier stages of the bill.

The holder of bills of exchange brought proceedings against the drawer, acceptor and indorsers of the bills, and sought summary judgment under Ord. 14. The defendants sought leave to defend on the ground of fraud and illegality in relation to the issue, acceptance and negotiation of the bills. In an affidavit in reply the plaintiff set out the circumstances in which it had discounted the bills, supported by contemporary documents, which made it clear that the plaintiff was in no way involved in, and had no notice of, any fraud. This evidence was not seriously challenged. *Held,* that the plaintiff was entitled to summary judgment. (*Wallingford* v. *Mutual Society* (1880) 5 App. Cas. 685, *Millard* v. *Baddeley* [1884] W.N. 96, *Powszechny Bank Zwiazkowy W Polsse* v. *Paros* [1932] 2 K.B. 353, and *Alexander* v. *Rayson* [1936] 1 K.B. 169 considered.)

BANK FÜR GEMEINWIRTSCHAFT AKTIENGESELLSCHAFT v. CITY OF LONDON GARAGES [1971] 1 W.L.R. 149, C.A.

641. Cheque—conversion—negligence by drawer

[Cheques Act 1957 (c. 36), s. 4 (1); Law Reform (Contributory Negligence) Act 1945 (c. 28).] P, stockbrokers, employed a Mr. Blake as a temporary accountant. P's practice was to draw cheques in favour of their clients in an abbreviated form, *e.g.,* payable to " . . . Brown." Blake opened an account at D. Bank in the name of " J. A. G. Brown," an Australian, and forged nine references purporting to be from " J. Blake, D.Sc., Ph.D." D assumed in the absence of further information requested from the " referee " that he and " Brown " were professional men, newly arrived from Australia, and made no further inquiries. Blake converted cheques drawn by P and paid them into his account. P claimed the value of the cheques from D. *Held* (1) that D, as bankers, were guilty of negligence and not protected by s. 4 (1) of the Cheques Act 1957; (2) that the Law Reform (Contributory Negligence) Act, 1945 applied to the tort of conversion, that P were guilty of contributory negligence and could recover only 90 per cent. of the damages which would otherwise be awarded: LUMSDEN & CO. v. LONDON TRUSTEE SAVINGS BANK [1971] 1 Lloyd's Rep. 114, Donaldson J.

642. —— forgery—forged indorsement. See [Can.] ONTARIO WOODSWORTH MEMORIAL FOUNDATION v. GROZBORD [1967] 210.

643. —— —— joint account. See JACKSON v. WHITE & MIDLAND BANK [1967] 180.

644. —— " holder for value." See DIAMOND v. GRAHAM [1968] 202.

645. —— holder in due course—paid into overdrawn account

[Bills of Exchange Act 1882 (c. 61), ss. 27 (1) (3), 29, 30 (2); Cheques Act 1957 (c. 36), s. 2.]

The holder of a cheque who has a lien on it is deemed to have taken it for value and to be a holder in due course.

M had a large overdraft at the plaintiff bank. The bank received cheques to the value of £2,850 drawn by the defendants payable to M for hire-purchase transactions. The bank decided to honour two cheques of M amounting to £345, which they would not otherwise have done. The transactions were fraudulent and M was prosecuted and liquidated. The defendants stopped payment on the cheques. The bank claimed that they had given value for the cheques and were holders in due course and not merely agents for collection. It was found that the bank took the cheques in good faith and had no notice of any defect in M's title. *Held,* that a holder of a cheque with a lien on it the annotations to the Law Reform (Contributory Negligence) Act in *Halsbury's Statutes of England*, but to be sure that nothing has been missed, it is wise to check both, since their approach is different. The listing of relevant periodical articles in the *Current Law Statute Citator* is especially useful. At the time of writing, the statute citator section in the annual cumulative *Current Law Citator* noted post-1971 cases in which the Law Reform (Contributory Negligence) Act was considered and also recorded changes to section 4 of the Act in 1976 and to sections 1 and 5 in 1978 (see Illustration 38). For further updating, see the statute citator section in the loose-leaf service to *Current Law Statutes*.

In addition to the Current Law Service, there is a Scottish Current Law Service. If a library does not subscribe to both, it usually chooses the Scottish edition since, in addition to Scottish material, it includes everything in the English edition as well.

(f) Statutory Instruments

Rules and regulations made under the authority of a statute are found in volumes called *Statutory Instruments*; before 1949, the term *Statutory Rules and Orders* was used. Revised editions are published from time to time, but the latest consolidation and many of the volumes published since then are out of print, and you will probably find that your law school library does not have a complete set. If you need information concerning a statutory instrument, a good source is *Halsbury's Statutory Instruments*, a companion work to *Halsbury's Statutes of England*. *Halsbury* does not contain the full text of all statutory instruments in force, but it does provide a complete classification of those that are of general application throughout England and Wales or that, while applying partly or principally outside England and Wales, have reciprocal force therein. Some instruments of local application are also included. The text of a selection of rules, orders, and regulations is also given. The choice is made with the needs of the practising lawyer in mind.[37]

---

37 *Halsbury's Statutory Instruments*, Vol. 1, 4th Re-issue (London: Butterworths, 1979), Introduction, p. v.

ILLUSTRATION 38
Current Law Citator, 1983

STATUTE CITATOR 1972–83   **1945**

CAP.

7 & 8 Geo. (1943–44)—cont.

31. Education Act 1944—cont.
s. 90, repealed in pt.: 1980,c.20,schs.1,7.
s. 91, repealed: 1972,c.70,sch.30; ss. 6, 68, 88, 114, sch. 1, amended: *ibid.*, s.192,sch.30.
s. 94, amended: orders 74/1291; 77/1861; 81/241; 82/222.
s. 95, repealed in pt.: 1980,c.20,sch.1.
s. 97, repealed: 1980,c.20,sch.7.
s. 99, see *Meade* v. *Haringey London Borough Council* [1979] 1 W.L.R. 637, C.A.
s. 99, repealed in pt.: 1980,c.20,sch.1.
s. 100, regs. 72/1678; 73/370, 1535; 75/1054, 1198, 1929, 1964; 76/1191; 77/278; 78/1145; 79/1552; 80/1861; 81/786, 1086, 1788, 1839; 82/106; 83/74, 169, 1017.
s. 100, repealed in pt.: 1980,c.20,sch.7.
s. 102, amended: 1975,c.2,s.3; 1980, c.20,sch.3; repealed in pt.: *ibid.*,sch.1.
s. 103, amended: 1975,c.2,s.3; 1980, c.20,sch.1.
s. 105, repealed in pt.: *ibid.*
ss. 106, 108–110, sch.7, repealed: S.L.R. 1975.
s. 107, repealed: S.L.R. 1978.
s. 111, order 78/467; regs. 81/1839.
s. 114, regs. 82/1730.
s. 114, amended: 74/595; 1980,c.20, ss.24,34,sch.1; repealed in pt.: S.L.R. 1975; 1980,c.20,schs.1,7; 1981,c.60,sch. 3.
s. 120, repealed in pt.: S.L.R. 1978; 1980,c.20,sch.1.
sch. 1, repealed in pt.: 1980,c.20,sch.7.
sch. 2, repealed in pt.: *ibid.*,sch.1.
sch. 3, amended: *ibid.*,sch.3; repealed in pt.: *ibid.*,schs.1,7.
sch. 4, repealed: *ibid.*,s.4,sch.7; *repealed in pt.: *ibid.*,sch.1.
sch. 8, amended: 1972,c.44,sch.; repealed in pt.: S.L.R. 1978.
34. Validation of War-time Leases Act 1944.
repealed: S.L.R. 1976.
36. Housing (Temporary Accommodation) Act 1944.
repealed: 1972,c.46,sch.11; c.47,schs.8,11.
38. India (Miscellaneous Provisions) Act 1944.
repealed: S.L.R. 1976.
43. Matrimonial Causes (War Marriages) Act 1944.
ss. 1, 2, repealed: S.L.R. 1975.
s. 5, repealed in pt.: *ibid.*
s. 8, repealed: 1973,c.36,sch.6.
iv. City of London (Various Powers) Act 1944.
s. 9, repealed in pt.: regs. 77/1341.

8 & 9 Geo. 6 (1944–45)

5. Representation of the People Act 1945.
repealed: S.L.R. 1978.
s. 34, repealed (S.): order 74/812.

CAP.

8 & 9 Geo. (1944–45)—cont.

7. British Settlements Act 1945.
orders 75/1211; 76/52; 77/423; 82/824.
repealed: S.L.R. 1976.
10. Compensation of Displaced Officers (War Service) Act 1945.
ss. 1, 6, 8, 9, repealed in pt.: S.L.R. 1975.
ss. 2–5, sch., repealed: *ibid.*
s. 10, amended: 1973,c.36,sch.6.
12. Northern Ireland (Miscellaneous Provisions) Act 1945.
ss. 1, 2, repealed: 1973,c.36,sch.6.
s. 8, repealed: 1978,c.23,sch.7.
15. Public Health (Scotland) Act 1945.
s. 1, regs. 75/308; 76/1240.
s. 1, amended: 1982,c.48,sch.6.
16. Limitation (Enemies and War Prisoners) Act 1945.
s. 1, amended: 1973,c.52,sch.4.
s. 2, amended: 1973,c.18,sch.2; 1980, c.58,sch.3.
ss. 2, 4, amended: 1974,c.39,sch.5.
18. Local Authorities Loans Act 1945.
order 74/989.
s. 2, regs. 74/989; 82/1089.
s. 8, repealed: 1972,c.70,sch.30.
19. Ministry of Fuel and Power Act 1945.
s. 1, repealed in pt.: regs. 74/2012.
21. Wages Councils (Northern Ireland) Act 1945.
s. 10, S.Rs. 1979 Nos. 347, 359, 360.
26. Camps Act 1945.
repealed: 1973,c.39,sch.1.
28. Law Reform (Contributory Negligence) Act 1945.
see *De Meza and Stuart* v. *Apple, Van Staten Shena and Stone* [1974] 1 Lloyd's Rep. 508.
s. 1, see *Boothman* v. *British Northrop* [1972] 13 K.I.R. 112, C.A.; *Parnell* v. *Shields* [1973] R.T.R. 414; *Toperoff* v. *Mor* [1973] R.T.R. 419; *McGee* v. *Francis Shaw & Co.* [1973] R.T.R. 409.
s. 1, repealed in pt.: 1978,c.47,sch.2.
s. 4, repealed in pt.: 1976,c.30,sch.2.
s. 5, amended (S.): 1978,c.47,sch.1.
33. Town and Country Planning (Scotland) Act 1945.
repealed: 1972,c.52,sch.23.
sch. 6, see *Renfrew's Trs.* v. *Glasgow Corporation*, 1972 S.L.T. 2; *Smith & Waverley Tailoring Co.* v. *Edinburgh District Council*, 1976 S.L.T.(Lands Tr.) 19; *Apostolic Church Trs.* v. *Glasgow District Council*, 1977 S.L.T. (Lands Tr.) 24; *Apostolic Church Trustees* v. *Glasgow District Council (No. 2)*, 1978 S.L.T. (Lands Tr.) 17; *Birrell* v. *City of Edinburgh District Council*, 1982 S.L.T. 111.
37. Education (Scotland) Act 1945.
sch. 4, amended: 1972,c.44,sch.; repealed in pt.: S.L.R. 1978.

4

Legal Encyclopedias and Digests

1. GENERAL

In Chapters 2 and 3 we have been speaking chiefly about primary sources of the law. Some secondary materials or finding aids, such as indexes, annotation services, and statute citators, were mentioned, but we have still to deal with the important multi-volume sets of legal encyclopedias and digests. It should be emphasized that these works are not primary sources of the law; their purpose is to summarize the law and direct you to the primary sources. If you want to cite a case in court, you will not refer to a digest of it, but to the account given in the law reports.

If you are looking for a specific case or statute and have a complete citation for it, you can go directly to the volume of reports or statutes containing it. However, if you do not have the complete citation, or if you are not looking for a specific case or statute, but want to know the law relating to a particular problem, your task is more difficult. It is here that legal encyclopedias and digests are likely to be helpful.

Before proceeding further, something should be said about the difference between a legal encyclopedia and a digest. The term "abridgment" should also be mentioned, as you will find references to it from time to time. In a sense, both digests and encyclopedias are abridgments of the law; they summarize it under subject headings. The subjects are arranged alphabetically, and there is a wide range of headings, some general, others more specific. You will find, for instance, a section dealing with tort and other sections relating to specific torts such as negligence. If you look up a subject that is not dealt with separately, you may find a reference to the section of the work in which information on it is included.

Encyclopedias generally deal with both case and statute law. They state the law in the form of essays or articles, with footnotes citing the cases and/or statutes on which it is based. Digests are usually restricted to case law, though they may include references to statutes, if a case involves statutory interpretation. They give brief summaries of individual cases, together with citations, so that you can look up the reports if you wish. If a case is very similar to one already digested, a summary of it may not be included; in this instance, only the citation is given. One useful feature of a digest is that if a case is reported in more than one series of reports, all sources are listed. Thus if your library does not have one of the series of reports, or if the volume you need is in use, an alternate citation may lead you to a report of the case in another series.

American writers on legal bibliography usually make a definite distinction between encyclopedias and digests. In England, a similar distinction is made, though it does not seem to be quite so clear cut. The term "digest" is generally used in the same sense as in the United States, while either "abridgment" or "encyclopedia" denotes the essay type. *The Digest* (better known by its earlier name, *English and Empire Digest*) is an example of the former, while *Halsbury's Laws of England* represents the latter. In Canada, we tend to use all three terms interchangeably, for the *Canadian Abridgment* is really a digest, and the *Canadian Encyclopedic Digest,* an encyclopedia.

In Chapters 2 and 3, Canadian and English source books are treated in separate sections. Since some of the English encyclopedias and digests deal with Canadian as well as English law, it is preferable to discuss them in conjunction with Canadian works of a similar nature rather than separately. The remainder of this chapter is therefore devoted mainly to a discussion of how to make effective use of Canadian and English abridgments of the law.

2. FINDING CASE CITATIONS

Suppose you are looking for a report of a case, but you lack the complete citation; let us take *MacLeod v. Roe* as an example. We will assume that you know it is a Canadian case, but you are not sure of the jurisdiction or the court. You are aware that the case dealt with the question of whether the owners of a roller skating rink were liable for injuries suffered by a skater in a fall and you think it was decided some years ago. How can you find it? Let us try the *Canadian Abridgment.*

(a) Canadian Abridgment and Canadian Current Law

The current edition of the *Canadian Abridgment* is the second. Its 38 main volumes, dealing with substantive law, and three practice volumes, numbered separately, were published between 1966 and 1974. They are kept current by a loose-leaf cumulative supplement, the digests and citations in which are later updated, if necessary, and published in bound permanent supplements. There has also been a beginning to replacing volumes in the main set by revised volumes. The first volumes to be replaced are volumes 9 to 11, dealing with criminal law. These three volumes have been replaced by seven volumes numbered R9, R10, R11, and R11A through R11D. Volume 22, containing labour law, landlord and tenant and limitation of actions, is being replaced by five volumes numbered R22 and R22A through R22D. Revised volumes have a red Abridgment label on the spine instead of a green one.

The title pages of the main volumes of the second edition of the *Canadian Abridgment* describe it as "A Digest of Reported Decisions of the Supreme and Exchequer Courts of Canada and of all Courts of the Common Law Provinces including Appeals to the Privy Council and also Decisions from the Courts of Quebec of Universal Application". This description is amended in the revised volumes to read as follows: "A Digest of Reported Decisions of all Courts of the Common Law Provinces of Canada including

Appeals to the Privy Council and decisions in federal matters from the Courts of Quebec". This new title may give the erroneous impression that decisions of the Supreme and Exchequer (now Federal) Courts are no longer included, whereas in fact they are.

Between 1974 and 1980 there were published numerous finding aid volumes, which assist the reader in using the *Canadian Abridgment*. These include a Consolidated Table of Cases, Cases Judicially Considered, Statutes Judicially Considered, Words and Phrases Judicially Considered, and a General Index. As well, an *Index to Canadian Legal Literature* was published in 1981. The finding aid volumes, like the main set, are kept current by both loose-leaf updating (some in the Cumulative Supplement binders, others in the Appendix binders), permanent bound volumes and revised volumes. The only revised finding aid volume published to date is "Words and Phrases". The primary finding aid is the loose-leaf "Key and Research Guide". The Key consists of a subject titles table and a Key classification table, and the research guide explains how to use the *Canadian Abridgment*. *Canadian Current Law*, published monthly, further updates the *Abridgment*.

Since you are interested in a particular case, which you know is not very recent, the obvious place to begin is with the original two-volume Consolidated Table of Cases, which lists cases digested in the main set and the First Permanent Supplement, 1974. You will find *MacLeod v. Roe* listed in volume 2, which covers the letters M-Z. The entry reads as follows: MacLeod v. Roe 30.1615 (see Illustration 39). This means that the case is digested or otherwise referred to in paragraph 1615 of volume 30.

If you now look up paragraph 1615 in volume 30, you will find that you are in a section of the volume dealing with "Dangerous Premises," a heading under the title "Negligence". Paragraph 1615 gives quite an extensive digest of the case in which you are interested (see Illustration 40). From it you should be able to determine whether it is worthwhile to read a report of the case. If it is, the citations following the digest will enable you to find it. Had the case related to other subjects besides negligence involving dangerous premises, there would have been additional digests elsewhere in the *Abridgment*. In this situation, the Consolidated Table of Cases would have listed more than one digest reference. (See for instance, the reference to *McLeod v. Sweezy* in Illustration 39.)

From the information that you now have, you can tell that the case of *MacLeod v. Roe* was decided by the Supreme Court of Canada, and you can go directly to the 1947 volume of the *Supreme Court Reports* or to the third volume for 1947 of the *Dominion Law Reports* to read the judgment. You also know that the decision reversed an earlier judgment of an appeal court in one of the western provinces and that this appeal court's decision affirmed the trial court's decision. If you wish to read the earlier judgments, you can go to the volumes cited.

The Consolidated Table of Cases in the *Canadian Abridgment* is the best place to look if you have little information about a case. If you had known from the outset that the case of *MacLeod v. Roe* was decided by the Supreme

ILLUSTRATION 39
Canadian Abridgment (2nd), Consolidated Table of Cases, Volume 2

CONSOLIDATED TABLE OF CASES

MacLeod v. Dom. (Town) School Commrs.
  7.1544; 14.2561; 23.3377; 35.579
McLeod v. Domville 15.789
McLeod v. Doucette 2.243; 5.3388
McLeod v. Dunlap P1.1803
McLeod v. Eberts 2.2419; 5.1141
McLeod v. Egan S3.52157
McLeod v. Emigh 12.896; 32.2513
McLeod v. Firth 16.2105
McLeod v. Forsyth 12.1009
McLeod v. Fortune 5.3167; 16.770;
  17.2813; 37.449; P3.910
McLeod v. Fuoco 30.1518
McLeod v. Gibson 14.1433
McLeod v. Gillies 16.524, 2283, 2870
McLeod v. Girvin Central Telephone Assn.
  16.465
McLeod v. Grant S3.66611
MacLeod v. Great West Distributors Ltd.
  and Whyte & Co. P1.170
MacLeod v. Green P3.1129
McLeod v. Hamilton 5.2875
MacLeod v. Harbottle 22.1004, 1049
Macleod v. Hartigan 27.790
McLeod v. Heathcote P2.2827; P3.2492,
  2563
McLeod v. Higginbotham 1.2150
McLeod v. Hughes 17.407
McLeod v. Ins. Co. 15.1443; 20.3261;
  21.1172; P3.2711
McLeod v. Kings 7.955; 21.672; 32.3045
McLeod v. Krysko 14.1982, 1990; 21.2697;
  34.2424
MacLeod v. Kuhlmann 27.393
McLeod v. Lab. Rel. Bd. (Sask.) S3.52071
McLeod v. Lawson 14.45; 21.1883;
  25.1927, 2015; **37.1035**
McLeod v. Lee 27.867
McLeod v. McGuirk 3.1690; 17.1406;
  22.2573
McLeod v. McKenzie 14.603
Macleod v. McLean 22.3793; 29.1652
McLeod v. McLellan 4.1469, 2065
McLeod v. McLeod (1852), 9 U.C.Q.B.
  331 35.1055
McLeod v. McLeod (1918), 25 B.C.R. 430
  12.1058; 24.1384
McLeod v. McLeod (1929), 24 Alta. L.R.
  565 33.2948, 2954
Macleod v. Macleod, [1931] 1 W.W.R. 811
  (Alta.) 6.2621; 24.1757, 2424
McLeod v. McLeod, [1931] 2 D.L.R. 364
  (N.S.) 24.918, 1249
McLeod v. McLeod, [1935] O.R. 329
  24.392
Macleod v. Macleod (1954), 13 W.W.R. 269
  (B.C.) 24.1052
MacLeod v. MacLeod (1968), 67 W.W.R.
  111 (B.C.) 24.2345

McLeod v. McLeod (1970), 2 R.F.L. 386
  (Man.) S3.61485
McLeod v. McMillan 31.2568
McLeod v. McNab 38.439, 493
McLeod v. McRae 22.2886, 2957, 2989,
  3059; 34.2878
McLeod v. Meek 30.1793; 37.676; P2.1421,
  1432
McLeod v. Mercer 5.3684; 31.2033
McLeod v. Merriman 25.2193
McLeod v. Minister of Customs and Excise
  18.1726, 1995, 2461; 36.1532
McLeod v. M.N.R. 18.1726, 1997, 2136,
  2368; 36.1546
McLeod v. Murray 21.605, 2817
McLeod v. N.B. Ry. 6.1770, 1838
McLeod v. News Co. P1.1802
McLeod v. Noble (1897), 24 O.A.R. 459
  1.879; 14.962; 19.1878, 2126; 21.1898;
  32.966; **P3.855**
McLeod v. Noble (1897), 28 O.R. 528
  14.940, 1245; 19.2185
McLeod v. O'Keefe 13.879
McLeod v. Ont.-Minnesota Pulp & Paper
  Co. 35.2525
McLeod v. Paul 6.2976
McLeod v. Pearson 15.582 694, 709, 3169,
  3173; 22.2714, 3001, 3277, 3305; 26.670
Macleod v. Peterson 7.3064
McLeod v. Pye 2.755
MacLeod v. R. 6.1046, 1576; 15.859, 3083;
  S2.19341
MacLeod v. Royal Trust Co. 16.1930
MacLeod v. Roe 30.1615
McLeod v. St. John Gen. Hospital
  S3.95373
McLeod v. St. Paul Fire etc. Ins. Co.
  20.3301
McLeod v. Salmon Arm S. Trustees 1.768;
  32.1255; 35.81
McLeod v. Sandall 16.924; 29.484, 495,
  1914
McLeod v. Sault Ste. Marie P.S. Bd. 5.75;
  31.1891
McLeod v. Savoy 15.749
MacLeod v. Sawyer and Massey Co.
  34.2789
Macleod v. Scramlen 31.2731
McLeod v. Security Trust Co. 24.1253
McLeod v. Sexsmith P3.283
MacLeod v. Sing Lung Co. P1.2392
McLeod v. Sweezey 1.2016; 17.500;
  25.2045
McLeod v. Sydney 18.1169
McLeod v. Toronto Gen. Trusts Corpn.
  15.305, 1187; 38.220
McLeod v. Truax 19.267; 33.1911
McLeod v. Union Estates Ltd. 30.1286
McLeod v. United Canners Ltd. 8.1805

39

ILLUSTRATION 40
Canadian Abridgment (2nd), Volume 30

DANGEROUS PREMISES   [1612-1616]

become an actual hidden danger. *Held* further, the limitation provisions in s. 31 of the London Waterworks Act, 1873 (Ont.), c. 102, and s. 32 of the Public Utilities Act, R.S.O. 1950, c. 320, were not applicable to this case. What was complained of in this action was not anything done under either of these statutes, nor was it leaving unperformed a statutory duty, or anything that ought to be done to complete performance of a statutory duty. It was not anything done or omitted to be done in the exercise of the functions of a public utility. What was complained of was a failure of duty in relation to a public park maintained by the city, and plaintiff's action was based upon the common law liability of the occupant of premises.

MACKINDER v. LONDON, [1953] O.R. 52, [1953] 1 D.L.R. 452 (C.A.).

1612. A person was fatally injured by a fall while walking in a park maintained by defendant municipal corporation. It was contended that he was an invitee, and that, even were he not, defendant corporation owed him a higher duty in the matter of care than that owed to a mere licensee. *Held*, the contention could not be maintained, and the action should be dismissed.

RICHARDSON v. WINDSOR, [1942] O.R. 1, [1942] 1 D.L.R. 500.

1613. Ice show — Injuries suffered by spectator when proceeding to seat — Slipping on ice — Spectator as invitee — Judgment for plaintiff.

ASHBURY v. VICTORIA, [1953] 4 D.L.R. 476 (B.C.).

1614. Roller skating rink — Injury to patron — Duty of management. The law as to the duties of an invitor to an invitee was applied to a case where plaintiff, a patron of a roller skating rink, was injured when he caught his skate upon a balloon or other novelty which, having been distributed to the patrons, was lying on the skating surface of the rink on a New Year's Eve—which fact was well known to plaintiff.

STREET v. COLAVECCHIO, [1952] 2 D.L.R. 654 (Ont.).

1615. While plaintiff was skating at defendants' roller skating rink she fell and was injured as the result of one of her skates coming off. It was found that the skate had come off because defendants' employee, whose duty it was to attach the skates, had failed to attach it securely to plaintiff's shoe

with a toe strap. The skates were supplied by defendants and plaintiff paid a fee for their use and the use of the rink. Toe straps were supplied only to patrons who made a deposit as security for their return. A sign to this effect was posted near the skate wicket, but plaintiff did not see it and, having roller skated only a few times previously, did not know that toe straps were used. *Held*, defendants were not liable. The skates not being defective, defendants could not be made liable for the injuries suffered by plaintiff even if the skates might have been made safer for roller skating. In furnishing the skates and fastening them to plaintiff's shoes defendants did not undertake that under no circumstances would they become loose or come off. The obligation assumed by defendants, at its highest, did not go beyond furnishing and attaching skates which could be used with reasonable safety if ordinary and usual skill and care were exercised by the skater. There was no evidence that, either in the general experience of roller skating or in the opinion of persons who had closely observed its practice, the absence of straps rendered these skates less than reasonably safe for use; nor, assuming such a duty, was there evidence that defendants were responsible for that absence. The question was not whether plaintiff actually knew or did not know that straps could be obtained; the question was, did the management of the rink take reasonable steps to bring the fact of their availability to the notice of its patrons; and, considering the necessary mode of carrying on a business of this nature, it had clearly discharged that duty. There was, moreover, nothing whatever to make it appear that plaintiff, under any circumstances, would have used straps. The skates were complete without straps, for which, in fact, they were not designed, and nowhere in the United States or Canada were straps used more than occasionally or otherwise than as a special safeguard.

MACLEOD (SILVER GLADE ROLLER BOWL) v. ROE, [1947] S.C.R. 420, [1947] 3 D.L.R. 241, reversing [1946] 3 W.W.R. 522, [1947] 1 D.L.R. 135, which affirmed [1946] 2 W.W.R. 482.

1616. Hockey arena — Injury to spectator — Duty of invitor. There is no absolute warranty on the part of an occupier of premises who invites others to use the premises to see a game, race or other spectacle, that the premises are safe. He is under a duty only to see that reasonable

Court of Canada, you could have quickly located a report of it by using the *Supreme Court of Canada Reports Service.*[1]

We should now try to find a more recent case, because depending on the date, there may be variation in the procedure. Let us take *Murdoch v. Murdoch,* a well-known case originating in Alberta which concerns a wife who, on separating from her husband, claimed a half interest in a ranch owned by him. Assume you remember that the case was decided in the 1970s – thus, it may be listed in the *Canadian Abridgment's* original two-volume Consolidated Table of Cases or in volume 3, which covers the years 1975 to 1982 and includes cases digested in the revised Criminal Law volumes. In fact, you will find the case listed in volume 2 (see Illustration 41), but unlike the reference to *MacLeod v. Roe* in the same table, this one begins with a letter rather than a number. "S3.91476" refers you to volume 3 of the First Permanent Supplement 1974, paragraph 91476. When you look it up (see Illustration 42), you will find a digest of the case, together with a citation that refers you to reports of it in three series of reports – the *Western Weekly Reports, Reports of Family Law,* and the *Dominion Law Reports.* The notation "(Can.)" at the end of the citation indicates that it is a decision of a federal court. From the subject matter you can infer that it is the Supreme Court of Canada rather than the Federal Court, but "S.C.C." would have been a more precise notation. ("S.C.C." has been adopted as the appropriate notation in later volumes of the *Abridgment.*) It happens that there is also a listing for *Murdoch v. Murdoch* in volume 3 of the Consolidated Table of Cases, but if you check the references to it, you will find that it is a different and later, though related, case.

Let us now take a still more recent case as an example. *Re Philip,* a Manitoba case of the late seventies that raised the question of whether a will, partly printed and partly in the testator's handwriting, could be regarded as a holograph will, is listed in volume 3 of the Consolidated Table of Cases (see Illustration 43). The notation 2S5.92323 refers to paragraph 92323 in volume 5 of the Second Permanent Supplement (see Illustration 44). "Man. C.A." at the end of the citation is rather misleading because it refers to the case reported in [1979] 3 W.W.R. 554 and really belongs at the end of that part of the citation. The decision it reversed was a Surrogate Court case. The *Abridgment* now places the Province and the court in parentheses at the end of each court level in the citation. The case now would be cited as *Re Philip,* [1979] 3 W.W.R. 554 (Man. C.A.), reversing [1978] 4 W.W.R. 148, 4 E.T.R. 1 (Man. Surr. Ct.).

At the time of writing, the latest permanent supplement published was the Third Permanent Supplement dated 1982. As we have seen, volume 3 of the Consolidated Table of Cases also ends at 1982. If looking for a later case you should go to the table of cases and supplementary table of cases in the *Canadian Abridgment*'s loose-leaf Cumulative Supplement binders. If the case is digested in the Cumulative Supplement, it will be listed in the table of cases. If it has not yet been cumulated there, it may be listed in the supplemen-

---

1   See pp. 8-10, above.

ILLUSTRATION 41
Canadian Abridgment (2nd), Consolidated Table of Cases, Volume 2

CONSOLIDATED TABLE OF CASES

Munson, Re   14.2048; 38.1786
Munson v. Collingwood   29.2613; 32.1118;
   35.111
Munson v. Hall   31.441
Munson v. Poirier and LaPlante   27.245,
   1729
Munton, Re   20.2805
Munton v. Edmonton and Findley   27.1708;
   29.2904
Munz v. Munz   S3.49989, 62288
Murakami v. Henderson   13.679
Muranyi v. Vallance Coal & Cartage Co.
   13.447, 475; 23.2422; P1.174
Murcar v. Bolton   33.2776
Murch v. Murch   20.2754
Murch v. Toronto   1.1810; 4.266; 6.896
Murcheson v. Donohoe   21.1701
Murchie, Ex parte (1914), 42 N.B.R. 475
   14.1738
Murchie, Ex parte (1914), 42 N.B.R. 529
   9.65; 23.1215; 28.317
Murchie, Ex parte (1914), 42 N.B.R. 541
   21.2770; 32.856
Murchie, Ex parte (1914), 43 N.B.R. 115
   28.389, 506
Murchie v. Canterbury   29.2719
Murchie v. Mail Publishing Co.   7.2117;
   P1.1410
Murchie v. Scott   35.1299; 36.2141
Murchie v. Theriault   26.1248, 2107
Murchison v. Bank of N.S.   2.3526
Murchison v. Marsh   21.843
Murdoch, Re   19.510, 545; 21.14; 38.79
Murdoch v. A.G. B.C.   21.1367; 25.1363
Murdoch v. Belloni   26.1661, 2221
Murdoch v. Davis   27.596
Murdoch v. Grant   15.1573, 2683
Murdoch v. Guardian Ins. Co.   20.1615
Murdoch v. Guar. Trust Co.   19.2745
Murdoch v. Hill   P3.2410
Murdoch v. Hughes   12.619
Murdoch v. Man. South Western
   Colonization Ry.   8.1973
Murdoch v. Minneapolis Threshing Machine
   Co.   21.3879; P1.820
Murdoch v. Murdoch   S3.91476
Murdoch v. Pitts   22.3489
Murdoch v. Ransom   24.492
Murdoch v. West   7.3830; 15.354; 16.2123
Murdoch v. Windsor & Annapolis Ry.
   34.93
Murdock, Re   15.3948; 24.32; S3.56241,
   56251, 56252
Murdock v. Borysuk   P2.1063
Murdock v. Kilgour   12.2246; 19.1619
Murdock v. O'Sullivan   27.1236; 30.291
Murdock v. Patton   22.3649; P1.2529, 2530,
   2674
Murdock v. Richards   35.559

Murdock (John) Ltée v. Commn. de Rel.
   Ouv.   22.175
Murdy v. Burr   19.803
Murfina v. Sauvé   10.3745
Murgatroyd v. Stewart   38.2406
Murison v. Boyd   12.554
Murison v. Murison   16.44
Murne v. Morrison   29.538, 1078; 36.1467,
   1516
Murney v. Markland   4.3627
Murphy, Ex parte (1917), 38 D.L.R. 625
   (N.B.)   10.3284
Murphy, Ex parte (1921), 49 N.B.R. 280
   12.3612; 23.13, 1186
Murphy, Ex parte, [1936] S.C.R. 609
   3.2388
Murphy, Ex parte, [1936] S.C.R. 613
   3.3472
Murphy, Re (1894), 26 O.R. 163   9.3077,
   3128; 11.8122, 8312, 10115; 32.395,
   600
Murphy, Re (1896), 28 N.S.R. 196
   11.8284; 32.649
Murphy, Re (1902), 7 Terr. L.R. 271
   35.1301, 1333
Murphy, Re (1904), 4 O.W.R. 281
   20.2878
Murphy, Re (1910), 8 E.L.R. 586 (P.E.I.)
   21.87
Murphy, Re (1910), 15 B.C.R. 401   1.3215
Murphy, Re (1911), 9 E.L.R. 410 (P.E.I.)
   38.14
Murphy, Re (1922), 55 N.S.R. 267   38.164
Murphy, Re, [1926] 4 D.L.R. 1136 (P.E.I.)
   20.2847
Murphy, Re (1930), 43 B.C.R. 203
   25.1059
Murphy, Re (1931), 2 M.P.R. 440 (P.E.I.)
   11.7841; 32.2556
Murphy, Re (1931), 55 C.C.C. 113 (B.C.)
   25.1060
Murphy, Re (1932), 41 O.W.N. 98
   14.2438, 2535; 20.2863
Murphy, Re, [1943] O.W.N. 603   38.861;
   P1.2126
Murphy, Re, [1946] O.W.N. 419   19.938
Murphy, Re, [1950] 4 D.L.R. 182 (N.S.)
   38.1100
Murphy, Re (1952), 30 M.P.R. 61 (N.S.)
   11.9554; 23.1420, 1538, 1558
Murphy, Re (1954), 35 M.P.R. 238 (Nfld.)
   38.530
Murphy, Re (1956), 2 D.L.R. (2d) 132
   (N.S.)   7.3817; 17.1968
Murphy, Re, [1965] 4 C.C.C. 137 (Nfld.)
   10.7140
Murphy, Re (1970), 3 N.S.R. (2d) 293
   S2.43767
Murphy v. Barnabé Motors Ltd.   23.3099
Murphy v. Boulton   P3.2583

ILLUSTRATION 42
Canadian Abridgment (2nd), First Permanent Supplement 1974, Volume 3

TRUSTS AND TRUSTEES   [91488]

been held on a resulting trust or under the terms of an express oral trust.

DAVID v. SZOKE (1973), 39 D.L.R. (3d) 707 (B.C.).

91452. (III, 6)
tees prior to execution of will — Trustees named as executors — Whether trust enforceable — Wills Act, R.S.B.C. 1960, c. 408. The residuary clause of the last will of deceased read: "(e) To pay or transfer the residue of my estate to my Trustees . . . subject to the Trusts that I have indicated to them." The day before signing his will deceased had written to the two trustees named therein advising them that he had appointed them as his trustees, that he was leaving the residue of his estate to them and adding: "I direct that you transfer the said residue of my estate to the Provincial Committee of the Communist Party of Canada, or its successor." *Held*, there was a secret trust communicated to the trustees prior to the execution of the will. There had been no contravention of the Act. The trust was not rendered unenforceable by reason only that the trustees of the secret trust were also the trustees and executors named in the will. The secret trust was not so vague as to be void for uncertainty.

RE D'AMICO, [1974] 2 W.W.R. 559, 42 D.L.R. (3d) 759 (B.C.).

91458. (III, 7)
Construction — Charitable trusts — Whether words "charitable and benevolent" constituting valid charitable trust — Whether organizations merging to operation of will continuing to exist. The testatrix left the residue of the estate to be used for "charitable and benevolent" purposes by various named organizations some of which had since merged with other organizations. The executor applied for an order construing whether the gifts under the residue were good charitable gifts and whether the organizations which had merged ceased to exist and thus would not be entitled to the gift. *Held*, the words "charitable and benevolent" should read conjunctively and differed from the cases where the words were "charitable or benevolent" and therefore constituting one class of objects which should possess two attributes. The organizations did not cease to exist on merger and therefore were entitled to the gifts.

RE SHORTT (1974), 2 O.R. (2d) 329, 42 D.L.R. (3d) 673.

IV Resulting Trusts

91476. (IV, 3)
Wife's claim to beneficial interest in ranch property registered in husband's name — Contribution in labour to acquisition of property — Whether resulting trust. Appeal from the dismissal of a wife's claim to a beneficial one-half interest in a ranch property consisting of land and other ranch assets owned and registered in the name of the husband. There was no evidence of any agreement between the parties which might support her claim either on the basis of partnership or otherwise and the present appeal turned on the question whether a trust arose in the wife's favour by reason of her contribution over the years by way of labour to the creation of the assets in which she now claimed an interest. *Held* (by a majority), the appeal should be dismissed. The trial Judge had found that the wife's contributions in labour consisted of no more than was to be ordinarily expected of a ranch wife and that there was no financial contribution. It could not be said that there was any common intention that the beneficial interest in the property was to belong solely to respondent, in whom the legal estate was vested. The evidence did not support the existence of a resulting trust.

MURDOCH v. MURDOCH, [1974] 1 W.W.R. 361, 13 R.F.L. 185, 41 D.L.R. (3d) 367 (Can.).

91477. (IV, 3)
Matrimonial home — Title to property held by husband as required by Veterans' Land Act, R.S.C. 1970, c. V-4 but wife depositing initial down payment — Wife indirectly contributing by spending own money on day-to-day expenses enabling husband to expend his entire salary on improving house — Husband holding property on implied trust as to one-half interest in favour of wife.

RE WHITELEY, No. 55919/2.

V Constructive Trusts

91488. (V)
Constructive trust — Grantee named in deed to house providing part of purchase price — Grantee's brother providing the larger part of purchase price and taxes but not named in the deed — Presumption that grantee holding house in trust for himself and brother.

WOOLNOUGH v. WOOLNOUGH (1970), 3 N.S.R. (2d) 521.

ILLUSTRATION 43
Canadian Abridgment (2nd), Consolidated Table of Cases
Volume 3 (1975-1982)

CONSOLIDATED TABLE OF CASES

Petrofina Can. Ltd. v. Air Canada
3S5. 90309/48, 90429/222

Petrofina Can. Ltd. v. Chmn., Restrictive
Trade Practices Comm. 3S5. 88819

Petrofina Can. Ltd. v. Gionet 2S1. 12610

Petrofina Can. Ltd. v. Havard Mfg.
Corp. 3S5. 90279/21, 90429/130

Petrofina Can. Ltd. v. Lynn 2S3. 50596;
2S5. 87158

Petrofina Can. Ltd. v. Markland Devs.
Ltd. 2S4. 69803; 2S5. 83846/11,
84278

Petrofina Can. Ltd. v. Moncton
2S4. 71951/6

Petrofina Can. Ltd. v. Restrictive Trade
Practices Comm. 2S5. 88831

Petrofina Can. Ltée v. Travailieurs Unis
du Pétrole, Loc. 3 2S4. 52485

Petrogas Processing Ltd. v. Pub. Utilities
Bd. 3S4. 64378

Petropolis v. R. R11A. 11331, 11406,
11478; R11C. 18314

Petrov v. Legault R11D. 20784

Petrovitch v. A.G. R11C. 17145

Petryga v. Alberta 3S1. 9339

Petryga v. Petryga 3S4. 61700

Petryshyn v. Petryshyn 2S4. 55879/42

Pettigrew v. Pettigrew 3S3. 42964/26

Pettipas v. Roop 3S2. 28470; 3S3. 46085

Pettipas v. Watson 2S3. 30228/1

Pettis v. McNeil 2S3. 29393/28;
2S5. 91269

Pettit and Ont. College of Nurses, Re
2S4. 63493

Petts and Alta. Teachers' Assn., Re
2S1. 695

Petts v. Unemployment Ins. Umpire
2S1. 695

Petty v. Bishop 2S5. 94741

Petty v. MacKay 3S4. 63533

Peugeot Can. Ltd. v. Darte 2S4. 65305

Peugnet, Re R11A. 10935

Pfeifer v. Pfeifer 3S3. 42964/49

Pfeiffer and Commr. of N.W.T., Re
2S3. 50305/77, 50703/1; 2S5. 78923

Pfeutzenreuter v. Pfeutzenreuter
2S4. 58958

Pfizer Co. v. Dept. M.N.R. 2S3. 27959;
2S5. 86708

Pfizer Co. v. Nestlé-LeMur Ltd.
3S5. 90429/22

Pfizer Co. v. Pierre Fabre S.A.
3S5. 90429/44

Pflueger v. South Alta. Land Registration
Dist. 2S5. 81706

Pfundt v. Min. of Govt. Services
3S1. 9388

Phalen v. Solicitor Gen. of Can.
3S1. 1143/97

Phaneuf v. R. 2S3. 39295

Pharmacie Belisle Pharmacy Ltd. v.
Mineau 2S5. 96975, 96976

Pharmacies Modernes Inc., Re 2S1. 4544

Phelan, Ex parte R11A. 10857

Phelps, Re R11A. 11751, 13166;
R11B. 13910; R11D. 21049

Phibbs v. Chee Choo 2S5. 83671

Phibbs v. Choo 2S5. 83671, 97389

Philbin v. Rutley 2S4. 66890

Philco Int. Corp. v. Reg. T.M.
3S5. 90310, 90490

Philip, Re 2S5. 92323

Philip v. M.N.R. 3S3. 40057

Philipchalk v. Victoria 3S4. 71643

Philipp v. Southam 3S1. 6486; 3S5. 98751

Philipp Bros. v. Torm A/S, D/S
3S5. 97373

Philipzyk v. Edmonton Real Estate Bd. etc.
Ltd. 2S1. 2713; 2S3. 28886;
2S5. 79293

Phillion v. R. 2S3. 32366, 32367

Phillips and Coughlin, Re 3S5. 91919/4

Phillips and Coughlin (No. 2), Re
3S5. 91919/5

Phillips, Ex parte R11B. 16776;
R11C. 17009

Phillips, Re R11C. 17006

Phillips v. Alexander 3S2. 28784;
3S5. 84494

Phillips v. Bongard Leslie & Co.
3S5. 92217

Phillips v. C.N.R. 2S5. 74855

Phillips v. Conroy 3S4. 71033

Phillips v. Day & Ross Ltd.
2S3. 28997/1; 2S5. 74395/18

Phillips v. Evdokimoff 2S5. 84521

Phillips v. Gallagher 3S2. 29130

Phillips v. Kranjcec 2S4. 53402/7;
2S5. 97828/27

Phillips v. Phillips 3S3. 43281;
3S4. 55876, 56331

Phillips v. R. 2S5. 97458/10, 97462/3;
R10. 5191

Phillips v. Regina Bd. of Educ.
2S5. 74551, 74911/13

Phillips v. Reg., Mortgage Brokers Act
2S5. 79297

Phillips v. Roy 2S4. 66955

Phillips v. Spooner 2S5. 92248;
3S4. 56033; 3S5. 92247

ILLUSTRATION 44
Canadian Abridgment (2nd), Second Permanent Supplement, 1979
Volume 5

[92308]   WILLS

"absolutely" was confirmed by the evidence of the solicitor who drew the will. It was concluded, therefore, that B, the survivor, received an absolute devise and therefore notwithstanding the irrevocable agreement, she did nothing which was in contradiction of the joint and mutual will, but indeed carried out its terms in that she had absolute control over how the property should be devised.

RE OHORODNYK (1979), 4 E.T.R. 233 (Ont. H.C.).

II Form

92308.   (II, 1)

Form — Printed form will — Testatrix's signature not in place designated for signature — Signature conforming with placement requirements of Wills Act — Lack of evidence of due execution as existence, identity and whereabouts of witnesses unknown — Presumption of due execution applicable — Apparent "from the face of the will" that testatrix intended to give effect to document she signed as her will — Fact that date on will post-dating testatrix's death indicating mistake and not fatal to validity — Wills Act, R.S.O. 1970, c. 499, s. 11(1), (2).

RE RIVA (1978), 3 E.T.R. 307 (Ont. Surr. Ct.).

92320.   (II, 2)

Holograph will made shortly before visit to foreign country — Will not conditional on death during trip.

LANDOLFO v. HUEBNER, [1975] W.W.D. 66, 53 D.L.R. (3d) 730 (*sub nom.* RE HEUBNER). Affirmed (*sub nom.* RE HEUBNER AND LANDOLFO) [1976] W.W.D. 89 (Can.).

92321.   (II, 2)

Paper written and signed by deceased referring to existing but invalid form of will — Admissibility to probate — Wills Act, R.S.S. 1965, c. 130. Deceased completed, in August 1972, a printed form of will by which he made a complete disposition of his estate. He signed the document but his signature was not witnessed. In October 1972 he wrote in his own handwriting a paper in which he stated that he had placed in his bank safety deposit box certain title documents and insurance policies and "My will dated 19th August 1972", made a disposition of jewellery and directed that his remains be cremated. He signed the paper. *Held*, the second document was a holograph will in conformity with the requirements of the Act, and it incorporated by reference the earlier so-called will, which was in existence at the time and was sufficiently identified. The holograph will, to-

gether with the document referred to therein, should be admitted to probate.

RE CHAMBERLAIN, [1976] 1 W.W.R. 464 (Sask.).

92322.   (II, 2)

Form — Holograph — Testatrix filling in blanks on printed stationer's form — Requirements for valid will — Circumstances from which testamentary intention may be inferred — Cy-près doctrine applied — Wills Act, R.S.A. 1970, c. 393, s. 7. A testatrix purported to make a will by simply filling in the blanks on a printed stationer's form. Looking at only the handwritten portions of the purported will, the attempt to name executors was unsuccessful as the names standing alone were meaningless. Furthermore, there were no effective words of disposition. The latter defect, although usually fatal, was not so in this case for the Court was entitled to infer the deceased's testamentary intention by reason of the fact that she obtained, filled in, and signed her purported will in a stationer's will form and because she made a residual gift of her estate. On an application for advice, *held*, the handwritten portions constituted a testamentary paper.

RE SHORTT (1977), 4 Alta. L.R. (2d) 152, 9 A.R. 51 (Surr.Ct.).

92323.   (II, 2)

Form — Holograph — Will partly handwritten and partly printed stationer's form — Inference that testator did not intend to incorporate printed words — Administration with will annexed granted — Wills Act, R.S.M. 1970, c. W150, s. 7. Deceased made a will on a stationer's will form which was partly printed and partly in her handwriting. There were no witnesses. Letters of administration were refused. On appeal, *held* (by a majority), the appeal should be allowed. As deceased had not filled in the blanks on the form the Court could infer that she did not intend to incorporate the printed words on the will form, but intended to use it as a guide in making a holograph will.

RE PHILIP, [1979] 3 W.W.R. 554, reversing [1978] 4 W.W.R. 148, 4 E.T.R. 1 (Man. C.A.).

92339.   (II, 4)

Form — Execution — Attestation — Whether valid. The testator signed a will and then called two witnesses and asked them to sign. The testator did not acknowledge his signature. On probate, *held*, the will was valid. An acknowledgement was sufficient where a testator said "this is my will", or words to that effect, even tary table; if so, the number given will be a digest number in a monthly issue of *Canadian Current Law*. The cases digested in *Canadian Current Law* are later incorporated into the *Canadian Abridgment*'s Cumulative Supplement of Case Law and eventually into the next bound Permanent Supplement.

As an example of a recent case already digested in the Cumulative Supplement and therefore listed in the table of cases at the time of writing, let us take *Hanna v. Hanna,* an Ontario case relating to an adult child's duty to maintain a parent. Illustration 45 shows the listing in the table of cases; the number 43368 refers to a paragraph in the Cumulative Supplement (see Illustration 46).

Also at the time of writing, *Kingsbury v. Min. of Soc. Services for Prov. of Sask.,* a Charter case concerning the mobility rights of a thirteen-year old ward of the Alberta Minister of Social Services (the ward ran away to Saskatchewan) was listed in the Cumulative Supplement's supplementary table of cases (see Illustration 47). The number 963 refers to the number assigned to the digest in [1984] *Canadian Current Law.* On the spine of each issue of *Canadian Current Law* you will find the range of digest numbers contained in that issue. You will find that digest 963 is included in the February issue (see Illustration 48). The citation beneath the digest tells you that the case is reported in one of the new services devoted exclusively to Charter cases – the *Canadian Rights Reporter.*

For cases too recently reported and digested to be listed in the supplementary table of cases in the Cumulative Supplement binders to the *Canadian Abridgment,* look at the individual table of cases in subsequent issues of *Canadian Current Law.* Thus, if the supplementary table lists cases digested in the current year's January-June issues of *Canadian Current Law,* turn to the individual table of cases commencing with the July issue.

(b) Other Canadian Search Tools

Finding citations through the use of the tables of cases in the *Canadian Abridgment* and *Canadian Current Law* has been dealt with at length because of their extensive coverage of both jurisdiction and report series. But no matter how comprehensive such publications aim to be, errors and omissions are bound to occur. You should, therefore, be aware of alternative places to look if you do not find what you want there or if, on occasion, you do not have access to these publications.

We have already mentioned the *D.L.R. Annotation Service,* which cumulates annually – you can check its Table of Cases to the third series or, for earlier cases, the Table of Cases to the second series, which is bound separately. As noted earlier, a fourth series began in 1984.[2] Presumably the 1985 *D.L.R. Annotation Service* will begin to list cases in that series and annotations to them.

---

2   See pp. 11, 17, above.

ILLUSTRATION 45
Canadian Abridgment (2nd), Cumulative Supplement, Volume 1

TABLE OF CASES

ILLUSTRATION 46
Canadian Abridgment (2nd), Cumulative Supplement, Volume 2

[X.4]   INFANTS AND CHILDREN   [43368-43441]

Nova Scotia Court's maintenance order — Order registered in New Brunswick being photocopy not bearing Judge's actual signature — Therefore no valid registration of foreign order — Court having no jurisdiction to enforce order — Child and Family Services and Family Relations Act, S.N.B. 1980, c. C-21, ss. 6, 9.

M.G.P. v. T.V.D. (1983), 46 N.B.R. (2d) 15, 121 A.P.R. 15 (Q.B.).

43368. (X.5)
Maintenance — Child's duty to maintain parent — Husband applying for support against wife and adult children — Application dismissed — No interim interim parental support ordered — Court having jurisdiction to make such order prior to return of motion — Children having no surplus income — Unfair to disturb children's financial arrangements on sketchy information before Court — Family Law Reform Act, R.S.O. 1980, c. 152, ss. 17-19.

HANNA v. HANNA (1983), 33 R.F.L. (2d) 335 (Ont. H.C.).

XI   Guardianship

43373. (XI.1)
Guardianship — General — Provincial Court order giving wife custody of child with specified access to husband exercisible only in city of Calgary — Order not depriving husband of joint guardianship of child — Husband taking child to British Columbia — Husband found not guilty at trial of taking child with intent to deprive parent having lawful care or charge — Appeal allowed — Husband's right of custody limited by provincial Court order — Taking child out of city constituting "taking" within meaning of s. 250 of Criminal Code — Joint guardianship no defence to charge — Criminal Code, R.S.C. 1970, c. C-39, s. 250.

R. v. ENKIRCH, [1983] 1 W.W.R. 530, 31 R.F.L. (2d) 25, 23 Alta. L.R. (2d) 47, 1 C.C.C. (3d) 165, 41 A.R. 387, 142 D.L.R. (3d) 490 (C.A.).

43374. (XI.1)
Guardianship — General — Grandparents voluntarily assuming guardianship of child following parent's death — Court awarding minor daughter of deceased $50,575 damages for loss of benefit of dependency — Defendants appealing — Appeal dismissed — Contributions made by grandparents not being valid consideration in relation to claim for loss of dependency — Families Compensation Act, R.S.B.C. 1960, c. 138. The maternal grandfather of the infant child brought an action against defendants for the wrongful death of the child's mother in a traffic accident. The grandparents voluntarily assumed guardianship of the child following the mother's death. Defendants appealed an award of damages of $50,575. *Held*, the appeal should be dismissed. The contributions made by the grandparents were not to be considered in relation to the claim for loss of dependency. The acceptance of the guardianship was a gratuitous and voluntary act. Furthermore, it would be contrary to public policy and would reflect badly on the administration of justice to encourage people to refrain from accepting the duties of guardianship until all claims for compensation on behalf of children had been finally settled or litigated.

STONEHOUSE v. GAMBLE (1982), 31 R.F.L. (2d) 385, 44 B.C.L.R. 375, 24 C.C.L.T. 133 (C.A.).

43375. (XI.1)
Guardianship — General — Child adopted by maternal grandmother, an alcoholic — Custody order made in favour of Ministry of Social Services, and subsequently renewed — Provincial Court making guardianship order in favour of Minister under s. 56(1) of Act during term of renewed custody order on ground that "security and development" of child in danger — Appeal Court reversing guardianship order and directing new hearing — "Best interests of the child", as defined in Act, of primary concern — Security and development of child only one factor to be considered in determinating custody — Child and Family Services and Family Relations Act, S.N.B. 1980, c. 2.1, ss. 31(1)(c), 56(1).

D.A.M. v. R. (1983), 47 N.B.R. (2d) 41, 124 A.P.R. 41 (C.A.).

43390. (XI.2)
Guardianship — Parent as guardian — Child born March 1972 — Mother not requesting child maintenance from father and having no contact with him — Father being unemployed and unknown to child — Mother bringing application to have father declared deprived of all paternal rights and accessorily to have child's name changed to mother's name — Application dismissed — Evidence failing to establish sufficient grounds to grant paternal authority deprivation as paternal authority to be annulled only in grave circumstances — Best interests of child guiding Court — Court declining to grant order only to obtain change of name — Civil Code of Lower Canada, arts. 56.1 [en. 1980, c. 39, art. 7], 56.3 [en. 1980, c. 39, art. 7], 245(e) [rep. 1980, c. 39, art. 14] — Civil Code of Quebec, art. 654 — Code of Civil Procedure, arts. 813.3, 826.

ST-HILAIRE c. MENARD (1982), 31 R.F.L. (2d) 373 (C.S. Qué.).

43441. (XI.5)
Guardianship — Official guardian — Natural mother suffering from chronic alcoholism — Superintendent granted permanent custody and guardianship of child pursuant to Family and

ILLUSTRATION 47
Canadian Abridgment (2nd), Cumulative Supplement, Volume 1

SUPPLEMENTARY TABLE OF CASES

Keenan v. Keenan (1983), 36 R.F.L. (2d) 333 4146
Keenan v. Keenan (1983), 49 N.B.R. (2d) 228 4173
Keenan (Alvin) Ltd. v. Sun Alliance Ins. Co. (1984), 4 C.C.L.I. 261 6921
Keenberg v. Royal Ins. Co. of Can. (1983), 23 Man. R. (2d) 267 .... 1770, 1871, 2149, 2398, 2403, 2404
Kehler v. Klumper (1983), 23 Man. R. (2d) 196 .... 804, 805
Keirouz v. Co-operators Ins. Assn., [1983] I.L.R. 1-1712 2890
Kelleher v. Meadows (1983), 24 Man. R. (2d) 148 1746
Kelly v. Phoenix Assur. Co. of Can. (1984), 4 C.C.L.I. 172 .... 6979, 6986
Kelly v. Village of Vanderhoof Works Dept. (1984), 5 C.H.R.R. D/2159 8345
Kelly, Douglas & Co. v. Can. Allied Mfrs. Wholesale & Retail Union, [1981] 1 W.L.A.C. 612 7090
Kelly Douglas Co. v. Can. Allied Mfrs. Wholesale & Retail Union, [1981] 2 W.L.A.C. 260 10106
Kelly (Leonard P.) Ltd. v. Haldimand-Norfolk, Reg. Mun. of (1983), 27 L.C.R. 113 163
Kelowna v. C.U.P.E., Loc. 338 (1983), 13 L.A.C. (3d) 285 9009
Kemaldean v. Edmonton (1984), 52 A.R. 97 .... 8333, 8340, 8766
Kendal-Parliament Hldgs. Ltd. v. Toronto (1983), 15 O.M.B.R. 222 4332
Kennedy, Re (1984), 1 O.A.C. 317 5390
Kennedy v. A.G. B.C., [1983] 6 W.W.R. 673 1932
Kennedy v. Sarnia Bd. of Commrs. of Police (1984), 1 O.A.C. 317 5390
Kennedy v. Vancouver (1983), 45 B.C.L.R. 175 700
Kennedy Park Fam. Clothing Ltd. v. Haidinyak (1983), 4 C.L.R. 129 10686
Kenny v. Kenny (1983), 47 N.B.R. (2d) 345 641
Kenora Dist., C.A.S. and S., Re (1983), 42 O.R. (2d) 474 1346
Kent v. Kent (1983), 54 N.B.R. (2d) 158 9926, 10214
Kent v. O.P.S.E.U., Loc. 132 (1983), 10 L.A.C. (3d) 203 2227
Kent Drugs Ltd. v. Kronson (1983), 23 Man. R. (2d) 161 .... 827, 828
Kenton Natural Resources Corp. v. Burkinshaw (1983), 47 A.R. 321 951
Kentz v. Breitkreuz (1983), 27 Sask. R. 268 2041
Kepron v. Vogt (1983), 25 Man. R. (2d) 110 .... 4324, 4414
Kerber v. Kerber (1983), 35 R.F.L. (2d) 184 .... 1459, 1467
Kerkhoff (J.C.) & Sons Const. Ltd. v. Pennyfarthing Dev. Ltd. (1984), 84 C.L.L.C. 16,025 8888
Kerkhoff (J.C.) & Sons Contr. Ltd. v. XL Ironworks Co. (1983), 26 C.C.L.T. 1 .... 1834, 1841, 2154
Kernahan & Graves Real Estate Co. v. Nat. Trust Co. (1983), 3 D.L.R. (4th) 175 4514
Kerr v. M.N.R. (1984), 84 D.T.C. 1094 5893
Ketchum v. Hislop (1984), 54 B.C.L.R. 327 .... 11085, 11193
Ketra Uebersee Tpt. GmbH & Co. KG c. Perras, Fafard, Gagnon Inc., [1983] R.D.J. 459 8394
Khan v. Pfuegel (1984), 44 C.P.C. 154 10469, 10477
Khan v. R. (1984), 12 C.C.C. (3d) 193 10787
Khirkhanan v. Khirkhanan (1983), 44 O.R. (2d) 476 .... 6368, 6378
Kidd v. M.N.R., [1983] C.T.C. 2747 2946
Kidd v. Southam Press Ltd. (1983), 1 C.C.E.L. 167 .... 1446, 1449, 1451
Kierans v. Kierans (1984), 38 R.F.L. (2d) 445 7184
Kierans v. Kierans (1984), 45 C.P.C. 84 10699
Kieswetter v. Kieswetter Cartage & Excavating Co. (1983), 38 C.P.C. 170 5274
Kimberly-Clark of Can. Ltd. v. U.P.I.U., Loc. 655 (1983), 10 L.A.C. (3d) 241 2229
Kimco Steel Sales Ltd. v. Latina Ornamental Iron Work Ltd. (1984), 3 P.P.S.A.C. 237 9255, 9256
Kimura v. Min. of Govt. Services (1983), 28 L.C.R. 170 .... 3517, 3518, 3522
Kinaschuk and Weiser, Re (1983), 3 D.L.R. (4th) 521 .... 5391, 6157
Kindersley & Dist. Co-op Ltd. v. Bowman (1983), 25 Sask. R. 213 .... 1063, 1064
King v. Gull Bay Indian Band (1983), 38 C.P.C. 1 .... 4900, 5275
King v. Larlee (1984), 54 N.B.R. (2d) 32 8716
King v. Meadow Ford Sales Ltd. (1983), 25 Sask. R. 301 .... 1651, 1655
King v. R. (1984), 27 M.V.R. 212 .... 8477, 8607
King v. Solna Offset of Can. Ltd. (1984), 3 O.A.C. 178 9049
King George Private Hosp. v. Hosp. Employees' Union Loc. No. 180, [1981] 1 W.L.A.C. 94 .... 5012, 5084
King Nursing Home Ltd. and Grossman, Re (1983), 43 O.R. (2d) 355 3334
King (Pat) Real Estate Ltd. v. Corkum (1983), 59 N.S.R. (2d) 74 .... 888, 890, 1236
King Planning Area Official Plan Amendment 22, Re (1983), 15 O.M.B.R. 258 .... 5188, 5189
Kingsbury v. Min. of Soc. Services for Prov. of Sask. (1983), 4 C.R.R. 151 963
Kingston v. Homestead Land Hldgs. Ltd. (1983), 15 O.M.B.R. 127 2372
Kingsway Tpts. Ltd. v. I.B.T., Loc. 938 (1983), 10 L.A.C. (3d) 440 3106
Kinloch v. Tarasoff (1984), 33 Sask. R. 66 .... 9047, 9048
Kirkpatrick v. Maple Ridge (1983), 49 B.C.L.R. 134 .... 5179, 5182, 5186, 5217, 5218
Kirkwall Const. Ltd. v. Vancouver Gen. Hosp. (1984), 84 C.L.L.C. 16,015 5018
Kirsch v. Safeco Ins. Co. of Amer. (1984), 6 C.C.L.I. 68 9964
Kirsch Hldgs. Ltd. v. Ins. Corp. of B.C. (1984), 6 C.C.L.I. 68 9964
Kiss v. Palachik (1983), 47 N.R. 148 .... 2268, 2269

51

ILLUSTRATION 48
Canadian Current Law, February, 1984

[1984] C.C.L. 963   **CONSTITUTIONAL LAW**

963. (XXIV.1.d.ii)
Constitution Act, 1982 — Charter of Rights and Freedoms — Mobility rights — Residence — Thirteen-year-old ward of Alberta Minister of Social Services running away to Saskatchewan — Application to restrain defendant from returning child to Alberta — No violation of s. 6(2) mobility rights — Rights subject to reasonable limit prescribed by law of legal guardian's right to determine residence of child — Application dismissed — Canadian Charter of Rights and Freedoms, 1982, ss. 1, 6(2)(a).

KINGSBURY V. MIN. OF SOC. SERVICES FOR PROV. OF SASK. (1983), 4 C.R.R. 151 (Sask. Q.B.).

964. (XXIV.1.e.i)
Constitution Act, 1982 — Charter of Rights and Freedoms — Legal rights — Life, liberty and security — Ss. 250(2), (2.1) of Act inconsistent with s. 7 of Charter insofar as making driving while disqualified absolute liability offence — Absolute liability offences prima facie violating fundamental principles of penal liability — Only to be used when penalties for breach minimal and regulatory scheme impossible to enforce without them — Insofar as ss. 250(2), (2.1) of Act make offence of driving while disqualified absolute liability, offence not having minimal penalties inconsistent with s. 7 of Charter and of no force and effect — Offence held not to be absolute liability offence but one of strict liability allowing accused certain defences — Canadian Charter of Rights and Freedoms, 1982, s. 7 — Highway Traffic Act, R.S.M. 1970, c. H60, ss. 250(2), (2.1).

R. v. BLACKBIRD (1983), 22 M.V.R. 130 (Man. Prov. Ct.).

965. (XXIV.1.e.i)
Constitution Act, 1982 — Charter of Rights and Freedoms — Legal rights — Life, liberty and security — Code provision regarding sexual intercourse with female under 14 excluding mistake as defence — Charter not preventing Parliament from creating offence and excluding mistake as defence — Canadian Charter of Rights and Freedoms, 1982, s. 7 — Criminal Code, R.S.C. 1970, c. C-34, s. 146(1).

R. v. VILLENEUVE (1983), 4 C.R.R. 1 (Ont. C.A.). Leave to appeal to S.C.C. granted (1983), 4 C.R.R. 1n.

966. (XXIV.1.e.i)
Constitution Act, 1982 — Charter of Rights and Freedoms — Legal rights — Life, liberty and security — Applicant pretrial detainee alleging respondent violating principles of fundamental justice by depriving applicant of liberty — Respondent limiting number of "open visits" without affording prisoners hearing — Application for relief dismissed — Director having no duty to afford hearing — Principles of fundamental justice not imposing procedural standards on official having statutory authority to set rules of institution — Canadian Charter of Rights and Freedoms, 1982, s. 7.

SOENEN V. DIR. OF EDMONTON REMAND CENTRE (1983), 48 A.R. 31 (Q.B.).

967. (XXIV.1.e.ii)
Constitution Act, 1982 — Charter of Rights and Freedoms — Legal rights — Unreasonable search or seizure — Material illegally seized under defective search warrant — Application for return of material seized allowed — Charter prohibiting retention of material by Crown even if already tendered as evidence at preliminary inquiry — Criminal Code, R.S.C. 1970, c. C-34, s. 443(1) — Canadian Charter of Rights and Freedoms, 1982, ss. 8, 24.

R. v. TAYLOR (1983), 35 C.R. (3d) 80, 25 Sask. R. 145 (Q.B.).

968. (XXIV.1.e.ii)
Constitution Act, 1982 — Charter of Rights and Freedoms — Legal rights — Unreasonable search or seizure — Tax investigator with Department of National Revenue searching and seizing corporate taxpayer's records under s. 231(1)(d) of Income Tax Act without warrant — Whether such proceedings contrary to unreasonable search and seizure provisions of s. 8 of Charter — In circumstances public interest in efficient tax system outweighing taxpayer's expectation of privacy — Income Tax Act, S.C. 1970-71-72, c. 63, s. 231(1)(d) — Canadian Charter of Rights and Freedoms, 1982, s. 8.

NEW GDN. REST. & TAVERN LTD. V. M.N.R., 83 D.T.C. 5338, [1983] C.T.C. 332 (Ont. H.C.).

969. (XXIV.1.e.ii)
Constitution Act, 1982 — Charter of Rights and Freedoms — Legal Rights — Unreasonable search or seizure — Writs of assistance under Narcotic Control Act violating s. 8 of Charter, as no objective and independent review of reasonable belief — Canadian Charter of Rights and Freedoms, 1982, s. 8 — Narcotic Control Act, R.S.C. 1970, c. N-1, s. 10(1)(a). S. 10(1)(a) of the Narcotic Control Act, which authorizes a peace officer to search a dwelling house pursuant to a writ of assistance, offends s. 8 of the Charter, since there is no objective and independent verification of the grounds underlying the reasonable belief authorizing the search.

R. v. CUFF (1983), 34 C.R. (3d) 344 (B.C. Co. Ct.).

Another place you might look is the *Dominion Report Service,* published by CCH Canadian Limited. It consists of a loose-leaf service for current material, which is later refiled in transfer binders or replaced by bound volumes if your library purchases them (bound volumes used to be supplied as part of the annual update service). There is a Finding Lists volume for 1968-1979, which includes a consolidated case table covering those years. For later cases you must at the present use the case tables in the annual volumes and loose-leaf service. However, beginning in 1985, a cumulative table, which is updated annually, is to be made available as an optional extra. You may want to check whether your law school library subcribes to it.

Taking as an example one of the cases we found through the *Canadian Abridgment*'s tables of cases, look up *Re Philip.* As in the Carswell publications, you will find it under "Philip, Re" in the consolidated case table in the volume of Finding Lists, 1968-1979 (see Illustration 49). The notation (79) 94-304M tells you that the case is digested in the 1979 volume in paragraph 94-304 and that it is a Manitoba case. This is confirmed in Illustration 50. Note that numbers in the sequence are used at the beginning of the paragraphs and for additional guidance in finding them, at the foot of the pages. Disregard the numbers at the top of the pages; retained from the loose-leaf service that keeps the set current, their use was for purposes of filing. In the digest of *Re Philip* (Illustration 50), see the following note: "For the facts and decision under appeal see (78) D.R.S. ¶94-249. This refers you to a digest of the facts and decision in the Surrogate Court case (see Illustration 51), from which there was a successful appeal to the Manitoba Court of Appeal.

In its loose-leaf volume, the *Dominion Report Service* sometimes digests a case before it is reported. In this situation, a full citation cannot be given. See, for instance, in Illustration 52 the digest of *Law Society of Upper Canada v. Skapinker,* a case in which the Supreme Court of Canada ruled that the Law Society's requirement that candidates for admission to the Ontario bar be Canadian citizens or other British subjects (the correct term now is Commonwealth citizens) was not in conflict with the Charter's guarantee of mobility rights. Note that the case is listed in the 1984 table of cases under both Law Society of Upper Canada and Skapinker (see Illustrations 53 and 54), thus making it easy to locate the digest. The year and numbers are the same in the loose-leaf service as they will be when bound.

If you think that a case has been reported in a particular series that has a consolidated table of cases, you may go directly to it. Or if you know the jurisdiction and approximate date, you may, for cases likely to be reported in a Maritime Law Book series, go to the table of cases in the appropriate index and digest volume.[3] For a western case, depending on the date you may try one of the consolidated indexes to the *Western Weekly Reports.*[4] If you are looking for a case on a subject dealt with in a series of topical law reports, you

---

3   See pp. 26-29, above.
4   See p. 23, above.

ILLUSTRATION 49
Dominion Report Service, Finding Lists 1968-1979
Consolidated Case Table

336   **Dominion Report Service**

Paragraph

Petersen—continued
v. Bezold et al. .... (71) 94-179
v. Peterson, Re ......(79) 15-804; (71) 53-408
v. Saskatchewan Government Ins.
  Office .... (69) 86-573
et al. v. Spilde ....(72) 86-1128
Howell and Heather (Canada) Ltd
  et al. v. Rempel et al ....(74) 86-1434
  et al. Rempel et al. v. .... (73) 53-771
  et al. Walsh v. ....(72) 86-1176

Electronic Die Co. Inc. et al. v.
  Plastiseal Inc. .....(73) 1-1127; (74) 1-1375

Pethick v. Pethick .: .... (78) 54-111

Petijevich v. Law .... (68) 86-510

petits Profits (Les) INC. V. Rhéaume (68) 1-158

Petranik v. Dale et al. .(73) 70-380; (76) 70-253

Petricia, R. v. ....(74) 15-2594

Petrie, R. v. .... (69) 15-397

Petritz v. M.N.R. .... (73) 80-640

Petrofina Canada Ltd..
  Lincoln Lions Club Inc. v. ....(78) 1-948
  R. v. .... (75) 15-524
  Stevens v. .... (75) 90-029
  v. Les travailleurs unis du pétrole.
    local 3 .... (78) 60-114
  v. Markland Development Ltd. ...(78) 70-623
  (City of) Moncton .... (76) 26-420
  v. Moneta Porcupine Mines Ltd. et
    al. .... (70) 70-129
  v. Restrictive Trade Practices
    Commission, Director of
    Investigation and :Research and
    Attorney General of
    Canada .... (79) 54-738, F.C.C.; C.A.

Pétroles Inc. (Les),
  v. Francois Nilon Ltée .... (71) 86-943
  v. Gravel (Dame) .... (69) 86-562

Petropoulos, Re .... (74) 1-1255

Petryczka and Petryczka, Re .... (73) 21-678

Petryshen R. v. .... (69) 15-496

Petryshyn v. Petryshyn .... (78) 21-962

Pettigrew v. Pettigrew .... (72) 21-587

Pettigrew
  v. Pettigrew .... (72) 21-587
  R. v. .... (79) 17-735, O.

Pettinicchi, R. v. .... (71) 15-949

Pettipiece, R. v. ....(72) 15-1602

Petty v. Bishop et al. .... (77) 53-703

Petzoldt, R. v. ....(73) 15-2186

Paragraph

Peugeot Canada Ltd. v.. :Darte
  et al. .... (77) 70-341

Pezzo, R. v. ....(73) 15-1910

Pfaff; MacEachern v. .... (76) 21-137

Pfeffer et al.. R. v. .... (76) 16-178

Pfeiffer
  and Commissioner of Northwest
    Territories, Re .... (77) 53-913
  R. v. ....(79) 17-833, A.
  et al. v. Morrison et al. ....(74) 86-1423

Pfeutzeureuter v. Pfeutzeureuter (79) 21-995, M.

Pfizer Co. Ltd.
  v. Deputy Minister of National
    Revenue For Customes and
    Excise .... (76) 80-268
  v. M.N.R. (Deputy) .... (73) 80-694

Pflueger et al. v. South Alberta Land
  Registration District et al. .... (77) 70-370

Pfrimmer Estate, Re ...(68) 94-059; (69) 94-081

Phaneuf
  v. Sylvestre .... (76) 70-176
  Estate v. .... (78) 80-457

Pharmacie Belisle Pharmacy Ltd. v.
  Mineau et al.; Gauthier,
  Third Party .... (78) 53-998

Pharmaco (Canada) Ltd., Noxzema
  Chemical Co. of Canada Ltd. v. .(73) 1-1141

Pharmo Products Ltd..
  R. v. .... (75) 15-005; 15-006; 15-007

Pharo, R. v. ....:................. (71) 15-956

Phase III Productions Inc. et al.,
  Herrboldt v. ....(79) 54-736, B.C.

Phelps,
  R. v. ....(72) 15-1700
  et al., R. v. ....(73) 15-1959

Phibbs v. Chee Choo .... (77) 70-299

Phil Olson gencies et al.. R. v. ....(71) 15-1100

Philbin
  et al., R. v. .... (78) 17-154
  and Henderson, R. v. .... (78) 17-039

Philco-Ford of Canada Ltd.,
  Vanderhoek v. ....(79) 54-653, O

Philip,
  Re .... (79) 94-304, M
  Abbey Inc., Lester et al. v. ....(76) 43-163
  Morris Inc. v. Rothmans of Pall Mall
    Canada Ltd. ....(77) 1-726

Philippon et al. v. Legate et al. ..... (70) 53-289

ILLUSTRATION 50
Dominion Report Service, 1979

1874   Dominion Report Service—Cited 79 DRS

Held: There was no requirement that the executors appoint additional executors. The provisions in the will for the appointment of additional executors to replace the executors nominated were directory only and not mandatory. The land in question was not yet vested in the legatees. The provision in the will impliedly authorized the executors to use their discretion in the realization of the estate.

BECKER AND BRITISH CANADIAN PITWOOD LTD. v. CLELAND'S ESTATE ET AL.; CLELAND'S ESTATE v. MELVIN ET AL., (1978) 23 N.B.R. (2d) 631 (Q.B.).

[¶ 94-302, S.] Beneficiaries—Appeal by legitimate child of intestate's illegitimate daughter — Difference between legitimate and illegitimate children abolished — Appeal allowed—*Intestate Succession Act*, R.S.S. 1965, c. 126, ss. 2(b), 5, 17 [re-en. 1971, c. 18, s. 1], 17A [en. 1973-74, c. 51, s. 1], 18 [repealed 1971, c. 18, s. 1].

This was an appeal from a decision rejecting the application of the legitimate child of the intestate's illegitimate daughter to inherit and administer the estate. The intestate had publicly acknowledged his illegitimate daughter during his lifetime and therefore had she survived the intestate she would have inherited his estate. The legitimate child submitted that she was entitled to inherit because her mother qualified as if she were legitimate.

Held: The appeal was allowed. Any difference between legitimate and illegitimate children was eliminated by the statutory provision that an illegitimate child shall be treated as if he were the legitimate child of his mother.

LAMONT v. THOMPSON, [1979] 1 W.W.R. 760 (C.A.).

[¶ 94-303, B.C.] Intestate succession—Illegitimate son of illegitimate half-brother not entitled to share of intestate's estate—*Administration Act*, R.S.B.C. 1960, c. 3, ss. 91-94 [all re-en. 1972, c. 3, s. 2], 94A [en. 1972, c. 3, s. 2], 105 [am. 1966, c. 1, s. 12], 108, 113, 116—*Administration Act*, R.S.B.C. 1948, c. 6, s. 123, 124—*English Law Act*, R.S.B.C. 1960, c. 129—*Inheritance Act*, 1883 (Imp.), c. 106.

The Official Administrator applied for directions as to the administration of the estate of the deceased who died intestate. At issue was whether the illegitimate son of the deceased illegitimate half-brother of the intestate was entitled to a share of the intestate's estate.

Held: The illegitimate son of the illegitimate half-brother was not entitled to a share of the intestate's estate. If he had been alive, the illegitimate half-brother would have been entitled to share in the intestate's estate because s. 113 of the *Administration Act* deemed an illegitimate child to be the legitimate child of his mother. However, the common law with respect to illegitimate children of a father was not altered by the *Administration Act*. Consequently, the word "children" was interpreted to mean legitimate children and the illegitimate son was not entitled to share in the estate.

MANSON v. HAYNES ET AL., [1979] 1 W.W.R. 542 (S.C.).

[¶ 94-304, M.] Letters of administration with will annexed—Will partly handwritten and partly printed on stationers' form—Holograph will—Appeal allowed.

This was an appeal against the dismissal of an application for letters of administration with the deceased's will annexed. For the facts and decision under appeal see (78) D.R.S. ¶ 94-249.

Held (one diss.): The appeal was allowed. As the deceased had not filled in the blanks on the stationers' will form and had repeated prepositions included in the printed form, it was concluded that the deceased had not intended to adopt or incorporate the printed words on the form.

RE PHILIP, [1979] 3 W.W.R. 554 (C.A.).

¶ 94-302

ILLUSTRATION 51
Dominion Report Service, 1978

[¶ 94-248, N.S.] Estate and inheritance taxes—Succession duties payable by beneficiary of each specific bequest in absence of provision in will to the contrary—Interest payable to beneficiary of each specific bequest from end of executor's year at rate of 5 per cent as determined by s. 3 of *Interest Act*, R.S.C. 1970, c. I-18.

This was an application by the executor of a deceased person's estate for directions in the administration of the estate. The first question was whether succession duties were chargeable by the Province against the estate charged to and paid from the residue of the estate remaining after the payment of individual specific bequests and legacies or should succession duty with respect to each specific bequest and legacy be paid by the beneficiary of each such specific individual bequest or legacy, or charged against each such individual specific bequest or legacy? The second question was whether interest was payable from the estate to the beneficiary of each individual specific bequest or legacy on the amount of such bequest or legacy, and, if so, from what date and what rate?

Held: Under s. 9 of c. 17 of the Acts of 1972, *An Act Respecting Succession Duties,* the burden of the duty fell on the beneficiary. The testator could relieve the beneficiary of that burden. There was no provision in the will which would indicate an intention on the part of the testator to relieve the beneficiaries of their statutory duty to pay succession duties. The succession duties were chargeable against the specific bequests. Interest was payable to the beneficiary of each specific bequest from the end of the executor's year. The rate of interest was determined by s. 3 of the *Interest Act* at 5 per cent.

RE LYNCH'S ESTATE, (1975) 25 N.S.R. (2d) 13 (S.C.).

[¶ 94-249, M.] Application for letters of administration with will annexed—Will partly handwritten and partly printed on stationers' form — Not holograph will — Application refused—*Wills Act*, R.S.M. 1970, c. W-150, s. 7.

This was an application for letters of administration with the deceased's will annexed. The will was an undated document, on a stationers' will form, partly printed and partly in the handwriting of the deceased and signed by her. While the will form contained an attestation form, there were no witnesses to the signature of the deceased and the will (or, more precisely, the handwritten portion of the document) was therefore being propounded as a holograph will. There was evidence that the will was completed sometime between September, 1972, and July 6, 1976; that all of the handwriting, signatures and initials in the will were those of the deceased; that the deceased was of full age of 18 years throughout the period in question; and that throughout that period the deceased was of sound mind, memory and understanding. Counsel for the applicant contended that the testamentary intention (or lack of it) could be determined by the handwritten portion and extrinsic evidence but that resort might not be had to the portion of the document not in the deceased's handwriting. The document was found sometime after the death of the deceased in a box in a bureau drawer in the deceased's bedroom.

Held: The application was dismissed. The evidence invited only one conclusion, that the will document was intended by the deceased to be "a deliberate or fixed and final expression of intention as to the disposal of property upon death". Section 7 of the *Wills Act* required a person's holograph will to be "wholly in his own handwriting" and the courts had consistently interpreted that requirement as admitting only the maker's own handwriting and nothing else. In this matter the deceased intended to adopt or to incorporate, at the very least, the printed words preceding the handwritten words disposing of her home, contents and other personal property and specific bequests and the printed words preceding the handwritten disposition of the residue of her estate.

RE PHILIP, [1978] 4 W.W.R. 148 (Surr. Ct.).

[¶ 94-250, S.] Application to remove executor—Executor wasting assets of estate and not passing accounts — Executor not "competent" within s. 61 of *Surrogate Court Act*, R.S.S. 1965, c. 75—Application allowed.

This was an application for the removal of the executor of a deceased person's estate and the appointment of the applicant in his place and stead and to order the executor to file and pass his accounts up to and including the date of revocation of the grant of

ILLUSTRATION 52
Dominion Report Service (Loose-leaf), July 1984

Government   23,819

to work in any province unrestricted by any law of that province which was directed to restricting the right of the permanent resident to do so. (3) The third approach was to separate clauses (a) and (b) as though the conjunction "and" were missing, but to read (b) as requiring a mobility aspect. This approach would cover the case of a person residing in one province but commuting to perform work in an adjoining province whether or not the permanent resident had previously or subsequently moved to the second province for the purpose of undertaking or continuing to undertake the work in question. After reviewing the jurisprudence respecting the use of headings in the interpretation of statutes the Court concluded that, at the very minimum, the headings in the Charter had to be considered in the process of discerning the meaning and application of the Charter provisions. If the section, when read as a whole, was clear and without ambiguity the heading would not operate to change that clear and unambiguous meaning. However, a court should not, by the adoption of a technical rule of construction shut itself off from whatever small assistance might be gathered from an examination of the heading as part of the entire constitutional document. The expression "Mobility Rights" must mean rights of the person to move about, within and outside the national boundaries. A division into clauses (a) and (b) was superfluous if one right only was being created as suggested by the first interpretation. Moreover, the first interpretation of s. 6(2)(b) was inconsistent with s. 6(3) which subjected the "*rights*" specified in subsection (2) to certain limitations. (The Court's emphasis). The second interpretation, which was necessary to create a free standing "right to work" provision out of clause (b) failed to account for the presence of the phrase "in any province" in clause (b). A reading out of the phrase "in any province" would create a result verging on the absurd and clause (b) alone among the rest of s. 6 would be out of context under the heading "Mobility Rights". Further, if clause (b) were reduced by the deletion of the phrase "in any province" the citizen or permanent resident would not have a clear and unambiguous right to commute across a provincial boundary to engage in regular work. Many considerations led to the adoption of the third interpretation: (1) the clause was thereby accorded a meaning consistent with the heading of s. 6 ("Mobility Rights"); (2) the transprovincial border commuter was accorded the right to work under (b) without the need of establishing residence in the province of residence; (3) there was a separation of function and purpose between (a) and (b) and the need for separate clauses was demonstrated; and (4) the presence of s. 6(3). The conclusion was further supported in the writings of all of the authors whose works were brought to the attention of the Court. As a result s. 6(2)(b) did not establish a separate and distinct right to work divorced from the mobility provisions in which it was found. The rights in (a) and (b) related to the movement to another province, either for the taking up or residence, or to work without establishing residence. Clause (b) did not give an independent constitutional right to work as a lawyer in the province of residence so as to override s. 28(c). As *obiter* the Court indicated that the record of the appellant on the issue of s. 1 of the Charter would have made it difficult to determine the issue as to whether a reasonable limit on a prescribed right had been demonstrably justified. The decision of the trial judge was restored.

LAW SOCIETY OF UPPER CANADA v. SKAPINKER, May 3, 1984.

[¶ 27-067, M.]   **Municipalities — Repair of roads — By-laws — By-laws amending city policy to reduce level of maintenance for gravel roads — Residents on gravel streets seeking to have by-law declared null and void and claiming policy discriminatory — Appeal dismissed —** *City of Winnipeg Act,* S.M. 1971, c. 105, ss.352, 519(1).

This was an appeal from a judgment which held that a municipal by-law was valid. The by-law resulted in the deterioration of the condition of the granular surface roads along which the plaintiffs resided. For a summary of the trial decision see 84 DRS ¶ 26-902.

Held: The appeal was dismissed. The Court of Appeal agreed with the decision of the trial judge but added a few words on the plaintiffs' main arguments. The by-law was not discriminatory. The plaintiffs argued that the city could not pass a by-law which required them to pay for the maintenance of other streets while not requiring the ratepayers in other areas to pay for the maintenance of their streets. The by-law did not require the plaintiffs to pay for maintenance of other city streets. It was the policy of the city and not the by-law, that dictated that paved streets throughout the city were to be maintained at the expense of the city at large.

ILLUSTRATION 53
Dominion Report Service (Loose-leaf), October 1984

Table of Cases—1984 **60,707**

Paragraph

Laurie, R. v. .... (84) 18-213, Nfld.

Laurier, R. v. .... (84) 17-959, O.

Lauze et al., Turner (G.W.) Ltd. v. .... (84) 2-702, M.

Lauzon, R. v. ... (84) 18-167, Q.; 18-329, O.

Laval (City), Batsos v. ... (84) 18-196, Q.

Laverty and Laverty Re .... (84) 2-538, O.

Lavery v. Sherway Contracting (Windsor) Ltd. et al. .. (84) 54-869, O.

Lavigne v. Home Insurance Co. .... (84) 43-385, N.B.

Lavigne v. **Lavigne** ...... (84) 22-443, B.C.

Laviolette and Lund, R. v. .... (84) 17-596, P.E.I.

Lavoie v. Poirier .... (84) 3-021, O.

Law v. Kingston General Hospital et al. .... (84) 54-849, O.

Law v. Solicitor General of Canada et al. .... (84) 27-129, F.C.C.; C.A.

Lawlor et al., Roderick Davis & Sons Ltd. v. .... (84) 2-494, Nfld.

Lawrence's Estate et al. v. Good .... (84) 86-655, M.

Lawrick Estate, Re .... (84) 55-245, S.

Law Society of Alberta,
- v. Black et al. .... (84) 55-169, A.
- Black et al. v. (No. 2) ... (84) 54-793, A.
- Continental Insurance Co. v. .... (84) 43-465, A.
- Petrashuyk v. .... (84) 27-143, A.

Law Society of British Columbia
- Donald v. .... (84) 27-088, B.C.
- Hoem v. .... (84) 27-209, B.C.

Law Society of Manitoba v. Giesbrecht .... (84) 54-980, M.

Law Society of Upper Canada
- Re Emerson .... (84) 27-183, O.
- McKeown v. .... (84) 26-969, O.
- v. Skapinker (84) 27-066, S.C.C. from O.

Lawson Motors (1978) Ltd. et al., Canadian Pacific Ltd. v. .... (84) 2-675, N.B.

Paragraph

Layman v. St. John's (City) et al. .... (84) 27-214; 27-215, Nfld.

Layte, R. v. .... (84) 18-077, O.

Lazarenko, Re .... (84) 27-089, A.

LDARC Corp. v. London (City) et al. .... (84) 80-635, O.

Leachman v. MacLachlan (84) 90-546, B.C.

Leader Terrazzo Tile Mosaic Ltd. et al., Merker v. .... (84) 54-918, O.

Leal v. Leal .... (84) 22-203, B.C.

Lean, R. v. .... (84) 17-414, S.

Lebel v. R. et al. .... (84) 18-030, Q.

Leblanc, Canada Mortgage and Housing Corp. v. .... (84) 71-039, N.B.

LeBlanc v. Dalfen et al... (84) 70-942, N.B.

LeBlanc v. Goodwin et al.. (84) 86-640, N.B.

Le Blanc v. MacLaren Plansearch Ltd. and et al. ...... (84) 48-793, N.B.

Le Blanc, R. v. .... (84) 17-453, N.S.; 17-590, N.B.; 18-209, N.S.

Leblanc v. Trust General du Canada .... (84) 71-040, N.B.

Le Blanc and Mollins et al., Re .... (84) 2-805, N.B.

LeBlanc, Mollins and Leblanc, New Brunswick (Province) and Federal Business Development Bank, Re .... (84) 3-025, N.B.

Leblond v. Ottawa Board of Education .... (84) 90-550, O.

Lechasseur v. R. et al. .... (84) 18-031, Q.

Lecky Paper Ltd., Grays Harbor Paper Co. v. .... (84) 55-124, B.C.

Ledoux v. Ledoux .... (84) 2-955, B.C.

Ledyit and Alford, Re ...... (84) 22-577, O.

Lee et al. v. Block Estates Ltd. .... (84) 2-949, B.C.

Lee v. Pankowski et al. .... (84) 54-795, M.

Leeco v. Regional Administrative School Unit No. 3 School Board .... (84) 48-611, P.E.I.

ILLUSTRATION 54
Dominion Report Service (Loose-leaf), October 1984

Table of Cases—1984   60,761

Paragraph

Sinclair, R. v. .... (84) 18-241, N.S.

Sinclair, Thorne Riddell Inc.
v. .... (84) 2-846, O.

Sinclair et al. v. Tomic
et al. .... (84) 54-652, A.

Singbeil, R. v. .... (84) 17-521, M.

Singer v. Singer .... (84) 54-982, O.

Singh v. Hooper et al. ..... (84) 54-718, O.

Singh v. Incardona .... (84) 54-870, O.

Singh v. Minister of Employment and
Immigration ...... (84) 26-877; 26-884;
26-900; 26-944; 26-972; 27-122;
F.C.C.; C.A.

Singh et al. v. Minister
of Employment and
Immigration   (84) 26-883, F.C.C.; T.D.

Singh v. Nicholls et al. ..... (84) 86-683, O.

Singh, R. v. .... (84) 17-883, O.

Singh (Balwant) v. Minister of
Employment &
Immigration   (84) 27-026, F.C.C.; T.D.

Sinitoski, R. v. .... (84) 17-541, A.

Sinnott v. Sinnott ...... (84) 22-578, Nfld.

Sirois v. Club Jeunesse Outaouais
Inc. and Unitours Canada
Ltée .... (84) 2-598, Q.

Sirois et al. v. Fédération des
enseignants du Nouveau-Brunswick
et al. .... (84) 90-616, N.B.

Sisters of the Immaculate Conception
et al., Re Samson ... (84) 27-222, B.C.

Sivret, Minister of Justice
v. .... (84) 17-747, N.B.

Sivyer Steel Corp., N.A.S. Management
Services Corp. .... (84) 2-416; 2-417, S.

625 President Kennedy Building Ltd.
v. Union Kennedy Co.; First
Quebec Co. et al. ...... (84) 60-285, Q.

Sjoden, R. v. .... (84) 17-828, A.

Skagway Terminal Co. Ltd. et al.
v. The Ship "Gayong", Ssang
Yong Shipping Co. Ltd.
et al. .... (84) 54-583, F.C.C.; T.D.

Skalbania and N. M. Skalbania
Ltd., Re .... (84) 2-567, B.C.

Paragraph

Skapinker, Law Society of Upper
Canada v.   (84) 27-066, S.C.C. from O.

Skeena Management Services Ltd.
et al., Attorney General of
Canada v. .... (84) 2-961, B.C.

Skeena Northern Boat Ltd. v.
Minister of National
Revenue .... (84) 80-505, T.C.C.

Skellet v. Kline .... (84) 86-582, O.

Skinners Marine Inc., A-1 Steel
Works v. .... (84) 55-185, O.

Sklar Construction Ltd., Sim
Construction (Y.K.) Ltd.
v. .... (84) 54-633, N.W.T.

Skogman v. R. .... (84) 18-190, S.C.C.
from B.C.

Skulsh v. Insurance Corp. of
British Columbia .... (84) 43-490, B.C.

Slack Transport Ltd. v. General
Concrete Ltd. et al. .... (84) 3-055, O.

Slater, R. v. .... (84) 18-258, A.

Slattery Management and Realty
(1978) Ltd. et al. v. Archie Colpitts
Ltd. et al. .... (84) 2-637, N.B.

Slauenwhite, Re .... (84) 3-022, N.S.

Slice Construction Ltd.
v. Ottawa (City) ...... (84) 27-200, O.

Sliwa and Ed Sliwa Agencies
Ltd. v. Minister of National
Revenue .... (84) 80-486, T.C.C.

Sloan et al. v. Dierden and Canada
Permanent Trust Co. . (84) 71-029, B.C.

Sloan v. Sloan et al. ...... (84) 22-198, O.

Sloboda et al., Don Bosco Agencies
Ltd. v. ...... (84) 26-918, F.C.C.; T.D.

Slugoski, R. v. .... (84) 18-219, S.

Slusarchuk v. Da Cunba
et al. .... (84) 90-521, O.

Small v. Brock et al. ...... (84) 94-251, M.

Small v. Northern Horizon Resource
Corp. .... (84) 54-818, B.C.

Small, R. v. .... (84) 17-748, N.S.

Smallwood v. Attorney General of
Canada et al. .... (84) 54-649, Nfld.

(10)   Sma

may try its cumulative table of cases.[5] There are numerous possibilities with which you should become familiar.

Two services that are useful if you are looking for information on a very recent case are the *All-Canada Weekly Summaries* (for civil cases) and the *Weekly Criminal Bulletin,* both published by Canada Law Book Limited. They do not, however, give citations. Their purpose is to provide digests of cases *before* they are reported. Indeed, some of the cases may not be reported, for the cases digested in the two services are all those submitted for *possible* inclusion in the *Dominion Law Reports* and *Canadian Criminal Cases.* If you have immediate need for a report of a case digested in *All-Canada Weekly Summaries* or the *Weekly Criminal Bulletin,* a photocopy service is available. Details are noted on the front of each issue.

The current issues of *All-Canada Weekly Summaries* and the *Weekly Criminal Bulletin* are filed in loose-leaf binders. Arrangement is by jurisdiction (Canada, followed by the provinces in alphabetical order) and by subject within the jurisdiction. Interim cumulative subject indexes and tables of cases are issued at regular intervals. Later, bound volumes are published. Citations to published reports are not added to the bound volumes. It must be emphasized that the chief advantage of these services is the swift digesting of recent decisions. Their purpose is different from that of *Canadian Current Law,* which does not digest a case until it is reported. *Canadian Current Law* tells you where to find the first published report of a case.

The "Weekly Digest" in *Ontario Lawyers Weekly,* a newspaper that Butterworths began to publish in 1983, is another source of digests of recently decided Ontario cases, including appeals to the Supreme Court of Canada. Arrangement is by subject. Like *All-Canada Weekly Summaries* and the *Weekly Criminal Bulletin,* it summarizes decisions before they are reported and offers a full text photocopy service. The digests are later consolidated and republished separately from the newspaper. If a case has by then been reported, the citation is added to the table of cases at the end of the volume. The first volume in the series, dated 1984, prints digests published in the first two volumes of the newspaper covering the period, May 1983 to April 1984.

Carswell also publishes a number of weekly digests. The *Alberta Weekly Law Digest* and the *British Columbia Weekly Law Digest* are both pre-reporting services consisting of digests of all available judgments of the courts of those provinces plus decisions of the Supreme Court of Canada and the Federal Court in cases originating in those provinces. Refusal of leave to appeal to the Supreme Court of Canada is also noted. The *Weekly Digest of Family Law* contains digests of all the most recent family law digests available in Canada, and the *Weekly Digest of Civil Procedure* provides digests of all Ontario Supreme and District Court cases in that subject area.

---

5   See pp. 29, 32-33, above.

(c) The Digest

This publication used to be called the *English and Empire Digest,* and this title still appears on the spine and title page of many of the volumes. The transformation of the Empire into the Commonwealth and the entry of the United Kingdom into the European Economic Community are presumably the reasons for this rather belated change. In the volumes that use the new title, *The Digest* is described in a sub-title as "Annotated British, Commonwealth, and European Cases". The title, *The Digest,* is used consistently in the illustrations that follow even though some of the volumes from which they are reproduced still bear the earlier title. You will probably not go to *The Digest* if you are looking for the citation to a Canadian case because you are likely to have access to the many available Canadian finding aids. However, you will use it to find information about English cases and cases from other Commonwealth (or former Commonwealth) countries. It may also prove useful if you are looking for a case and do not know whether it is Canadian, English or from another Commonwealth jurisdiction.

Suppose you are looking for the well known English case *Central London Property Trust Ltd. v. High Trees House Ltd.* You know that it was decided shortly after the Second World War, for it concerned the question of whether the owner of some London flats who had agreed to a reduction in rent when the tenants were away during the war could, on their return, recover the full rent stipulated in the lease for the time the flats were empty.

If you look at *The Digest* on the shelves of your law library, you will see that most of the volumes have green bands on the spine, whereas a few have blue bands. This is because the blue-band edition is gradually being replaced by a green-band edition and the latter is now nearing completion. (Any remaining blue-band volumes will have the title *English and Empire Digest*; the less recently published green-band ones also have the older title.) Some reorganization and rearrangement of subject titles is taking place; thus, the numbers of the blue-band volumes no longer necessarily equate, title by title, with the new green-band volume numbers. For instance, the title "Employment" in green-band volume 20 for the most part replaces "Master and Servant" in blue-band volume 34, though the section of the Master and Servant title dealing with industrial injuries and workmen's compensation is replaced by the new "National Health and Social Security" title in green-band volume 35.

A consolidated table of cases is contained in volumes 52-54 of the blue-band edition. Published in 1968, it covers cases to the end of 1966 – those digested in the main blue-band volumes and in Continuation Volumes A and B. Although most of the blue-band volumes have been replaced, you will have to use this consolidated table of cases until the green-band edition is complete and a new consolidated table of cases to the green-band edition is published in 1986.[6]

---

6   *The Digest: A User's Guide* (London: Butterworths, 1983), p. 15.

Since you know that the case in which you are interested was decided before 1967, you will look it up in the blue-band consolidated table. It is listed on page 475 of volume 52 (see Illustration 55). "21 Estpl. 376" refers you to page 376 of volume 21, under the subject heading "Estoppel," – "31 L. & T. 247" to page 247 of volume 31, under the subject heading "Landlord and Tenant". If volumes 21 and 31 of the blue-band edition were still current, you could go directly to the pages noted, but on checking you will find that both these volumes have been replaced by green-band ones. There is no change of title as in the Master and Servant/Employment situation noted above, but the page numbers you have will be incorrect. Therefore, you will have to look up the case again in the table of cases at the front of the appropriate green-band volumes. Looking at volume 21, you will find two references to *Central London Property Trust Ltd. v. High Trees House Ltd.* in the table of cases (see Illustration 56). Note at the top of the columns of numbers the word "CASE". This indicates that "53" and "64" are case or paragraph numbers, not page numbers as "376" and "247" are in the consolidated table of cases in blue-band volume 52 (see again Illustration 55). Looking up cases 53 and 64 in green-band volume 21 you will find that the two digests are not identical because they relate to different points of law, but the citations are the same (see Illustrations 57 and 58). At the end of paragraph 64 are annotations, and the two digests are connected by "see" references. The digest in paragraph 64 is also published on page 478 of green-band volume 31(1) under the title "Landlord and Tenant" (see Illustrations 59 and 60). However, the annotations in paragraph 64 of green-band volume 21 are more up to date because it was published more recently (1981) than green-band volume 31(1) (1973). In the table of cases in green-band volume 31(1), references are to pages, not to case numbers (see again Illustrations 59 and 60). The change to listing by case numbers rather than by page numbers appears to have been made at the same time as the change from the title *English and Empire Digest* to that of *The Digest.* Another change made at this time relates to the numbering of Scottish, Irish, and Commonwealth (that is, other than English) cases. Formerly, the numbers assigned to them were in a different sequence from those assigned to English cases. This confusing practice has now been discontinued. For a comparison of the old and new practices, see Illustrations 61 and 62.

If you are looking for a case reported later than 1966, you should consult the table of cases at the front of the Cumulative Supplement, a volume that is replaced annually. Until you become accustomed to it, you may find it a little difficult to use because some of the references are to paragraphs in the Supplement and others to green-band volumes in the main set.

Take another well known English case, *Padfield v. Minister of Agriculture, Fisheries, and Food,* decided by the House of Lords in 1968. You will find it listed in the table of cases in the 1984 Cumulative Supplement (see Illustration 63). We will use just the first reference as an example, 1(1) (Reissue) Admin. L. 606. This refers you to the title, "Administrative Law," in green-band volume 1(1). (The publisher, Butterworths, calls the blue-band volumes a replacement edition – it replaced the original edition – and the

ILLUSTRATION 55
The Digest, Blue-band Volume 52

Centaur Co. v. American Druggists Syndicate (Can.): **46** Trade Mks. 17

Centaur Cycle Co. v. Hill (Can.): **39** S. Goods 585, 590, 816

Central Advance & Discount Corpn., Ltd. v. Marshall (1939): **35** Money 246, 247

Central African Trading Co. v. Grove (1879): **40** Set-off 448

Central & District Property, Ltd. v. I. R. Comrs. (1966): **B** Coys. 100

Central Argentine Ry., Ltd. v. Marwood (1915): **41** Ship. 321

Central Bahia Ry. Co., Ltd., Re (1902): **9** Coys. 614; **10** Coys. 1135

Central Bank, Re, Ex p. Burk (Can.): **3** Bank. 166

——, Re, Ex p. Harrison & Standing (Can.): **3** Bank. 167

——, Re, Ex p. Morton (Can.): **8** Chos. 545

——, Re, Ex p. Reid (Can.): **3** Bank. 332

——, Re, Canada Shipping Co.'s Case (Can.): **3** Bank. 312, 327

——, Re, Henderson's Case (Can.): **3** Bank. 163, 166

——, Re, Lye's Claim (Can.): **10** Coys. 924

——, Re, Morton & Block's Claims (Can.): **3** Bank. 212

——, Re, North America Life Insce. Co.'s Case (Can.): **3** Bank. 163

—— v. McKeen (Can.): **21** Exon. 712

Central Bank & Hogg, Re (Can.): **9** Coys. 270

Central Bank of Canada, Re (Can.): **10** Coys. 913, 914, 924

——, Re, Baines' Case (Can.): **3** Bank. 163; **9** Coys. 377

——, Re, Cayley's Case (Can.): **3** Bank. 247, 332

——, Re, Hogaboom v. Receiver-General of Canada (Can.): **10** Coys. 1003

——, Re, Home Savings & Loan Co.'s Case (Can.): **3** Bank. 166; **9** Coys. 412

——, Re, Wells & MacMurchy's Case (Can.): **3** Bank. 342

——, Re, Yorke's Case (Can.): **3** Bank. 342; **10** Coys. 988, 991

—— v. Earle (Can.): **22** Evid. 532

—— v. Ellis (1893) (Can.): **21** Exon. 736

—— v. —— (1896) (Can.): **21** Exon. 778

—— v. Garland (Can.): **6** B. of Exch. 181

—— v. Osborne (Can.): **40** Set-off 464

Central Bank of India, Ltd. v. Shamdasani (P. D.) (Ind.): **3** Bank. 348

Central Bank of London, Ex p., Re Fraser (1892): **4** Bkpcy. 353; **36** Prtnrs. 445

—— v. Hawkins (1890): **7** B. of Sale 96

Central Board of Education for Nelson v. Roberts (N.Z.): **30** L. & T. 455

Central Broadcasters, Ltd. v. South Australia Deputy Federal Taxation Comr. (Aus.): **28** Inc. T. 125

Central Burnaby Citizens' & Ratepayers' Assocn., Re (Can): **38** Pub. Hlth. 170

Central Canada Ry. Co. Arbitrations, Re (Can.): **11** Comp. Pche. 160

Central Canadian Securities, Ltd. v. Brown (Can.): **40** S. Land 125

Central Control Board (Liquor Traffic) v. Cannon Brewery Co., Ltd. (1919): **17** Defence 438; **44** Stats. 297

Central Darjeeling Tea Co., Ltd., Re (1866): **10** Coys. 1139

Central De Kaap Gold Mines, Re (1899): **9** Coys. 481; **10** Coys. 1077

Central Dri Wall Co., Ltd. v. Bodnar and Booth (Can.): **B** Exon. 254

Central Electricity Authority v. British Oxygen Co., Ltd. (1956): **20** Electric 226

Central Electricity Board v. Yorkshire Electric Power Co. (1943): **20** Electric 225

Central Electricity Generating Board v. Halifax Corpn. (1962): **32** Limit. of A. 384

—— v. Jennaway (1959): **20** Electric 222

Central Employment Bureau for Women & Students' Careers Assocn. (Inc.), Re (1942): **8** Char. 317

Central Essex Light Ry. Case (1908): **46** Tram. 339, 340

Central Freehold Estates (Leeds), Ltd. v. Leeds Corpn. (1965): **B** Housg. 337

Central Gas Utilities, Ltd. v. Canadian Western Natural Gas Co. & Gibson (1964) (Can.): **B** Tort 686

—— v. —— (1965) (Can.): **B** Tort 686

Central Grain Co. v. C. P. Ry. Co. (Can.): **8** Carr. 23, 28

Central Hotel & Homfray & Bral, Re (Can.): **31** L. & T. 250

Central Housing & Planning Authority v. Griffith (W. Indies): **A** Housg. 658

Central Illawarra Shire Council, Re, Ex p. Ballantine (Aus.): **26** Housg. 689

Central India Mining Co. v. Société Coloniale Anversoise (1920): **2** Aliens 220

Central Jewish Institute, v. Toronto (City) (Can.): **38** Pub. Hlth. 166

Central Klondyke Gold Mining & Trading Co., Ltd., Re, Savigny's Case (1898): **9** Coys. 269

——, Re, Thomson's Case (1898): **9** Coys. 136

Central Land Board v. Saxone Shoe Co., Ltd. (1955): **45** T. & C. P. 372

Central London Electricity, Ltd. v. Berners (1945): **10** Coys. 823

Central London Property Trust, Ltd. v. High Trees House, Ltd. (1947): **21** Estpl. 376; **31** L. & T. 247

Central London Railway Bill, Re (1901): **36** Parl. 386

Central London Ry. Co. v. Hammersmith B. C. (1904): **36** Nuis. 341

—— v. I. R. Comrs. (1936): **28** Inc. T. 182

—— v. London (City) Land Tax Comrs. (1911): **26** Hghys. 335; **30** Land Tax 339, 349

Central Marine Engine Works v. Amalgamated Ry. Co.'s (1930): **38** Rates 526

Central Mortgage & Housing Corpn. v. Hankins & Hankins (Can.): **A** Housg. 659

—— v. Ward (Can.): **35** Mtge. 757

Central Motor Engineering Co. v. Galbraith (Scot.): **4** Bkpcy. 185, 203, 457.

Central Motors, Glasgow, Ltd. v. Cessnock Garage & Motor Co. (Scot.): **3** Bailmt. 80

Central Newbury Car Auctions, Ltd. v. Unity Finance, Ltd. (1956): **21** Estpl. 485

Central News Co. v. Eastern News Telegraph Co. (1884): **18** Discy. 90

Central Ontario Ry. Co. v. Trusts & Guarantee Co. (Can.): **35** Mtge. 630

Central Press Assocn. v. American Press Assocn. (Can.): **18** Discy. 239

Central Printing Works, Ltd. v. Walker & Nicholson (1907): **10** Coys. 807; **18** Distr. 326

Central Queensland Meat Export Co. v. Gallop (1892): **50** Pldg. 120

Central Ry. Co. of Venezuela (Directors, etc.) v. Kisch (1867): **9** Coys. 95, 97, 103, 105, 106, 114, 115, 116, 132, 138, 144, 258, 647; **35** Misrep. 63, 72; **50** Pldg. 23

Central S. M. T. Co., Ltd. v. Lanarkshire C. C. (Scot.): **45** Tort 295

Central South African Rys. v. Adlington & Co. (S. Af.): **8** Carr. 73

—— v. Geldenhuis Main Reef G. M. Co., Ltd. (S. Af.): **19** Easmt. 189

ILLUSTRATION 56
The Digest, Green-band Volume 21

xix   Vol 21 Table of Cases   Commercial Bank

CASE

Central Bank v McKeen (CAN) **2275**
Central Bank of Canada v Ellis (1893) (CAN) . . **3811**
—— v —— (1896) (CAN) **4207**
Central London Property Trust Ltd v High Trees House Ltd (1946) **53, 64**
Central Newbury Car Auctions Ltd v Unity Finance Ltd (1956). **1510**
Century Indeminity Co v Rogers and Fitzgerald (CAN) **3624**
Chadwick v Holt (1856) **4014**
—— v Manning (1896). **1150**, 1292
Chalmers v Chalmers (1930) **276**
—— v Machray (CAN) **455**
Chamberlain and Sproat v Wall and Lloyd (1920) . **4137**
Chambers v Coleman (1841) 3234, **3237**
—— v Corbeau, Imperial Bank of Canada, Garnishee (CAN) **4001**
Chandler (Doe d) v Ford (1835) **955**, 1047
Chant v Rhodess (NZ) **458**
Chapman v Bowlby (1841) **2055**, 2122
—— v Callis (1862) **3759**
Charrington & Co, ex p (1888) **2520**
Chasteauneuf v Capeyron (1882) **2661**
Chatterton v Watney (1881) **3637, 3747**
Cheatle v Piddocke (1843) **1954**
Chekaluk v Webster (CAN) **739**
Chemidus Wavin Ltd v Societe Pour La Transformation et L'exploitation Des Resines Industrielles SA (1978) **1775**
Cherniak Estate, Re (CAN) **2731**
Chesley, R v (CAN) **857**
Chester (Goodtitle d) v Alker and Elmes (1757) . **3345**
Chestolowsky v Chestolowsky (CAN) **3584**
Chew Deb v Davie (CAN) **3992**
Chew Lumber Co v Howe Sound Lumber Co (CAN) **1526**
Chick v Smith (1840) 2004, **2401**
Childers v Wooler (1859) **3067**
Childrens v Saxby (1683) **3046**
Chippendale's Case (AUS) **1405**
Chisholm v Morse (CAN) **593**
Cholmondesley (Marquis) v Clinton (Lord) (1817). 987, **1037**
—— (Marquis) v —— (Lord) (1820) **1037**
Choquet, Re (16/78) (1978) **1671**, 1674
Christie v Secretan (1799) **202**
Christmas (Doe d) v Oliver (1829) **1088**
Christopherson v Burton (1848) **2472**, 3255
Christy v Tancred (1842) **459**
Chugg Estate, Re Lang v Chugg (CAN). . . . **152**
Church v Arnold (AUS) **4201**
Churchill v Bank of England (1843). **4079**
—— v McRae and Cowie (CAN) **653**
—— v Siggers (1854) **2388**
Cicognia v McHeather (CAN) **3649**
Cinzano Francesco & CIA GmbH v Hauptzollamt Saarbrucken (13/70) (1970) **1664**
Citizens' Bank of Louisiana v First National Bank of New Orleans (1873) **1285**
Citizens Light and Power Co v St Louis Town (CAN) 335
Clarke, Re (1898). **2039**
—— v Clement and English (1796) **2034**
—— v Creighton (CAN). **1982**
—— v Hall (1888) (IR) **1008**
Clarkson and Forgie v Wishart and Myers (CAN). **2537**
Clatton, Re Richardson v Greaves (1861) . . . **3936**
Claydon v Finch (1873). **3459**

CASE

Cleghorn v Des Anges (1819). **3252**, 3272
Clements, ex p (1901) **1990**
——, Re, ex p Clements (1901) **1990**
——, Re, ex p —— v Davis (1901). **1990**
——, Re, ex p Davis (1901) **1990**
—— v Davis, ex p (1901) **1990**
Clemow v Geach (1870) **995**
Clerk v Withers (1704) **1994**, 2095, 2936, 3090, 3206, 3236
Clifford v Phillips (1907) (1908) . 183, 237, **296**, 811
—— v Timms (1907) (1908) . . 183, 237, **296**, 811
Clifton Securities Ltd v Huntley (1948). . . . **2311**
Clinch v Smith (1840) **2401**
Clinton v Sellars (CAN) **2160**
Clissold v Cratchley (1910). . . . **2377**, 3034, 3069
Clough v London & North Western Railway Co (1871). **1496**
Cloutte v Storey (1911). 158, **352**
Clutterbuck v Jones (1812). **3548**
Clyne v Yardley (NZ) **320**
Coast Lumber Co v Bates (CAN) **1060**
Coate's Case (1876) **4046**
Cobbett, Re (1861) **2069**
Cobbold v Chilver (1842) **2052**
Cobbold and Woolley v Morgan (1888) . . . **2427**
Cochlin v Massey-Harris (CAN) **2953**
Cochrane v Hamilton Provident Loan Soc (CAN). **136**
Cockburn v Jeanotte (CAN) **2526**
Cocks v Great Western Railway Co (1886) . . **1987**
—— v —— (1887) **1987**
Coddrington v Lloyd (1838) **2440**
Codrington v Lloyd (1838) **2440**
Codville & Co v Haygarth (CAN). **1397**
Coenen v Social-Economische Raad (39/75) (1976). **1756**
Cogswell (Doe d) v Smith (CAN) **3372**
Cohen v Beadell (1891). **4095**
—— v De las Rivas, ex p Durham Sheriff (1891). **2208**
—— v Hale (1878) **3641**
—— v Jonesco (1926) **143**
—— v Lapin (AUS) **591**
—— v McCord (S) & Co Ltd (CAN). **397**
Cole v Bank of Montreal (CAN) **828**
—— v Terry (1861) **2268**
Coleman v Dunlap (CAN). **3198**
—— v Rawlinson (1858) **2673**, 3158
Coles v Coates (1840) **2193**
—— v Coles (1956) **3416**
Collett v Foster (1857) **2445**
Collier v Walters (1873) **436**
Collingridge v Paxton (1851) **2610**, 2617
Collins v Cave. **600**
—— v Gough (1785) **627**
—— v Hall (CAN). **4148**
—— v Smith (1896). **1539**
Collins & Co Ltd v Rossia Insce Co of Petrograd (1926). **3848**
Colls v Coates (1840) **2193**
Colonial Bank of Australasia v Cooper (AUS) . . **2763**
Colonial Bank of New Zealand v Bennet (NZ) . **1532**
Colonial Footwear Ltd, Re, ex p Sussman (CAN) : **1552**
Colonial Securities Co v Taylor (CAN) **3295**
Colston v Gardner (1681) **3497**
Columbia Graphophone Co v Union Bank of Canada (CAN) **1527**
Combined Weighing & Advertising Machine Co, Re (1889) **3862**
Commercial Bank v Van Norman (CAN) . . . **2211**

References are to case numbers

ILLUSTRATION 57
The Digest, Green-band Volume 21

Nature, classification and principles of estoppel   Case **53**

sterling. The Court of Appeal reversed the judge's decision and the buyers appealed: *Held* the appeal would be dismissed for the following reasons—(1) since all the relevant facts and correspondence were set out in the special case, the construction of the sellers' letter of 30 September was a question of law and not of fact and accordingly the courts were not precluded by the umpire's findings from considering the meaning of the letter; (2) the letter, whether read by itself or read with the other correspondence, could not be construed as stating that, in relation to contracts already entered into, the price could be treated as expressed in sterling of the same nominal amount and that future contracts might be made for the sale of cocoa for sterling; it amounted to no more than a representation that the sellers would accept payment in Lagos of the sterling equivalent of the price calculated in Nigerian pounds; furthermore even if it could be said that the meaning of the letter was ambiguous and that the buyers could reasonably have understood it to contain a representation that the money of account could be treated as expressed in sterling, it could not give rise to an estoppel because, to do so, a representation must be clear and unequivocal and, if a representation failed to comply with that requirement, it mattered not that the representee should have misconstrued it and relied on it; (3) the exchange of letters of 20 and 30 September could not constitute a variation of the contract since the parties were not ad idem, the buyers meaning one thing by their request and the sellers another by their acceptance of it; accordingly, the letters being insufficiently unambiguous to constitute a variation of the contract, their combined effect was not sufficiently unambiguous or precise to form the basis of a promissory estoppel whereby, although the letters did not amount to a variation of the money of account, the sellers were estopped by their letter of 30 September from denying that they did.
Woodhouse AC Israel Cocoa Ltd, SA v Nigerian Produce Marketing Co Ltd [1972] 2 All ER 271, [1972] AC 741, [1972] 2 WLR 1090, 116 Sol Jo 392, [1972] 1 Lloyd's Rep 439, HL
ANNOTATIONS **Apld** WJ Alan & Co Ltd v El Nasr Export & Import Co [1971] 1 Lloyd's Rep 401; Halfdan Grieg & Co A/S v Sterling Coal & Navigation Corpn [1973] 1 All ER 545; Finagrain SA Geneva v P Kruse Hamburg [1976] 2 Lloyd's Rep 508 **Apld** dictum Lord Hailsham LC Secretary of State for Employment v Globe Elastic Thread Co Ltd [1979] 2 All ER 1077

53 —— Need not be of existing fact—Distinguish estoppel in pais As to estoppel, this representation with reference to reducing the rent was not a representation of existing fact, which is the essence of common law estoppel; it was a representation in effect as to the future—a representation that the rent would not be enforced at the full rate but only at the reduced rate. At common law, that would not give rise to an estoppel, because, as was said in *Jorden v Money* (1854) [no 1144 post] a representation as to the future must be embodied as a contract or be

nothing. So at common law it seems to me there would be no answer to the whole claim.
What, then, is the position in view of developments in the law in recent years? The law has not been standing still even since *Jorden v Money* [supra]. There has been a series of decisions over the last fifty years which, although said to be cases of estoppel, are not really such. They are cases of promises which were intended to create legal relations and which, in the knowledge of the person making the promise, were going to be acted on by the party to whom the promise was made, and have in fact been so acted on. In such cases the courts have said these promises must be honoured. There are certain cases to which I particularly refer: *Fenner v Blake* (1900) [LANDLORD AND TENANT vol 31 (2) (reissue) no 7183], *Re Wickham* (1917) [no 1197 post], *Re William Porter & Co Ltd* (1937) [no 61 post] and *Buttery v Pickard* (1946) [no 63 post]. Although said by the learned judges who decided them to be cases of estoppel, all these cases are not estoppel in the strict sense. They are cases of promises which were intended to be binding, which the parties making them knew would be acted on and which the parties to whom they were made did act on. *Jorden v Money* [supra] can be distinguished because there the promisor made it clear the she did not intend to be legally bound, whereas in the cases to which I refer the promisor did intend to be bound. In each case the court held the promise to be binding on the party making it, even though under the old common law it might be said to be difficult to find any consideration for it. The courts have not gone so far as to give a cause of action in damages for breach of such promises, but they have refused to allow the party making them to act inconsistently with them. It is in that sense, and in that sense only, that such a promise gives rise to an estoppel. The cases are a natural result of the fusion of law and equity; for the cases of *Hughes v Metropolitan Railway Co* (1877) [no 55 post], *Birmingham & District Land Co v London & North Western Railway Co* (1888) [LANDLORD AND TENANT vol 31 (2) (reissue) no 7089] and *Salisbury v Gilmore* (1942)[LANDLORD AND TENANT vol 31 (2) (reissue) no 5216] show that a party will not be allowed in equity to go back on such a promise. The time has now come for the validity of such a promise to be recognised. The logical consequence, no doubt, is that a promise to accept a smaller sum in discharge of a larger sum, if acted on, is binding, notwithstanding the absence of consideration, and if the fusion of law and equity leads to that result, so much the better. At this time of day it is not helpful to try to draw a distinction between law and equity. They have been joined together now for over seventy years, and the problems have to be approached in a combined sense (*Denning J*).
Central London Property Trust Ltd v High Trees House Ltd (1946) [1956] 1 All ER 256 n, [1947] KB 130, [1947] LJR 77, 175 LT 332, 62 TLR 557, see no 64 post.

ILLUSTRATION 58
The Digest, Green-band Volume 21

Cases **63–65**   Vol 21 Estoppel 1

December 1939, sent to Mrs A indicating that a certain sum (which included interest accrued prior to 1927), was due to her, was sufficient acknowledgement to take the pre-1927 interest out of the operation of the Limitation Act; (5) as regards the interest accrued due to A before 1927, in view of the fact that the amount outstanding as shown in the accounts included such interest, and as those accounts had been passed by the company annually since 927, it was impossible to say that, because during the last six years the acknowledgments had been made by a board to estates of which they were trustees, the board was acting without the authority of the company.

Ledingham v Bermejo Estancia Co Ltd, Agar v Bermejo Estancia Co Ltd [1947] 1 All ER 749

ANNOTATION **Apld** Re Transplanters (Holding Co) Ltd [1958] 2 All ER 711

63 —— —— —— —— **Reduced rent** Plaintiff demised a house to defendant, in 1936 for fourteen years at an annual rental amounting to 30s a week. In 1940, defendant's business being adversely affected by war conditions, she informed plaintiff that she must either terminate the lease at the end of the fifth year, as she was entitled to do, or pay a reduced rent; and it was agreed that she should pay a rent of 15s a week. As conditions improved, defendant voluntarily increased her weekly payments until she was once again, in 1944, paying 30s a week. Plaintiff having claimed arrears of rent at 30s a week from October 1941, to November 1944: *Held* (1) the lease had not been determined by the agreement for payment of reduced rent, so that the claim was prima facie valid; but (2) plaintiff was estopped by that agreement, on which defendant had relied when she could otherwise have terminated the lease, from subsequently claiming arrears of rent at the full rate.

Buttery v Pickard (1946) 174 LT 144, 62 TLR 241, 90 Sol Jo 80

64 —— —— —— —— By a lease under seal dated 24 September 1937, plaintiff company let to defendant company (a subsidiary of plaintiffs) a block of flats for a term of ninety-nine years from 29 September 1937, at a ground rent of £2,500 a year. In the early part of 1940, owing to war conditions then prevailing, only a few of the flats in the block were let to tenants and it became apparent that defendants would be unable to pay the rent reserved by the lease out of the rents of the flats. Discussions took place between the directors of the two companies, which were closely connected, and, as a result, on 3 January 1940, a letter was written by plaintiffs to defendants confirming that the ground rent of the premises would be reduced from £2,500 to £1,250 as from the beginning of the term. Defendants thereafter paid the reduced rent. By the beginning of 1945 all the flats were let but defendants continued to pay only the reduced rent. In September 1945, plaintiffs wrote to defendants claiming that rent was payable at the rate of £2,500

a year and, subsequently, in order to determine the legal position, they initiated friendly proceedings in which they claimed the difference between rent at the rates of £2,500 and £1,250 for the quarters ending 29 September and 25 December 1945. By their defence defendants pleaded that the agreement for the reduction of the ground rent operated during the whole term of the lease and, as alternatives, that plaintiffs were estopped from demanding rent at the higher rate or had waived their right to do so down to the date of their letter of 21 September 1945: *Held* (1) where parties enter into an arrangement which is intended to create legal relations between them and in pursuance of such arrangement one party makes a promise to the other which he knows will be acted on and which is in fact acted on by the promisee, the court will treat the promise as binding on the promisor to the extent that it will not allow him to act inconsistently with it even although the promise may not be supported by consideration in the strict sense and the effect of the arrangement made is to vary the terms of a contract under seal by one of less value; (2) the arrangement made between plaintiffs and defendants in January 1940, was one which fell within the above category and, accordingly, that the agreement for the reduction of the ground rent was binding on plaintiff company, but that it only remained operative so long as the conditions giving rise to it continued to exist and that on their ceasing to do so in 1945 plaintiffs were entitled to recover the ground rent claimed at the rate reserved by the lease.

Central London Property Trust Ltd v High Trees House Ltd (1946) [1956] All ER 256 n, [1947] KB 130, [1947] LJR 77, 175 LT 332, 62 TLR 557. See no 53 ante

ANNOTATIONS **Apld** Ledingham v Bermejo Estancia Co; Agar v Bermejo Estancia Co [1947] 1 All ER 749 **Consd** Wallis v Semark [1951] 2 TLR 222; Lyle-Mellor v A Lewis & Co (Westminster) Ltd [1956] 1 WLR 29; Slough Estates Ltd v Slough BC (no 2) (1967) 19 P&CR 326 **Expld** Beesly v Hallwood Estates Ltd [1960] 2 All ER 314 **Consd** Slough Estates Ltd v Slough BC (no 2) (1967) 19 P&CR 326; W J Alan & Co Ltd v El Nasr Export & Import Co [1971] 1 Lloyd's Rep 401 **Apld** Re Wyvern Developments Ltd [1974] 2 All ER 535; Evenden v Guildford City Association Football Club Ltd [1975] 3 All ER 269; Argy Trading Development Co Ltd v Lapid Development Ltd [1977] 3 All ER 785

65 —— —— —— **Contract date for delivery** Where, as a condition of its performance, time is of the essence of a contract for the sale of goods and, on the lapse of the stipulated time, the buyer continues to press for delivery, thus waiving his right to cancel the contract, he has a right to give notice fixing a reasonable time for delivery, thus making time again of the essence of the contract, which, if not fulfilled by the new time stipulated, he will then have the right to cancel. The reasonableness of the time fixed by the notice must be judged as at the date when it is given.

In similar circumstances, in the case of a contract for work and labour done, the person who has

12

ILLUSTRATION 59
The Digest, Green-band Volume 31(1)

CAPITAL | VOL. 31—TABLE OF CASES | xxvi

	PAGE
Capital & Counties Bank, Ltd. v. Rhodes (1903)	884
Capital & Counties Properties, Ltd. v. Butler (1944)	1048
Capital & Provincial Property Trust, Ltd. v. Rice (1950), (1951)	1061
Capital Brewing Co., Ltd. v. R. (Can.)	481
Caplan (I. & H.), Ltd. v. Caplan (1961)	955
—— v. —— (No. 2) (1963)	951
Caponhurst v. Caponhurst (1661)	712
Cappello v. Bell (Can.)	924
Capron v. Capron (1874)	519
Car Owners Assocn. v. McKercher (Can.)	848
Cardshops, Ltd. v. Davies (1971)	961
Carden v. Butler (Ir.)	657
Cardiff Corpn. v. Crosta (1921)	1051
—— v. Isaacs (1921)	1051
Cardwell v. Lucas (1836)	132
Carey v. Bostwick & Higgins (Can.)	511
Cargill v. Phillips (Scot.)	1016
Carith v. Read (1595)	345
Carleton v. Herbert (Ir.)	891
Carlisle (Earl) (Doe d.) v. Woodman (1807)	781
Carlisle Café Co. v. Muse Bros. & Co. (1897)	234
Carlisle Corpn. v. Blamire (1807)	722
Carlton v. Bowcock (1884)	36, 39
Carmichael v. Dolmage & MacInnes (Can.)	680
Carnarvon (Earl) v. Villebois (1844)	863
Carne v. Mitchell (1846)	97, 98
Carnegie v. Waugh (1823)	528
Carolan v. Brabazon (Ir.)	98, 588
Carpenter v. Collins (1605)	246, 251
—— v. Hall (Can.)	862, 875
—— v. Parker (1857)	358
Carr v. Benson (1868)	218
—— v. Cubitt (1844)	127
—— v. Levingston (1865)	57
—— v. Lynch (1900)	61
Carrell v. Carson (Nfld.)	862
—— v. Read (1595)	345
Carrick v. Miller (Scot.)	797
Carrington v. Roots (1837)	217
Carrington Mfg. Co., Ltd. v. Saldin (1925)	78
Carroll v. Empire Limestone Co. (Can.)	29
—— v. Routledge (Ir.)	598
—— v. Williams (Can.)	64
Carson v. Veitch (Can.)	570
—— v. Wood (Aus.)	847
Carstairs v. Taylor (1871)	321, 649
Cartan v. Bury (Ir.)	91, 95
Carter v. Aldous (Aus.)	760
—— v. Carter (1829)	499, 505
—— v. Cummins (1695)	514
—— v. Ely (Dean) (1834)	85
—— v. Fennell (Ir.)	396
—— v. Green (1950)	1102
—— v. Hibblethwaite (Can.)	701
—— v. Irving Oil Co. (Can.)	124
—— v. Love (1594)	867
—— v. Pryke (1791)	484
—— (Doe d.) v. Roe (1842)	255
—— v. S. U. Carburetter Co. (1942)	974, 987
—— v. Salmon (1880)	199, 200
—— v. Williams (1870)	389
Cartwright v. Pingree (1675)	877
—— v. Hoogstoel (1911)	54, 86
—— v. Miller (1877)	53, 63
—— v. McPherson (Can.)	804
—— v. Pingree (1765)	877
—— v. Pinkney (1675)	877
—— v. Russell (1912)	404
Cartwright's Case (1598)	117, 472
Carvick v. Blagrave (1820)	38
Carwardine v. Wood (1923)	1018
Cary v. Jenkings (1722)	506
Cascade Brewery Co., Ltd. v. Barker (Aus.)	691
Case v. Stephens (1731)	578, 582
Casey v. Hanlon (Can.)	162
Castle v. Rohan (Can.)	607
Castle (Henry) & Sons, Ltd., Re, Mitchell v. Castle (Henry) & Sons, Ltd. (1906)	837
Castle Laundry (London), Ltd. v. Read (1955)	950
Castleton (Doe d.) v. Samuel (1804)	768
Castor v. Brisbane City Council (Aus.)	207
Catley v. Arnold (1859)	272
Catt v. Tourle (1869)	331, 335
Cattell v. New Zealand Native Land Settlmt. Co., Ltd. (N.Z.)	494
Cattley v. Arnold (1859)	267, 272
Catto v. Curry (1926)	987, 1000, 1119, 1121, 1123
Caulfield v. Farr (Ir.)	266
Causeway Shopping Centre, Ltd. v. Muise (Can.)	129
Cavaleiro v. Puget (1865)	60, 172
Cavalier v. Pope (1906)	651
Cavaliero v. Slater (1854)	528
Cave v. Brookesby (1636)	360, 361
—— v. Horsell (1912)	408
Caverhill v. Orvis (Can.)	159
Cayley v. Walpole (1870)	53, 54, 55, 57
Cecil's Case (1566)	153
Central Estates (Belgravia), Ltd. v. Woolgar (1971)	177
—— v. —— (No. 2) (1972)	828
Central Hotel & Homfray & Brae, Re (Can.)	481
Central London Property Trust, Ltd. v. High Trees House, Ltd. (1946)	478
Central Trust Co. v. Ross Drug Co. (Can.)	66
Cessford v. Dover Harbour Board (1898)	365
Chadburn (Doe d.) v. Green (1839)	267
Chadwick v. Clarke (1845)	114
—— v. Kerschstien (Can.)	804
—— v. Marsden (1867)	240
—— v. Pearl Life Insce. Co. (1905)	572
Chaine v. Croker (Ir.)	754
Chaku Modan Isana v. Dullabh Dwarka (Ind.)	922
Chalcot Developments, Ltd. v. De Gray (1967)	1023
Chalcots (or Chalcot or Chalcott) Developments, Ltd. v. De Gray (1967)	1023
Chalcott Developments, Ltd. v. De Gray (1967)	1023
Chalkley, Ex p. (1948)	1129
Challis Avenue (10a) Pty., Ltd. v. Seddon (Aus.)	691
Challoner v. Davies (1698)	713, 860
—— v. Ware (1627)	814
Chamberlain v. Farr (1942)	1038
Chamberlayne v. Collins (1894)	437
Chambers v. Gaussen (Ir.)	295
—— v. Kingham (1878)	886
—— v. Mason (1604)	476
Chancellor v. Poole (1781)	728
Chandler v. Strevett (1947)	1097
Chandless (Doe d.) v. Robson (1826)	812
Chandless-Chandless v. Nicholson (1942)	818
Chandmal v. Bachraj (Ind.)	783
Chandos v. Brownlow (Ir.)	280
Chandri v. Daji Bhau (Ind.)	252
Chaplain v. Southgate (1717)	360
Chaplin v. Reid (1858)	670
—— v. Smith (1926)	684
Chapman v. Bluck (1838)	128
—— v. Dalton (1565)	282
—— v. Earl (1968)	1073, 1075
—— v. Honig (1963)	789

ILLUSTRATION 60
The Digest, Green-band Volume 31(1)

[Sect. 3.   *Reservation of rent: Sub-sect.* 8, cont.]

of £2,500 and £1,250 for the quarters ending Sept. 29 & Dec. 25. 1945. By their defence defts. pleaded that the agreement for the reduction of the ground rent operated during the whole term of the lease &, as alternatives, that pltfs. were estopped from demanding rent at the higher rate or had waived their right to do so down to the date of their letter of Sept. 21, 1945:—*Held:* (1) where parties enter into an arrangement which is intended to create legal relations between them & in pursuance of such arrangement one party makes a promise to the other which he knows will be acted on & which is in fact acted on by the promisee, the ct. will treat the promise as binding on the promisor to the extent that it will not allow him to act inconsistently with it even although the promise may not be supported by consideration in the strict sense & the effect of the arrangement made is to vary the terms of a contract under seal by one of less value; (2) the arrangement made between pltfs. & defts. in Jan., 1940, was one which fell within the above category &, accordingly, that the agreement for the reduction of the ground rent was binding on pltf. co., but that it only remained operative so long as the conditions giving rise to it continued to exist & that on their ceasing to do so in 1945 pltfs. were entitled to recover the ground rent claimed at the rate reserved by the lease.— CENTRAL LONDON PROPERTY TRUST, LTD. *v.* HIGH TREES HOUSE, LTD. (1946), [1956] All E. R. 256, n; [1947] K. B. 130; [1947] L. J. R. 77; 175 L. T. 332; 62 T. L. R. 557.

Annotations:—**Apld.** Ledingham *v.* Bermejo Estancia Co., Agar *v.* Bermejo Estancia Co., [1947] 1 All E. R. 749. **Consd.** Wallis *v.* Semark, [1951] 2 T. L. R. 222; Lyle-Mellor *v.* A. Lewis & Co. (Westminster), Ltd., [1956] 1 W. L. R. 29; Slough Estates, Ltd. *v.* Slough B. C. (No. 2) (1967), 19 P. & C. R. 326. **Refd.** Foot Clinics (1943), Ltd. *v.* Cooper's Gowns, Ltd., [1947] K. B. 506; *Re* Venning (1947), 63 T. L. R. 394; Perrott & Co. *v.* Cohen, [1951] 1 K. B. 705; Mitas *v.* Hyams, [1951] 2 T. L. R. 1215.

3934. Lease of licensed premises—Rent reduced if beer supplied by lessor—Right of lessee to purchase elsewhere.]—The lease of a public-house contained a covenant that the lessee & his assigns would, during the term, purchase all beer required for the business from the lessors, a proviso for re-entry on non-payment of rent, or non-performance of the covenants, & a provision for reduction of the rent so long as the lessee should purchase beer from the lessors:—*Held:* the covenant to purchase beer was an absolute one, & the lessee had not the alternative of dealing with a rival brewer & paying the unreduced rent.— HANBURY *v.* CUNDY (1887), 58 L. T. 155.

3935. —— Effect of assignment.]—A covenant by the lessee contained in the lease of an hotel that he will not during the term created by the lease buy, receive, sell, or dispose of, in, upon, out of, or about the premises any wines or spirits other than shall have been *bonâ fide* supplied by or through the lessor, a wine & spirit merchant, his successors or assigns, is a covenant which runs with the land, & is binding on the assigns of the lessee, even though such assigns are not mentioned; & where such covenant is coupled with a proviso for abatement from the rent so long as the lessee shall well & truly observe the covenant, the assigns of the lessee are entitled to the benefit of the proviso, & may claim the abatement, notwithstanding that the ownership of the business of the lessor & the ownership of the reversion have been severed by a sale of the business, while they continue to obtain wines & spirits from the purchasers of the business.—WHITE *v.* SOUTHEND HOTEL CO., [1897] 1 Ch. 767; [1895–9] All E. R. Rep. 500; 66 L. J. Ch. 387; 76 L. T. 273; 45 W. R. 434; 13 T. L. R. 310; 41 Sol. Jo. 384, C. A.

Annotations:—**Refd.** Levin *v.* American & Colonial Distributors, Ltd., [1945] Ch. 225; Regent Oil Co., Ltd. *v.* J. A. Gregory (Hatch End), Ltd., [1965] 3 All E. R. 673.

SCOTTISH, IRISH AND COMMONWEALTH CASES

*1330. Whether operating as new demise.]—Before the expiry of the lease an arrangement was made between the co. & the landlord for a reduction of the rent after the expiry of the lease, nothing being said as to the other terms:— *Held:* the arrangement made imported the terms of the old lease, so far as applicable.—*Re* CANADA COAL CO., DALTON'S CLAIM (1895), 27 O. R. 151.—**CAN.**

*1331.]——.]—An agreement between a landlord & tenant for the increase or reduction of rent does not of itself create a new tenancy.—CLARK *v.* CHITTICK (1934), 42 Man. L. R. 205.—**CAN.**

*1332. ——.]—A verbal agreement to accept a lesser rent than that mentioned in an agreement to grant a lease, followed by acceptance thereof, is not, *per se,* an abandonment of the former contract; nor does it operate **as a** substitution of a new agreement for the former one; or as the creation of a new tenancy, in which the old tenancy merged.—CLARKE *v.* MOORE (1844), 1 Jo. & Lat. 723.—**IR.**

*1333. Lease of licensed premises—Rent reduced if prohibitory law passed—Local option bye-law.]—The lease contained a clause providing for a rebate in the rent, if any prohibitory law passed. A local option bye-law had been passed, & then 8 Edw. 7, c. 54, s. 11 (Dom.), was enacted:—*Held:* the tenant was entitled to a rebate.— HESSEY *v.* QUINN (1909), 13 O. W. R. 907; 18 O. L. R. 487.— **CAN.**

*1334. In case of damage by fire—Binding on assignee of lessor.]—A., the assignee of the lessor, sued B., the lessee of a grist mill, in debt for rent. The lease contained the following covenant: " The lessor, for himself, his assigns, etc., covenants, that during all the time the grist mill shall be unfit for working, in consequence of damage or loss by fire, a fair reduction & allowance shall be made in the rent ": —*Held:* the assignee as well as the original lessor was bound.—McGILL *v.* PROUDFOOT (1847), 4 U. C. R. 33.— **CAN.**

*1335. ——.]—Pltf. co. leased to deft. the half of a shop in which deft. carried on the business of selling *lingerie.* The other half was occupied by deft. co. There was a term in the lease that should the premises be damaged by fire the rent should be reduced for the time occupied in repairing such part or parts " as may be rendered untenantable & incapable for use & occupancy by the lessee." A fire took place on pltf.'s premises from which smoke penetrated to deft.'s shop, disfiguring the walls & ceiling:—*Held:* the damage was caused by the fire, &, having regard to the nature of the goods dealt in by deft., the premises were so injured by fire as to render them " untenantable & incapable " for use & occupancy by the lessee.—UNITED CIGAR STORES, LTD. *v.* BULLER & HUGHES, [1931] 2 D. L. R. 144; 66 O. L. R. 593.—**CAN.**

*1336. Rent payable in advance—Contingent alteration in rent.]—A proviso in an hotel lease, under which rent was payable in advance, to the effect that upon the happening of a named event a new rental shall be fixed, applied only to rent which by the terms of the lease should become payable after the happening of the event mentioned.—*Re* LITTLE & BEATTIE (1917), 38 O. L. R. 551; 34 D. L. R. 217.—**CAN.**

*1337. Whether agreement presumed—Where reduced rent accepted—Want of consideration.]—WESTERN TRANSFER CO. *v.* FRY (1920), 55 D. L. R. 291.—**CAN.**

*1338. ——.]—A bill will not lie by a tenant against his landlord for specific performance of a promise in writing signed by him to reduce the rent of premises demised by indenture, in consideration of previous expenditure on them & a fall in the value of the land though there had been an acceptance of the reduced rent for seven years.— FITZGERALD *v.* PORTARLINGTON (LORD) (1835), 1 Jo. Ex. Ir. 431.—**IR.**

*1339. ——.]—MORGAN *v.* RAINSFORD (1845), 8 I. Eq. R. 299.—**IR.**

*1340. ——.]—An agreement to reduce rent was presumed from the receipt of the reduced rent, which was consistent with the recital in a settlement.—ENRAGHT *v.* HAUGHTON (1845), 8 I. Eq. R. 274.—**IR.**

B. By Statute

See Landlord & Tenant (Requisitioned Land) **Act,** 1942 (c. 13), s. 8; 18 HALSBURY'S STATUTES (3rd Edn.), 526 *et seq.*

ILLUSTRATION 61
The Digest, Green-band Volume 31(1)

LEASES [975–997 : *291–*299]   121

it was concurred in by the *cestuis que trust* & sanctioned by the ct., & had proved beneficial to the trust estate, it must be considered as binding on the *cestuis que trust* & the trust estate was liable for the rent in arrear & the dilapidations.—NEATE v. PINK (1851), 3 Mac. & G. 476 ; 42 E. R. 344 ; *sub nom.* NEATE v. PINK, *Ex p.* FLETCHER & YATES, 21 L. J. Ch. 574 ; 16 Jur. 69 ; *sub nom.* PINK v. NEATE, 18 L. T. O. S. 57, L. C.

986. —— From co-executor.]—COWPER v. FLETCHER, No. 949, *ante*.

SCOTTISH, IRISH AND COMMONWEALTH CASES

***298.** Power to grant lease with option to purchase.]—An option to purchase clause in a lease made by an administratrix declared to be null & void.—ST. GERMAIN v. RENEAULT (1909), 12 W. L. R. 169.—CAN.

SUB-SECT. 10. INFANTS

See INFANTS, Vol. 28 (2) (Reissue), Nos. 559 *et seq.*

SUB-SECT. 11. LAND SEIZED IN EXECUTION

See EXECUTION, Vol. 21 (Repl.), Nos. 1864, 1959 *et seq.* (lease by sequestrator), No. 1995 (lease by owner of sequestrated land), Nos. 1812 *et seq.* (sequestration generally), Nos. 1547, 1548 (tenant by elegit), Nos. 1369 *et seq.* (elegit generally).

SUB-SECT. 12. MENTAL PATIENTS

LAW. *See* HALSBURY'S LAWS (3rd Edn.), Vol. 23, pp. 415, 424.
STATUTES. *See* Mental Health Act, 1959 (c. 72), s. 103 ; 25 HALSBURY'S STATUTES (3rd Edn.), 131, 132.
CROSS-REFERENCES. *See* MENTAL HEALTH, Vol. 33 (Repl.), Nos. 1133 *et seq.*

987. Power of committee to grant—Necessity for leave of court.]—The committee of a lunatic cannot make leases, or incumber the estate, without the leave of the ct.—FOSTER v. MARCHANT (1684), 1 Vern. 262 ; 23 E. R. 784.

988. ——.]—Covenant upon a lease made by the committee of a lunatic, by pltf. as the committee will not lie, for a committee cannot make such lease at law.—KNIPE v. PALMER (1760), 2 Wils. 130 ; 95 E. R. 725.

Annotation :—**Refd.** Pitman v. Woodbury (1848), 3 Exch. 4.

989. —— Mining lease.]—Agreement by the committee of a lunatic that coal under the lunatic's estate should be worked by the owner of the adjoining land, established under the circumstances.—*Ex p.* TABBERT (1801), 6 Ves. 428 ; 31 E. R. 1127.

990. ——.]—Where a lunatic was bound by covenant to grant a renewal of a lease, the expenses incurred by the lessee in applying to the ct. for a direction to the committee to execute a lease instead of the lunatic, must be borne by the lunatic's estate.—*Ex p.* BARNES (1848), 17 L. J. Ch. 436, L. C.

Annotation :—**Refd.** Wortham v. Dacre (1856), 2 K. & J. 437.

991. —— Lease of easement.]—*Re* ARNOTT (1891), 35 Sol. Jo. 623, C. A.

992. Agreement by committee to grant—Specific enforcement.]—*Re* WYNNE, No. 510, *ante*.

993. Power of committee of mentally disordered tenant for life—Whether trustee under Settled Land

---

Act necessary.]—Where a tenant for life is a lunatic, & his committee desires to exercise the powers of leasing given by Settled Land Act, 1882 (c. 38), & no trustees of the settlement are in existence new trustees must be appointed for the purposes of the Act.—*Re* TAYLOR (1883), 52 L. J. Ch. 728 ; 49 L. T. 420 ; 31 W. R. 596, C. A.

994. —— ——.]—The person appointed to act, under Lunacy Act, 1890 (c. 5), s. 116, as committee of the estate of a person lawfully detained as a lunatic though not so found by inquisition may by leave of a judge exercise the power of leasing vested in the lunatic as tenant for life under Settled Land Act, 1882 (c. 38).—*Re* SALT, [1896] 1 Ch. 117 ; 65 L. J. Ch. 152 ; 73 L. T. 598 ; 44 W. R. 146 ; 40 Sol. Jo. 113, C. A.

Annotations :—**Consd.** *Re* S. B., [1906] 1 Ch. 712. **Refd.** *Re* A., [1904] 2 Ch. 328.

995. Infant entitled in remainder—Lease for life of mentally disordered person approved.]—An application having been made under Infants Property Act, 1830 (c. 65), s. 23. for a lease of property belonging to a lunatic for life, with remainder to an infant, at rack rent, for a term of twenty-one years. The ct. refused to make such order, but directed a lease to be granted for twenty-one years determinable on the lunatic's death, & without a covenant for quiet enjoyment.—*Re* WHITE (1853), 21 L. T. O. S. 82 ; 1 W. R. 294, L. JJ.

996. Guardian appointed under statute.]—*Re* VENNER'S SETTLED ESTATES (1868), L. R. 6 Eq. 249 ; 16 W. R. 1033.

Annotation :—**Refd.** *Re* Clough's Estate (1873), L. R. 15 Eq. 284.

SCOTTISH, IRISH AND COMMONWEALTH CASES

***299.** Power of committee to grant.]—SARABJIT SINGH v. CHAPMAN (1886), 1. L. R. 13 Calc. 81 ; L. R. 13 Ind. App. 44.—IND.

SUB-SECT. 13. MARRIED WOMEN

LAW. *See* HALSBURY'S LAWS (3rd Edn.), Vol. 23, p. 416.
STATUTES. *See* Law Reform (Married Women & Tortfeasors) Act, 1935 (c. 30), s. 1 ; 17 HALSBURY'S STATUTES (3rd Edn.), 128; Married Women (Restraint upon Anticipation) Act, 1949 ; 17 HALSBURY'S STATUTES (3rd Edn.), 131.

SUB-SECT. 14. MORTGAGORS AND MORTGAGEES

See MORTGAGE, Vol. 35 (Repl.), Nos. 1514 *et seq.*

SUB-SECT. 15. OWNERS OF RENTCHARGE

STATUTE. *See* Law of Property Act, 1925 (c. 20), s. 121 (4) ; 27 HALSBURY'S STATUTES (3rd Edn.), 530.

997. After entry for non-payment.]—A fine levied to the grantee of a rentcharge with a power limited by way of use to enter on non-payment of the rent " & retain until he be fully satisfied " conveys to him on entry an estate in possession of which his lessor may maintain ejectment.—HAVERGILL (OR HAVERGIL) v. HARE (1616), Cro.

ILLUSTRATION 62
The Digest, Green-band Volume 20

The contract of employment   Cases 2399–2408

c By third party

LAW See Halsbury's Laws (4th edn) vol 16 para 502

2399 Right to give directions—Thames water-men—Members of Watermen's Company
Martin v Temperley (1843) 4 QB 298; 3 Gal&Dav 497; 12 LJQB 129; 11 LT 159; 7 JP 145; 7 Jur 150; 114 ER 912

2400 —— Servants of stevedore under control of ship's officers Where a stevedore had contracted to discharge a vessel for a lump sum, the fact that the master of the vessel had control over the incidents of the discharge held not to make the servants of the stevedore the servants of the shipowners so as to free the stevedore from liability for their negligence.
Cameron v Nystrom [1893] AC 308; 62 LJPC 85; 68 LT 772; 57 JP 550; 7 Asp MLC 320; 1 R 362, PC

2401 Right to appoint—Servant hired by bailiff The employer of the servant is the master for whose service he is retained, and not the bailiff of the farm, who in fact hires the servant.
R v Hoseason (1811) 14 East 605; 104 ER 734

2402 Right to dismiss—Servant of contractor Defendant had the power of insisting on the removal of careless or incompetent workmen, but this power of removal does not vary the case. The workman is still the servant of the contractor only, and the fact that defendants might have insisted on his removal, if they thought him careless or unskilful, did not make him their servant (*Rolfe B*).
Reedie v London & North Western Ry Co Hobbit v Same (1849) 4 Exch 244; 6 Ry&Can Cas 184; 20 LJ Ex 65; 13 Jur 659; 154 ER 1201

2403 —— Sub-contractor
Moore v Palmer no 2371 ante

Scottish, Irish and Commonwealth Cases

2404 Engagement on one employer's work—At another's plant Where operations conducted by B Company at the plant of A Company were carried out by employees hired by A Company and subject to discharge and supervision by A Company, which also paid their wages, although charging the money so expended back to B Company: *Held* the employees were employees of A Company and were properly included in a bargaining unit of its employees. *USWA Local 1005 v Steel Co of Canada* [1944] 2 DLR 583; [1944] OR 299; [1944] OWN 281 (CAN)

2 REMUNERATION

A In general

LAW See Halsbury's Laws (4th edn) vol 16 paras 501, 502

CROSS REFERENCES See no 2744 et seq post (remuneration other than wages), nos 2527, 2528 post (opportunity of earning gratuity at end of employment: consideration), no 2529 post (employment without wages in expectation of testamentary bequest)

2405 Remuneration by commission—Taxi driver—Employee
Challinor v Taylor (1971) [1972] ICR 129; 116 Sol Jo 141

B By third party

LAW See Halsbury's Laws (4th edn) vol 16 para 502
CROSS REFERENCE See MINES vol 33 (Repl) no 1209 et seq (relationship of master & servant between party serving & party served where filler paid by collier.)

2406 Relationship of master and servant—Between party serving and party served—Coachman paid by job-master In a suit of subtraction of legacy, a coachman, a married man, originally hired by, and who had lived five years with, testatrix, residing over her stables in town, occasionally accompanying her into the country, where he lived in the house, though, like all her servants, on board-wages; waiting sometimes at table, and remaining with her though she changed her job-man: *Held* although the several job masters paid him his wages and board-wages, except 3s per week extra in the country, and found him in liveries, entitled under a bequest to each of my servants living with me at the time of my death £10 and executrix condemned in full costs.
Howard v Wilson (1832) 4 Hag Ecc 107; 162 ER 1387

2407 —— —— Servant paid by fellow servant Respondents, potters, engaged appellant to work for them, at specified work, in their manufactory, for a year, at daily wages. The same day respondents engaged R to work for them by piece-work for the same period. The work which appellant had to do was, in fact, included in the piece-work of R, and R paid appellant's wages out of the amount paid by respondents to R for the piece-work: *Held* the contract of master and servant subsisted between respondents and appellant, notwithstanding the fact of the payment of his wages by the hands of R, and, consequently appellant was liable to be convicted, under 4 Geo 4 c 34 (repealed), for neglecting his service with respondents.
Willett v Boote (1860) 6 H&N 26; 30 LJMC 6; 3 LT 276; 25 JP 40; 158 ER 11

Scottish, Irish and Commonwealth Cases

2408 Liability of master to servant for remuneration—Notwithstanding judgment recovered by servant against third party. *Herod v Ferguson* (1894) 25 OR 656 (CAN)

ILLUSTRATION 63
The Digest, Cumulative Supplement, 1984

[153] **Table of Cases** **Parker**

Pace (formerly Doe), R v (1968) (Can): 45 Str Traf *512f
Pachal's Beverages Ltd (in Bkpcy) Re (1969) (Can): 4 (Reissue) Bkpcy *1078
——, Re (1972) (Can): 4 (Reissue) Bkpcy *1326
Pachonik, R v (1973) (Aus): 22 Evid *27872
Pacific Elevators Ltd v Canadian Pacific Ry Co (1974) (Can): 17 Damgs *151a
Pacific Engineering Ltd v Pine Point Investments Ltd & North West Trust Co (1968) (Can): 18 (Reissue) Discy *323
Pacific Leasing Corpn Ltd v Fire Valley Land & Cattle Co Ltd & Jordan (1969) (Can): 26 (Reissue) H Pchse *5286
Pacific Logging Co Ltd v A-G of BC (1971) (Can): 38 (Reissue) Rates *2593
Pacific Molasses Co & United Molasses Trading Co Ltd v Entre Rios Compania Naviera SA, The San Nicholas (1976): 11 Confl 837a
Pacific Press Ltd v Vancouver Typographical Union Local 226, Vancouver Mailers' Union Local 70 & Vancouver Newspaper Printing Pressmen's Union Local 25 (1970) (Can): 45 Trade *608aq
Pacific Produce Delivery & Warehouses Ltd v Labour Relations Board (1974) (Can): 45 Trade *613bbf
Pacific Produce Delivery & Warehouses Ltd & Retail Wholesale & Dept Store Union Local No 580, Re (1974) (Can): 45 Trade 613bbf
Pacific Wash-A-Matic Ltd v Booth (RO) Holdings Ltd (1978) (Can): 12 Contr *2453a
Pacific Wind (Ship) v Johnson, Ferguson, George, Bond & Reilly (1967) (Can): 42 Ship *1829a
Paclantic Financing Ltd v Moscow Narodny Bank Ltd (1982): 37 (3) (Reissue) Prac & Proc 3130
Paczy v Haendler & Natermann GmbH (1979): 3 Arbn 448a
Paddison, R v (1973): 14 (1) (Reissue) Crim 34
Padfield v Minister of Agriculture Fisheries & Food (1968): 1 (1) (Reissue) Admin L 606; 16 (Reissue) Cr Pract 3659; 25 (Reissue) Food 1148
Padolecchia v Leis (1967): 11 (Reissue) Confl 1029, 1175
—— v Padolecchia (orse Leis) (1967): 11 (Reissue) Confl 1029, 1175
Paduch, R v (1973): 45 Str Traf 322nn
Page v Freight Hire (Tank Haulage) Ltd (1981): 20 (Reissue) Empt 4519
—— v Page (1981): 27 (2) H&W 6962A(13)
——, Re (1973) (Can): 51 (Reissue) Wills *9261
——, R v (1971): 15 (Reissue) Crim 12,140
——, R v (1968) (Can): 14 (1) (Reissue) Crim *1928
—— v Solr (1971) (1972) (Can): 43 Solrs *371a
Page Estate, Re (1969) (Can): 23 (Reissue) Exors 7697
Page One Records Ltd v Britton (trading as The Troggs) (1967): 28 (2) (Reissue) Injon 702
Pagebar Properties Ltd v Derby Investment Holdings Ltd (1973): 40 S Land 1072b, 1106a
Paget-Cooke v Paget-Cooke (1973) (Aus): 27 (1) H&W *2097a
Pagett, R v (1983): 15 Crim 9381b
Pagnan (R) & Fratelli v Corbisa Industrial Agropacuaria Ltda (1971): 39 S Goods 2768a
Paine, R v (1973) (Can): 45 Str Traf *1035rzb
Painter & Davis, R v (1849): 34 (Reissue) Money 4743
Pais v Pais (1970): 27 (1) (Reissue) H&W 3475, 3476
Paithouski, Re (1976) (1978) (Can): 51 (Reissue) Wills *10,507
Pajelle Investments Ltd v Herbold (1975) (Can): 31 (2) L&T *1730a
Pal & City of Toronto, Re (1971) (Can): 45 T&CP *18c
Palace-Clark v Standen (1963): 15 (Reissue) Crim 9103
Palamisto General Enterprises SA v Ocean Marine Insce Co Ltd (1972): 29 (Reissue) Insce 3132; 37 (1) (Reissue) Pldg 1540
Palazzo v Copeland (1976) (Scot): 15 Crim *5921a
Palfrey, R v (1970): 45 Str Traf 3220b, 3222a
Palin, R v (1969): 14 (1) (Reissue) Crim 3399
Pallett, R v (1970) (Can): 14 (2) (Reissue) Crim *5489
Pallister v Waikato Hospital Board (1974) (NZ): 29 (Reissue) Insce *3692
Palmco Shipping Inc v Continental Ore Corpn, The Captain George K (1970): 41 Ship 3395a
Palmdale Insurance Ltd, Re (1982) (Aus): 29 Insce 927a
Palmer ex p (1969): 14 (2) (Reissue) Crim 7426
—— v Bank of NSW (1975) (Aus): 50 (Reissue) Wills *131
—— v Barclays Bank Ltd (1971): 35 (Reissue) Mtge 3280
—— v Guadagni (1906): 37 (1) (Reissue) Pldg 1542
—— v Peabody Trust (1974): 31 (2) L&T 7979a
—— v R (1971): 15 (Reissue) Crim 9967
——, R v (1969) (Can): 15 (Reissue) Crim *8676
——, R v (1964) (W Indies): 15 (Reissue) Crim *6780
Palmer's Appln (1970): 36 (2) (Reissue) Pats 96
Palmer & Southwood, Re (1976) (Can): 21 (Reissue) Exon 2032
Palmer-McLellan (United) Ltd v Minister of National Revenue (1969) (Can): 28 (1) (Reissue) Inc T *692
Palvolcyi v Palvolcyi (1967): 27 (2) (Reissue) H&W 8174
Pambakian v Brentford Nylons Ltd (1978): 20 (Reissue) Empt 3168
Pamplin v Gorman (1980): 45 Str Traf 393b
Pan American World Airways Inc v Aetna Casualty and Surety Co (1975): (USA): 29 (Reissue) Insce 3309
Pan American World Airways Inc v Dept of Trade (1976): 8 (2) Civil Av 6Aa
Panalpina Services Ltd v Transport & General Workers Union (1972): 45 Trade 1498a, 1498b, 1522
Panamanian Oriental SS Corpn (or Co) v Wright (1971): 29 (Reissue) Insce 2425, 2481, 2767
Panayiotou, R v (1973): 15 (Reissue) Crim 8090b
Panchaud Frères SA v Etablissements General Grain Co (1970): 39 S Goods 1046a
Pandiak, R v (1967) (Can): 28 (2) (Reissue) Infts *1403
Pando Compania Naviera SA v Filmo SAS (1975): 3 (Reissue) Arbn 656
Pane Niagara Enterprises Ltd & City of Niagara Falls, Re (1968) (Can): 45 T&CP *54daa
Panfab Corpn Ltd, Re Duro Lam Ltd v Last (1971) (Can): 5 (Reissue) Bkpcy *3765
Panipatsek E7–614 (1971) (Can): 15 (Reissue) Crim *5903
Panko v Simmonds (1983) (Can): 43 Solrs *183a
Panneton, Re (1971) (Can): 7 (Reissue) B of Sale *314
Pannett v McGuinness (P) & Co Ltd (1972): 36 (1) (Reissue) Negl 748
Panorama Developments (Guildford) Ltd v Fidelis Furnishing Fabrics Ltd (1971): 9 (Reissue) Coys 3518; 12 (Reissue) Contr 534
Pantanassa, The Norsk Bjergningskompagni A/S v SS Pantanassa (Owners) her cargo & freight (1970): 41 Ship 3392a
Panzavecchia v Piche (1972) (Can): 28 (2) Infts *1047a
Pao On v Lau Yiu (1979): 12 (Reissue) Contr 1899a
Papadopoulos R v (1979) (NZ): 30 Juries *351a
Papal, Re (1973) (Aus): 14 (1) (Reissue) Crim *986
Papatheodorou v Papatheodorou (1971) (Can): 27 (1) (Reissue) H&W *93
Papavasiliou, R v (1970) (Can): 14 (1) (Reissue) Crim *2273
Paper Sales Corpn Ltd v Miller Bros Co (1962) Ltd (1975) (Can): 1 (2) (Reissue) Agcy *3019
Papineau, R v (1980) (Can): 16 Cntmpt *483a
Papp v Papp (1970) (Can): 27 (2) (Reissue) H&W *2431
Papparis v Charles Fulton & Co Ltd (1981): 20 (Reissue) Empt 3408
Papps v Evers (1980): 46 Trusts 3596a
Papworth v Coventry (1967): 45 Str Traf 12a
Paquette, R v (1976) (Can): 14 (1) Crim *314b
Paradise Beach & Transportation Co Ltd v Price-Robinson (or Robinson) (1968): 32 (Reissue) Limit of A 4902
—— v Robinson (1968): 32 (Reissue) Limit of A 4902
Paradise Motor Co Ltd, Re (1968): 9 (Reissue) Coys 2351; 25 (Reissue) Gifts 4653, 154a
Paragon Holdings Ltd, Re (1961): 10 (Reissue) Coys 6367, 6708
Paragon Properties Ltd v Magna Envestments Ltd (1972) (Can): 17 (Reissue) Damgs *19
Parallel Productions Ltd v Goss Contracting Co Ltd & McAuley (1968) (Can): 17 (Reissue) Damgs *325
Paramount Petroleum & Mineral Corpn Ltd v Imperial Oil Ltd (1970) (Can): 34 (Reissue) Mines 1790
Paras v Paras (1971) (Can): 27 (2) (Reissue) H&W *2437
Parfums Marcel Rochas Vertriebs-GmbH v Bitsch (1/70) (1970): 21 (Reissue) EC 1809
Parghi v Parghi (1973): 27 (1) H&W 2643b
Parikh v Birmingham North General Comrs (1976): 28 (1) Inc T 2023a
—— v Currie (1978): 28 (1) Inc T 2098b
—— v Curry (1978): 28 (1) Inc T 2098b
—— v General Comrs for Birmingham North Division (1976): 28 (1) Inc T 2023a
Paris v Machnick (1972) (Can): 40 S Land *1937a
Paris Investments Ltd v Davies Taxi Ltd & Robertson (1969) (Can): 46 Trade Mks *569a
Parish, R v (1967) (1968) (Can): 15 (Reissue) Crim *7833
Parisien, R v (1971) (Can): 37 (3) (Reissue) Prsns 5340
Park, Re IR Comrs v Park (1970): 16 (Reissue) Cr Pract 2509; 21 ED 425Aa
—— (No 2) Re —— v —— (1972): 21 ED 104b, 200b
—— v Hicks (1979): 45 Str Traf 425n
——, In the estate of, Park v Park (1953): 37 (1) (Reissue) Pldg 1299
—— v National Coal Board (1981): 37 (3) (Reissue) Prac & Proc 3246
Park Ct Hotel Ltd v Trans-World Hotels Ltd (1970): 46 Trade Mks 1569b
Park Street Securities Ltd v Albert William Roe (1982): 3 Bank 3582a
Park Valley Enterprises Ltd, R v (1971) (Can): 30 (Reissue) Intox *1577
Parkash v Irani Finance Ltd (1969): 35 (Reissue) Mtge 5345
Parkasho v Singh (1967): 11 (Reissue) Confl 995
Parke, Davis & Co v Probel (24/67) (1968): 21 (Reissue) EC 1781
Parker, Re (1972) (Can): 23 (Reissue) Exors 7669
——, Re (1973) (Can): 32 (Reissue) Limit of A *2059
—— v Boughey (1862): 34 (Reissue) Money 4773
—— v British Airways Board (1982): 46 Trov 578a
—— v Clark (1960): 12 (Reissue) Contr 9, 959
—— v Great Western Ry Co (1844): 38 (Reissue) Rys 855
—— v O'Connor (1974): 31 (2) L&T 4876c
—— v Parker (1972): 27 (1) (Reissue) H&W 2640, 2641, 2642, 2643
—— v —— (1967) (NZ): 27 (1) (Reissue) H&W *1337
——, R v (1969): 14 (1) (Reissue) Crim 3520; 14 (2) (Reissue) Crim 7128
——, R v (1970): 14 (2) (Reissue) Crim 5479, 6192, 7464
——, R v (1977): 15 (Reissue) Crim 12,692
——, R v (1968) (NZ): 14 (2) (Reissue) Crim *4237

green-band volumes a reissue edition.) Look up paragraph 606 in that volume and you will find the information you want (see Illustration 64).

For a more recent case, *Laker Airways Ltd. v. Dept. of Trade,* the procedure is somewhat different. Begin, as with the *Padfield* case, by looking it up in the table of cases in the latest Cumulative Supplement (see Illustration 65). Because the word "Reissue" is not included, "8(2) Civil Av." refers you to the update of green-band volume 8(2) in the noter-up section of the Cumulative Supplement under the subject heading "Civil Aviation". Paragraph 10 Ab gives you the name and date of the case in which you are interested, but not a full citation (see Illustration 66). Instead, it directs you to Continuation Volume E. (It also cites a 1983 case in which *Laker* was judicially considered, thus updating the annotations to *Laker* in Continuation Volume E.) This continuation volume covers the years 1976-1979. If you look up volume 8(2) Civ. Av., case 10 Ab in Continuation Volume E, you will find after a lengthy digest, only part of which is shown in Illustration 67, a list of several series in which the *Laker* case is reported.

A case too recent to be included in a continuation volume is treated differently. Suppose you are interested in a 1982 case, *Clay v. Pooler,* which involved a claim for damages under the Fatal Accidents Act 1976. The table of cases in the 1984 Cumulative Supplement directs you to "36(1) Negl 1473 ea" (see Illustration 68). When you look up the case in the noter-up section of the Supplement, you will find a digest followed by a citation (see Illustration 69).

(d) English Finding Aids Other than the Digest

The tables of cases in *The Digest* are not the only places to find citations to English cases. The consolidated indexes (formerly called digests) to the *Law Reports* contain tables of cases – most of these volumes cover a ten-year period, though some, such as the first (1865-90), cover a longer time. They now include not only cases reported in the *Law Reports, Weekly Law Reports,* and *Industrial Cases Reports,* but also additional cases reported in the *All England Law Reports, Lloyd's Law Reports, Tax Cases* and *Tax Case Leaflets, Local Government Reports, Criminal Appeal Reports,* and *Road Traffic Reports.* The latest permanent consolidation is updated by a soft-cover "Red Index" now covering 1981-83 and by a still later "Pink Index", which is replaced frequently.

The three-volume Consolidated Tables and Index to the *All England Law Reports* covers the years 1936-81. The table of cases is contained in volume 1. These volumes are updated on a regular basis.

The *Current Law Citator* and, for recent cases, the monthly parts of *Current Law* are other sources where you can find citations. Like *The Digest, Current Law* notes not only cases reported in the major series, but those reported in a great many others as well.

ILLUSTRATION 64
The Digest, Green-band Volume 1(1)

104   VOL. 1 (1)—ADMINISTRATIVE LAW: PART II

Sect. 8. *Construction of powers, etc.: Sub-sect.* 2,
cont.]

(1907), 96 L. T. 762; 71 J. P. 265; 23 T. L. R.
440; 51 Sol. Jo. 409; 5 L. G. R. 584, C. A.

Annotation:—**Refd.** Webb *v.* Minister of Housing & Local
Govt., [1965] 2 All E. R. 193.

See, also, Nos. 627, 687 *et seq., post*; PUBLIC
HEALTH & LOCAL ADMINISTRATION, Vol. 38 (Repl.)
No. 393.

606. Objects of statute frustrated.]—Applts.,
members of the south east regional committee of
the Milk Marketing Board, made a complaint to the
Minister of Agriculture, Fisheries & Food, pursuant
to Agricultural Marketing Act 1958, s. 19 (3) (*b*),
asking that the complaint be referred to the committee of investigation established under that
enactment. The complaint was that the board's
terms & prices for the sale of milk to the board did
not take fully into account variations between
producers & the cost of bringing milk to a liquid
market. In effect the complaint was that the price
differential worked unfairly against the producers
in the popular south east region, where milk was
more valuable, the cost of transport was less & the
price of land was higher. There had been many
previous requests to the board, but these had failed
to get the board, in which the south east producers
were in a minority, to do anything about the
matter. The Minister declined to refer the matter
to the committee. By letters of May 1, 1964, &
Mar. 23, 1965, he gave reasons which included that
(in effect) his main duty had been to decide the
suitability of the complaint for such investigation,
but that it was one which raised wide issues &
which he did not consider suitable for such investigation, as it could be settled through arrangements
available to producers & the board within the milk
marketing scheme; that he had unfettered discretion, & that, if the complaint were upheld by the
committee, he might be expected to make a statutory order to give effect to the committee's recommendations:—*Held:* the matter would be remitted
to the Queen's Bench Div. with a direction to
require the Minister to consider applts.' complaint
according to law, for the following reasons—(1) (*a*)
where a statute conferring a discretion on a Minister
to exercise or not to exercise a power did not
expressly limit or define the extent of his discretion
& did not require him to give reasons for declining
to exercise the power, his discretion might nevertheless be limited to the extent that it must not be
so used, whether by reason of misconstruction of the
statute or other reason, as to frustrate the objects
of the statute which conferred it; (*b*) although the
Minister had full or unfettered discretion under
Agricultural Marketing Act 1958, s. 19 (3) he was
bound to exercise it lawfully, *viz.*, not to misdirect
himself in law, nor to take into account irrelevant
matters, nor to omit relevant matters from consideration; (*c*) the complaint in the present case
was a substantial & genuine complaint, neither
frivolous, repetitive nor vexatious; the reasons of
the Minister for not referring the matter to the
committee of investigation (*viz.* the complaint
raised wide issues, that his discretion was unfettered so that, in effect, it was sufficient that he
should *bona fide* have considered the matter) were
not good reasons in law, & indeed left out of
account the merits of the complaint & showed that
he was not exercising his discretion in accordance
with the intention of s. 19 of 1958 Act; (2) the
fact that a Minister gave no reasons for his decision, whether or not to exercise a discretionary
power conferred on him by statute, would not pre-

vent the ct. from reaching a conclusion in a proper
case that a prerogative order should issue.

Per LORD UPJOHN: there may be good policy
reasons for refusing an investigation [under s. 19
(3) of 1958 Act], but policy must not be based on
political considerations, which are pre-eminently
extraneous.—PADFIELD *v.* MINISTER OF AGRICUL-
TURE, FISHERIES & FOOD, [1968] 1 All E. R. 694;
[1968] A. C. at p. 1016; [1968] 2 W. L. R. at p.
936; 112 Sol. Jo. 171, H. L.

Annotations:—**Apld.** Congreve *v.* Home Office, [1976] 1 All
E. R. 697; Laker Airways, Ltd. *v.* Dept. of Trade, [1977]
2 All E. R. 182.

SECT. 9. **EXEMPTION FROM LIABILITY**

SUB-SECT. 1. POWERS, ETC. EXERCISED
WITHOUT NEGLIGENCE

LAW. *See* HALSBURY'S LAWS (4th Edn.), Vol.
1, paras. 200 *et seq.*

CROSS-REFERENCES. *See,* NEGLIGENCE, Vol.
36 (1) (Reissue) No. 1 (escape of water from
main), No. 199 (overflow of canal water),
No. 834 (sparks from steamboat);
STATUTES, Vol. 44 (Repl.) Nos. 1471 *et seq.*
(exercise of statutory powers); RAIL-
WAYS & CANALS, Vol. 38 (Repl.) Nos. 582
et seq. (generally).

**607. No liability without proof of negligence—
Road watercourse.]**—One who in the exercise of a
public function without emolument, which he is
compellable to execute, acting without malice, &
according to his best skill & diligence & obtaining
the best information he can, does an act which
occasions consequential damage to a subject is not
liable to an action for such damage.

The trustees of a turnpike road, empowered to
make watercourses to prevent the road from being
overflowed, directed their surveyor to present a
plan for carrying off the water of an adjacent
brook; he recommended, & on that recommendation they adopted & caused him to make a wide
channel from the road, gradually narrowing, &
conducting the water into the ordinary fence
ditches of pltf.'s land which were insufficient to
discharge it, & his land was consequently overflowed:—*Held:* no action lay against the chairman of the trustees who signed the order for
cutting this trench.

Deft. . . . executes a duty imposed on him by
the legislature which he is bound to execute. He
exercises his best skill, diligence & caution in the
execution of it, & we are of the opinion that he
is not liable for an injury, which he did not only
not foresee, but could not foresee (GIBBS, C.J.).—
SUTTON *v.* CLARKE (1815), 6 Taunt. 29; 1 Marsh.
429; 128 E. R. 943.

Annotations:—**Distd.** Jones *v.* Bird (1822), 5 B. & Ald. 837.
Apld. Boulton *v.* Crowther (1824), 2 B. & C. 703. **Consd.**
Hall *v.* Smith (1824), 2 Bing. 156; Smith *v.* Shaw (1829),
L. & Welsb. 98. **Apld.** Grocers' Co. *v.* Donne (1836), 3
Bing. N. C. 34. **Distd.** Smith *v.* Kenrick (1849), 7 C. B.
515; Scott *v.* Manchester Corpn. (1857), 22 J. P. 70;
Whitehouse *v.* Fellowes (1861), 10 C. B. N. S. 765. **Expld.**
Mersey Docks Trustees *v.* Gibbs (1866), 11 H. L. Cas. 687.
Refd. Blakemore *v.* Glamorganshire Canal Co. (1829),
3 Y. & J. 60; R. *v.* Eastern Counties Ry. (1842), 6 Jur.
557; Dawson *v.* Paver (1847), 5 Hare, 415; *Re* Cooling
& G. N. Ry. (1849), 19 L. J. Q. B. 25; Metcalf *v.*
Hetherington (1855), 24 L. J. Ex. 314; Holliday *v.* St.
Leonard's, Shoreditch, Vestry (1861), 11 C. B. N. S. 192;
Clothier *v.* Webster (1862), 12 C. B. N. S. 790; Coe *v.*
Wise (1864), 5 B. & S. 440; Tobin *v.* R. (1864), 16 C. B.
N. S. 310; East Fremantle Corpn. *v.* Annois, [1902] A. C.
213; Roberts *v.* Charing Cross, Euston & Hampstead Ry.
(1903), 87 L. T. 732; Maxey Drainage Board *v.* G. N. Ry.
(1912), 76 J. P. 236; Boynton *v.* Ancholme Drainage &
Navigation Comrs., [1921] 2 K. B. 213; Howard-Flanders
v. Maldon Corpn. (1926), 70 Sol. Jo. 544; Dormer *v.* New-
castle-on-Tyne Corpn., [1940] 1 K. B. 586; Provender
Millers (Winchester), Ltd. *v.* Southampton C. C., [1940]
Ch. 131.

ILLUSTRATION 65
The Digest, Cumulative Supplement, 1984

[123] **Table of Cases** **Lally**

Kunstler v Kunstler (1969): 30 (Reissue) Jdgmts 325; 37 (2) (Reissue) Prac & Proc 2239
Kurt Kampffmeyer Muhlenvereinigung KG v EC Council and EC Commission (56–60/74) (1976): 21 (Reissue) EC 1865
Kushner v Merrill Lynch Royal Securities Ltd (1974) (Can): 43 Solrs *1386a
Kutassy v Isagold Holdings Ltd (1972) (Can): 31 (2) (Reissue) L&T *1931
Kutz, R v (1971) (Can): 45 Str Traf *1064b
Kuwait Government v Sir Frederick Snow & Partners (1983): 3 Arbn 2044a
Kuyken v Rijksdienst voor Arbeidsvoorziening (66/77) (1977): 21 (Reissue) EC 1733; 35 (Reissue) Nat Health & Soc Sec 7020
Kuziak v Romuld (1966) (Can): 20 (Reissue) Elect *528
Kwasnie v Penthouse Towers Ltd (1972) (Can): 36 (1) (Reissue) Negl *557
Kwasnitza, R v (1970) (Can): 45 Str Traf *1046bf
Kyle v Bearss (1975) (Can): 45 Time *37a
—— v McCullagh & McCullagh & Corpn of Delta (1969) (Can): 45 Str Traf *202j
Kyling, R v (1970) (Can): 14 (2) (Reissue) Crim *4839
Kynaston v Secretary of State for Home Affairs (1981): 34 (Reissue) Ment Hlth 450
Kyowa's Appln (1968): 36 (2) (Reissue) Pats 1526
—— (1969): 36 (2) (Reissue) Pats 1430
Kyte v GLC (1974): 20 (Reissue) Empt 3344

L

L, Re [1968] 1 All ER 20: 32 (Reissue) Legn & Affln 170; 28 (2) (Reissue) Infts 2243; 37 (2) (Reissue) Prac & Proc 2446
——, Re (1968) 112 Sol Jo 254; 34 (Reissue) Ment Hlth 634; 47 Trusts 2993a
—— (minors) Re (1974): 28 (2) Infts 1237a
—— (minor) Re (1978): 28 (2) Infts 2248b
—— v L (1968): 28 (2) (Reissue) Infts 2245
—— v —— (1969): 27 (2) (Reissue) H&W 7564; 28 (2) (Reissue) Injon 1137
—— v L (1969) (NZ): 27 (1) (Reissue) H&W *1046
L (AC) (infant) Re (1971): 28 (2) Infts 2441a
LB (Plastics) Ltd v Swish Products Ltd (1979): 13 Copyrt 1054(2)
LCC v Cross (1892): 38 (Reissue) Pub Hlth 797
—— v Davis, LCC v Rowton House Co (1897): 38 (Reissue) Pub Hlth 821
—— v Hancock & James (1907): 38 (Reissue) Pub Hlth 743
—— v Hirsch & Co (1899): 38 (Reissue) Pub Hlth 214
—— v Illuminated Advertisements Co (1904): 38 (Reissue) Pub Hlth 741
—— v Wandsworth BC (1903): 38 (Reissue) Pub Hlth 73
—— v Worley (1894): 38 (Reissue) Pub Hlth 800
LEP Air Services Ltd v Rolloswin Investments Ltd (1971): 26 (Reissue) Guar 764
LH v LHH (1971) (Can): 27 (1) H&W *1488a
LM v Director of Child Welfare (1968) (Can): 32 (Reissue) Legn & Affln *181
LRC International Ltd v Lilla Edets Sales Co Ltd (1973): 46 Trade Mks 2040d
LTSS Print & Supply Services Ltd v Hackney (London Borough of) (or Hackney London BC) (1976): 45 T&CP 86f
—— v Hackney London BC (1976): 45 T&CP 86f
Labatt's Saskatchewan Brewery Ltd v Harrisons & Crosfield (Canada) Ltd (1969) (Can): 3 (Reissue) Bailmt *2272
L'Abbe v Southam Press Ltd (1970) (Can): 32 (Reissue) Libel *1513
Labbe & Cormier v Savard & Cyr (1967) (Can): 22 (Reissue) Evid *1654
Labelle & Tp of Valley East, Re (1970) (Can): 45 T&CP *68b
Labenstoff v Smith (1969) (Can): 45 Str Traf *652a
Laberge, R v (1977) (Can): 14 (2) Crim *4024a
Laboratoire Pentagone, Ltee v Parke Davis & Co (1968) (Can): 28 (2) (Reissue) Injon *730
Laborde v Bendas (1972) (Can): 14 (1) (Reissue) Crim *1079
—— v Roberts (1967) (W Indies): 22 (Reissue) Evid *743
Laborde & R, Re (1972) (Can): 14 (1) (Reissue) Crim *1079
Labour Dept v Aloua (1975) (NZ): 2 (Reissue) Aliens *836
—— v Green (1973) (NZ): 14 (1) (Reissue) Crim *45
Labour Relations Act, Re, Bakery & Confectionery Workers' International Union of America Local 389 v Paulin Chambers Co Ltd & Manitoba Labour Board (1967) (Can): 45 Trade *613b
——, Re CAE Industries Ltd Electronics Division (Western) v Manitoba Labour Board & United Automobile Aerospace, Agricultural Implement Workers of America (UAW) Local 144 (1969) (Can): 45 Trade *607ga
Labour Relations Board & A-G (BC) Re, Re Simon Fraser University (1966) (Can): 45 Trade *613g
Labour Relations Board & Western Publishers (Prince Albert) Ltd, R (Saskatoon Printing Pressmen & Assistants' Union No 204) v (1967) (Can): 45 Trade *607h
Labour Relations Board of Province of Saskatchewan v R (1969) (Can): 45 Trade *607ab
Labour Relations Board of Saskatchewan, R (United Steelworkers of America) v (1969) (Can): 45 Trade *607ab
——, R (Piggott Construction Ltd) v (1973) (Can): 45 Trade *607eeb
Labour Relations Board of Sakatchewan & Main, R (Retail Wholesale & Dept Store Union & Gilbey) v (1969) (Can): 45 Trade *607ef
Labour Relations Board, Woodlands Enterprises Ltd & Construction & General Workers Local Union No 890, R (International Woodworkers of America Local 1—184) v (1969) (Can): 45 Trade *613k
Labourers' International Union of North America Local 183 ex p (1969) (Cam): 45 Trade *607aa
LaBrash v LaBrash (1973) (Can): 27 (2) H&W *2993b
La Caisse Populaire Notre Dame, Ltee v Moyen (1967) (Can): 8 (2) (Reissue) Comwlth *871
Laceward Ltd, Re (1981): 43 Solrs 1612b
Lacey v Lacey (1970) (Can): 27 (1) (Reissue) H&W *1394
——, v (1971) (Can): 45 Str Traf *1035rp
Lachman v Lachman (1970) (Can): 27 (1) (Reissue) H&W *1368
Lacis v Cashmarts (1969): 15 (Reissue) Crim 11,030
Lack v Doggett (1970) 46 Tax Cas at p 512: 28 (1) Inc T 2109a
Lack (Frederick) Ltd v Doggett (1970) 46 Tax Cas at p 532: 28 (1) Inc T 1994a
Lackner v Neath (1966) (Can): 45 Str Traf *765b
Laconia, The (1977): 41 Ship 539d
Laczko v Patterson (1971) (Can): 40 S Land *880a
Ladbroke Racing Ltd v Arnott (1983) (Scot): 20 Empt 3356B
—— v Mason (1978): 20 (Reissue) Empt 3337
Ladd v Jones (1975): 29 (Reissue) Insce 5423
Ladefoged Niels v Joseph H (SS) (1970) (Can): 1 (1) (Reissue) Adm *1078
Ladelpha v Myre (1974) (Can): 33 (Reissue) Med *2398
——, R v (1970) (Can): 33 (Reissue) Med *2396
Ladenbau (G&K) (UK) Ltd v Crawley & de Reya (a firm) (1978): 43 Solrs 1020a
Ladoceur v Jopka & Govt of Manitoba (1968) (Can): 45 Str Traf *765e
Ladyman v Wirral Estates Ltd (1968): 31 (2) (Reissue) L&T 7741
LaFarge Canada Ltd v Bldg Material Construction & Fuel Truck Drivers' Union Local 213 (1972) (Can): 45 Trade *699u
Laferte ex p (1837): 34 (Reissue) Money 4801
Lafleur ex p (1967) (Can): 28 (1) (Reissue) Inc T *1470
Lafleur Estate v R (1973) (Can): 28 (1) Inc T *1369d
Lafrance, R v (1972) (Can): 14 (1) (Reissue) Crim *254
—— v R (1973) (Can): 15 (Reissue) Crim *8179
Laga, The (1966): 41 Ship 2450a
Lagace v Minister of National Revenue (1968) (Can): 28 (1) (Reissue) Inc T *403
Lagasse v Ritchot (RM of) (1973) (Can): 36 (1) (Reissue) Negl *380
Laguerre's Patent (1970) (1971): 36 (2) (Reissue) Pats 2931
Lagunas Nitrate Co v Lagunas Syndicate (1899): 34 (Reissue) Mines 1422
Lahey v Hartford Fire Insce Co (1968) (1969) (Can): 29 (Reissue) Insce *4446
Laidlaw v Lions Gate Hospital Hiddleston (1969) (Can): 33 (Reissue) Med *2327
Lain ex p (1965): 14 (2) (Reissue) Crim 7499; 16 (Reissue) Cr Pract 4358
Laing v IR Comrs (1967) (Scot): 28 (1) (Reissue) Inc T *679
Laing's Trustees v Horsburgh (1965) (Scot): 51 (Reissue) Wills *14,028
Laird, R v (1968): 33 (Reissue) Mags 982
Lajoie, R v (1970) (Can): 14 (2) (Reissue) Crim *2853
——, R v (1971) (Can): 14 (2) (Reissue) Crim *5366
—— v R (1973) (Can): 14 (2) (Reissue) Crim *5366
Lakatosh v Ross (1974) (Can): 20 (Reissue) Empt 2324
Lake v Bayliss (1974): 40 S Land 1557a
—— v Bennett (1970): 31 (1) (Reissue) L&T 1489
—— v Essex CC (1979): 20 (Reissue) Empt 3277
——, R v (1976): 14 (1) Crim 2255a
—— v R (1969) (Can): 14 (2) (Reissue) Crim *5569
Lake Apartments Ltd v Bootwala (1973) (Can): 35 (Reissue) Mtge 3313
Lake Atlin, The (1972): 40 Set-off 505a
Lake Bosomtwe (No 2) The (1971) (Can): 1 (1) (Reissue) Adm *1084
Lake Louise Ski Lodge Ltd, Cooper & Boyle v R (1968) (Can): 11 (Reissue) Comp Pche *139c
Lake Ontario Cement Co v Golden Eagle Oil Co Ltd (1974) (Can): 12 Contr *408a
Lake Ontario Cement Ltd, R v (1973) (Can): 36 (1) (Reissue) Nuis *306
Lakehead Registered Nursing Assistants Bargaining Assocn, Re (1969) (Can) 45 Trade *613ba
Lakelse Dairy Products Ltd v General Dairy Machinery & Supply Ltd & Mueller (Paul) Co of Canada (1970) (Can): 39 S Goods *364b
Lakeport Navigation Co Panama SA v Anonima Petroti Italiana SpA, The Olympic Brilliance (1982): 43 (Reissue) Ship 10184
Laker Airways Ltd v Dept of Trade (1977): 8 (2) Civil Av 10Ab
Lakhani v Hoover Ltd (1978): 20 (Reissue) Empt 3297
Lakshmijit v Sherani (1973) (Fiji): 32 (Reissue) Limit of A *2580
Lal v Minister of Manpower & Immigration (1972) (Can): 2 (Reissue) Aliens *992
—— v R (1976) (Fiji): 14 (2) (Reissue) Crim *4456
Laliberte v R (1967) (Can): 30 (Reissue) Intox *1570
——, R v (1967) (Can): 30 (Reissue) Intox *1570
Lally v Kensington and Chelsea Royal Borough (1980): 26 (Reissue) Housg 5333

ILLUSTRATION 66
The Digest, Cumulative Supplement, 1984

Vol 8 (2)—Civil Aviation   **80**

restoration to the register and this was permitted on condition that the court was satisfied that the third company was a person aggrieved within a provision of the Australian legislation corresponding to the Companies Act 1948, s 353(6). The second company contended that the assignment was invalid, and thus the third company could not bring itself within the section, due to the public policy rule that a bare right of action could not be assigned. In order to be assignable it had to be associated with the assignment of some other form of property. Held in determining the validity of such an assignment the whole transaction had to be examined. Where the assignee had a genuine and substantial interest in the litigation or a bona fide commercial interest in accepting the assignment the cause of action might have been validly assigned. An assignee who was a creditor of the assignor, as the third company was in this case, held such an interest and the assignment was valid. Where the assignor company had been struck off the register as defunct, the assignee, as a creditor, was a person aggrieved. The assignor's name would be restored to the register. RE TIMOTHY'S PTY LTD AND THE COMPANIES ACT [1981] 2 NSWLR 706 (AUS)

Part IV—What amounts to an Assignment

SECT 1 **STATUTORY ABSOLUTE ASSIGNMENTS** (p 519)

CROSS REFERENCE See BANKRUPTCY & INSOLVENCY No 8358a (assignment by trustee in bankruptcy to bankrupt of right to sue: covenant by bankrupt to pay trustee percentage of proceeds of action if successful)

226 Folld Care Shipping Corpn v Latin American Shipping Corpn, The Cebu [1983] 1 All ER 1121
243 Apld Swiss Bank Corpn v Lloyds Bank Ltd [1980] 2 All ER 419
273 Expld Helstan Securities Ltd v Hertfordshire CC [1978] 3 All ER 262
297 Apld dictum Lord Wrenbury, Swiss Bank Corpn v Lloyds Bank Ltd [1981] 2 All ER 449

312 Consd Helstan Securities Ltd v Hertfordshire CC [1978] 3 All ER 262

Part V—Notice of Assignment

355a *Equitable assignment of option—No notice given to grantor of option— Purported exercise of option unenforceable* WARNER BROS RECORDS INC v ROLLGREEN LTD (1975) See Continuation Vol D
442 Distd Midland Bank Trust Co Ltd v Hett Stubbs & Kemp (a firm) [1978] 3 All ER 571

Part VI—Effect of Assignment

596 Apld Warner Bros Records Inc v Rollgreen Ltd [1975] 2 All ER 105

Part VII—Assignment subject to Equities

644 Apld Re Islington Metal and Plating Works Ltd [1983] 3 All ER 218
651a *Whether assignee affected by rights—Assignment of debt due by company—Claim under hire purchase agreement made before receiver appointed—Debtor not entitled to set-off against claim under assigned debt* BUSINESS COMPUTERS LTD v ANGLO-AFRICAN LEASING LTD (1977) See Continuation Vol E
652 Apld Business Computers Ltd v Anglo-African Leasing Ltd [1977] 2 All ER 741
653 Apld Business Computers Ltd v Anglo-African Leasing Ltd [1977] 2 All ER 741
656 Distd Aries Tanker Corpn v Total Transport Ltd [1977] 1 All ER 398 **Apld** Helstan Securities Ltd v Hertfordshire CC [1978] 3 All ER 262 [1978] 3 All ER 262
657 Generally Distd Aries Tanker Corpn v Total Transport Ltd [1977] 1 All ER 398

CIVIL AVIATION

Part II—Administration and Finance

SECT 1 **IN GENERAL** (p 592)

6Aa *Airline operating permit—Validity of condition as to payment of commission* PAN AMERICAN WORLD AIRWAYS INC v DEPT OF TRADE (1976) See Continuation Vol E
*13a *Air carrier licences—Power of Canadian Transport Commission to cancel* CANADIAN TRANSPORT COMMISSION v WORLDWAYS AIRLINES LTD (1975) CAN See Continuation Vol E

SECT 3 **THE CIVIL AVIATION AUTHORITY**
SUB-SECT 1 GENERALLY (p 594)

10Aa *Air operations certificate—Provisional suspension—Notice & reasons for suspension need not be given* R v CIVIL AVIATION AUTHORITY ex p NORTHERN AIR TAXIS LTD (1975) See Continuation Vol E
10Ab *Designated operator—Power to withdraw designation—Mandatory direction imposing fetter on authority's discretion—Validity* LAKER AIRWAYS LTD v DEPT OF TRADE (1977) See Continuation Vol E **Apld** R v Police Complaints Board ex p Madden R v Police Complaints Board ex p Rhone [1983] 2 All ER 353

Part III—Aerodromes and Land

11(1) *Aerodrome owned by British Airports Authority— Authority increasing landing and take-off charges— Foreign aircraft operators bringing action challenging validity of increase—Operators meanwhile paying at old rate and withholding increase—Whether operating permit granted by Secretary of State conferring absolute right as against authority to use its aerodromes—Whether authority's right to detain aircraft precluding it from*

seeking injunction The British Airports Authority was a body constituted under the Airports Authority Act 1975 to manage certain aerodromes, including the aerodrome at Heathrow, of which it was the beneficial owner in possession and for which it held a licence granted under art 68 of the Air Navigation Order 1976, which required it at all times when its aerodromes were available for the take-off and landing of aircraft to make them so available to all persons on equal terms and conditions. The authority was entitled to charge landing fees in respect of, inter alia, the use of its aerodromes for the landing and take-off of aircraft. Under s 14 of the Civil Aviation Act 1968 the authority was empowered to detain and sell any aircraft in respect of which default was made in the payment of the fees. The plaintiffs were a number of airline operators from contracting states (ie states which were parties to the 1944 Chicago Convention) engaged in operating scheduled passenger flights using Heathrow airport and which held permits granted under art 77 of the 1976 order. Article 77 provided that aircraft such as those operated by the plaintiffs could not, without the permission of the Secretary of State and in accordance with any conditions to which such permission was made subject, take on board or discharge passengers or cargo in the United Kingdom when carried for hire or reward. In April 1980 the authority introduced new landing fees which were

ILLUSTRATION 67
The Digest, Continuation Volume E, 1976-1979

made between the debtor & the assignor before the date of the assignment. For the purposes of set-off against an assignee, there was no distinction between the assignment of a single debt & the assignment of a number of debts which took place on the appointment of a receiver by a debenture holder. Since defts.' right to claim £30,000 had not accrued due by June 17, the date when defts. had received notice of the appointment of the receiver & therefore of the assignment to the debenture holders of BCL's assets including the debt of £10,587.50, & the debt of £30,000 claimed by defts. & the debt of £10,587.50 owed by them to BCL had arisen under different contracts, it followed that defts. were not entitled to set-off their claim for £30,000 against the claim by the receiver for the debt of £9,110.30 & the receiver was therefore entitled to recover that sum from defts.—BUSINESS COMPUTERS, LTD. v. ANGLO-AFRICAN LEASING, LTD., [1977] 2 All E. R. 741; [1977] 1 W. L. R. 578; 121 Sol. Jo. 201.

CIVIL AVIATION

Part II.—Administration and Finance

SECT. 1.   IN GENERAL (p. 592)

6Aa. Airline operating permit—Validity of condition as to payment of commission.]—(1) Under Air Navigation Order & the Chicago Convention there is no restriction on the powers of the Secretary of State to impose conditions when granting operating permits & this includes power to impose a condition as to the amount of commission payable to travel agents; (2) the Bermuda Agreement does not form part of the law of England & cannot restrict any powers of the Secretary of State.— PAN AMERICAN WORLD AIRWAYS, INC. v. DEPT. OF TRADE (1976), 119 Sol. Jo. 657; [1976] 1 Lloyd's Rep. 257, C. A.

*13a. Air carrier licences—Power of Canadian Transport Commission to cancel.]—The determination by a statutory tribunal to whom the matter has been entrusted for determination that the cancellation of all or part of a licence is required by public convenience & necessity is not a question of fact but rather involves the forming of an opinion by such a tribunal based upon an existing state of facts. Where the tribunal has formed such an opinion & there is evidence to support it, the ct. should not substitute its opinion for that of the tribunal. Moreover, where more than a year's notice of a possible cancellation is given, the tribunal's decision cannot be attacked on the ground of lack of proper notice.— CANADIAN TRANSPORT COMMISSION v. WORLDWAYS AIRLINES, LTD. (1975), 55 D. L. R. (3d) 389.—CAN.

SECT. 3.   THE CIVIL AVIATION AUTHORITY

SUB-SECT. 1.   GENERALLY (p. 594)

10Aa. Air operations certificate—Provisional suspension—Notice & reasons for suspension need not be given.]—R. v. CIVIL AVIATION AUTHORITY, Ex p. NORTHERN AIR TAXIS, LTD. (1975), 119 Sol. Jo. 591; [1976] 1 Lloyd's Rep. 344, D. C.

10Ab. Designated operator—Power to withdraw designation—Mandatory direction imposing fetter on authority's discretion—Validity.]—In Oct. 1972 pltfs. were granted an air transport licence by the Civil Aviation Authority (the CAA) under Civil Aviation Act 1971 to provide a low cost passenger air service, known as Skytrain, for a period of 10 years from Jan. 1, 1973 between London & New York. Relying on the grant pltfs. purchased several wide-bodied aircraft & trained crews with a view to operating Skytrain. In Feb. 1973 the British govt. served a formal notice on the U.S. govt. designating pltfs. as a scheduled carrier in accordance with a treaty between the two countries, the Bermuda Agreement 1946. Under the provisions of that treaty the designation would enable pltfs. to obtain a foreign air carrier permit from the U.S. Civil Aeronautical Board (the CAB), "without undue delay". In Mar. 1974 the CAB granted pltfs. such a permit subject to the signature of the President of U.S. In Feb. 1975 the British Airways Board asked the CAA to revoke the licence granted to pltfs. on the ground that since 1972 there had been a substantial decrease in the volume of air traffic coupled with a large increase in costs. The CAA refused. In July 1975, following a change in aviation policy, the Secretary of State reversed the decision to allow Skytrain to come into operation. That decision was communicated to the CAB which then withdrew its permit before it had received the President's signature. In 1976, in purported exercise of the power conferred by s. 3 (2) of 1971 Act, the Secretary of State for Trade published a White Paper setting out new policy "guidance" to be followed by the CAA in performing its functions under the Act. The White Paper stated, inter alia, that pltfs.' designation as a scheduled service operator under the Bermuda Agreement should be cancelled & that, unless British Airways consented, "in the case of long-haul scheduled services . . . the [CAA] should not . . . licence more than one British airline to service the same route . . .". The new policy guidance was approved by Parliament, in accordance with s. 3 (3) of 1971 Act, although the House of Lords requested the Secretary of State to withdraw the instruction to the CAA to revoke pltfs.' licence. Pltfs. brought an action for a declaration that the new policy guidance was ultra vires the powers conferred on the Secretary of State on the ground that it conflicted with the general objectives of 1971 Act contained in s. 3 (1), that the licence granted to pltfs. to operate Skytrain from Jan. 1, 1973 remained in force & that the Secretary of State was not entitled to revoke pltfs.' designation: —Held: pltfs. were entitled to the relief sought because—(1) although s. 3 (2) of 1971 Act empowered the Secretary of State to give guidance to the CAA with respect to the functions conferred on it by s. 3 (1) that could not be construed as conferring on the Secretary of State power to give the CAA directions which, by granting a monopoly

* * *

way as to deprive a subject of a right conferred on him by statute. It followed therefore that, once pltfs. had been granted a licence under 1971 Act, they could only be deprived of that licence in accordance with the provisions of the Act & it was an improper exercise of the prerogative power in effect to nullify that licence by withdrawing pltfs.' designation as a scheduled air carrier under the Bermuda Agreement.—LAKER AIRWAYS, LTD. v. DEPT. OF TRADE, [1977] 2 All E. R. 182; [1977] Q. B. at p. 684; [1977] 2 W. L. R. 234; 121 Sol. Jo. 52, C.A.

* An asterisk indicates a Scottish, Irish or Commonwealth case.

ILLUSTRATION 68
The Digest, Cumulative Supplement, 1984

Clarke | Table of Cases | [72]

Clarke (HF) Ltd v Thermidaire Corpn Ltd (1973) (Can): 45 Trade *100d
Clarks of Mave Ltd v Bankers' Union [1979]: 20 Empt 3678
Clarkson, R v (1971): 14 (1) (Reissue) Crim 591
——, R v (1977): 14 (1) Crim 62a
Clarkson Co Ltd v Canadian Indemnity Co (1979) (Can): 29 (Reissue) Insce 5517
—— v Zhelka (1967) (Can): 4 (Reissue) Bkpcy *109
Clarkson International Tools Ltd v Short (1973): 20 (Reissue) Empt 3431
Clarksons Holidays Ltd, R v (1972): 46 Trade Mks 1100c
Claro (Rene) (Haute Coiffure) Ltd v Hallé Concerts Soc (1969): 31 (2) (Reissue) L&T 7720, 7740
Claudius Ash Son & Co Ltd v Invicta Manufacturing Co Ltd (1912): 37 (1) (Reissue) Pldg 1553
Claverie & TFM Act, Re (1970) (Aus): 24 (Reissue) Exors 7603
Claxton v Claxton (1972) (Aus): 27 (2) H&W *3004a
Clay v Pooler (1982): 36 (1) Negl 1473ca
Clay (Charles) & Sons Ltd v British Rys Board (1971): 31 (2) (Reissue) L&T 6244
Clay Cross (Quarry Service) Ltd v Fletcher (1979): 20 (Reissue) Empt 4484
Claydon & Quann Agencies Ltd, Re (1972) (Can): 26 (Reissue) Housg *5359
Clayton v Albertsen (1972): 42 Ship 8762a
—— v Chief Constable of Norfolk (1983): 14 (1) Crim 2232a
—— v Chief Constable of Norfolk and another appeal (1983): 33 Mags 991a
—— v Gothorp (1971): 28 (1) Inc T 1226a, 1697a
—— v Investments (JNZ) Ltd (1969) (Can): 36 (1) (Reissue) Negl *1854
—— v Lavender (1965): 28 (1) (Reissue) Inc T 1218
——, R v (1973) (NZ): 45 Str Traf *1153p
—— v Victoria (State of) (1968) (Aus): 36 (1) (Reissue) Negl *1288
Clayton's Deed Poll, Re (1979): 19 (Reissue) Educ 4232
Clear, R v (1968): 15 (Reissue) Crim 11,633
—— v Smith (1980): 35 (Reissue) Nat Health & Soc Sec 6989
Cleary v Cleary (1974): 27 (1) H&W 2629b
—— v Cleary & Hutton (1974): 27 (1) H&W 2629b
—— v English China Clays Ltd (1974): 20 Empt 2658
Cleary v IR Comrs (1967): 28 (1) (Reissue) Inc T 1753
—— v Public Service Appeal Board (1973) (Can): 11 Const L *59e
Cleaveley, R v (1966) (Can): 14 (2) (Reissue) Crim *3495
Cleaver, Re (1981): 50 (Reissue) Willis 158
Cleaver v Insley (1981): 50 (Reissue) Wills 158
Cleghorn, R v (1967): 14 (1) (Reissue) Crim 2790
Clein, R v (1975): 14 (1) (Reissue) Crim 2014
Clemens v Clemens Bros Ltd (1976): 9 Coys 4083a
Clement v Leslies Storage Ltd & MacDonnell (1979) (Can): 36 (1) Negl *3022a
Clement-Clarke International Ltd v Manley (1979): 20 (Reissue) Empt 3455
Clement-Davis v Inter GSA (1979): 43 Solrs 1612a
Clements v Doherty (1975) (NI): 14 (1) Crim *515a
——, R v (1967) (Can): 8 (2) (Reissue) Comwlth *720
—— v Rydeheard (1978): 3 Auct 2626a
Clemons v Stewart (1969): 36 (1) (Reissue) Nuis 128
Clendenning & Bd of Police Comrs for City of Belleville, Re (1976) (Can): 22 Evid *2361a
Cleobulos Shipping Co Ltd v Intertanker Ltd, The Cleon (1983): 43 (Reissue) Ship 10090
Cleon, The (1983): 43 (Reissue) Ship 10090
Clerco Compana Naviera SA v Food Corpn of India, The Savvas (1982): 43 (Reissue) Ship 10785
Clerk to Lancashire Police Committee, R v ex p Hook (1980): 33 (Reissue) LG 180
Clerkenwell Stipendiary Magistrate, R v ex p Mays (1975): 33 (Reissue) Mags 1351
Cleveland, Re (1966) (Can): 51 (Reissue) Wills 13010
Cleveland Petroleum Co Ltd v Dartstone Ltd (1969): 45 Trade 130aa
Cleveleys Investment Trust Co v IR Comrs (1975): 28 (1) Inc T 1453h
Cliff v Comr of Police of the Metropolis (1973): 15 (Reissue) Crim 8048
Clifford, R v (1969) (Can): 14 (2) (Reissue) Crim *4874
—— v Walker (1972): 37 (3) (Reissue) Prac & Proc 5086
Clifford Maersk, The (1982): 45 Time 346a
Clifford's Settlement Trusts, Re Heaton v Westwater (1980): 40 Sttlmts 1166c
Clifton Place Garage Ltd, Re (1970): 10 (Reissue) Coys 5910
Clifton Steam Trawlers Ltd v MacIver (Duncan) Ltd (1953) (Scot): 42 Ship *2366
Clinch v IR Comrs (1973): 28 (1) Inc T 1592b
Clinton, R v (1971) (Can): 30 (Reissue) Intox *1483
Clipper Maritime Co Ltd v Mineralimportexport, The Marie Leonhardt (1981): 28 (2) Injon 79t; 37 (3) (Reissue) Prac & Proc 3437
Clissold & Testator's Family Maintenance Act, Re (1970) (Aus): 24 (Reissue) Exors 7566
Clixby v Pountney (1968): 28 (1) (Reissue) Inc T 2000
Clode v Barnes (1974): 46 Trade Mks 1142d
—— v LCC (1914): 26 (Reissue) Hghys 3238
Clore (dec'd), Re (1982): 23 Exors 8542; 26 G&E Tax 156a
Clore v IR Comrs (1967): 28 (1) (Reissue) Inc T 1474
Close, Re (1972) (NI): 17 (Reissue) Defence *34
—— v Globe & Mail Ltd (1967) (Can): 45 Trade *608ae
Clothier, Re (1970) (1971) (NZ): 37 (1) (Reissue) Perps *945
Clothing Reference, Re (1966): 45 Trade 235db
Cloudfoam Ltd v Toronto Harbour Comrs (1969) (Can): 1 (1) (Reissue) Admin L *276
Cloudfoam Ltd & Federal By-Products Corpn v Toronto Harbour Comrs (1969) (Can): 1 (1) (Reissue) Admin L *276
Clough v Clough (1968): 37 (1) (Reissue) Pldg 1644
Cloverlawn Investments Ltd v Corpn of District of Burnaby (1972) (Can): 45 T&CP *54dd
Clowes ex p (1977): 14 (2) Crim 7499a
Clowser v Chaplin (1981): 45 Str Traf 330a (ii)
Club Coffee Co Ltd v Moore-McCormack Lines Inc, Moore-McCormack Lines (Canada) Ltd & Eastern Canada Stevedoring (1963) Ltd (1968) (Can): 41 Ship *540a
Club Two Ltd v Ongakusha Ltd (1983): 45 Trade 288e
Cluney, R v (1971) (Can): 45 Str Traf *1035qcc
Clyde & Co v Secretary of State for the Environment (1977): 45 T&CP 46c
Clyne v East (1967) (Aus): 8 (2) (Reissue) Comwlth *1091
—— v Stamp Duties Comr (1967) (Aus): 39 Revenue *415a
Coach, R v (1971) (Can): 45 Str Traf *1035qiii
Coalite & Chemical Products Ltd v Treeby (1971): 28 (1) Inc T 1453d
Coard v National Westminster Bank Ltd (1980): 24 Exors 7712a
Coast Ferries Ltd v Century Insce Co of Canada (1974) (Can): 29 (Reissue) Insce *2344
—— v Coast Underwriters Ltd (1971) (Can): 29 (Reissue) Insce *2249
Coast Homes Ltd, Re (1972) (Can): 5 (Reissue) Bkpcy *3730
Coast Lines Ltd v Hudig & Veder Chartering NV (1972): 11 (Reissue) Confl 834; 37 (2) (Reissue) Prac & Proc 1848
Coast Realties Ltd v Nolan (1971) (Can): 35 (Reissue) Mtge 3156
Coastal Equipment Agencies Ltd v Comer (Ship) (1970) (Can): 1 (1) (Reissue) Adm *792
Coates v Crispin (CJ) Ltd (1973): 20 (Reissue) Empt 4647; 45 Trade 1510b
—— v Modern Methods and Materials Ltd (1982): 20 Empt 3388a
Coats's Trustees v Lord Advocate (1965) (Scot): 21 ED *137a
Cobb v Whorton (1971): 39 Revenue 141a
—— v Williams (1973): 45 Str Traf 205d
Cobbold v Time Canada Ltd (1980) (Can): 44 Sp Pfce *57a
Cobiac v Liddy (1969) (Aus): 45 Str Traf *1053d
Coburg Hotel v LCC (1899): 38 (Reissue) Pub Hlth 740
Coburn v Coburn (1971) (Can): 27 (2) (Reissue) H&W *2948
Coca-Cola Co v William Struthers & Sons Ltd (1968) (Scot): 46 Trade Mks *167a
Coca-Cola Export Corpn v Registrar of Trade Mks (1969) (E Af): 46 Trade Mks *65g
Cochlan Estate, Re (1969) (Can): 29 (Reissue) Insce *3406
Cochrane v IR Comrs (1974) (Scot): 28 (1) Inc T *1135Ac
—— (District Assessor for District of) v Trans-Canada Pipe Lines Ltd (1971) (Can): 38 (Reissue) Rates 2737
Cochrane's Exors v IR Comrs (1974) (Scot): 28 (1) Inc T *1135Ac
—— v Lord Advocate (1974) (Scot): 28 (1) Inc T *1135Ac
Cockburn, R v (1968): 15 (Reissue) Crim 11,072
Cockle's Will Trusts, Re (1967): 51 (Reissue) Wills 8536
Cocks v Thanet District Council (1982): 26 Housg 5335a
Coco v AN Clark (Engineers) Ltd (1969): 28 (2) (Reissue) Injon 914
Cocomile v Toronto (Municipality of Metropolitan) (1968) (Can): 11 (Reissue) Comp Pche *228
Codd, Re (1975): 47 Trusts 2219b
Codd's Will Trusts, Re National Westminster Bank Ltd v Codd (1975): 47 Trusts 2219b
Coderque v Mutual of Omaha Insce Co (1970) (Can): 18 (Reissue) Discy *391
Coditel v SA Cine Vog Films (62/79) (1980): 13 Coprt 707A
Coe, R v (1969): 14 (1) (Reissue) Crim 1877; 14 (2) (Reissue) Crim 5489, 6303; 33 (Reissue) Mags 570
——, R v (1971) (Can): 14 (1) (Reissue) Crim *1272
Coenen v Payne (1974): 37 (3) (Reissue) Prac & Proc 3383
—— v Sociaal-Economische Raad (39/75) (1975): 21 (Reissue) EC 1756
Coffey v Coffey (1968) (Can): 27 (2) (Reissue) H&W *2935
Coffey's Registered Designs (1982): 46 Trade Mks 1261a
Cofone v Spaghetti House Ltd (1980): 20 (Reissue) Empt 4604
Cogan, R v (1975): 14 (1) (Reissue) Crim 691
Cogan Ltd & City of Toronto, Re (1974) (Can): 45 T&CP *62ca
Cohen, Re Cowan v Cohen (1973): 8 (1) (Reissue) Char 55
—— v Calgary (City) & Carma Developers (1967) (Can): 45 T&CP *54db
—— v Cohen (1970) (1971) (Can): 27 (2) (Reissue) H&W *2952
—— v Daily Telegraph Ltd (1968): 32 (Reissue) Libel 2331
—— v Mirror Newspapers Ltd (1968) (Aus): 32 (Reissue) Libel *917
—— v Nessdale Ltd (1981): 44 Sp Pfce 212a
—— v Nessdale Ltd (1982): 12 Contr 602c
—— (George) 600 Group Ltd v Hird (1970): 45 Str Traf 235ab
Cohn, Re National Westminster Bank Ltd v Cohn (1974): 51 (Reissue) Wills 13,841
Coin Sales Corpn's Appln (1970): 36 (2) (Reissue) Pats 1714
Colahan, Re Molloy v Hara (1967) (Ir): 51 (Reissue) Wills *10,224
Colbeam Palmer Ltd v Stock Affiliates Pty Ltd (1968) (Aus): 46 Trade Mks *341b

ILLUSTRATION 69
The Digest, Cumulative Supplement, 1984

small notional sum representing the pocket money he would have received from the husband over and above his upkeep and maintenance and that accordingly the proportion of the damages awarded under the 1976 Act which were attributable to the son should be £7,000, and the widow's proportion of those damages should not include the cost of the son's upkeep. *Held* (1) The proportion of the damages awarded under the 1976 Act which were attributable to the son was to be assessed on the basis of his estimated genuine dependency and not merely on his 'pocket money' dependency. Bearing in mind his extreme youth and that there would be a long dependency, the amount of his dependency and thus his damages under the 1976 Act should be £5,000 and the widow's damages under that Act.

(2) The living expenses which had to be deducted from the husband's lost earnings in the lost years in assessing the recoverable damages under the 1934 Act had to be calculated on the same basis as was used in calculating the family's dependency under the 1976 Act. It followed that only the husband's own living expenses, and not the expenses of maintaining his family, could be deducted from his lost earnings in the lost years in assessing the damages under the 1934 Act and that, as his own living expenses had been agreed at 30% of his future earning for the purpose of the claim under the 1976 Act, the same proportion of his earnings was deductible as living expenses for the purpose of the claim under the 1934 Act. It followed that the same figure, £49,000, was recoverable under the 1976 Act as was recoverable under the 1934 Act. The £49,000 recoverable under the 1934 Act therefore comprised the husband's estate.

(3) Since the deceased had died intestate the widow's and the son's damages under the 1934 Act were to be determined according to the division of the estate on the intestacy. Under the intestacy the widow was entitled to the first £25,000 of the husband's estate and to a life interest in half the remainder of the estate, ie in £12,000 (the reversion to that half of the remainder going to the son) and the son, in addition to the reversion, was entitled to the other half of the remainder on the statutory trusts. It followed that under the 1934 Act and the effect of the intestacy the widow was entitled to damages of £36,750, namely £25,000 plus £11,750 as representing the value of her life interest less the value of the son's reversion (£250), and the son was entitled to damages of £12,250, namely £250, the value of his reversion on the widow's life interest, and £12,000, being the value of his entitlement under the intestacy to the other half of the remainder on the statutory trusts. Deducting the wife's damages under the 1934 Act (£36,750) from her damages under the 1976 Act (£42,500), it followed that she was entitled to £5,750 under the 1976 Act in addition to her damages under the 1934 Act. However, the amount of the son's damages under the 1934 Act extinguished his damages of £5,000 under the 1976 Act. Accordingly, the widow was entitled to judgment for the total sum of £54,750, namely (i) her damages of £36,750 under the 1934 Act (ii) her damages of £5,750 under the 1976 Act and (iii) the son's damages of £12,250 under the 1934 Act. BENSON v BIGGS WALL & CO LTD [1982] 3 All ER 300
Folld Harris v Empress Motors Ltd [1982] 3 All ER 306

Apld Harris v Empress Motors Ltd [1982] 3 All ER 306 **Folld** Clay v Pooler [1982] 3 All ER 570

1473ea ——— ——— ——— ——— The plaintiff's husband died as a result of a road accident and she brought a claim for damages under the Fatal Accidents Act 1976 on behalf of herself and her two daughters and under the Law Reform (Miscellaneous Provisions) Act 1934 on behalf of the deceased's estate. Liability was admitted but the question arose as to the calculation of the deceased's probable living expenses which were to be deducted from his probable earnings during the lost years in assessing the amount of any dependency under the 1976 Act. *Held* since money coming to a dependant from the deceased's estate was taken into account in computing the damages to be awarded under the 1976 Act, and therefore a dependent wife might get less from the estate than her entitlement under that Act, the defendant might have to make up the difference and pay more in damages than he would have had to had an award of damages been made in relation to one only of the claims; accordingly, the defendant had a direct interest in the computation of the two claims and in the distribution between dependants of the Fatal Accidents Act fund. The computation of the deceased's probable living expenses in the lost years was the same calculation as that used to arrive at personal living expenses in assessing dependency in respect of a claim under the 1976 Act. Further, since insurance moneys paid as a result of the deceased's death had to be disregarded in assessing damages under the 1976 Act, the appropriate procedure to be adopted where a deceased died intestate and his estate consisted partly of damages awarded under the 1934 Act and partly of such insurance moneys, was to divide the estate in accordance with the rules of intestacy and then deduct from each beneficiary's share a proportion of the insurance moneys in proportion to the amount of his share in the estate. CLAY v POOLER [1982] 3 All ER 570

1473f ——— ——— ——— ——— In assessing the damages recoverable by a deceased's estate under the Law Reform (Miscellaneous Provisions) Act 1934 for the deceased's loss of earnings in the 'lost years', ie the period of the deceased's pre-accident earning life expectancy, the deceased's living expenses in those years, which have to be deducted from his net earnings in those years in assessing the recoverable damages, are to be calculated on the same basis as a deceased's living expenses are calculated under the Fatal Accidents Act 1976 in assessing, on the basis of the deceased's future earnings, the amount of a claimant's dependency under the 1976 Act. The deductible living expenses from the earnings in the lost years for the purpose of the 1934 Act are, therefore, merely the living expenses which the deceased would have spent on himself and are not the whole of his expenditure on himself and his family during the lost years. It follows that the basis for an award of damages for lost earnings in the lost years under the 1934 Act is not confined to that proportion of the deceased's earnings which he would have been likely to save, or put indirectly into building up his wealth, after deducting the whole of his expenditure on himself and his family.

Faced with the situation that a plaintiff by suing under both the 1976 Act and the 1934 Act may be awarded a total sum larger than that which she could

3. SOLVING A LEGAL PROBLEM

(a) General

Important as it is to know how to look up reports of specific cases, much of your work in the study and practice of law will be concerned with the more complex task of solving legal problems. You may not know the names of any cases that will help you with a particular problem, so you cannot approach your research through a table of cases. You will have to try a different method.

Let us take a hypothetical case and consider how you would go about looking up the law concerning it. Suppose that a client (we will call him A) comes to you with the following set of facts.

A is the owner of a company that employs B as a salesman. A's company provides B with a car to make calls and deliveries and for limited personal use. On the day in question, B had been making calls in a town some distance away. It had been a long and trying day, and before setting out on his return journey, B stopped at a bar, where he had a few drinks. At this time his day's work was not finished as he had promised to call on a customer who lived on the outskirts of his home town. After leaving the bar, B picked up a hitchhiker, C, whose destination was the same as B's. According to B, C complained as soon as he was in the car that B was in no condition to drive. B, noting that the car's supply of gas was getting low, stopped at a service station to have the tank filled and suggested to C that if he did not like his driving, he should get out and find other transportation. C declined to do so. After leaving the service station, the car driven by B was involved in an accident, in which C was injured. Since the car that B was driving is owned by A's company, C is now suing not only B, but also A's company. A wants to know whether C's action against the company is likely to succeed. He hopes you can provide him with an adequate defence against it.

There are several questions to be considered. Does the owner of the car, as distinct from the driver, owe a duty of care at common law? Has the common law rule pertaining to this situation been modified by statute? If the owner owes a duty of care, does the fact that the driver of the car was an employee of the owner make any difference? What is the common law rule regarding this situation and has it been modified by statute? In accepting a ride from a person whose ability was clearly impaired by the use of alcohol and by remaining in the car when he had an opportunity to leave, was the hitchhiker guilty of contributory negligence? If so, what effect, at common law, does his contributory negligence have on the outcome of the case? Finally, has the common law rule relating to contributory negligence been modified by statute?

Let us begin with the question as to whether the owner of the car, as distinct from the driver, owes a duty of care at common law. The duty of care is a matter dealt with under the law of negligence, and for general guidance you may go to a text book on this subject. Assume, however, that you are practising law in Ontario and have decided to begin your research with the *Canadian Encyclopedic Digest (Ont. 3rd)*.

(b) The Canadian Encyclopedic Digest and Other Canadian Search Tools

The third Ontario edition of this legal encyclopedia began publication in 1973; by 1982 all 34 volumes, with one exception, had been published. The exception, volume 15, which is to contain the title, Income Tax, is scheduled for publication in 1985.

Unlike previous editions, the third is being issued in loose-leaf form, and is being updated on a regular basis. Supplements printed on yellow pages used to be filed at the front of each volume, but beginning with those published in 1984 there is a separate supplement for each title within a volume, and it is inserted at the beginning of the title. If a major revision relating to the law on a particular subject takes place, a completely new set of white main pages is issued. Sometimes the contents of a volume become so thick that a second volume lettered "A" has to be added to the set. For instance, volume 1 and 7 have expanded so much that there are now as well volumes 1A and 7A. With both the original pages and the replacements, the date of issue appears at the lower right hand corner of the front of each sheet. This method of updating makes *C.E.D. (Ont. 3rd)* a permanent work of reference. There will be no need to issue further completely new editions.

A useful feature of *C.E.D. (Ont. 3rd)* is the KEY, which consists of four parts: a contents key, a statutes key, a titles key, and a key-words index. The contents key contains a consolidation of the tables of contents of all titles in *C.E.D. (Ont. 3rd)* together with cross-references. The statutes key lists statutes alphabetically, indicating the volumes, titles, and paragraphs of *C.E.D. (Ont. 3rd)* in which references to them occur. In the titles key, the subject titles used in *C.E.D. (Ont. 3rd)* are listed, showing the volumes in which they appear and giving the respective title numbers. Subject titles that were used in *C.E.D. (Ont. 2nd)*, but that have been removed or incorporated into other titles in *C.E.D. (Ont. 3rd)*, are printed in italics, with *see* references being given, where appropriate, to their location in the third edition. The key-words index gives a detailed listing of topics, showing the volume and title numbers where they are discussed in *C.E.D. (Ont. 3rd)*.

The KEY used to be published in the same volume as the *C.E.D. Desk Book*, which contained useful reference materials of general interest to the legal practitioner in Ontario. Because the KEY has grown in size, the reference materials are now published in a separate volume called *The Lawyer's Desk Book*. Both the KEY and the *Desk Book* are replaced annually.

Because the first 30 volumes (with the exception of volume 15) of *C.E.D. (Ont. 3rd)* were published while the current revision of Ontario statutes was the *Revised Statutes of Ontario, 1970,* many titles in the set still refer to that revision. To assist readers in converting citations to or from the *Revised*

Statutes of Ontario, 1980, Carswell has provided *C.E.D. (Ont. 3rd)* subscribers with a volume of concordance tables, 1980-1970 and 1970-1980.

Depending on the nature of your research, you may go directly to a volume and title that you know and find what you want through the table of contents or index to that title. On the other hand, you may begin with the appropriate section of the KEY. Perhaps the key-words index requires a little more explanation. You should use it when you are starting your research without the aid of a known statute and are also uncertain of the subject title under which the information you need is likely to be found. Think of the words relevant to your subject and look them up in the key-words index. You will probably find one or more entries directing you to the volume and title that you need. You should next consult the index to that title. It will direct you to the paragraph or paragraphs that are likely to contain the information for which you are looking. Even if you know the title under which the main discussion occurs, the key-words index may still be helpful in directing you to references under other titles that may be relevant to your problem.

There are several ways in which you might begin your research on your client A's problem. Remember that you want to know whether the owner of the car, as distinct from the driver, owes a duty of care at common law. You might look up "duty of care" in the key-words index. The entry there notes that the subject is dealt with generally in volume 23, title 101, and that duty of care to passengers is considered in volume 4, title 23 (see Illustration 70). The second entry sounds promising, but on looking up title 23 in volume 4, you will find that it deals with "carriers". A carrier, whether common or private, is a person who carries for hire, and since neither the owner nor the driver in our hypothetical case was a carrier, the statements regarding duty of care to passengers in title 23 may not be relevant. You may, therefore, decide to try the general reference under "duty of care" in the key-words index; it, we have seen, is 23.101. Title 101 in volume 23 you will find to be "Negligence," the subject under which you would expect duty of care to be treated. Having located this title, you may either glance through the tables of contents at the beginning or look up "duty of care" in the index at the end of the title. Let us use the table of contents approach.

There are several entries that may be helpful; try first "III. Elements of Negligence, 2. Breach of Duty, §15." Refer to this paragraph and you will find that it tells you that "the duty to take care is the duty to avoid doing or omitting to do anything, the doing or omitting to do which may have as its reasonable and probable consequence injury to others, and the duty is owed to those to whom injury may reasonably and probably be anticipated if the duty is not observed." It is emphasized in the next paragraph that where there is no duty, there can be no negligence. As general statements these are useful, but they give you no guidance as to whether the owner of a car, as distinct from the driver, owes a duty of care to a passenger. You therefore go to another section that might be helpful. "V. General Principles and Defences, 10. Liability of Two or More Defendants, – §110". Here again the statements are general and give you little help with your specific problem. It seems probable that "IX.

ILLUSTRATION 70
Canadian Encyclopedic Digest (Ont. 3rd)
The Key to Volumes 1 to 34, 1985

THE KEY TO C.E.D.

doubtful title 29-130
dower 28-123
   Indians, and 16-77
   legacy in lieu of 12-59
   limitation period 19-87
   writ of assignment 12-58
double aspect rule 4-30
double jeopardy 7-39
draft wills
   admissibility 34-150
drainage 9-50, 28-122
drawbacks 8-41
drawings 13-62, 13-65, 24-107
Driver Improvement Program 14-70
driver's licences 14-70
driving instructor's licences 14-70
driving negligently or
     dangerously 7A-39.1
driving offences 30-132.1
driving timber 31-137
   see floating and driving timber
driving while disqualified 7A-39.1
drugging with intent 7A-39.1
drugs
   horse-races 13-67
   prescription 20-92
   regulation 23-100, 27-119
drunkards
   contracts 5-32
drunkenness 7-39
dual citizenship 4-27
due diligence 10-54
duration
   agency of 1-4
   annuity, of 1A-7
   contracts, of 5-32
   execution, of 12-58
   extended benefit period 33-145
duration of statutes 31-136
duress 5-32, 13-65, 29-127, 33-144
duties binding
   Crown, on 8-41
   Indians, on 8-41
duties of agent 1-4
duties of holders
   see rights and duties of holders
duty 8-41
duty and liability
   barristers, of 3-16
   broker and customer 30-132
   parents and guardians, of 10-52
   police, of 26-113
   sheriffs and bailiffs 30-133
duty of care
   generally 23-101
   passengers, to 4-23
duty of executor 12-59
duty to act fairly 1-3
duty to client 3-16

duty to extinguish fires 13-63
duty to give hearings 1-3
duty to inform oneself 9-47
duty to warn of fires 13-63
Dyer v. Dyer, rule in 33-144
dying declaration 11-57
earliest time for 9-48
earnings
   see also earnings, allocation; and
     interruption of earnings 33-145
   allocation 33-145
   children, of 16-78
easements 9-51
   affected by boundaries 3-19
   condominiums, and 4-27.1
   contracts for 31-135
   equity, and 10-55
   highways, over 14-71
   injunction re 16-79
   limitation period 19-87
   mining 20-94
   nuisance and 23-102
   perpetuities and
     accumulations 25-109
   public utilities 27-120
ecclesiastical tribunals 4-26
economic interest, interference
     with 31-139
economic law 17-81
economic loss, pure, damages
     for 31-139
education 4-30, 16-77, 16-78
Education Act 20-94
educational allowances 1A-9
educational broadcasting 28-121
effect of non-registration or defective
   registration
   bills of sale, of 3-18
ejectment 28-123
ejusdem generis rule 31-136
elderly offenders 30-132.1
election 34-150, 34-151
   accused, by 7-39
   affirm, to 13-65
   equitable 10-55
   estoppel by 10-56
   injunction re 16-79
   remedy 29-127
Election Acts
   see strict construction 31-136
elections
   contributions 10-53
   controverted 10-53
   expenses 10-52
   gambling on result 13-67
   municipal 10-53, 22-98
   officers of association, of 1A-10
   rights of mental incompetents 20-93
   school boards 10-52

504

Ownership and Use of Goods and Dangerous Agencies" will provide more assistance, for it includes a subsection dealing with motor vehicles. However, when you look up "3(g) Motor Vehicles," paragraphs 317 to 326, you will find nothing about the specific topic in which you are interested. A footnote reference to "Highway Traffic" and the directive "See the text generally for cases arising from the use of motor vehicles, most of which cases relate to factual situations that occurred in Ontario," give you the clue that you should be looking at the title "Highway Traffic" instead of the title "Negligence". If you had begun your research by looking up "motor vehicles" instead of "duty of care" in the key-words index, you would have found immediately that the topic is treated generally in volume 14, title 70 (see Illustration 71). On looking it up, you would have found that title 70 is "Highway Traffic". The sub-heading, "negligence 23-101" under "motor vehicles" in the key-words index might, however, have led you instead to the negligence title.

Assume now that by whatever method of research you have arrived at 14 *C.E.D. (Ont. 3rd)* and are looking at "Title 70, Highway Traffic". You might check the table of contents at the front of the title, where you will find that section X is headed "Civil actions" and that its first two sub-headings are "Liability for loss or damage" and "Meaning of owner" (see Illustration 72). In fact, the information you want is contained in the first two paragraphs under "Liability for loss or damage". Paragraph 234 tells you that at common law the driver owes a duty to use reasonable care for the safety of a gratuitous passenger, but that the owner, if not driving the vehicle, is not liable merely because he is the owner. It goes on to explain in what circumstances the owner may be liable (see Illustration 73). The preceding paragraph – 233 – states the current statutory provisions in Ontario. Under s. 166(1) of the Highway Traffic Act, the driver's duty of care is the same as it was at common law, but the owner's has been changed. Both owner and driver are now equally liable for loss or damage sustained by any person by reason of negligence in the operation of a motor vehicle unless the vehicle was without the owner's consent in the possession of some person other than the owner or his chauffeur. (Clearly this exception does not apply to your client A, since B was driving the car with the authorization of the company.) It is further explained in paragraph 233 that an earlier statutory exception to this rule with regard to gratuitous passengers was repealed in 1977, but continues in force regarding a cause of action arising before the date. Under the repealed provision, the owner or driver of a motor vehicle was not liable for loss or damage sustained by a gratuitous passenger unless it was caused or contributed to by the gross negligence of the driver (see again Illustration 73). Title 70, Highway Traffic, is one that has been revised recently (see notes in lower right hand corners of Illustrations 72 and 73) so it refers to the Highway Traffic Act in the *Revised Statutes of Ontario, 1980.* With regard to the gross negligence provision, it must, however, refer back to the numbering in the *Revised Statutes of Ontario, 1970* because this provision was repealed before the *Revised Statutes of Ontario, 1980* came into force.

ILLUSTRATION 71
Canadian Encyclopedic Digest (Ont. 3rd)
The Key to Volumes 1 to 34, 1985

THE KEY TO C.E.D.

ILLUSTRATION 72
Canadian Encyclopedic Digest (Ont. 3rd)
Volume 14 – Table of Contents to Title 70

CLASSIFICATION OF TITLE

ILLUSTRATION 73
Canadian Encyclopedic Digest (Ont. 3rd)
Volume 14 – Title 70

X Civil Actions

1. LIABILITY FOR LOSS OR DAMAGE

§233 The owner of a motor vehicle is liable for loss or damage sustained by any person by reason of negligence in the operation of the motor vehicle unless the motor vehicle was without the owner's consent in the possession of some person other than the owner or his chauffeur, and the driver of a motor vehicle not being the owner is liable to the same extent as the owner.[1]

> 1.   Highway Traffic Act, s. 166(1). In respect of passengers, s. 132(3) of R.S.O. 1970, c. 202 was repealed in 1977 but continues in force regarding a cause of action arising before 1977, c. 54, s. 16 came into force. The subsection read: "(3) Notwithstanding subsection 1 [now s. 166(1)], the owner or driver of a motor vehicle, other than a vehicle operated in the business of carrying passengers for compensation, is not liable for any loss or damage resulting from bodily injury to, or the death of any person being carried in, or upon, or entering, or getting on to , or alighting from the motor vehicle, except where loss or damage was caused or contributed to by the gross negligence of the driver of the motor vehicle." The effect of the repeal is to establish absence of negligence as the standard of care to be exercised by drivers towards gratuitous passengers.

§234 At common law the driver of an automobile owes a duty to a passenger being carried gratuitously in the automobile to use reasonable care for his safety, and if as a result of negligent driving the passenger is injured the driver is liable to him for the damages suffered. If the automobile belongs to someone other than the driver that person is not liable at common law merely because he is the owner; his liability, if it exists, must be found in a relationship between him and the driver which renders him liable for the latter's negligence or in a relationship between the owner and the passenger which imposes on the former a duty to take care for the safety of the latter.[2]

> 2.   *Co-operators Ins. Assn. v. Kearney*, [1965] S.C.R. 106 at 127. For example, at common law the owner of a motor vehicle was liable for the negligence of his driver or chauffeur occurring in the course of the employment, and the ordinary principles of the law of master and servant applied in such a case. But the owner was not liable for the negligence or other default of one who was using the vehicle simply with his permission and, a fortiori, without his permission: see *Bernstein v. Lynch* (1913), 28 O.L.R. 435 (C.A.); *Lowry v. Thompson* (1913), 29 O.L.R. 478 (C.A.). However, the enactment of the predecessor of this section imposed upon the owners of motor cars a civil liability in excess of the common law liability, the aim being to place responsibility where it would be effective, by casting the burden of ensuring safety, so far as possible, upon the owner who has dominion over the vehicle and who has it in his power to choose the person to whom he entrusts it, and mkaing him responsible for all loss and damage sustained in the operation of the vehicle: see *Falsetto v. Brown*, [1933] O.R. 645 (C.A.); *Downs v. Fisher* (1915), 33 O.L.R. 504 (C.A.); *Thompson v. Bourchier*, [1933] O.R. 525 (C.A.).

You now know that before the repeal of the gross negligence provision in Ontario's Highway Traffic Act, your client A would not have been held liable for C's injuries unless it was found that they were caused or contributed to by the gross negligence of the driver B. Now A may be liable if B's conduct was simply negligent. Assuming that the accident occurred after the repeal of this provision, the defence of your client is likely to be more difficult than it would have been had the accident occurred earlier.

For additional related information you may want to read subsequent paragraphs in the section "Civil Actions" in title 70 in 14 *C.E.D. (Ont. 3rd)* and you should also check the yellow page supplement for any updating. To be sure that *C.E.D. (Ont. 3rd)* has accurately described the provisions in s. 166(1) of the Highway Traffic Act you should also check the official text in the *Revised Statutes of Ontario, 1980.* In fact, you will find that the wording in the two is identical.

Of course, you will check the *Ontario Statute Citator* or the table of public statutes in the latest annual volume of the *Statutes of Ontario* and bills that have been passed, but are not yet included in the statute books, to make sure that there have been no recent amendments to s. 166. But it appears that, in preparing your case, you will have to consider the possibility of proving that the accident and C's resulting injuries were not caused by B's negligence.

Before considering what constitutes negligence in the operation of a motor vehicle and trying to determine whether B's conduct could be so described, it is, however, necessary to take another factor into account. Now that it is known that the owner of the car will be held liable for the hitchhiker's injuries if they were caused, or contributed to, by the driver's negligence, it becomes relevant to find out whether the fact that the driver was an employee of the owner will have any effect on the outcome of the case. Was the driver, at the time the accident occurred, acting as an agent of the owner? For guidance on this point, you might turn to "Title 4 – Agency" in volume 1 of *C.E.D. (Ont. 3rd).* If you did not know the title to consult, you might have used the key-words index, but assume that, in this case, you have gone directly to the title "Agency". Look first at the "Classification of Title" at the beginning. Section VII dealing with "Rights and Liabilities between Principal and Third Person" will probably be the most helpful; two entries under this heading seem most likely to give you information on the point of law in which you are interested. They are "3. Principal's liability for agent's unauthorized acts, §338" and "4. Principal's liability for agent's negligence, §343" (see Illustration 74). The numbers 338 and 343 refer to paragraphs. Look first at paragraph 338. It tells you that "a principal is liable for the unauthorized acts of an agent done in the course of an authorized employment" and that "the doctrine applies to incorporated companies as well as to individuals". This statement seems to relate directly to your problem, for presumably giving a ride to the hitchhiker was an unauthorized act of the driver done in the course of his authorized employment; he was still engaged in making calls on behalf of his principal, the company, at the time he picked up C. But when you read the definition of an unauthorized act in paragraph 338, you will be less convinced that the term

ILLUSTRATION 74
Canadian Encyclopedic Digest (Ont. 3rd)
Volume 1, Title 4

AGENCY

(d) Officer of company, §110
(e) Insurance agent, §112
(f) Other examples, §124
6. Apparent or ostensible authority, §128

V Rights and Liabilities Between Principal and Agent, §148
1. Agent's duties, §148
(a) To perform personally, §148
(b) To follow instructions, §158
(c) To exercise care and skill, §169
(d) To act in good faith, §175
(e) Secret profits, §181
(f) Full disclosure, §192
2. Liabilities of agent, §207
(a) To account, §207
(b) With respect to principal's property, §213
3. Indemnity of agent, §217
4. Agent's lien, §220

VI Remuneration of Agent, §221
1. Earning of commission, §221
(a) Right to commission, §221
(b) Disentitlement to commission, §232
(c) Agent the effective cause of sale, §240
(d) Finding purchaser ready, willing and able, §258
(e) Special and general employment, §263
(f) Principal's right of independent sale, §266
(g) Where sale not carried out, §268
(h) Time in relation to commission, §285
2. Principal's interference or breach of agency contract, §292
3. Commission on sale of real estate, §310

VII Rights and Liabilities between Principal and Third Person, §321
1. Principal's liability for agent's fraud and misrepresentation, §321
2. Knowledge of agent attributed to principal, §331
3. Principal's liability for agent's unauthorized acts, §338
4. Principal's liability for agent's negligence, §343
5. Principal's liability for agent's contracts, §344
6. Payment by third person to agent, §348
7. Estoppel of third person as against principal, §353
8. Third person's liability for agent's breach of duty to principal, §354

C.E.D. (3rd) Title 4 2

"unauthorized act" applies to B's action in picking up C. "An unauthorized act is within the scope of an agent's employment when it is so directly incidental to some act or class of acts which the agent was authorized to do that it may be said to be a mode, though an improper mode, of performing them." (See Illustration 75.) Note that cases that support the statement made in paragraph 338 are cited in footnotes to this paragraph; at this point, you will probably want to read them to see whether they give you further guidance. Alternatively, before going directly to reports of the cases, you might look up digests of them in volume 1 of the *Canadian Abridgment (2nd)*. This will give you an idea of whether they are likely to be helpful. Moreover, since the *Canadian Abridgment* digests cases from all Canadian jurisdictions, you may find grouped with those for which you are looking, persuasive authorities from other jurisdictions that are not given in the mainly Ontario-based *C.E.D.* Remember, though, that if a case relates to several aspects of the law, it may be digested more than once in the *Canadian Abridgment*. For instance, the case *Sheppard Publishing Co. v. Press Publishing Co.*, which is listed in three footnotes to paragraph 338 under title 4 – Agency – in *C.E.D. (Ont. 3rd)*, is digested four times, from different points of view, in volume 1 of the *Canadian Abridgment (2nd)*, once under "Actions" and three times under "Agency". The digest contained in paragraph 2508 is most relevant to your problem. This is mentioned simply to emphasize that if you are interested in a particular point of law, you must be sure you are looking at the correct group of digests.

More relevant to your problem is paragraph 343, which deals with "Principal's liability for agent's negligence". "A principal is liable for the negligence of his agent in the course of his employment, whether or not he has authorized the negligent act, and even if he has expressly forbidden it." (See Illustration 76.) Whether or not B's action in picking up C was "an unauthorized act" as defined in paragraph 338, it seems clear from the first sentence in paragraph 343 that A's company will be held liable for C's injuries if it can be proved that B's conduct in driving the car while intoxicated constituted negligence. Once again, however, the second sentence may give you hope that you can provide A's company with an adequate defence, for "the principal is not liable for negligence committed beyond the scope of the agency, unless he has expressly authorized the acts to be done, or has subsequently adopted them for his own use and benefit".

Since paragraph 343 relates directly to the point of law in which you are interested, it is important that you read the cases cited in footnote 42 (see again Illustration 76) to see if there are any distinguishing factors that are likely to be helpful in your defence of A's company. The main line of defence seems to be that although B picked up the hitchhiker during his working hours and while engaged in carrying out his agency, giving a ride to a hitchhiker was outside the scope of his agency, rather than an unauthorized act within the scope of his authorized employment. It may also be helpful for you to see whether the cases cited in footnote 42 have been judicially considered in later cases. Look them up in the cases judicially considered volumes in the second

ILLUSTRATION 75
Canadian Encyclopedic Digest (Ont. 3rd)
Volume 1, Title 4

PART VII – PRINCIPAL AND THIRD PERSON   §340

§337 Where a commercial partnership was dissolved and a company formed, notice of change given to the plaintiff's selling agent was held notice to plaintiff.[30]

> 30. *Malkin & Co. v. Crossley* (1923), 32 B.C.R. 207 (C.A.); see also *Gelhorn Motors Ltd. v. Yee* (1969), 71 W.W.R. 526 (Man. C.A.) (the mere fact that one member of the supplier's accounting staff received a cheque signed in the corporate name of the buyer did not fix the supplier with knowledge that the original partnership had been superseded and taken over by the company).

3. PRINCIPAL'S LIABILITY FOR AGENT'S UNAUTHORIZED ACTS

§338 A principal is liable for the unauthorized acts of an agent done in the course of an authorized employment;[31] the doctrine applies to incorporated companies as well as to individuals.[32] An unauthorized act is within the scope of an agent's employment when it is so directly incidental to some act or class of acts which the agent was authorized to do that it may be said to be a mode, though an improper mode, of performing them.[33]

> 31. *Sheppard Publishing Co. v. Press Publishing Co.* (1905), 10 O.L.R. 243 (C.A.); *Craig v. Sauve and Payette*, [1939] O.W.N. 591 (C.A.). See also *Can. Laboratory Supplies Ltd. v. Engelhard Industs. of Can. Ltd.*, [1979] 2 S.C.R. 787; varied on rehearing on other grounds, [1980] 2 S.C.R. 450 (employee of appellant purchasing metal from respondent as part of employee's fraudulent scheme; title passing to appellant upon delivery in ordinary course of filing of proper purchase orders; employee having no authority to make such transactions; appellant's agent referring respondent to employee amounting to holding out to respondent that employee had apparent authority).
>
> 32. *Sheppard Publishing Co. v. Press Publishing Co., ante.*
>
> 33. *Sheppard Publishing Co. v. Press Publishing Co., ante,* at p. 249. See also as regards the liability of a principal for the negligence of his agent, below, §343.

§339 The measure of the principal's liability is the same as if the agent's wrongful act had been committed by himself and is the amount of loss suffered as a result of it.[34]

> 34. *Sheppard Publishing Co. v. Press Publishing Co., ante,* at p. 252.

§340 A company is liable for purchases made by its agent in excess of the quantity authorized if the agent has acted within his apparent authority and the limitation upon it has not been communicated.[35] Where an agent, authorized to purchase an object for his principal, buys something entirely different, the transaction is enforceable by the innocent vendor; the agent has received exactly what he bargained for, and there is no mistake as to the subject-matter.[36] An agent employed to sell

173

ILLUSTRATION 76
Canadian Encyclopedic Digest (Ont. 3rd)
Volume 1, Title 4

4. PRINCIPAL'S LIABILITY FOR AGENT'S NEGLIGENCE

§343   A principal is liable for the negligence of his agent in the course of his employment, whether or not he has authorized the negligent act, and even if he has expressly forbidden it.[42] But the principal is not liable for negligence committed beyond the scope of the agency, unless he has expressly authorized the acts to be done, or he has subsequently adopted them for his own use and benefit.[43]

42.   *Consol. Mining & Smelting Co. v. Murdoch*, [1929] S.C.R. 141, leave to appeal to Privy Council granted, [1929] W.N. 237 (P.C.). See also *Rosen v. Kitchener*, [1935] O.R. 522 (S.C.); *Majorcsak v. Na-Churs Plant Food Co.; Lammens v. Majorcsak*, [1968] S.C.R. 645; *G.R. Young v. Dom. Ins. Corp.*, [1979] I.L.R. 1-1157 (B.C. S.C.); *Fenn v. Peterborough* (1979), 25 O.R. (2d) 399 (C.A.).

As to a principal's liability for acts of an independent contractor, see *Kerr v. T.G. Bright & Co.*, [1939] S.C.R. 63.

For the liability of a master for the acts of his servant, see *Yepremian v. Scarborough Gen. Hosp.* (1980), 28 O.R. (2d) 494 (C.A.).

43.   *Kelly v. Wawanesa Mut. Ins. Co.* (1979), 30 N.S.R. (2d) 294 (C.A.); *O'Donnell v. Lumbermen's Mut. Casualty Co.*, [1979] I.L.R. 1-1057 (Ont. Co. Ct.).

5. PRINCIPAL'S LIABILITY FOR AGENT'S CONTRACTS

§344   When a person contracts in the name of another and gives the name of his principal, the contract so made is considered the contract of the principal, and involves no liability on the part of the agent, unless the other circumstances of the case lead to the conclusion that he has either expressly or impliedly incurred, or intended to incur, such personal responsibility.[44] The onus of establishing the authority of an agent is upon the person who seeks to bind the principal.[45]

44.   *Bell v. Rokeby* (1905), 15 Man. R. 327 (K.B.); and see *Carlstadt Dev. Co. v. Alta. Pac. Elevator Co.* (1912), 4 Alta. L.R. 366 (S.C.) (sale in name of agent known to vendor's agent); *Armstrong v. Oliver Ltd.*, [1933] 2 W.W.R. 462 (Sask. C.A.) (liability of principal for storage of goods by agent on third party's premises; absence of privity of contract); *Metz v. Con-Stan Can. Inc.* (1982), 16 Sask. R. 270 (Q.B.) (Canadian subsidiary company of American corporation managing plaintiff, promoting her, and finally terminating her employment on authorization of joint board of directors of both companies; Canadian company agent of American corporation; action for wrongful dismissal only against the latter); cp. *Saab Inc. v. Shipping Ltd.*, [1976] 2 F.C. 175 (T.D.); affirmed [1979] 1 F.C. 461 (C.A.). See also §§357-362.

45.   *Stevens v. Merchants Bank* (1920), 30 Man. R. 46 (C.A.) (bank manager guaranteeing repayment of loan from third party to bank's customer); *Tanouye v. KJM Devs. Ltd.* (1981), 25 A.R. 200 (Q.B.).

As to the authority of an agent, see §§77-85, 93-96, 128-147.

Similarly the principal may sue, e.g., for the price of goods sold by the agent to the third party, in which event the third party cannot set-off a claim against the agent to such action by the principal; nor is it material whose agent the third party thought him edition of the *Canadian Abridgment*. The four-volume main set lists judicial considerations to the end of 1973. Information on later judicial considerations is contained in permanent supplements to these volumes and in the "Cases Judicially Considered" section in the loose-leaf Appendix, which consists of a white page annual release and a coloured page Quarterly Release. For still more recent information, see the "Cases Judicially Considered" tables in the monthly issues of *Canadian Current Law*. Note that the tables of cases judicially considered in the *Canadian Abridgment* list not only Canadian cases, but also cases decided in other jurisdictions that are cited in Canadian cases.

The fact that only cases are cited in the footnotes to paragraphs 338 and 343 in title 4 of *C.E.D. (Ont. 3rd)* indicates that the liability of principals for the actions of their agents is governed entirely by common law; there has (or had at the time these paragraphs were written) been no modification by statute. Note the date (month and year) on the front of each sheet in the lower right hand corner (see again Illustrations 75 and 76). In fact the May 1984 revision of title 4 – Agency arrived as I was updating this section of Chapter 4; thus, at the time of writing there was no yellow page supplement at the beginning of the title to check for more recent information. At a later date it will be necessary to look up paragraphs 338 and 343 in such a supplement for more recent cases relevant to the subject and to be sure that no statutory provision has been passed concerning it. To update the yellow page supplement or the main pages until a supplement appears, check the monthly issues of *Canadian Current Law*.

When your research on the agency aspect of your problem is complete, you will probably not be sure whether you can provide A's company with an adequate defence on the grounds that B, in picking up the hitchhiker, was acting outside the scope of his agency. In case you cannot, it is important that you consider other possible defences. One of these is that B's conduct was not negligent. Thus, your next task is to find out what constitutes negligence in the operation of a motor vehicle.

To determine this, you will want to read cases in which the facts were similar to those in the situation you are considering. When the gratuitous passenger-gross negligence provision was in force, your best plan would have been to check what was then s. 132(3) of the Highway Traffic Act in the *Ontario Statute Citator* or in the statutes judicially considered tables in the *Canadian Abridgment (2nd)* and *Canadian Current Law*. Now, however, it is better to avoid cases in which gross negligence was an issue and to concentrate on those in which it was sufficient to prove ordinary negligence. The accident need not involve injuries to a gratuitous passenger, since whether the injuries were suffered by a gratuitous passenger, or indeed by a passenger at all, has become irrelevant. An accident in which a pedestrian or an occupant of another vehicle was injured by a car in which the driver was under the influence of alcohol would be relevant. If you find such a case in which the driver has had a few drinks but, in spite of this, was not found negligent, it may help in your client's defence.

To find such cases, use the general index to the *Canadian Abridgment (2nd)*. It is not a key-words index, so if you look up "alcohol" or "intoxication", you will find nothing. There is a subject heading "intoxicating liquors," but it is clear from the entries under it that it does not relate to your problem. You might try "motor vehicles". There are many entries under this subject heading, including "care, duty of – *see care, duty of*". This directs you to "care, duty of," as a main heading, rather than as a sub-heading under "motor vehicles". Look up that heading in the general index and you will find a sub-heading "disabilities of driver," one of which is "intoxication" (see Illustration 77). Several paragraphs in volume 27, the volume devoted to the subject "motor vehicles", are listed. (You would have found the same entries if you had gone directly to the index at the back of volume 27.) Look them up and see if any are likely to be helpful. You will note from the index entries that two of the numbers relate to cases that deal with the meaning of intoxication. They may be especially useful. Illustrations 78 and 79 show some of the digests to which the index refers you. Those most likely to relate to your problem have been underlined. You should read the full reports of these cases and, if they are relevant, see if they have been judicially considered in later cases. You should also check volume 4 (1975-79) of the general index, which supplements the original three volumes, and the cumulative supplement for later cases on the same subject. The digest of the case in paragraph 1499 (see again Illustration 79) shows you that sometimes it is necessary to refer to a case in a jurisdiction outside Canada – in this case the United States – for guidance if nothing on the subject can be found in Canadian cases.

After all your research, you will probably be uncertain whether B's conduct in driving the company car will be held to have been negligent. You will prepare a good case attempting to prove that it was not, but in the event that you lose on this point, what are the chances of proving that C, the hitchhiker, was guilty of contributory negligence? And if C is so judged, what effect does this have on the company's liability?

In your general research on the duty to take care and your study of what constitutes negligence in the operation of a motor vehicle, you undoubtedly came across references to contributory negligence. If you go back to the article on negligence in volume 23 of *C.E.D. (Ont. 3rd)*, you will find from the table of contents at the beginning that Section VI deals with contributory negligence. Subsection 1, beginning with paragraph 142, pertains to contributory negligence at common law. "Simply stated," it declares, "the common law rule was to the effect that a plaintiff in a negligence action was wholly debarred from recovery if it could be shown that his own negligence contributed in any way to the accident giving rise to his claim." This common law rule has, however, been modified by legislation, and subsection 3, beginning at paragraph 173, outlines the provisions of Ontario's Negligence Act. As a result of its provisions, states paragraph 173, "a finding of contributory negligence on the part of the plaintiff is no longer a complete bar to his claim." Paragraph 174 explains the matter further:

ILLUSTRATION 77
Canadian Abridgment (2nd), General Index, Volume 1

CARE, DUTY OF

care, duty of—cont.
  motor vehicle operator, of—cont.
    animals on highway, for—cont.
      small animals, stopping to avoid
        27.1696
      strayed animals 27.1675, 1676,
        1691-3
    breach of
      emergencies, in
        "agony of collision" 27.1726-36,
          1747, 1755, 1767; S3.67385
        create, duty not to 27.1743-9
        immediate or abnormal hazard
          27.1738-42
        obligation in 27.1725
        reasonable care, duty to use
          27.1754-62
        standard of care required 27.1730,
          1731, 1737
        voluntary risk to avoid, incurring
          27.1749-53
      inevitable accident, in
        blowout 27.1777
        brakes, failure of 27.2773-6;
          S3.67587
        burden of proof 27.1766, 1767
        definition 27.1763-7
        evidence 27.1784-8, 1790
        liability for 27.1780
        mistake of driver 27.1781
        non-repair of highway 27.1782,
          1783
        pleadings 27.1786, 1789
      steering mechanism failing 27.1778
      sudden fog 27.1779
      sudden unconsciousness of driver
        27.1768-72
    cyclists
      door of vehicle opening on 27.1670-2
      intersection, at 27.1660, 1661
      overtaken by vehicle 27.1662-5
      parking on highway S3.66860
      rights and duties of 27.1656
      statutory rules, application of
        27.1654, 1655
      through streets, entering 27.1668,
        1669
      turns, making 27.1657-9
      turns, vehicles making 27.1666-8
    dangerous highways, on
      condition of road, driver's duty as to
        27.1532-50; S3.67509, 67559
      construction work, where 27.1551-7
    degree of care required
      attention diverted 27.1467, 1468
      backing vehicle 27.1470-4
      children on highway S2.67609
      circumstances as varying 27.1429,
        1430, 1435-9
      disabled vehicle stopped on road
        shoulder S3.67384

elbow projecting 27.1463
failure to report traffic sign down
  27.1477
hands off wheel 27.1460-2, 1469
injured person lying in street
  S3.67538
lack of attention 27.1475, 1476
obedience of others, right to assume
  27.1447-9
pedestrian highway, towards
  S3.67586
starting vehicle in gear 27.1464-6
statutory rules, compliance with
  27.1440, 1441
towed vehicles 27.1456-9; S3.67409
traffic, special duty in 27.1442-6
unreasonable user of highway
  27.1450-5
disabilities of driver
  handicapped, when 27.1492
  health unsound, driving when
    27.1487-9; S3.67434
  intoxication 27.1492-7, 1500, 1501
    meaning of 27.1498, 1499
  sleepy, driving when 27.1490, 1491
  standard of skill and experience
    27.1478-86
highways, on—see duty and standard of
  care
lookout, keeping
  see also passengers; pedestrians;
    railway crossings; rules of the
    road
  approaching traffic, for 27.1594-6,
    1600, 1601; S3.67386
  children, for 27.1597, 1598
  eyes on road, keeping 27.1570-3
  intersection, at 27.1574-8, 1590,
    1595; S3.67534, 67535
  primary duty, as 27.1558-62
  pulling out from curb 27.1599
  rear-end collisions 27.2583-8, 1600;
    S3.67537
  stalled vehicles, for 27.1591, 1592;
    S3.67536
  stationary objects, for 27.1581-3
  unlighted obstructions, for 27.1579,
    1580, 1589, 1593
  view obscured 27.1563-9
speed, rate of
  see also offences and penalties, under
    motor vehicles; passengers,
    gratuitous, under motor vehicles;
    rules of the road
  blinding headlights, speeding with
    27.1633, 1634
  close to vehicle ahead, driving too
    27.1626-8, 1630
  contributing to negligence, as
    27.1631, 1632
  defective equipment 27.1614

212

ILLUSTRATION 78
Canadian Abridgment (2nd), Volume 27

[1490-1495]   MOTOR VEHICLES

could not escape responsibility merely by convincing himself that he had no serious ailment or no knowledge of the risk. It was not the want of care at the exact time of the accident that was the overall operative factor in cases of this kind, but the question of whether or not defendant had knowledge of some serious defect which might have led to a grave risk in certain circumstances. The deceased had failed to do what a reasonable man would have done in his place, namely, to refrain from driving the car on the particular occasion. TURNER'S TRANSFER LTD. v. ANDERSON (1962), 48 M.P.R. 84, 37 D.L.R. (2d) 399 (N.S. C.A.).

1490. Continuing to drive when becoming sleepy. A motorist who knows or should realize that he is tending to fall asleep is negligent in continuing to drive while in that condition. Therefore where his defence to an action for damages is that he was asleep at the time of the accident the onus is on him to show that his state of unconsciousness resulted from such sudden, unexpected and overpowering causes that he had no opportunity of averting the accident by guarding against the physical or mental condition which caused him to go to sleep. *Semble*, there should be corroboration of such a contention. LAJIMODIERI v. PRITCHARD AND DUFF, [1938] 1 W.W.R. 305 (Man.).

1491. A motor car in which plaintiff was riding as a passenger overturned, and plaintiff was injured. The driver had been up for at least 36 hours, and had been driving almost continuously for 17 or 18 hours on busy highways before the accident occurred. Judgment was recovered against the driver on grounds other than his unfitness to drive for want of rest. Fisher J.A., pointed out that it would not be speculation or conjecture, but a reasonable inference, to hold that the driver was either unfit, or that it was in the circumstances dangerous for him to drive, but that if the maxim *volenti non fit injuria* had been pleaded and argued he would have held plaintiff not entitled to recover, because he willingly and knowingly associated himself with danger in submitting to be driven by a person in the condition of this driver. ANDANOFF v. SMITH AND NADEFF, [1935] O.W.N. 415 (C.A.).

1492. Driver having artificial hand — Negligent in starting car when intoxicated and with handicap — Car owner not

negligent in allowing driver to sit in front seat with key in ignition. MACDONALD v. MITCHELL (1969), 2 N.B.R. (2d) 165, 10 D.L.R. (3d) 240, varying 1 N.B.R. (2d) 563 (C.A.).

1493. Intoxication as affecting driver's liability — Effect of statutory provisions. In this case, the situation in which a driver found himself was attributed by the Court to lack of attention and care on the driver's part in the management of the car, due at least in part to intoxication. *Held*, it was this negligence on the part of defendant amounting to gross negligence which brought about the accident and resulting injuries to plaintiff. Per Mitchell J.A.: "I have reached my conclusion from considerations quite apart from the fact that the defendant was guilty of a breach of s. 59 of the [Vehicles and Highway Traffic] Act, 1924 (Alta.), c. 31, which forbids intoxication on the part of a person whilst driving a motor vehicle, though I think that circumstance might in itself be sufficient to render the defendant liable." BURGESS v. HODGINSON, [1929] 2 W.W.R. 21, [1929] 3 D.L.R. 133 (Alta.).

1494. In an action arising out of a motor vehicle collision the trial Judge made no finding as to whether defendant driver was intoxicated on the grounds that such evidence was irrelevant since intoxication was not negligence. On appeal, *held*, a new trial should be ordered solely on the issue of liability. While intoxication was not *per se* negligence and it would have to be shown that the intoxication resulted in the negligence which caused the accident, evidence of intoxication was relevant to the weight and credibility of the driver's testimony and would thus be relevant to the question of liability. GUZYK v. LANE AND PEDERSON (1962), 37 D.L.R. (2d) 480 (B.C. C.A.).

1495. Conflicting evidence — Weight accorded evidence of party who had been drinking — Conduct of driver after accident. Where, in an action for damages arising out of an automobile accident, there is conflicting evidence, greater weight should be given to the evidence of the party who had not been drinking than to that of the party who is shown to have indulged even in moderate drinking, because of the effect such drinking would have on his powers of observation and his skill and efficiency as a driver in an emergency. In this case, the conduct of the driver of one ot the

ILLUSTRATION 79
Canadian Abridgment (2nd), Volume 27

DUTY OF CARE   [1496-1500]

cars in leaving the scene of the accident without reporting to the police, and in leaving the city immediately, was considered to be such as to impair confidence in his credibility.

VALIN v. EMPEY, [1942] 1 W.W.R. 381 (Alta.).

1496. Defendant appealed against a judgment arising out of an automobile collision on the grounds, *inter alia*, that the trial Judge erred in holding s. 48*a* of the Automobile Accident Insurance Act, R.S.S. 1953, c. 371 as enacted by 1957, c. 100, s. 1 (which provided for the conclusive proof in a civil action of a driver's impairment by filing his conviction therefor) retrospective. *Held*, the appeal should be dismissed. S. 48*a* provided that evidence is admissible to prove a conviction of defendant under s. 222 or 223 of the Criminal Code, 1953-54 (Can.), c. 51, and that the proof of such conviction shall be conclusive evidence that the person so convicted was at the time of the offence operating a vehicle while under the influence of intoxicating liquor or drugs to such an extent as to be for the time being incapable of the proper control of the vehicle. As the section related to procedure only and no vested right was affected the section was retrospective.

ROBERTSON v. WRIGHT (1958), 26 W.W.R. 337, 16 D.L.R. (2d) 364 (Sask. C.A.).

1497. Sufficiency of evidence as to intoxication. The fact that a person was in company with others who were intoxicated and had the opportunity, had he so desired, to get in that condition, did not justify a finding that he was intoxicated while driving a car at the time an accident occurred. Nor could the fact that he had been in a beer parlour that evening be regarded as *prima facie* evidence of intoxication. A smell of liquor on his breath was not noticed; and there was evidence that he was sober, and no evidence that he had been drinking or was intoxicated, save his own admission that he had had a drink of ale earlier in the evening. *Held*, a finding that he was driving while intoxicated was not justified on the evidence.

PEAT v. WALSH, 54 N.B.R. 36, [1927] 2 D.L.R. 1120 (C.A.).

1498. Meaning of "intoxication". There are degrees of "intoxication" and pliable definitions of the word. A person is "intoxicated" within the meaning of a statutory condition in a policy of automobile insurance, relieving the insurer from liability

when the car is being driven by a person while intoxicated, when such person is not in a fit state to drive a car because of the too free use of liquor.

McKNIGHT v. GEN. CASUALTY INS. CO., [1931] 2 W.W.R. 315, 44 B.C.R. 1, [1931] 3 D.L.R. 476, affirming [1930] 3 W.W.R. 73, 43 B.C.R. 177, [1930] 4 D.L.R. 816 (C.A.).

1499. Per Macdonald J.: "I have not been afforded any judicial definition of 'intoxication', in Canada." He quoted as follows from 33 Corpus Juris at p. 802, as to the law in the United States: "'Intoxication' is a broad and comprehensive term, having a different meaning to different persons. . . . In the absence of any controlling definition, the word should be given a reasonable interpretation, having reference to the purpose of the instrument in which it is used. . . . According to some definitions the words may be applied to any mental exhilaration, however slight, produced by alcohol without regard to its effect on the judgment or reasoning process." And from *Elkin v. Buschner*, 16 Atl. R. 102, at 104: "Whenever a man is under the influence of liquor, so as not to be entirely himself, he is intoxicated. Although he can walk straight, attend to his business, and may not give any outward and visible signs to the casual observer that he is drunk, yet if he is under the influence of the liquor so as not to be himself, so as to be excited from it, and not to possess that clearness of intellect and control of himself that he otherwise would have, he is intoxicated."

GEN. CASUALTY INS. CO. v. LAMBERT, [1930] 2 W.W.R. 548, 43 B.C.R. 133, [1930] 3 D.L.R. 1007.

1500. In an action upon a policy of automobile insurance, the trial Judge found, on the evidence, that the insured was, at the time an accident occurred, driving while intoxicated, and that by reason of the quantity of liquor he had consumed, he was unable to drive with safety. These findings, in the light of the trial Judge's reasons were held clearly to involve the conclusion that the accident was due to such intoxication. The fact that the insured was "manifestly" intoxicated while driving disentitled him, on grounds of public policy, from recovery

Where the court is unable to determine that the ultimate fault or neglect of any one of the parties was the direct or proximate cause of the damage to the exclusion of fault or neglect on the part of each of the others and finds that it was contributed to by the fault or neglect of each of the parties to the action in different degrees, in such circumstances, the Ontario Legislature has imposed upon the court the duty of determining the degree in which each party was at fault or negligent, although it must have anticipated that it cannot be done with mathematical precision and that such determination can only be attempts at fair estimates.

Paragraph 175 explains that the Negligence Act was designed to cover only cases in which contributory negligence was formerly a defence (more correctly an absolute defence) and should not be extended to other situations. It also notes that the words "fault" and "negligence" in the Act are synonymous and mean simply "negligence".

At the time of writing, the main pages of title 101 – Negligence were dated May 1979 and the yellow-page supplement, June 1984. If you check the supplement's entry for paragraphs 173-175, you will find references to recent cases to be added to the footnotes to these paragraphs. None of them, however, seems especially relevant to your problem. You will also want to look at the text of the Negligence Act in the *Revised Statutes of Ontario, 1980.* Entries for the Act in the *Ontario Statute Citator* and legislative bills should also be checked for possible amendments subsequent to the latest *C.E.D. (Ont. 3rd)* supplement.

When your research on this point is complete, you will know that if B's conduct is held to have been negligent, but you succeed in proving that C's negligence contributed to his own injuries, both your client A's company and B will have to pay a portion of the damages awarded by the court, the percentage depending on the degree of C's contributory negligence.

You will now have the answer to your questions regarding C's contributory negligence if it can be proved. It remains for you to determine your prospects of proving it. You will want to read cases decided under Ontario's Negligence Act or in other jurisdictions having similar statutory provisions relating to contributory negligence. You have seen some cited in the footnotes to the relevant paragraphs in *C.E.D. (Ont. 3rd).* Another place to look for the names of Ontario cases is under the Negligence Act in the *Ontario Statute Citator,* since it not only gives the text of amendments, but also notes judicial considerations from 1981 to date. The *Citator* will also refer you to a companion Canada Law Book publication, *Ontario Statute Annotations* for cases from 1930 to 1980. Another alternative – and indeed it is wise to check several sources – is to look up Ontario's Negligence Act in volume 2 of the *Canadian Abridgment's* Statutes Judicially Considered. This volume deals with the statutes of the various provinces. The Statutes Judicially Considered volumes are updated annually and quarterly in the loose-leaf Appendix and by bound permanent supplements.

You might also check the General Index to the *Canadian Abridgment* for cases dealing with contributory negligence. This will give you cases not only from Ontario, but also from other Canadian jurisdictions. Such cases may be persuasive if the statutory provisions relating to contributory negligence are the same.

You will notice that sometimes a defendant in a motor vehicle case pleads that the plaintiff, in accepting a drive from him, knowing that he was under the influence of alcohol, voluntarily assumed the risk involved. It may even happen that both this defence and that of contributory negligence are raised on the chance that if one fails, the other may succeed. If the court accepts the defence *volenti non fit injuria* (voluntary assumption of risk) the plaintiff's action fails, whereas if the plaintiff is found guilty of contributory negligence, the defendant may still be held to some degree liable for the plaintiff's injury and be required to pay a percentage of the damages. You will want to consider whether you should raise the defence of *volenti non fit injuria* on the grounds that the hitchhiker, in accepting a ride from a driver who was obviously under the influence of alcohol and in refusing to leave the car when he had an opportunity to do so, voluntarily assumed the risk involved.

The manner in which we have gone about solving this hypothetical legal problem is by no means the only way in which it can be approached. If you are practising law in one of the western provinces, you might have begun your research with *C.E.D. (Western)*. The third edition of this legal encyclopedia, which began publication with volume 12 (title 58 – Evidence) in 1978, is described on its title pages as "A complete statement of the law of the provinces of Western Canada as derived from the cases and statutes." Many additional volumes have now been published. The text is much the same as in *C.E.D. (Ont. 3rd)* – though there are differences – and the emphasis in footnotes is on cases decided or originating in the western provinces. *C.E.D. (West. 3rd)* is, like *C.E.D. (Ont. 3rd)*, being issued in loose-leaf form. Until all volumes of the third edition are issued, the second edition of the western service is used in conjunction with it.

(c) Halsbury's Laws of England

Whatever the province in which you are practising and however you begin your research, you may still want to check other legal encyclopedias and digests to be sure that you have missed no relevant point of law. Suppose, for instance, that you have decided to do some reading on contributory negligence and voluntary assumption or risk in the well-known English encyclopedia, *Halsbury's Laws of England*. The fourth edition of this work began publication in 1973; at the time of writing in 1984 all volumes except 45 and 51-52 had been published. Since the index at this time covered only volumes 1-32 and the title "Negligence" is contained in volume 34, your best plan would be to go to the index at the back of that volume. Volume 34 includes titles from "Negligence" to "Parliament," but the index is divided by title so that all entries relating to the negligence title are found together. There are entries under both "contributory negligence" and "*volenti non fit injuria*". You decide to look up the entry "contributory negligence, plea of, distinguished from maxim" under "*volenti non fit injuria*"; it directs you to paragraph 62. You look at it and as the next paragraph appears to relate closely to it, you continue reading and find a statement that a passenger who travels in a motor car does not necessarily accept the risk of negligent driving even though he knows that the driver is under the influence of alcohol. This is certainly relevant to your problem and you see that the statement is followed by footnote 7, which refers you to the case of *Dann v. Hamilton,* [1939] 1 K.B. 509, and to a later case in which it was judicially considered.

For references to still more recent cases (volume 34 of the fourth edition of *Halsbury's Laws* was published in 1980 and is up to date to 1 July of that year) you should consult the cumulative supplement. The 1984 supplement, which was current at the time of writing, cites under volume 34, paragraph 63, a 1981 case to be added to footnote 7 (see Illustration 80). For further updating, look up the same volume and paragraph numbers in the Key to the current loose-leaf service to *Halsbury's Laws of England* (the Key is included in the loose-leaf volume). At the time of writing there was one entry "D 104" under paragraph 63 (see Illustration 81). The prefix "D" followed by a number refers you to a paragraph in one of the monthly reviews filed in the current loose-leaf service. (An entry with the prefix "EE" would refer you to the Noter-Up, also in this service.) Paragraph 104 is found in the monthly review for November 1983. The case digested there does not seem very relevant to your problem, but note that an Australian case, digested in paragraph 105 relates to contributory negligence and intoxication in collision cases. The digest suggests that it may be helpful to you (see Illustration 82). Case D105 updates paragraphs 68 to 75 of volume 34, which you would probably also have read while doing research on contributory negligence.

To find out whether there have been Canadian cases dealing with the same subject, you can use the Canadian Converter volumes to *Halsbury's Laws of England,* but the process is rather complicated because they relate to the third edition rather than the fourth. To use them you must first see if the information on English law contained in the fourth edition is also included in the third edition, where the title "Negligence" is found in volume 28. In fact, you will find the statement in which you are interested (which appears in paragraph 63 of volume 34 of the fourth edition) in paragraph 88 on pages 82-83 of volume 28 of the third; the case of *Dann v. Hamilton* is cited in footnote (d). From there you can go to the relevant Canadian Converter volume. These volumes are lettered "A" and each covers five volumes of the third edition of *Halsbury's Laws.* Thus they are numbered 5A, 10A, 15A, *etc.* Since the title "Negligence" is contained in volume 28 of the third edition, you will find information concerning the Canadian law on this subject in volume 30A; now current is the seventh replacement dated 1984. Turn to volume 28, paragraph 88 in Canadian Converter volume 30A and you will find two Canadian cases cited under footnote (d) (see Illustration 83). They are *Stein v. Lehnert* (1962), 36 D.L.R. (2d) 159 (S.C.C.) and *Taylor v. Peterson* (1975), 12 N.S.R. (2d) 646. The letters "S.C.C." in the first entry tell you that it is a Supreme Court of Canada case; this makes it especially important that you read the report of it, if you have not already done so in your earlier research.

ILLUSTRATION 80
Halsbury's Laws of England, 1984 Cumulative Supplement

Part 2.   Situations in which a Duty of Care Arises

20   Who is a visitor
Note 2—*Greenhalgh v British Railways Board*, cited, applied in *Holden v White* [1982] QB 679, [1982] 2 All ER 328, CA (no duty owed by landowner to person who uses private right of way over land in exercise of dominant owner's rights).

21   Duty of occupier
Note 3—See also *Wheeler v Copas* [1981] 3 All ER 405 (ladder); *Kealey v Heard* [1983] 1 All ER 973 (scaffolding).

32   Liability of professional advisers
Text and Notes 2, 3—A local authority was further held liable when its building inspector negligently required the foundations of a building to be of a depth which was insufficient to satisfy the building regulations and to protect the building from damage by movement of the subsoil: *Acrecrest Ltd v WS Hattrell & Partners* [1983] QB 260, [1983] 1 All ER 17, CA.
Note 2—*Anns v Merton London Borough Council*, cited, did not approve *Sparham-Souter v Town and Country Developments (Essex) Ltd*, cited, as the main issue in the former case was whether any duty was owed by the local authority; see *Pirelli General Cable Works Ltd v Oscar Faber & Partners (a firm)* [1983] 2 AC 1, [1983] 1 All ER 65, HL.

33   Liability of owners after disposal of premises
Note 4—*Sparham-Souter v Town and Country Developments (Essex) Ltd*, cited, has now been overruled; see *Pirelli General Cable Works Ltd v Oscar Faber & Partners (a firm)* [1983] 2 AC 1, [1983] 1 All ER 65, HL.

37   Nature of duty
Notes 1, 10—See now *Lexmead (Basingstoke) Ltd v Lewis* [1982] AC 225, 1 All ER 1185, HL.

41   Articles entrusted to third persons
Note 1—See also *Wheeler v Copas* [1981] 3 All ER 405 (loan of ladder for building work).

53   The nature and scope of the duty
Text and Note 4—See *JEB Fasteners Ltd v Marks, Bloom and Co* [1983] 1 All ER 583, CA (duty of care owed by auditors).
Note 4—See also *Yianni v Edwin Evans & Sons (a firm)* [1982] QB 438, [1981] 3 All ER 592, where it was held that valuers instructed by a building society to value a property owed a duty of care to the prospective purchasers, because it was within the valuers' reasonable contemplation that carelessness on their part might be likely to cause the purchasers damage.

Part 3.   Civil Proceedings and Remedies

54   Proving negligence
Text and Notes 11–13—See *Clark v Maclennan* [1983] 1 All ER 416 (onus of proof shifted to defendant where departure from accepted practices shown).

57   Inference of defendant's negligence
Note 3—See *Kealy v Heard* [1983] 1 All ER 973 (planks placed on scaffolding by unknown workman collapsed when plaintiff walked on them).

60   Occurrences that cannot without carelessness
Notes 1, 6—See *Kealey v Heard*, para 57, note 3, ante.

63   Application of the defence
Note 7—See also *Ashton v Turner* [1981] QB 137, [1980] 3 All ER 870.

66   Limitation of actions
Text and Notes—Legislation relating to limitation of actions consolidated by Limitation Act 1980; see LIMITATION OF ACTIONS.
Text and Note 1—Now ibid, s 2.
Notes 2, 4, 6, 7—Now ibid, ss 11, 12, 33.

3

ILLUSTRATION 81
Halsbury's Laws Current Service

VOLUME 33—cont.			Key			VOLUME 35	
PARA.	KEY NO.	PARA.	KEY NO.	PARA.	KEY NO.	PARA.	KEY NO.
771	D1593	914	EE67	5	G80b	**Open Spaces and**	
774	D685	916	HH101	5	G382	**Historic Buildings**	
774	G431	925	D134	5	EE1922	420	EE826
778	D1861	925	D1853	6	D804	421	EE827
779	D554	927	EE1484	6	G80b	427–429	EE828
779	D1131	927	HH102	6	G81	429A	EE829
779	G430	928	D840	6	G212	430	EE830
781	G432	929	EE70	6	G382	431	EE831
782–797	EE1307	930	EE71	7	G81	448	D1252
796	EE1308	931	EE72	7	EE1012	487	D1253
798–810	EE1309	932	EE73	8	D1056	556	EE1310
798	G104	933–941	HH103	8	D1195	562	EE832
800	D1275b	960	EE315	9	D1599b	590–652	EE833
805	G242	963–972	EE1810	10	D806	601	EE834
810	D1591	963	EE2034	10	D1103	637	EE1526
811–823	EE1044	973–989	EE971	11	D805	638	EE1527
812	D303	973–1012	EE611	11	D1103	639	EE1528
816	D303	973	HH220	11	EE391	640	EE1529
819	D303	982	EE1523	12	D268	654–656	EE835
821	G421	988	EE1524	12	D269	657	D656
834	D305	989	EE1525	12	D804a	657	EE836
834	D306	990–1001	EE1011	12	D1248	660	D656
834	D844	1015	D1004	12	D1249	662	G82
834	D1741	1021	D1794	12	D1712	662	EE837
834	EE572	1022	G422	12	G80a	674	EE838
839	D1741	1026	D1794	12	EE1112	675	EE1196
840	EE573	1027	D1067	18–30	D970	677	EE839
842	EE574	1028	D421	21	D271a	678	EE840
859	D679	1028	D1002a	22	D271a	683	EE841
859	D843	1028	D1067	22	D498	683A	EE842
859	D1003a	1028	D1670	30	D271a	685	EE1811
863	D1590	1028	G41	32	EE2112	686	EE1197
865	D548	1029	D421	33	D497	687–1000	EE835
871	EE610	1029	D1002a	36	EE1261		
874	EE1194	1038	D421	37	G81a	**Parliament**	
875	EE1195	1049	D421	40	G81a	1111–1113	EE1198
877	D1855	1049	D1275	44	D270	1112	EE1113
878–890	HH288	1049	EE214	53	D269	1123–1136	D1714
881	EE1045	1054	D1004	53	G212	1123	EE1870
882	EE1045	1054	D1794	57	D1248	1124	EE1871
892	D1856	1057	G41	59	D1248	1126	EE1872
892	EE575	1058	D1670	63	D104	1129	EE1873
893	EE576	1060	G422	65	D104	1135	EE355
894	D136	1066	D1067	67	D970	1136	EE1874
894	D300	1069	D1863	67	G211	1435	HH221
894	D1740			67	HH268	1486	EE1199
895	D301			68–75	D105	1501	D1834
895	D1856			68	D270		
895	G106	**VOLUME 34**		68	D803		
897	EE1482	**Negligence**		73	D1711	**VOLUME 35**	
898	D1740	2	D271	75	D1711	**Partnership**	
898	EE1046	4	G80b	76	D1711	97	D1713
899	EE1046	4	G81	94	G27	106	G85
901	EE1483	4	EE2111	96	G27	107	G85
903	EE448	5	D106			141	EE845
904	EE448	5	D271	**Nuisance**			
908	EE68	5	D497	317	D1104	**Patents**	
908	HH99	5	D969	332	D807	328	D1396
909	HH100	5	D1560	362	EE612	339	D658
913	EE66	5	D1712				

The prefixes D and G indicate the Reviews, and EE and HH the Noter-up

ILLUSTRATION 82
Halsbury's Laws Current Service

contending that the judge had not considered the desirability of maintaining the status quo, and that he should have interviewed the children. *Held*, the judge had considered the conflicting emotions involved and all the consequences of changing the past arrangements. He had exercised his discretion and decided it best not to see the children. The welfare report showed that one boy wanted to stay with his father and the other to go to his mother, and there was no perfect solution. The Court of Appeal would not substitute its opinion for that of the judge. He had not been plainly wrong in the exercise of his discretion or in his decision, and the appeal would be dismissed.

CLARKE-HUNT v NEWCOMBE (1983) 4 FLR 482 (Court of Appeal: CUMMING-BRUCE LJ and BUTLER-SLOSS J).

See Halsbury's Laws (4th edn), Vol 24, paras 546, 564

MORTGAGE

D102 Article

Further Implications of Section 36 of the Administration of Justice Act 1970, Alison Clarke: [1983] Conv (NS) 293.

NATIONAL HEALTH SERVICE

D103 District health authority—members—power to seek consent to termination of appointment—exercise of power

A district health authority took certain decisions in relation to cuts in health service funding. The regional health authority considered that the decisions were not in the interests of the health service and the chairman wrote to the members of the district authority asking them to support a resolution to rescind the decisions. He indicated that if they did not co-operate he would seek the consent of the Secretary of State to their removal from office, pursuant to the relevant regulations. He further asked them to inform him how they intended to vote. Two members of the district authority made an application for judicial review contending that the regional authority's action was ultra vires its powers. *Held*, the regulations empowered a regional authority to seek the removal of a district member who had voted for a course of action which the former held to be prejudicial to the health service, but they did not empower a regional authority to direct district members how to vote and such members were under no obligation to inform the regional chairman of how they intended to vote. It was not unreasonable for the regional authority to threaten to exercise that power, even though members might be pressurised into voting in a certain way. The chairman's letter did not amount to a premature exercise of that power as it did not indicate an immediate intention to seek a member's removal but merely warned that the power would be exercised under certain circumstances. Accordingly the regional authority had not acted ultra vires and the application would be dismissed.

R v NORTH WEST THAMES REGIONAL HEALTH AUTHORITY, EX PARTE NERVA (1983) Times, 20 October (Queen's Bench Division: FORBES J).

See Halsbury's Laws (4th edn), Vol 33, para 155

NEGLIGENCE

D104 Consent—volenti non fit injuria—knowledge of risk—subjective test

It has been held that where a defence of volenti non fit injuria is relied upon, the test of whether the plaintiff had a full appreciation of the nature and extent of the risk is a subjective one, although the test of whether he consented to run that risk is objective. Furthermore, in assessing damages for personal injuries, there must be a real risk that the plaintiff will lose his present job in the future, before damages for handicap on the labour market may be awarded.

LATCHFORD v SPEDEWORTH INTERNATIONAL LTD (1983) Times, 11 October (Queen's Bench Division: HODGSON J). *Harrison v Vincent* [1982] RTR 8, CA, 1981 Halsbury's Abridgment

ILLUSTRATION 82 (Cont'd.)

para 2091 and *Moeliker v A Reyrolle & Co Ltd* [1977] 1 All ER 9, CA, 1976 Halsbury's Abridgment para 782 applied.

See Halsbury's Laws (4th edn), Vol 34, paras 63, 65

D105   Contributory negligence—intoxication in collision cases—relevant consideration

Australia

It has been held that intoxication of a party to a collision on a highway is a relevant consideration when determining the question of contributory negligence, if such intoxication is proved to have caused the intoxicated party to pay insufficient regard to his own safety at the time of the collision.

KILMINSTER v RULE (1983) 32 SASR 39 (Supreme Court of South Australia).

See Halsbury's Laws (4th edn), Vol 34, paras 68–75

D106   Duty of care—employer—duty to provide handrail

It has been held that where there is a foreseeable risk that an employee, in the course of his employment, might slip on steps and injure himself, the employers have a duty at common law (i) to take precautions against his slipping and (ii) to provide, for example, a handrail which could prevent injury in the eventuality of his slipping.

HALSEY v SOUTH BEDFORDSHIRE DISTRICT COUNCIL (1983) Times, 18 October (Queen's Bench Division: KILNER BROWN J).

See Halsbury's Laws (4th edn), Vol 34, para 5

D107   Duty of care—highway authority—flood control

In overtaking a car, a van driver hit a large pool of water, caused by flooding, and lost control of the van. Two men were killed and three others injured. In answer to allegations of negligence, the van driver contended that the highway authority was liable for what had occurred. *Held*, the flooding was a serious hazard which could reasonably have been predicted having regard to the prevailing weather conditions and the low lying nature of the road; the authority had direct knowledge of the serious extent of the flood from both the police and their own employees. They had failed to take any proper steps to alleviate it and one flood sign sited in a nearby lay-by was not an adequate warning. They were accordingly liable in negligence, to be apportioned two-thirds to the authority and one-third to the van driver.

MORRIS v THYSSEN (GB) LTD (1983) 20 May (unreported) (Queen's Bench Division: BOOTH J).

See Halsbury's Laws (4th edn), Vol 21, para 198

D108   Remoteness of damage—foreseeability—act of third party—novus actus interveniens

Canada

The defendant was operating a tractor for the purpose of stockpiling gravel. He left it unattended while taking a break and left the key in the ignition and the cab unlocked. When he returned the tractor was missing. It had been set in motion by another person and had crashed into the side of the plaintiff's dwelling house. The plaintiff claimed damages. *Held*, there was no evidence to show that the defendant could reasonably have foreseen criminal intervention on the part of a third party. The damage was not caused by the defendant's negligence but by a novus actus interveniens. The plaintiff's claim would be dismissed.

HEWSON v CITY OF RED DEER (1977) 146 DLR (3d) 32 (Supreme Court of Alberta).

See Halsbury's Laws (4th edn) Vol 12, paras 1141, 1143

PARLIAMENT-

D108a   Bills in progress

Private members bills are marked * and are not included until read a second time.

ILLUSTRATION 83
Halsbury's Laws of England, 3rd ed.
Volume 30A – Seventh Replacement

85–90   HALSBURY—CANADIAN CONVERTER   **[Vol. 28**

Para. Nos.

85.   **Meaning of inevitable accident.**
See *Lapierre's General Trucking Ltd.* v. *Broad and Province of New Brunswick Board of School Trustees, District No. 29* (1977), 18 N.B.R. (2d) 680, affd. (1978), 21 N.B.R. (2d) 516; *Vandervolk* v. *Craig*, [1978] 5 W.W.R. 180 (Alta.); *Shaw* v. *Martin* (1979), 19 A.R. 45.

(*a*) See *Robinson* v. *Carter*, [1950] 2 W.W.R. 1077 (Alta.); *Carvalho* v. *Baldwin* (1962), 33 D.L.R. (2d) 21, 6 B.O.D. Repl., Key 255.

(*d*) But see *Edwards* v. *Arbeau* (1962), 38 D.L.R. (2d) 319 (N.B.).

86.   **Proof of inevitable accident.**
(*l*) See *Hatfield* v. *Pearson* (1956), 7 D.L.R. (2d) 593, 20 W.W.R. 580 (B.C.); *Rintoul* v. *X-Ray & Radium Industries Ltd.*, [1956] S.C.R. 674, 6 B.O.D. Repl., Key 252, 8 B.O.D. Repl., Key 2197; *Aubrey* v. *Harris* (1957), 7 D.L.R. (2d) 545, [1957] O.W.N. 133, 6 B.O.D. Repl., Keys 253, 354, 8 B.O.D. Repl., Keys 2113, 2199.

88.   **Application of the defence.**
See *Fairweather* v. *Canadian General Electric Co.* (1913), 28 O.L.R. 300, 7 B.O.D. Repl., Key 2724; *Lamu* v. *Joki*, [1938] 3 D.L.R. 754, 8 B.O.D. Repl., Key 1891; *Hill* v. *Baade*, [1933] 3 W.W.R. 592 (Sask.); *Carnegie* v. *Trynchy* (1966), 57 W.W.R. 305 (Alta.); *Benjamin* v. *Boutilier* (1970), 17 D.L.R. (3d) 611 (N.S.); *Myers and Myers* v. *Peel County Board of Education and Jowett* (1977), 2 C.C.L.T. 269 (Ont.); *Stermer* v. *Lawson*, [1977] 5 W.W.R. 628 (B.C.); *Ferris Estate* v. *Stubbs* (1977), 19 N.B.R. (2d) 651; *Shaw* v. *Martin* (1979), 19 A.R. 45.

(*q*) See *Jennings* v. *Davies*, [1934] 1 W.W.R. 686, affd. [1934] 2 W.W.R. 587 (Alta.); *Mahoney* v. *City of Guelph* (1918), 43 D.L.R. 490, 43 O.L.R. 313, 8 B.O.D. Repl., Key 1762; *Halaska* v. *University of Saskatchewan* (1965), 52 W.W.R. 608 (Sask.).

(*r*) *Lewitt* v. *Fletcher* (1975), 12 N.B.R. (2d) 221.

(*d*) *Stein* v. *Lehnert* (1962), 36 D.L.R. (2d) 159 (S.C.C.); *Taylor* v. *Peterson* (1975), 12 N.S.R. (2d) 646.

(*f*) See *Carl* v. *Warren*, [1959] O.W.N. 249; affd. [1960] O.R. 213, 7 B.O.D. Repl., Keys 2574, 2682, 2735.

90.   **Limitation of actions.**
(*t*) N.B.—See Limitations of Actions Act, R.S.N.B. 1973, c. L-8, ss. 5,9.
NFLD.—See Limitation of Actions (Personal) and Guarantees Act, R.S.N. 1970, c. 206. s. 2.
N.S.—See Limitation of Actions Act, R.S.N.S. 1967, c. 168, s. 2 (am. 1982, c. 33).
P.E.I.—Statute of Limitations, R.S.P.E.I. 1974, c. S-7 (am. 1978, c. 6).
SASK.—Limitation of Actions Act, R.S.S. 1978, c. L-15, s. 3.

(*u*) ALTA.—See Limitation of Actions Act, R.S.A. 1980, c. L-15, ss. 4, 5.
N.B.—See Limitation of Actions Act, R.S.N.B. 1973, c. L-8, ss. 5, 9.
SASK.—See Limitation of Actions Act, R.S.S. 1978, c. L-15, s. 3.

(*b*) ALTA.—See Limitation of Actions Act, R.S.A. 1980, c. L-15, s. 8.
N.B.—See Limitation of Actions Act, R.S.N.B. 1973, c. L-8, s. 18.
NFLD.—See Limitation of Actions (Personal) and Guarantees Act, R.S.N. 1970, c. 206, s. 4 (am. 1971, c. 71; 1979, c. 39).
N.S.—See Limitation of Actions Act, R.S.N.S. 1967, c. 168, s. 3.
SASK.—See Limitation of Actions Act, R.S.S. 1978, c. L-15, s. 6.

(*d*) CAN.—See Canada Shipping Act, R.S.C. 1970. c. S-9, s. 722.

(*g*) ALTA.—See Limitation of Actions Act, R.S.A. 1980, c. L-15, ss. 4, 5.
NFLD.—Trustee Act, R.S.N. 1970, c. 380, s. 23.
N.S.—See Survival of Actions Act. R.S.N.S. 1967, c. 298, s. 4.
ONT.—See Trustee Act, R.S.O. 1980, c. 512, s. 38.
SASK.—See Trustee Act, R.S.S. 1978, c. T-23, s. 59.

(d) Further Research

You decide to do further research on the cases relating to contributory negligence and voluntary assumption of risk that you have found cited in *Halsbury's Laws of England*. We will use an English case, *Dann v. Hamilton*, and a Canadian case, *Stein v. Lehnert*, as examples. On looking up the report of the former in [1939] 1 K.B. 509, you find that the defendant (the widow of the driver, who was killed in the accident that caused the plaintiff's injuries) raised the defence "*volenti non fit injuria*" alleging that when the plaintiff entered the car she knew that the driver was under the influence of drink to such an extent as to be incapable of having control of the car.

The judge rejected this defence, explaining that, as a matter of strict pleading, the plea "*volenti*" is a denial of any duty at all and, therefore, of any breach of duty, and that an admission of negligence cannot strictly be combined with the plea. In this respect, he went on, it differs from the plea of contributory negligence, which was not raised in this case. However, he admitted that in some extreme cases the maxim "*volenti*" might apply to negligence. If the driver's drunkenness was so glaring that to accept a lift from him was like engaging in a dangerous occupation, there was a possibility that it might apply. However, it was unnecessary to decide whether it would, since he considered the driver's state of intoxication fell short of this degree.

The case of *Dann v. Hamilton* will not encourage you to plead as a defence that C, the hitchhiker, was "*volens*", but you consider it worthwhile to check whether the case has been judicially considered. If you look it up in the *Current Law Case Citator, 1947 to 1976* (a bound volume), you will find various references to its having been applied, not followed, considered, referred to and doubted (see Illustration 84). (To update the *Current Law Case Citator*, you should look at the case citator section of the *Current Law Citator*, which is replaced annually and in the monthly parts of *Current Law*.) The *Citator* also directs you to an article on the case in volume 38 of the *Canadian Bar Review* at page 107, which indicates that there has been much discussion and criticism of the decision. In the article you will find reference to earlier articles, including one in volume 55 of the *Law Quarterly Review* at page 184.[7] This article deals with the difference between contributory negligence and "*volenti non fit injuria*" and argues that the plaintiff in *Dann v. Hamilton* was guilty of contributory negligence and that judgment should

---

7   This article was published in 1939. It is not listed in the *Current Law Citator*, which covers the period from 1947. However, it should also be noted that the *Canadian Bar Review* article includes references to articles published after 1947 that comment on *Dann v. Hamilton*, but that are not listed in the *Current Law Citator* under the name of that case. It appears that the *Citator* lists articles that deal specifically with the case, but not more general articles that comment on that case along with others. Nor is a short but important note on *Dann v. Hamilton* published in 1955 in volume 69 of the *Law Quarterly Review* listed in the *Citator*, but this may have been an oversight.

ILLUSTRATION 84
Current Law Case Citator 1947-76

CASE CITATOR 1947–76	DAN

Danchevsky v. Danchevsky [1975] Fam. 17; [1974] 3 W.L.R. 709; 118
S.J. 701; [1974] 3 All E.R. 934, C.A. .... *Digested, 74/2911*

Dando (S. L.) v. Hitchcock [1954] 2 Q.B. 317; [1954] 3 W.L.R. 76; 98
S.J. 423; [1954] 2 All E.R. 335; [98 S.J. 468; 104 L.J. 820], C.A. *Digested, 54/2863*

D'Andrea v. Woods [1953] 1 W.L.R. 1307; 117 J.P. 560; 97 S.J. 745;
[1953] 2 All E.R. 1028; 37 Cr.App.R. 182, D.C. .... *Digested, 53/844*

Dandrick v. Central Electricity Generating Board (1960) 12 P. & C.R. 137,
Lands Tribunal .... *Digested, 61/1254*

Dandy v. Regent Stevedoring Co. [1964] 2 Lloyd's Rep. 128 .... *Digested, 64/2552*

Daneau v. Gendron (Laurent); Union Insurance Society of Canton (Third
Party) [1964] 1 Lloyd's Rep. 220 .... *Digested, 64/3422*

D'Angibau, Re (1880) 15 Ch.D. 228 ..: .... *Distinguished, 9346*

Daniel, Re [1917] 2 Ch. 405 .... *Distinguished, 5326*

——, Re [1945] 2 All E.R. 101 .... *Considered, 10864*

—— v. Hotel Pacific Pty. [1953] A.L.R. 1043; [17 M.L.R. 272].

—— v. Jones (1877) 2 C.P.D. 351 .... *Commented on, 341*

—— v. Skyrme (1951) 101 L.J. 541, Cty.Ct. .... *Digested. 3789*

Daniell v. Daniell, The Times, February 2, 1954, C.A. ....
Reported, 54/947: Subsequent proceedings, 55/785: Distinguished, 54/952

—— v. —— (No. 2), The Times, January 20, 1955 ....
Reported, 55/785: Previous proceedings, 54/947

—— v. Rickett, Cockerell & Co. [1938] 2 K.B. 322 .... *Followed, 10053*

Daniels v. Angus [1947] N.Z.L.R. 329 .... *Digested, 7019*

—— v. Davison (1809) 16 Ves.Jun. 249 .... *Applied, 74/3963*

—— v. Fielding (1846) 16 M. & M. 200 .... *Applied, 70/1040*

—— v. Ford Motor Co. [1955] 1 W.L.R. 76; 99 S.J. 74; [1955] 1 All
E.R. 218, C.A. .... *Digested, 55/1079*

—— v. Heskin (1953) 87 I.L.T. 189 .... *Digested, 54/2288*

—— v. Jackson and Gordon Hotels, The Times, October 10, 1956 .... *Reported, 56/4965*

—— v. Jones [1961] 1 W.L.R. 1103; 105 S.J. 568; [1961] 3 All E.R.
24; [77 L.Q.R. 470], C.A. .... *Digested, 61/2326: Considered,* 65/1012; 71/3233

—— v. Leyland (Frederick) & Co. [1951] 1 Lloyd's Rep. 59 .... *Digested, 6717*

—— v. London Graving Dock Co. [1960] 2 Lloyd's Rep. 293 .... *Digested, 61/5827*

—— v. Peak [1964] R.V.R. 310; 10 R.R.C. 265; 190 E.G. 301; [1964]
R.A. 113, C.A.; affirming LVC/211/1962 [1963] J.P.L. 551; [1963]
R.C.N. 53; [1963] C.L.Y. 2946, Lands Tribunal .... *Digested, 64/3101*

—— v. United Dominions Trust [1951] 2 Lloyd's Rep. 553 .... *Digested, 52/3276*

—— v. Whetstone Entertainments and Allender, 106 S.J. 284; [1962] 2
Lloyd's Rep. 1, C.A. .... *Digested, 62/1140*

Daniels, Elliot & Hare v. Glover (Thomas) & Co. [1966] I.T.R. 283; [1966]
K.I.R. 116, Industrial Tribunal .... *Digested, 66/4473*

Daniels (H. E.) v. Carmel Exporters and Importers [1953] 2 Q.B. 242;
[1953] 3 W.L.R. 216; 97 S.J. 473; [1953] 2 All E.R. 401; [1953]
2 Lloyd's Rep. 103; [103 L.J. 503] .... *Digested, 53/159: Previous proceedings,* 53/158

Daniels' Application, Re, LP/35/1960 [1961] J.P.L. 258, Lands Tribunal *Digested, 61/7522*

Danish Bacon Co. Staff Pension Fund Trusts, Re, Christensen v. Arnett
[1971] 1 W.L.R. 248; *sub nom.* Danish Bacon Co. Staff Pension
Fund, Re, Christensen v. Arnett [1971] 1 All E.R. 486 .... *Digested, 71/8808*

Danish Mercantile Co. v. Beaumont [1951] Ch. 680; 95 S.J. 300; [1951]
1 All E.R. 925, C.A. .... *Digested, 7790: Approved,* 67/466

Danita, The. *See* Uglands Rederi A/S v President of India, The; Danita,
The.

Dankbars (an Infant), Re [1954] Ch. 98; [1953] 3 W.L.R. 957; 97 S.J.
811; 51 L.G.R. 666; *sub nom.* D. (an Infant), Re, 118 J.P. 25;
[1953] 2 All E.R. 1318, C.A. .... *Digested. 53/1039.* 2717

Danluck v. Birkner and Cassey [1947] 3 D.L.R. 337 .... *Digested, 6684*

Dann v. Hamilton [1939] 1 K.B. 509; [38 Can.B.R. 107] ...... *Applied,* 56/5855; 60/2121:
Not followed, 56/6078: *Considered,* 57/2460; 58/2308:
Referred to. 62/2095: *Doubted.* 71/7817

Dann's Application, Re [1966] F.S.R. 329; [1966] R.P.C. 532, Patents
Appeal Tribunal; reversing [1966] F.S.R. 81 .... *Digested, 66/9107*

Dansereau v. Berget [1954] A.C. 1; [1953] 3 W.L.R. 676; 97 S.J. 728;
sub nom. Dansereau v. Berget, Colin v. Berget [1953] 2 All E.R.
1058, P.C. .... *Digested. 53/1340*

Dansk-Franske Dampskibsselskab A/S Det v. Compagnie Financiere
d'Investissements Transatlantiques S.A. (Compafina). *See* Himmer-
land, The.

therefore have been entered for the defendant.[8] It also discusses American law on the subject and directs you to the American Law Institute's *Restatement of the Law of Torts.* Thus, your research can lead you to many sources, both primary and secondary.

If you now look up *Stein v. Lehnert* (1962), 36 D.L.R. (2d) 159, you will find that the correct name of the case in the Supreme Court of Canada is *Lehnert v. Stein* because the defendant in the original action was now the appellant, while the plaintiff was the respondent. This case is especially relevant to your problem because it deals with both contributory negligence and voluntary assumption of risk.

The plaintiff, when a gratuitous passenger in the defendant's car, had suffered serious personal injury in an accident. The trial judge held that the accident had been caused by the gross negligence of the defendant,[9] who had been intoxicated when the accident occurred. In spite of this, the judge dismissed the action on the grounds that the plaintiff was "*volens*" and he added that if he had not found her "*volens*" he would have found her guilty of contributory negligence and apportioned 75% of the responsibility to her. The plaintiff appealed to the Manitoba Court of Appeal, which held that she had not been "*volens*" but was guilty of contributory negligence to the extent of 25%. The Supreme Court of Canada upheld the judgment of the Manitoba Court of Appeal. It was held that the maxim "*volenti*" had no application since the burden lies on the defendant of proving that the plaintiff, expressly or by necessary implication, agreed to exempt the defendant from liability for any damage suffered by the plaintiff occasioned by the defendant's negligence.

If you want to check whether *Lehnert v. Stein* has been judicially considered you can look it up in the *Canadian Abridgment* (2nd) "Cases Judicially Considered" volumes. In the main volumes it is listed under both its original name, *Stein v. Lehnert,* and its name on appeal to the Supreme Court of Canada, *Lehnert v. Stein.* This, presumably, is a mistake, as a check of some of the *Stein v. Lehnert* entries indicates that it is the Supreme Court case that was judicially considered and it is cited as *Lehnert v. Stein.*

In the First and Second Permanent Supplements to "Cases Judicially Considered," there are entries only under *Lehnert v. Stein,* but curiously there is a return to the use of both names in the Third Permanent Supplement. Illustrations 86 and 88 give you some of the entries, whereas Illustrations 85 and 87 show a change adopted in the Third Permanent Supplement to "Cases

---

8   Remember that *Dann v. Hamilton* was decided and this article written before the passage in England of the Law Reform (Contributory Negligence) Act 1945. Therefore, if the plaintiff had been found guilty of contributory negligence, judgment would have been for the defendant.

9   The case was decided under s. 99(1) of Manitoba's Highway Traffic Act (R.S.M. 1954, c. 112) which provided that a gratuitous passenger in a motor vehicle who suffered injury, death, or loss in an accident had no cause of action for damages against the owner or operator "unless the accident was caused by the gross negligence or wilful and wanton misconduct of the owner or operator . . . and unless the gross negligence or wilful and wanton misconduct contributed to the injury, death, or loss. . . ." This provision was continued in R.S.M. 1970, c. H60, s. 145(1), but has now been repealed (S.M. 1980, c. 19, s. 1).

ILLUSTRATION 85
Canadian Abridgment (2nd), Cases Judicially Considered, Volume 1

PREFACE

This Table of Cases Judicially Considered is not an exhaustive list of every case mentioned in subsequent cases, but contains all cases subsequently considered which by reason of similarity of subject matter or principle involved can be considered useful material in researching on particular issues and points of law.

The terms used throughout the table (and their abbreviations) are as follows:

Affirmed	(Aff.)
Applied	(Apld.)
Considered	(Consd.)
Distinguished	(Dist.)
Followed	(Folld.)
Not followed	(Not folld.)
Obsolete	(Obsol.)
Overruled	(Over.)
Reversed	(Rev.)
Varied	(Var.)

The main work of the Table of Cases Judicially Considered cumulates all material to the end of 1973 and is being published in four volumes, of which this volume is the first. A supplement to the four volumes will be cumulated from year to year and included in the Canadian Abridgment Appendix binder. Tables of cases considered by Canadian courts in decisions reported since the cut-off date of Appendix releases will be found in the monthly issues of CANADIAN CURRENT LAW.

ILLUSTRATION 86
Canadian Abridgment (2nd), Cases Judicially Considered, Volume 4

CASES JUDICIALLY CONSIDERED

Steffler v. Miles, [1951] O.R. 647.
Consd. Re Young, [1955] O.W.N. 789.

Stegg and Codd, Re, [1967] 1 C.C.C. 79.
Apld. Goodwin v. MacMillan, 60 W.W.R. 47.
Apld. Re R. and Groves, 5 C.C.C. (2d) 90.

Steggles v. New River Co., 11 W.R. 234.
Apld. Conklin v. Dickson, 40 O.L.R. 460.

Steidel, Re, 5 Terr. L.R. 303; 309.
Apld. Crichton v. Zelenitsky, [1946] 2 W.W.R. 209.
Folld. Re Mikkelson, 1 S.L.R. 514.

Steiger & Feldbar Const. Co., Re, [1959] O.W.N. 338.
Dist. Re Mullin and Knowles, 51 D.L.R. (2d) 493.

Steil's Prohibition Application, Re, 49 W.W.R. 371.
Consd. Re Continental Explosives Ltd., 49 W.W.R. 762.

Steiman v. Gordon, [1933] 1 W.W.R. 315.
Folld. Tilley v. Berg, [1944] 3 W.W.R. 529.

Stein v. Bourassa, 18 R.L. 484.
Consd. Cote v. James Richardson Co., 38 S.C.R. 53.

Stein v. Hauser, 6 Sask. L.R. 383.
Apld. Hennig v. Trautman, [1926] 1 W.W.R. 912.
Folld. Wodell v. Potter, 64 O.L.R. 27.

Stein v. Lehnert, 37 W.W.R. 267; [1963] S.C.R. 38.
Consd. Campbell v. Royal Bank, 41 W.W.R. 91; 46 W.W.R. 79.
Apld. Dorn v. Stevens, 39 D.L.R. (2d) 761.
Apld. Prior v. Kyle, 47 W.W.R. 489; 52 W.W.R. 1.
Apld. Lackner v. Neath, 57 W.W.R. 496.
Folld. Gorman v. Hertz Drive Yourself Stations, 54 D.L.R. (2d) 133.
Apld. Farley v. Brandon, 56 W.W.R. 193.
Apld. Kowton v. Public Trustee of Alta., 57 W.W.R. 370.
Apld. Carnegie v. Trynchy, 57 W.W.R. 305.

Dist. Deauville v. Reid, 52 M.P.R. 218.
Apld. Lillie v. Sanderson, 60 W.W.R. 535.
Apld. Harris v. Toronto Transit Commn., 63 D.L.R. (2d) 450.
Apld. Rondos v. Wawrin, 68 D.L.R. (2d) 658.

Stein v. R., [1928] 2 W.W.R. 346; [1928] S.C.R. 553.
Apld. Lizotte v. R., 11 C.R. 357.
Consd. R. v. Andrews, 38 C.R. 316.
Dist. R. v. Boucher, 40 W.W.R. 663.
Apld. R. v. Burkart, 50 W.W.R. 515.
Apld. R. v. Bourget, [1973] 1 W.W.R. 425.

Stein v. Valkenhugsen, E.B. & E. 65.
Folld. Blanchard v. Jacobi, 43 O.L.R. 442.

Steinberg, Re, 3 D.L.R. (3d) 565.
Apld. Mitchell v. Mitchell, 3 N.S.R. (2d) 455.

Steinberg v. Blum, [1953] O.W.N. 246.
Not folld. Cohen v. Power, [1971] 2 O.R. 742.

Steinberg v. Cohen, 64 O.L.R. 545.
Dist. Sidmay v. Wehttam Invts. Ltd., [1967] 1 O.R. 508.

Steinberg v. R., [1931] O.R. 222.
Folld. R. v. Deacon, 87 C.C.C. 271.
Consd. R. v. McGrath, 102 C.C.C. 228.

Steinberg v. Scala (Leeds) Ltd., [1923] 2 Ch. 452.
Consd. LaFayette v. W. W. Distributors and Co., 51 W.W.R. 685.
Apld. Fannon v. Dobranski, 73 W.W.R. 371.

Steinberg v. Steinberg, 45 W.W.R. 562.
Dist. Spurgeon v. Aasen, 52 W.W.R. 641.

Steinberg's Ltee v. Comité Paritaire de l'Alimentation de Montreal, [1968] S.C.R. 971.
Apld. R. v. Riddell, 11 C.C.C. (2d) 493.

Steine v. Korbin, 9 W.L.R. 670.
Folld. Columbia Caterers v. Famous Restaurants, 1 D.L.R. (2d) 397; 4 D.L.R. (2d) 601.

ILLUSTRATION 87
Canadian Abridgment (2nd), Third Permanent Supplement,
Cases Judicially Considered 1981-1983, Volume 3

CASES JUDICIALLY CONSIDERED
JURISPRUDENCE CITÉE
1981–1983

Prepared in cooperation with La Société québécoise d'information juridique, this table cumulates the tables of cases considered in the Canadian Abridgment in 1981, 1982 and 1983. Bold face entries indicate the cited decision and any appeals from it; light face entries following them refer to the cases in which they are considered.

Set out below are the terms and abbreviations used throughout this table. The symbols in the circles indicate the subsequent treatment of the case in another decision. Those in the squares indicate the treatment of the case on appeal.

Ⓐ	*applied*	Aᶠ	*affirmed*
©	*considered*	Lʳ	*leave to appeal refused (New: January 1983)*
Ⓓ	*distinguished*	Rᵛ	*reversed*
Ⓕ	*followed*	Sˢ	*set aside/quashed (New: January 1983)*
Ⓝ	*not followed/overruled*	Vⁱ	*varied*
Ⓡ	*referred to*		

R., Re. See Lewis Insulations Ltd. v. Goodram Bros. Ltd.

R., Re (1976), 35 C.R.N.S. 343. Re Ewenin (1979), 4 Sask. R. 213 ©.

R., Re (1977), 12 Nfld. & P.E.I.R. 158. Re Butt (1980), 26 Nfld. & P.E.I.R. 515 Ⓐ.

R. v. 294555 Ont. Ltd. (1978), 39 C.C.C. (2d) 352. Cordon Bleu International Ltée v. F.G. Bradley Co. (1979), 60 C.P.C. (2d) 71 Ⓡ.

R. v. A. See R. v. Allan.

R. v. A. See Re A.

R. v. A. (1974), 26 C.C.C. (2d) 474. Re Kabesh (1983), 44 A.R. 126 Ⓡ.

R. v. A. & A. Jewellers Ltd., [1978] 1 F.C. 479. Flexi-Coil Ltd. v. Smith-Roles Ltd. (1981), 59 C.P.R. (2d) 46 Ⓐ. Fabricated Plastics Ltd. v. Scott (1981), 25 C.P.C. 198 Ⓐ. Lumonics Research Ltd. v. Gould (1983), 46 N.R. 483 Ⓡ.

R. v. A.B. (1955), 22 C.R. 353. Re Stillo and R. (1980), 56 C.C.C. (2d) 178 Ⓡ.

R. v. A.B.Z. See R. v. Z.

R. v. A.G. B.C., [1924] A.C. 213, [1923] W.W.R. 1252. A.G. Man. v. A.G. Can., [1981] 6 W.W.R. 1 Ⓡ.

R. v. A.G. Sask. (1982), 15 Sask. R. 341. R. v. Yanke (1983), 21 Sask. R. 345 Ⓐ.

R. v. A.I.K., [1982] 1 W.W.R. 666. R. v. A. (P.) (1982), 38 A.R. 539 ©.

R. v. A.I.R.B. See A.I.R.B. v. Stedelbauer Chevrolet Oldsmobile Ltd.

R. v. A.N. See R. v. Nowakowski.

R. v. A.N., [1978] 3 W.W.R. 222. R. v. Bucklaschuk, [1981] 1 W.W.R. 443 Ⓝ.

R. v. A.O. Pope Ltd. (1972), 5 N.B.R. (2d) 719. R. v. Phillips (1980), 33 N.B.R. (2d) 50 Ⓡ.
Aᶠ **5 N.B.R. (2d) 715.**

R. c. A.S., T.J. Montréal 500-24-000012-814, le 23 juin 1981. Protection de la jeunesse — 54, [1981] C.P. 2047.

R. v. Aalders (1979), 31 N.S.R. (2d) 518. R. c. Ducharme (1980), 8 M.V.R. 183 ©. R. v. Peladeau (1981), 57 C.C.C. 385 Ⓡ.

R. v. Abbey (1982), 29 C.R. (3d) 193. R. v. Campeau (1983), 42 A.R. 81 Ⓐ. R. v. Courville (1982), 2 C.C.C. (3d) 118 Ⓡ.

R. v. Abbey, [1983] 1 W.W.R. 251. R. v. Jordan (1983), 33 C.R. (3d) 394 Ⓓ.

R. v. Abbey, 21 C.R. (3d) 63.
Rᵛ **43 N.R. 30.**

R. v. Abbott, [1940] 3 W.W.R. 289. Eddy v. Eddy (1982), 51 N.S.R. (2d) 1 Ⓡ.

R. v. Abell. See Abell v. R.C.M.P. Commr.

ILLUSTRATION 88
Canadian Abridgment (2nd), Third Permanent Supplement,
Cases Judicially Considered 1981-1983, Volume 2

CASES JUDICIALLY CONSIDERED/JURISPRUDENCE CITÉE

Legault, Re (1977), 24 C.B.R. (N.S.) 83. Re Worlidge (1983), 46 C.B.R. (N.S.) 60 Ⓐ.

Legault c. Chateau Paint Works Ltd., [1960] C.S. 567. L. Martin & Fils Inc. c. Industries Pittsburg du Canada Ltée, [1982] C.S. 629.

Legault v. Cie D'Assurance Generale de Commerce (1968), 65 D.L.R. (2d) 230. Mississauga Assn. for the Mentally Retarded v. Hartford Fire Ins. Co., [1981] I.L.R. 1-1399 Ⓝ.

Legault c. Surprenant (1926), 40 B.R. 228. April c. Trust général du Canada, [1981] C.S. 576.

Leger c. Bélisle, [1976] C.S. 1805. Goyette c. Guinard, [1980] C.S. 265.

Leger v. Home Ins. Co. See Leger v. Royal Ins. Co.

Leger v. Poirier, [1944] S.C.R. 152. Re Dorion (1980), 27 Nfld. & P.E.I.R. 211 Ⓝ. Re Fergusson (1980), 40 N.S.R. (2d) 223 Ⓝ. Fafard c. L'Abbée, [1980] C.S. 833. Re Bisyk (No. 2) (1980), 32 O.R. (2d) 281 Ⓒ. Re Valko (1982), 18 Sask. R. 211 Ⓝ. Re Babcock (1982), 53 N.S.R. (2d) 716 Ⓒ. Re Kostynuik (1982), 18 Sask. R. 383 Ⓒ.

Leger v. Royal Ins. Co., 1 N.B.R. (2d) 1. Westwood Elec. & Appliance Service Ltd. v. Man. Pub. Ins. Corp., [1982] 4 W.W.R. 201 Ⓐ.

Leggat Case, Re. See Re Knowles.

Legge v. Lucci (1972), 3 Nfld. & P.E.I.R. 409. Hartery v. Monroe (1981), 32 Nfld. & P.E.I.R. 504 Ⓝ.

Legge v. Richards (1979), 34 N.S.R. (2d) 612. Hachey v. Dakin (1983), 57 N.S.R. (2d) 441 Ⓝ.

Leggott v. Barrett (1980), 15 Ch. D. 306. Dyform Enrg. Ltd. v. Ittup Hollowcore Int. Ltd. (1982), 19 B.L.R. 1 Ⓝ.

Legion Oils Ltd. v. Barron (1955), 16 W.W.R. 93. Misericordia Hosp. v. Acres Consulting Services Ltd. (1980), 14 Alta. L.R. (2d) 140 Ⓒ. Stevens v. Home Oil Co. (1980), 28 A.R. 331 Ⓝ.

Legislative Authority of Parliament in Rel. to Upper House, Ref. re, [1980] 1 S.C.R. 54. A.G. Man. v. A.G. Can., [1981] 6 W.W.R. 1 Ⓓ. Re Stony Plain Indian Reserve No. 135, [1982] 1 W.W.R. 302 Ⓕ.Reference re Effect & Validity of Amendments to Constitution of Can. Sought in Proposed Resolution for a Joint Address to Her Majesty the Queen Respecting Constitution of Can., (1981), 29 Nfld. & P.E.I.R. 503 Ⓒ. Reference re Amendment of the Constitution of Can. (No. 2) (1981), 118 D.L.R. (3d) 1 Ⓡ. Reference re Amendment of the Constitution of Can. (No. 3) (1981), 120 D.L.R. (3d) 385 Ⓡ.

Legislative competence of the Parliament of Canada to Enact Bill No. 9, Entitled "An Act to amend the Supreme Court Act" (Reference as to the), [1940] R.C.S. 49. P.G. du Québec c. P.G. du Canada, [1981] C.A. 80.

Legislative Jurisdiction over Hours of Labour (In the matter of), [1925] R.C.S. 505. Commission du salaire minimum c. Ville de Saint-Hubert, [1980] C.P. 68. Cie des chemins de fer nationaux du Canada c. Commission de la santé et de la sécurité du travail, [1981] C.S. 1095.

Legislative Privilege, Ref. re (1978), 18 O.R. (2d) 529. Re Univ. of Guelph and Can. Assn. of Univ. Teachers (1980), 29 O.R. (2d) 312 Ⓒ. Bisaillon c. Keable, [1980] C.A. 316. Solicitor-Gen. of Can. v. Royal Comm. of Inquiry into Confidentiality of Health Records in Ont. (1981), 62 C.C.C. (2d) 193 Ⓡ. Porter v. Porter (1983), 40 O.R. (2d) 417 Ⓒ. Bezeau v. Ont. Institute for Studies in Educ. (1982), 3 C.H.R.R. D/874 Ⓝ.

Legree c. Caissie (1958), 41 M.P.R. 298. C.P. Ltd. v. Paul (1981), 34 N.B.R. (2d) 382 Ⓐ.

Legris c. Commission des services juridiques C.P. Trois-Rivières 400-19-001 277-78, le 23 mars 1979. Fortin c. Centre communautaire juridique du Nord-Ouest (In re: Loi de l'aide juridique), [1980] C.P. 188.

Legros v. Evans (1977), 3 B.C.L.R. 395. Friedrich v. Chisan (1983), 42 B.C.L.R. 396 Ⓒ. Rushton v. Lake Ont. Steel Co. (1980), 29 O.R. (2d) 68 Ⓝ.

Lehar Investment Corp. c. Bigue, [1968] B.R. 489. Goldenhar c. Comcap Factors Inc., [1980] C.A. 140.

Lehman v. Hunter (1939), 13 M.P.R. 553. Re Appleby (1982), 42 N.B.R. (2d) 427 Ⓓ.

Lehndorff Mgmt. Ltd. v. Dartmouth (1975), 15 N.S.R. (2d) 40. Halifax Devs. Ltd. v. Dir. of Assessment (1983), 55 N.S.R. (2d) 455 Ⓝ. Donovan v. Director of Assessment for City of Halifax (1977), 41 N.S.R. (2d) 534 Ⓕ.

Lehndorff Mgmt. Ltd. v. L.R.S. Dev. Enterprises Ltd., [1980] 5 W.W.R. 14. O'Nory v. Patricia Properties Ltd. (1983), 144 D.L.R. (3d) 742 Ⓝ. Canalan Invt. Corp. v. Gibbons, [1983] 3 W.W.R. 225 Ⓓ.

Lehnert v. Nelson, Carveth and L. & R. Ltd., [1947] 2 W.W.R. 25. Duncan v. Braaten (1980), 21 B.C.L.R. 369 Ⓒ. Ouellet v. Uranium City Hotel Ltd. (1979), 5 Sask. R. 421 Ⓓ.

Lehnert v. Stein, [1963] S.C.R. 38. Schill v. Weimer (1980), 5 Sask. R. 112 Ⓡ. Pottage v. Patterson (1980), 24 B.C.L.R. 43 Ⓐ. Christie v. Toronto (1983), 20 M.P.L.R. 145 Ⓒ.

Judicially Considered" in the manner of indicating the type of judicial consideration (Illustration 85 shows the abbreviations formerly used; Illustration 87, those used in the Third Permanent Supplement.) The new practice is preferable to the old because it makes a clear distinction between appeals and judicial considerations. If the reference is to an appeal (that is, *the same case* in a higher court), the letter indicating the outcome of the appeal is placed in a square. If, on the other hand, the reference is to a case in which a *different earlier case* was judicially considered, the letter indicating the type of judicial consideration is placed within a circle. Compare not only Illustrations 85 and 87, but also the usage in Illustrations 86 and 88. For further updating to "Cases Judicially Considered," see the loose-leaf appendix to the *Canadian Abridgment* and the monthly parts of *Canadian Current Law.*

Alternatively, or as a further check, since the case of *Lehnert v. Stein* is reported in the *Dominion Law Reports,* you can use the *D.L.R. Annotation Service.* You may remember that this case served as an illustration of how to use that service.[10]

Cases such as *Dann v. Hamilton, Lehnert v. Stein,* and those in which these cases have been judicially considered should prove very helpful to you. Consider similarities and differences between them and the case you are considering. For instance, was B, the driver of the car, as much under the influence of alcohol as the driver in either of these cases? Probably not, since B was sufficiently sober to notice that the gas tank was nearly empty and to stop to have it filled. Might this be a factor in determining that his conduct was not negligent? (But remember that the defendant's conduct in *Lehnert v. Stein* had been held to constitute *gross* negligence.) Or, if negligence is established, would the lesser degree of intoxication suggest that C was not guilty of contributory negligence? In *Lehnert v. Stein* the passenger was a friend of the driver and was persuaded by him to accept a ride, whereas in our hypothetical case the passenger was a hitchhiker who was urged by the driver to leave the car. Does this make his contributory negligence greater than that of the passenger in *Lehnert v. Stein*? This is the type of question you have to take into consideration in preparing a defence for A's company.

You might also check other digests for cases relating to the various aspects of your problem. For instance, you might try *Butterworth's Ontario Digest.* This publication is described on its title pages as "being a statement of the case law of Ontario from 1901 with full annotations". The bound volumes in the set gradually have been replaced by loose-leaf volumes, and a general index to these replacement volumes has now been issued in loose-leaf volume 12. A "Publisher's Note" at the beginning of the volume tells us that the entries in the index refer to *Butterworth's Ontario Digest* and to the *Digest of Ontario Case Law,* a four-volume set dealing with Ontario case law to the end of 1900, which was reprinted by Butterworth's in 1974. References to *Butterworth's Ontario Digest* are made by volume and case number. Entries prefixed by the letters SI refer to the service issues that update *Butterworth's Ontario*

---

10   See pp. 17-21, above.

Digest. These service issues were at first filed at the end of each volume, but because they were becoming rather bulky, a permanent supplement numbered volume 13 and containing those for 1972 to 1977 inclusive was issued. Service issues from 1978 on continue to be filed in the main volumes. Entries in the general index (volume 12) for the *Digest of Ontario Case Law* are distinguished by the letters OD followed by a page number.

For information on very recent cases, you might consult *All-Canada Weekly Summaries,* described earlier in this chapter.[11] If you look up the heading "Motor Vehicles" and the sub-heading, "Contributory negligence," in the indexes in the bound volumes and current service, you may find summaries of some cases that are relevant to your problem. For instance, Illustration 89 shows an entry in the index to one of the 1984 volumes – volume 24 of the second series – which may be helpful. The entry refers you to page 512, where a digest of the Ontario case *Dillon v. Curry* begins (see Illustration 90). The digest continues on page 513, the name of the case being given at the end. Note that in this case drinking and failure to wear a seat belt were matters at issue. You have not considered whether the hitchhiker, C, was wearing a seat belt; presumably he was if this is not an issue in the case. If he was not, this would today certainly be considered a factor in determining whether he had been contributorily negligent. If, however, as in *Dillon v. Curry,* the passenger's seat belt was broken, the case against the owner would be strengthened. If you wish to have a copy of the full text of a case digested in *All-Canada Weekly Summaries,* it can be obtained quickly by completing and mailing the order card enclosed with each issue or by telephoning the Photocopy Department of Canada Law Book Limited. As noted earlier, details regarding this photocopying service are included on the front of each issue of *All-Canada Weekly Summaries.*

Illustration 91 shows a digest of another motor vehicle case – this one from British Columbia – in which alcohol and failure to wear a seat belt were issues. It is from *British Columbia Decisions – Civil Cases,* one of several services published by Western Legal Publications Ltd., which also seeks to digest cases soon after they are decided. Its digests are also arranged by subject, and a photocopying service providing the full text of the reasons for judgment is offered.

In the course of your research you have found definite answers to some of your original questions. You know the statutory provisions that relate to your client's problem and you have read many cases in which the facts are very similar to the one with which you are dealing. But whether B's conduct will be held to constitute negligence and, if so, whether C will be found guilty of contributory negligence cannot be definitely determined in advance. Careful research is a vital first step in solving a legal problem, but it must be followed by logical reasoning and skillful preparation and presentation of your case.

---

11   See p. 125, above.

ILLUSTRATION 89
All-Canada Weekly Summaries (Second Series), Volume 24 (1984)

MORTGAGES—*Continued*

Power of sale proceedings — Agreement of purchase and sale containing condition that no redemption be made by owner before closing — Mortgagor tendering redemption amount before closing.
Canada Permanent Trust Co. v. Rieckenberg and one other action (Ont. Dist. Ct.), 53

Prepayment — Whether mortgagors could waive, by provisions of renewal agreement, protection of s. 17 of Mortgages Act (Ont.).
Re Shaw et al. and Royal Trust Co. (Ont. Co. Ct.), 511

Priorities — Petitioner's mortgage registered May 25, 1978 — Modification agreement of petitioner containing higher interest rates dated August 26, 1980 but not registered — Judgments registered after September 24, 1982 — Whether mortgagee entitled to higher interest rate as set out in agreement.
Re Fraser Valley Credit Union and Carlson et al. (B.C.S.C.), 227

Priorities — Vendor taking back second mortgage — Vendor authorizing purchaser to place $50,000 first mortgage — Purchaser placing $60,000 first mortgage.
Settlers Savings & Mortgage Corp. et al. v. McCauley et al. (Alta. C.A.), 135

Priorities as between hydro company and mortgagee — Power Corporation Act (Ont.), s. 73.
Hudson v. Ontario Hydro (Ont. Small Claims Ct.), 381

Redemption — Interest rate lowered through modification agreements with mortgagor — Default occurred at lower rate — Whether subsequent mortgagee could redeem at lower rate.
Vancouver City Savings Credit Union v. Harrington et al. (B.C.S.C.), 473

Sale — Mortgagee wanting sale by sealed tender within 30 days — No prejudice to waiting until summer when better price might be available.
Liberty Investments Ltd. v. Rix et al. (B.C.S.C.), 276

MOTOR VEHICLES

Contributory negligence — Accident occurring while plaintiff had removed seat-belt momentarily.
Has et al. v. Cameron et al. (Ont. H.C.J.), 190

Contributory negligence — Child struck by automobile while walking along highway with her family.
Howes et al. v. Crosby et al. (Ont. C.A.), 302

Contributory negligence — Failure to back up motor vehicle properly resulting in motor vehicle projecting into roadway.
Doyle v. Lefebvre (B.C. Co. Ct.), 84

Contributory negligence — Plaintiff riding in defendant's automobile after both had been drinking — Failure to wear seat belt, which was broken.
Dillon v. Curry (Ont. H.C.J.), 512

Contributory negligence — Plaintiff's motorcycle colliding with vehicle entering roadway.
Reikki v. Vanderuyt et al. (B.C.C.A.), 328

Contributory negligence — Proceeding into intersection from stop sign — Improper look out.
Rose et al. v. Belanger (Man. Q.B.), 89

Contributory negligence — Seat-belt defence.
Savard v. Branigan (Ont. H.C.J.), 377

Contributory negligence — Seat-belt defence — Plaintiffs, driver and his young child, failed to wear their seat-belts, and were injured in head-on collision.
Harrington et al. v. Parker et al. (Ont. Co. Ct.), 253

ILLUSTRATION 90
All-Canada Weekly Summaries (Second Series), Volume 24 (1984)

---

512   ALL-CANADA WEEKLY SUMMARIES   24 A.C.W.S. (2d)

interest were repayable in exactly five years — Given male mortgagor's business experience he should have been reasonably familiar
with express terms of renewal agreement — Mortgagor, in this
factual situation, could waive by contract the provisions of the
Mortgages Act, or the *Interest Act* — Mortgagors' application for
declaration of their right to prepay mortgage in accordance with s. 17
of *Mortgages Act* dismissed. (43 pp.)

Re Shaw et al. and Royal Trust Co. (Mar. 19, 1984, Ont. Co. Ct.,
Scott Co. Ct. J.)

24:1086
**MOTOR VEHICLES — Contributory negligence — Plaintiff riding
in defendant's automobile after both had been drinking —
Failure to wear seat belt, which was broken.**
**DAMAGES (PERSONAL INJURY) — Multiple injuries — Severe
fractures and dislocations of both feet and right hip —
Permanent disability.**
**INTEREST — Prejudgment — Plaintiff's delays, non-disclosures
and failures to produce hampering preparation of defence and
reducing likelihood of informed settlement.**

Action for damages for personal injuries suffered by passenger in
automobile when it failed to negotiate curve at high speed and struck
telephone pole — Driver admitted liability but alleged that plaintiff
was contributorily negligent — Parties had spent evening together
and had been drinking — Plaintiff contended that his failure to wear
seat belt was due to fact it was broken rather than to fact second
passenger was seated on his knee in vehicle designed to carry only one
passenger — Plaintiff suffered compound subtalar fractured dislocation with medial dislocation of subtalar joint of right ankle and foot
and compound peritalar fractured dislocation with lateral dislocation
of subtalar joint of left foot — Right femur was driven through dome
of hip socket resulting in comminuted fracture involving posterior
portion of acetabulum — Hip was severely dislocated and source of
great pain — Surgery to both feet and hip was required — Both feet
were deformed, resulting in continuing pain and probability of future
surgery — Despite extensive course of physiotherapy plaintiff,

• • •

tiff's delays, non-disclosures and failures to produce hampered preparation of defence and reduced likelihood of settlement on informed
basis, interest on general damages to run from second anniversary of
date of writ. (65 pp.)

Dillon v. Curry (Mar. 30, 1984, Ont. H.C.J., Sutherland J.)

ILLUSTRATION 91
British Columbia Decisions – Civil Cases

```
                              Suppl. digest:  file under: 2837-01
                              Cited as: [1984] B.C.D. Clv. 3373-01

                 MOTOR VEHICLE (GENERAL)

PASSENGERS - GRATUITOUS

    (CONTRIBUTORY NEGLIGENCE - FAILURE TO CARE FOR OWN SAFETY -
RELEASE OF CLAIM, NEGATION OF)

A passenger who knows that the driver of a motor vehicle has
partaken of alcoholic beverages, but who (despite his own
semi-intoxicated state) is certain that the driver "is not
drunk" must be considered, to a minor degree, to be the author
of his own harm when an accident occurs and he is injured.  If
he is to be found additionally liable by reason of his failure
to wear an available and operative seatbelt, the defendant
driver has the onus of proving that the wearing of such would
have minimized the injury suffered.  Finally, an insurance
adjuster who obtains from a "simple" plaintiff a release of his
claim may find that in certain circumstances (i.e. unequal
bargaining power, as herein) the Court will not give effect to
such when the settlement agreed upon would, having regard to
the serious nature of the injury, be inequitable.


James Gush              Co. Ct. Yale      December 2, 1983

v.                      3794              Kamloops

James King et al                          Finch, J.

Decision:  Liability apportioned: 85% to the defendant:  15% to
      the plaintiff.

Facts:    The plaintiff, a simple young man without much
      education and with a drinking problem, went on "the rounds"
      with the defendant.  In the early morning hours of August
      17th, 1980, the vehicle in which they were riding (and
      which was driven by the defendant) left the road and
      overturned; the plaintiff was injured.  The explanation
      given by the defendant for the accident was that he reached
      for a dropped cigarette and the car moved off the road.

Reasons:    The Court deals with a number of matters raised
      vis-a-vis liability, its extent or, in fact, its complete
      absense in light of the plaintiff's execution of a release
      obtained by an experienced adjuster representing the
      insurer of the defendant.  These issues are addressed as
      follows: (1) Failure to wear a seat belt: failure does not
      give rise to an automatic finding of contributory
      negligence; it is incumbent upon the defendant to prove
      that the wearing of a belt would have prevented or
      minimized the plaintiff's injury; no such proof is made and
      the onus is not met.  (2) Failure by the plaintiff to take
      care for his own safety:  .....cont.

  J.M. Hogg for the Plaintiff

  J.A. Horne for the Defendant                    (8 pages)

                      B.C. Decisions - April, 1984
```

5

Reference Books, Treatises, and Periodicals

We have now dealt with the primary sources of the law and with those secondary works the main purpose of which is to summarize the law and direct you to the primary sources. This chapter will be concerned with other secondary works, most of which can be classified as either reference books, treatises, or periodicals.

The secondary works of which we spoke in earlier chapters are sometimes classed as finding aids or search tools, whereas treatises and periodical articles are referred to as commentaries on the law. This is not, however, a clear cut division, because a treatise, say on negligence, may perform much the same function as an article on negligence in a legal encyclopedia. Both are likely to summarize the law on the subject and direct you to the primary sources. Often, though, the authors of treatises and periodical articles also comment on the law and sometimes suggest changes that they consider desirable.

Reference books are not usually regarded as a separate classification, but since most law school libraries have what is termed a reference collection and many of the books in it do not fit neatly into any of the other categories, a few words will be said about the types of books generally included in such a collection.

1. REFERENCE BOOKS

Librarians sometimes use the word "reference" in relation to books that are available for use only in the library, that is, to distinguish them from those that may be borrowed. In this sense, all the books we have talked about in Chapters 2 to 4 could be called reference books, for few law libraries allow such books to circulate. In law libraries, however, the word "reference" is generally used in a more restricted sense. The reference collection includes, for example, language dictionaries, general encyclopedias, indexes to periodical literature, bibliographies, directories, and collected biographies of the "Who's Who" type. The extent to which general works of reference are included depends, to some extent, on the proximity of the law school library to the general university library. Some law school libraries have extensive collections of general reference works, whereas others keep such books to a minimum. We will concentrate our attention on legal reference works.

One type of legal reference book that should be mentioned is the law dictionary. To new law students, a good law dictionary is especially useful, for many legal words and phrases will be new to them. Until recently no Canadian law dictionary had been published, and the most frequently used in Canadian law school libraries are an English one, Jowitt's *Dictionary of English Law,* and an American one, *Black's Law Dictionary.* Smaller ones are Mozley and Whiteley's *Law Dictionary* and *Osborn's Concise Law Dictionary,* both published in England.

In 1980, Law and Business Publications (Canada) Inc. published *The Canadian Law Dictionary.* The publisher's aim seemed to be to produce a Canadian equivalent of Jowitt or Black, but unfortunately it did not succeed. Instead of adapting or rewriting definitions in order to make them applicable to Canada, the editors for the most part simply inserted Canadian citations into English or American definitions. More recently, in 1983, Barron's Educational Series, Inc., of Woodbury, New York, published a smaller *Canadian Law Dictionary,* adapted from Steven H. Gifis' *Law Dictionary* (1975). Although the Canadian edition, prepared by John A. Yogis, Q.C., a Professor of Law at Dalhousie University, may be regarded as a Canadian equivalent of Gifis, Mozley & Whiteley or Osborn, rather than of Black or Jowitt, it is a good basic work which law students in Canada's common law provinces are likely to find very useful.

Mention might also be made of two other small dictionaries of legal terms written primarily for non-lawyers, but useful as well for beginning law students. William J. Flynn's *A Handbook of Canadian Legal Terminology* was published by General Publishing Co. Limited in Don Mills, Ontario. The first edition appeared in 1976 and a revised and updated one in 1981. *Basic Canadian Legal Terminology* was published by McGraw-Hill Ryerson Limited, Toronto, in 1979. Written by J. Steven Williams, a lawyer who teaches legal courses at Cambrian College of Applied Arts and Technology in Sudbury, Ontario, it was prepared mainly for students at the community college level. A French version of Williams' book entitled *Terminologie juridique* was published by McGraw-Hill Ryerson in 1982. Law students should use books of this type with caution, as some of the definitions are over-simplified.

A related type of publication that is useful for Canadian law students and lawyers is the *Encyclopedia of Words and Phrases, Legal Maxims,* the third edition of which, edited by Gerald D. Sanagan, Q.C., was published by Richard de Boo Limited in 1979. Consisting of four volumes, it defines words and phrases interpreted by Canadian courts from 1825 to 1978.

Law lists and legal directories are other types of reference books with which law students should become familiar. They give the names of lawyers, law firms, judges, other court officials, faculties of law schools, *etc.* Most useful to Canadian students and lawyers are the *Canadian Law List* and the *Canada Legal Directory,* both of which are published annually.

Many law school libraries have in their reference collections printed catalogues of books in other law school libraries. Examples are the *Dictionary Catalog of the Columbia University Law Library* (28 volumes) and the Harvard Law School Library's *Catalog of International Law and Relations* (20 volumes). These are helpful if you need information concerning a book that your own library does not have, or if you want to know whether there are additional books in a particular subject area.

Probably the most useful reference books found in a law library are the indexes to legal periodical literature. More will be said of them later in this chapter.

Only a general idea of the contents of a reference collection has been given here. You will find it helpful to browse in this area of your library to see the types of books that are included.

2. TREATISES

In law libraries the word "treatise" is sometimes applied to both general textbooks on a legal subject and to monographs dealing with more specialized topics. On the other hand, some books on legal research refer to "textbooks and treatises," but do not draw any clear distinction between them.[1] The *Oxford English Dictionary* defines "treatise" as "A book or writing which treats of some particular subject; commonly (in mod. use always), one containing a formal or methodical discussion or exposition of the principles of the subject; formerly more widely used for a literary work in general." Its definition of textbook is "A book used as a standard work for the study of a particular subject; now usually one written specifically for this purpose; a manual of instruction in any science or branch of study, esp. a work recognized as an authority." It appears from these definitions that "textbook" is the narrower term and that "treatise" really includes a textbook. I am therefore using the term "treatise" in this inclusive sense.

Treatises, being secondary sources, are not, strictly speaking, authoritative in the legal sense. Some, however, are written by scholars of repute and, in time, come to be regarded as having a considerable degree of authority. Though not binding on the courts, a legal treatise of distinction may carry considerable weight. Some of the best known run to many editions, with new editors carrying on the work of the original authors; *Chitty on Contracts,* for instance, is now in its twenty-fourth edition. Note the lawyer's habit of referring to *Chitty on Contracts* or *Salmond on Torts,* instead of using the full title. (Indeed the later editions of Chitty use "*Chitty on Contracts*" on the title page.) Probably the practice originated because so many legal treatises had long titles and some of them were so similar that it was difficult to distinguish between them. Whatever its origin, the practice continues, and it is one that most law students adopt very early in their studies.

Until recently there were relatively few Canadian legal treatises and Canadian law students were, to a considerable degree, dependent on works written by English and American scholars. This situation has gradually

---

1   Morris L. Cohen, *Legal Research in a Nutshell,* 3rd ed. (St. Paul: West, 1978), pp. 291-4; J.A. Yogis and I.M. Christie, *Legal Writing and Research Manual,* 2nd ed. (Toronto: Butterworths, 1974), p. 48.

changed, as more Canadian law teachers and practising lawyers are writing books on various aspects of Canadian law.

In addition to legal treatises, you will find in your law school library books that are useful in your studies, but that cannot strictly be classed as law books. If your library uses the Library of Congress Classification for any part of its collections, it is likely that you will find these books classified as they would be in a general university library. Most law school libraries have many books in the "H" (Social Sciences) and "J" (Political Science) classifications. For instance, treatises on labour law will be included in whatever law classification is used by your library, but you will find other books on labour, not written primarily from a legal point of view, in "HD 4801-8943"; books included here relate to such matters as wages, hours, strikes, lockouts and arbitration and conciliation.

One type of book that is used a great deal in law schools and that has not yet been mentioned is the case book. It is a useful aid to study for it brings together cases or extracts from reports of cases on a particular subject. Some of these case books are published; others are prepared by law teachers for use only in their own classes and are not for general distribution. Case books are really collections of extracts from primary sources, sometimes with commentary or annotations, but, for convenience, libraries generally class them with treatises on the same subject.

Law students should be cautioned against relying too heavily on case books. Glanville Williams gives good advice on this subject. A case book, he says, saves the student "some of the trouble (beneficial, but time-consuming) of making his own notebook of cases". It also "does something to eliminate immaterial facts, thus helping in the search . . . for the facts that are legally material". He adds, however, that "the use of case books by no means dispenses with the need for reading the original reports". Some of the more important cases can profitably be read in full in the law reports, using the case book version only for their review. Moreover, in their reading, keen students will come across references to many cases not in the case book which they will want to read.[2] I would add that students need practice in looking up cases in the various series of law reports. Otherwise, when they begin to practise law, and the case books they used in law school go quickly out of date, they will lack the experience needed in using the law reports.

3. PERIODICALS

(a) General

Periodical literature forms an important secondary source of the law. There are many types of legal periodicals, some scholarly, others more popular in form and content. Some publish articles on any aspect of the law; others are restricted to a particular subject, such as criminal law or family law.

---

2   Glanville Williams, *Learning the Law,* 11th ed. (London: Stevens, 1982), pp. 52-53.

Periodicals are issued at regular intervals, monthly or quarterly, for instance. They are published by bar associations, law schools, and other groups.

There is a tradition, especially in the United States, of student editing of law reviews. The same practice is generally followed in Canadian law schools, and nearly every one now publishes at least one law review. Examples of other Canadian legal periodicals are the *Canadian Bar Review, Chitty's Law Journal,* and the *Criminal Law Quarterly.*

Most Canadian law school libraries also subscribe to many legal periodicals published in England, the United States, and other countries. The *Modern Law Review* and the *Law Quarterly Review* are examples of important English ones; among the leading American legal periodicals are the *Harvard Law Review* and the *Yale Law Journal.*

Periodical literature is so voluminous that, without adequate indexing, access to it would be very limited. Indexes to individual sets of periodicals, such as those provided for the *Canadian Bar Review,* the *Law Quarterly Review,* and the *Harvard Law Review,* are useful as far as they go, but if you want to find all the articles published on a particular subject, you need an index that refers you to many different journals. The same is true if you are looking for an article by a particular author and you do not know in what journal it was published. Fortunately there are such indexes.

(b) Index to Legal Periodicals

The American Association of Law Libraries began in 1908 to publish both this *Index*[3] and the *Law Library Journal.* At first the two were bound together. The first eighteen volumes of the *Index* (1908-25) cover one year each. There are triennial cumulations from 1926 to 1979 (18 volumes) and from 1979/80 to date there are annual, but no triennial cumulations.[4] Numbering of the cumulations is continuous; thus, the last triennial cumulation is numbered 18, the first permanent annual one, 19.

A long-term association between The H.W. Wilson Company and the American Association of Law Libraries in publishing the *Index to Legal Periodicals* ended in the late seventies. The H.W. Wilson Company continues to publish this *Index,* whereas the American Association of Law Libraries now sponsors the *Legal Resource Index* and the *Current Law Index,* published by Information Access Company of Belmont, California. At the time of writing, an online retrieval system called Wilsonline, offering access to

---

3   In the first three editions of *Using a Law Library* it was stated that the *Index to Legal Periodicals* appeared first in 1926. No one questioned this statement, but in May 1984, during the annual conference of the Canadian Association of Law Libraries at The University of Western Ontario, Paul Rothman of Fred B. Rothman & Co., Littleton, Colorado, pointed out to me that our Law Library did not have the pre-1926 volumes of the *Index to Legal Periodicals* (1908-1925). I had been misled by the number "1" on the first triennial cumulation.

4   The *Index* is published monthly, except September. It cumulates quarterly as well as annually.

Wilson indexes, had just been announced. The *Index to Legal Periodicals* will be included from August 1981. Beginning with the quarterly cumulative issue dated November 1983, the *Index* is being produced by The H.W. Wilson Company's computerized bibliographic system. An important change stemming from this development is that full bibliographic data is given under both author and subject entries, whereas before that date, it was given only under subject. The effect of this change will be seen in some of the examples that follow.

The *Index to Legal Periodicals* aims to index those legal periodicals from the United States, Canada, the United Kingdom, the Republic of Ireland, Australia, and New Zealand that regularly publish legal matter of high quality and permanent research value. The contents and arrangement of the *Index* have changed somewhat from time to time. For instance, the book review index did not begin until volume 6 (August 1940 to July 1943), and the subject and author indexes, now consolidated, were published as two separate indexes until the end of triennial cumulation 12 (August 1958 to August 1961).

If you are looking for an article and do not know the date of its publication, you may have to search through several cumulations before you find it. Suppose, however, that you have been referred to an article on the history of the business corporation in Ontario by R.C.B. Risk. You think it was published in the mid-1970s, so you look up Risk's name in the Subject and Author Index in triennial cumulation 17, covering the period September 1973 to August 1976. There you will find the following entry:

RISK, R.C.B.
  Corp. (N)
  Legal history (N,P)

This means that an article by Risk is indexed under the subject heading "Corporations". The "N" indicates that the first word (or the first important word) in the title of the article begins with the letter "N". Two articles by the same author are indexed under "Legal history". Since one of them begins with the letter "N" it may (and in fact is) the same one as is indexed under "Corporations". Under both subject headings you will find the article in which you are interested listed as follows:

Nineteenth-century foundations of the business
corporation in Ontario. R.C.B. Risk.
U. Toronto LJ23: 270-306 Summer '73.

Thus, the article you want is published in volume 23 of the *University of Toronto Law Journal,* beginning at page 270 and ending at page 306. (If you are puzzled by the abbreviated title of a journal, you will find its full name in the "Abbreviations of Periodicals Indexed" at the front of the volume.) This is generally all you need to know to find the article, but the date of the issue (Summer '73) in which it appeared is added, and this is useful if the volume has not been found.

You could also have found the article in question by looking under the appropriate subject headings, but if you know the name of the author and the title of the article, you can generally locate the information more quickly by looking under his or her name. In this case, to find the article by subject, you would have had to determine what the appropriate headings were and then look through all the titles until you came to the one you wanted, rather than only through those beginning with the letter "N".

A subject approach is necessary, however, if you are looking for all the articles available (or perhaps for recent articles) on a particular topic. If you are uncertain of the heading or headings under which to look, you may find useful the "List of Subject Headings" near the front of each volume. In addition to listing the subject headings used, it contains cross-references from headings not used, together with references from headings used to similar or more specific headings.

An example from the November 1983 quarterly cumulative issue (which will be incorporated into permanent bound cumulation 23) shows the effect of the recent change in the format of author entries. Suppose you are looking for an article by Peter Hogg on the patriation of the Canadian constitution written soon after the event took place. You will find the article listed under his name in the subject and author index in the November 1983 quarterly cumulative issue as follows:

Hogg, Peter W.
   Patriation of the Canadian constitution: has it been achieved? 8 Queen's L.J. 123-30 Fall '82/Spr. '83

Note the difference between this and the author entry for the Risk article above. In the latter case you had to go from the author to the subject entry to find the name of the article and where it was published. This is no longer necessary (though you can also find the article using a subject approach) but you still need to be aware of the technique in case you are looking for less recent articles.

After a significant case has been reported, comments and articles on it often appear in the law reviews. A useful feature of the *Index to Legal Periodicals* is its "Table of Cases Commented Upon." Since most comments appear within a year or two after the case is reported,[5] it is usually quite easy to find references to them in the table. For instance, if you look up the well known English case of *Hedley Byrne & Co. v. Heller & Partners Ltd.*[6] decided in 1963, in the "Table of Cases Commented Upon" in cumulation 13 (September 1961 to August 1964) and in cumulation 14 (September 1964 to August 1967) you will find lists of 1963-65 journals in which appeared comments or articles on this case. A "Table of Statutes Commented Upon" was recently added to the index; it appears first in cumulation 20 (September 1980-August 1981).

---

5   There may be references in articles to an important case years after it is decided, especially if the case has been judicially considered from time to time. *Dann v. Hamilton* is a good example. See page 170, above. However, most case comments appear soon after the decision is reported.

6   [1964] A.C. 465 (H.L.).

Book reviews usually appear within a two or three-year period after the publication of the book. If you want to find out whether a book has been reviewed, first check its date of publication (in your library's catalogue if it has the book or in a bibliography such as *Law Books in Print*). Then consult the book review index in the appropriate volumes and/or current parts of the *Index to Legal Periodicals*. For instance, Barry L. Strayer's *Judicial Review of Legislation in Canada* was published in 1968; you will find the following entry in cumulation 15 (September 1967 to August 1970):

Strayer, B.L.
Judicial review of legislation in Canada. 1968
    G.V. La Forest. Sask L Rev 34:352 Winter '69
    B. Laskin. U Toronto LJ 19:86 '69

A later review is listed as follows in the book review index in cumulation 16 (September 1970 to August 1973): of the triennial cumulations:

Strayer, B.L.
Judicial review of legislation in Canada. 1968
    J. Cavarzan. Can B Rev 49:387 My '71

(c) Current Index to Legal Periodicals

This is a mimeographed index issued weekly by the Gallagher Law Library of the University of Washington and the *Washington Law Review* in Seattle, Washington. It indexes, under broad general subject headings, the contents of 189 American law reviews. Its purpose is to keep current the *Index to Legal Periodicals,* though not all journals indexed there are included in the *Current Index to Legal Periodicals.* For instance, no Canadian or other Commonwealth legal periodicals are indexed in the latter.

(d) Legal Resource Index and Current Law Index

New in 1980, these two services, as noted above, are provided by Information Access Company of Belmont, California. *Legal Resource Index* includes comprehensive indexing of over 750 law journals selected by the Advisory Board on Indexing of Periodical Literature of the American Association of Law Libraries. This Board meets annually to consider proposals for the inclusion of new journals in *Legal Resource Index* (LRI) and its companion print service, *Current Law Index* (CLI).

The publication pattern of the print and microfilm services is different. In a note at the beginning of the volumes and parts, *CLI* is said to be published in "eight (8) monthly issues, three (3) quarterly cumulations and a single annual cumulation". (The terminology appears to me somewhat odd; "monthly" surely means twelve times a year and "quarterly" four times a year.) *LRI,* on the other hand, cumulates monthly. At the time of writing in November 1984, it covered the period January 1980 to October 1984. This gives it a decided advantage over *CLI,* where none of the cumulations covers more than one year. The microfilm service also includes some material not contained in *CLI*. Several law newspapers are indexed in *LRI*, as is relevant legal material from *Magazine Index* and *National Newspaper Index*. *LRI* is also available online through DIALOG.

LRI and *CLI*, like the *Index to Legal Periodicals*, index not only American law journals, but also those published in Canada and other countries. I have not found a statement of policy as to the countries included.

Both *LRI* and *CLI* include a subject index, author/title index, table of cases, and table of statutes. The last mentioned has been found very useful in The University of Western Ontario Law Library because it refers the user to articles and comments on many Canadian statutes – federal and provincial – that might otherwise be overlooked.

There is no separate book review index in these two services, but in fact book reviews are indexed in both the subject and author/title indexes. An interesting feature is the grading, according to the reviewer's opinion, of the item being reviewed. The grades and their meaning are as follows:

A = Excellent
B = Good
C = Competent
D = Below Average
F = Inferior

(e) Index to Periodical Articles Related to Law

Many articles related to law appear in the journals of other disciplines such as medicine, business, economics, and political science. The aim of the *Index to Periodical Articles Related to Law,* which began publication in 1958, is to index these articles. It used to index as well some of the less scholarly law journals, which did not meet the standards required for inclusion in the *Index to Legal Periodicals,* but beginning with volume 21 (1979) it no longer indexes law journals, bar association journals, or any periodicals that are directly law related. The title page now states that articles indexed are selected from journals not included in the *Current Law Index,* the *Index to Foreign Legal Periodicals* or the *Index to Legal Periodicals.* The *Index to Periodical Articles Related to Law* contains both subject and author indexes. A cumulative volume covering the first ten-year period was published in 1970. There are five-year cumulations covering volumes 11-15 (1969-1973) and volumes 16-20 (1974-1978). The index is published quarterly, with the fourth issue in each year being an annual cumulation.

(f) Index to Canadian Legal Literature (Canadian Abridgment)

As noted in Chapter 4, the *Canadian Abridgment,* second edition, includes an *Index to Canadian Legal Literature.*[7] It indexes not only Canadian

---

7   See p. 105, above.

legal periodicals (articles, annotations, and case comments), but also legal treatises published in Canada. The *Index* consists of a two-volume subject index and a third volume containing a subject key and an author index. The subject key lists headings under which the user might be likely to look in the subject index with "see" references to the headings actually used. The author index does not give complete bibliographical data; instead, it refers you to the volume and paragraph numbers in the subject index where this information is found. This has the disadvantage that if you are looking for an article or a book by a prolific author it may take some time to find it. The three-volume *Index to Canadian Legal Literature* was updated in volume 3 of the *Canadian Abridgment*'s Cumulative Supplement and in the monthly parts of *Canadian Current Law.*

Beginning in January 1985, the *Index to Canadian Legal Literature* is undergoing major changes. The volumes and supplement to the end of 1984 will form a separate set labelled 1981-1984 (the dates during which it was published, though many of the materials indexed are of much earlier date). The new *Index* will have four separate sections – a subject index, book review index, author index and table of casaes [commented on]. Entries in all these sections will contain complete bibliographic information; thus the disadvantage noted above with regard to the author index will no longer exist. The author index and table of cases [commented on] will not be included in *Canadian Current Law* or the quarterly releases in the *Canadian Abridgment* Cumulative Supplement; they will appear only in the annual cumulations. Another important change is in the subject headings used. Instead of following the *Canadian Abridgment* classification, as in the past, the *Index* will now use *Library of Congress Subject Headings,* supplemented by the National Library of Canada's *Canadian Subject Headings.* These various improvements should greatly increase the usefulness of the *Index to Canadian Legal Literature.*

(g) Index to Canadian Legal Periodical Literature

This index began as a project of the Canadian Association of Law Libraries; it is now published privately in Montreal. It indexes not only Canadian legal periodicals, but also articles related to law in non-legal Canadian journals. Thus, it aims to do for Canada what the *Index to Legal Periodicals* (or LRI/CLI) and the *Index to Periodical Articles Related to Law* together do for a wider community. Its author and subject indexes are separate and both contain complete information on the articles indexed. Also included are a table of cases [commented on] and a book review index. There is now a ten-year cumulation covering the period 1961-70, a five-year cumulation covering the years 1971-75, as well as annual cumulations for each of the years from 1976 to 1983.

The practice with regard to issuing interim indexes has varied from year to year. The present policy is described in the preface to the 1984 interim index current at the time of writing. It states that the *Index* is published quarterly with each issue cumulating the material from the previous issue within the year, the fourth issue being the annual bound volume. In addition to journal articles, the *Index to Canadian Legal Periodical Literature* indexes articles published in the topical law reports, as well as certain published lectures series and collections of essays on legal topics. Cassettes are now indexed if they contain material normally found in a law review.

The value of indexing legal material in non-legal periodicals can be seen by comparing the entries for Strayer's *Judicial Review of Legislation in Canada* in the book review indexes in the *Index to Canadian Legal Periodical Literature* with those already quoted from the book review indexes in the *Index to Legal Periodicals.* The book review index in the *Index to Canadian Legal Periodical Literature,* 1961-70, contains the following entry:

> STRAYER, B.L.
> Judicial review of legislation in Canada.
> 1968.
> > (1968) 11 Can. BJ 208
> > A. Gélinas. (1969) 12 Can Pub Admin 125
> > D. Gibson. (1969) 3 Manitoba LJ 107
> > P.W. Hutchins. (1970) 11 Cahiers 186
> > G.V. LaForest. (1969) 34 Sask L Rev 352
> > B. Laskin. (1969) 19 U Toronto LJ 86
> > P.H. Russell. (1969) 2 Can J Pol Sc 378

The book review index in the 1971-75 cumulation adds the following:

> STRAYER, B.L.
> Judicial review of legislation in Canada.
> 1968.
> > J. Cavarzan. (1971) 49 Can B Rev
> > 387-389
> > W.R. Lederman. (1970) 16 McGill LJ
> > 723-728

The reviews in *Canadian Public Administration* and the *Canadian Journal of Political Science* would have been missed if legal material in journals of other disciplines had not been indexed. In addition, book reviews in several Canadian law journals that were omitted from the *Index to Legal Periodicals* are listed. See the entries for the *Canadian Bar Journal* (superseded by the *Canadian Bar Association Journal* and subsequently by the newspaper *National*), *Cahiers* (full title, *Les Cahiers de Droit*), and the *McGill Law Journal.* (The *Index to Legal Periodicals* indexes all these journals, but does not list book reviews that are less than two full pages in length. Two of the foregoing reviews are just under two pages, but the review in the *McGill Law Journal* is longer. Why it was omitted is not clear.) If this example is in any way typical, it appears that the *Index to Canadian Legal Periodical Literature* gives much better coverage to Canadian legal periodical literature than does the *Index to Legal Periodicals.*

However, using two more recent books as examples brings different results. E.L. Picard's *Legal Liability of Doctors and Hospitals in Canada* was published by Carswell in 1978. (A second edition has now been published, but it is too early for book reviews of it.) A search of the book review indexes in the *Index to Legal Periodicals* and the *Index to Canadian Legal Periodical Literature* from 1979 to date brings to light the same three book reviews indexed in both. The second edition of S.M. Waddams' *Products Liability* was published by Carswell in 1980. Book reviews of it in the *Queen's Law Journal* and *Manitoba Law Journal* are indexed in the *Index to Canadian Legal Periodical Literature*. The same two reviews and an additional one in the *Law Quarterly Review* are indexed in the *Index to Legal Periodicals*. The *Law Quarterly Review* is published in England. Its review of the Waddams book is not indexed in the *Index to Canadian Legal Periodical Literature* because the latter indexes only Canadian publications. It is worth remembering that reviews of Canadian law books published in other countries are not indexed in the *Index to Canadian Legal Periodical Literature*. On the other hand, you are likely to find such reviews indexed in the *Index to Legal Periodicals* and the *Legal Resource Index/Current Law Index*.

(h) Index to Foreign Legal Periodicals

The title of this publication is somewhat misleading, for it indexes the contents of the main legal periodicals dealing with international law (public and private) and comparative law, in addition to those relating to the law of all countries of the world other than the United States, the British Isles, and the countries of the Commonwealth whose systems of law have a common law basis. In the fields of international and comparative law, there is some duplication between the *Index to Legal Periodicals, LRI/CLI* and the *Index to Foreign Legal Periodicals,* since all of them index international and comparative law journals published in common law countries. Published by the Institute of Advanced Legal Studies in London, in co-operation with the American Association of Law Libraries, the *Index to Foreign Legal Periodicals* first appeared in 1960. Subject, author, and book review indexes are included. There is also a geographical index, which groups by country or region the legal subjects under which articles on that subject and relating to the particular country or region will be found in the subject index.

There used to be three unbound parts a year with an annual bound volume cumulating and adding to them. There were also triennial cumulations. A change to computerized printing of the *Index to Foreign Legal Periodicals,* which began with the February, 1971 issue, had an effect on the publication of the triennial cumulations. Because it is not possible to combine traditional and computerized methods of printing within a cumulated volume, the fourth permanent cumulation covers only two years, 1969-70. The fifth permanent cumulation reverted to the three-year coverage. The last triennial cumulation is the seventh, dated 1977-79. Since 1980 there have been four unbound parts a year with no cumulations.

(i) Other Indexes

There are other indexes, such as Jones and Chipman's *Index to Legal Periodicals* (1866-1937) for older articles, which you may use from time to time. The *Index to Commonwealth Legal Periodicals,* described in the third edition of this book,[8] has now ceased publication. It was published from 1974 to 1981 by the Sir James Dunn Law Library at Dalhousie University. A cumulation covering the period September 1978 to August 1981 was published by Carswell in 1982.

---

8   Margaret A. Banks, *Using a Law Library,* 3rd ed. (Toronto: Carswell, 1980), p. 172.

6

Automated Legal Research

1. INTRODUCTION

A book published in the 1980s on the use of a law library would not be complete without some reference to automated legal research. Most Canadian law school libraries now have computer terminals, some provincial law associations are offering computer search services to their members, and there are lawyers who have terminals in their offices. Increasingly in the future, law students and lawyers are likely to make some use of the computer in solving legal problems. Realizing that doing automated legal research will soon be regarded as a normal part of a lawyer's skills, law schools are beginning to include some instruction in this field in their legal research programs. Providing instruction and assistance in the use of the computer are becoming accepted additions to the functions of many legal reference librarians.

The development of automated legal research has come at an opportune time, for the increase in the volume of legal materials has never been so rapid as it is now. An interesting example, given to me by the Canadian Law Information Council (CLIC) when I was preparing the third edition of this book, is the fact that for a three-year period beginning in 1977 the *All-Canada Weekly Summaries* noted about 13,000 cases whereas the *Dominion Law Reports* for a 25-year period noted about 15,000 cases. Even allowing for the *Dominion Law Reports'* selectivity this is a remarkable example of the increase of legal information. Access to this information is essential to the lawyer, but is increasingly difficult through traditional manual methods.[1] Automated legal research makes it possible to quickly acquire information that might continue to elude the student or lawyer after many hours of manual searching. This is not to say, however, that automated research will completely replace the manual method. Claude Fabien, author of a paper entitled "Computerized Legal Research In Canada," points out that "the two methods are complementary and necessary to one another."[2] In a study comparing automated and manual legal research, Michael Iosipescu and John Yogis state that "the computer is especially adapted to searching for the particular, as opposed to more general and abstract concepts."[3]

---

1   For a fuller discussion of this problem, see Philip Slayton, *Electronic Legal Retrieval* (Ottawa: Information Canada, 1974), pp. 7-9.
2   Claude Fabien, *Computerized Legal Research in Canada* (Ottawa: Canadian Law Information Council, 1979), p. 26.
3   Michael Iosipescu and John Yogis, *A Comparison of Automated and Manual Legal Research: A Computer Study* (Ottawa: Canadian Law Information Council, 1981), p. 31.

The use of the computer in legal information storage and retrieval has a twenty-five year history. The first system was developed by Professor John Horty of the University of Pittsburgh, beginning in 1959. It originated in a project relating to Pennsylvania's health law statutes. In 1968, the Health Law Project became the nucleus of a private company, Automated Law Searching, later renamed Aspen Systems Corporation. Aspen converted into machine readable form the U.S. Code and the statutes of all states. It became involved in other projects as well, but is best known for its work in full text storage and retrieval of statutes.

Encouraged by the results of the Pittsburgh Project, an English lawyer, Colin Tapper, began a series of experiments with case law retrieval, which became known as the Oxford Experiments. The approach varied somewhat from Horty's because of differences between legislative and judicial texts, which tend to involve different problems. "For instance," say Jon Bing and Trygve Harvold in a recent book, "the language of case law is more redundant, the obvious document unit (one decision) is not as semantically homogeneous as the obvious document unit of statutes (one article) etc."[4] The main purpose of Tapper's experiments was to compare the performance of computer-based and manual research. Full text and abstracts were used as a data base. Taking an average of all questions processed in the experiments, he found that of a total of 175 relevant documents, 100 were retrieved by conventional methods and 144 by computer. Looking at the situation from a different approach – that of all documents retrieved – it was found that, using manual research methods, 100 of 109 documents retrieved were relevant, whereas of 496 documents retrieved by the computer, only 144 were relevant.[5] This low percentage of relevancy has continued to be regarded as a problem with automated legal research, but the computer's printing speed and capacity for modification prevent it from being a major one. It can also be lessened by extreme care in formulating queries. This will be seen from the examples used later in this chapter. Indeed, Iosipescu and Yogis, in the sample problems they used in comparing automated and manual research, found that the two methods identified approximately the same number of irrelevant cases. Thus, they claim, "we have disproved the usual challenge that computers pull up volumes of irrelevant material that requires vast amounts of time to peruse."[6]

A profusion of projects followed these early experiments. There is neither space nor need to deal with all of them here, as the emphasis in this chapter will be on developments in Canada. Before proceeding to them, however, a few words should be said about some major systems that have developed in the United States and the United Kingdom – LEXIS, WESTLAW, and EUROLEX.

---

4   Jon Bing and Trygve Harvold, *Legal Decisions and Information Systems* (Oslo: Universitetsforlaget, 1977), p. 67.
5   Colin Tapper, *Computers and the Law* (London: Weidenfeld and Nicolson, 1973), p. 179; Bing and Harvold, p. 68.
6   Iosipescu and Yogis, p. 7.

(a) LEXIS

Writing in 1976, James A. Sprowl called LEXIS the most ambitious and comprehensive of all the full text document retrieval systems developed in recent years.[7] It evolved out of a joint venture between OBAR (Ohio State Bar Association Automated Research Corporation), a not-for-profit corporation of Ohio lawyers, and Mead Data Central, Inc., which became a subsidiary of the Mead Corporation. Documents in the LEXIS system are broken down into collections of related documents, which are called "libraries". Included in its federal "library" are the full text of the United States Code, Supreme Court decisions from 1925, decisions of the Court of Appeals from 1945, United States District Court decisions from 1960, and Court of Claims decisions, beginning in 1977.[8] Also included are specialized "libraries" of securities law, tax law, trade regulation and patent, trade mark, and copyright law, communications, labour, federal bankruptcy, and Delaware corporation law. They contain statutes, regulations, and court decisions going back to earlier dates than those in the general federal "library", administrative board decisions, and other relevant documents. State "libraries" offered by LEXIS include the full text of cases for all fifty states and the District of Columbia; the date at which coverage begins varies. The constitution and statutes are included for some states, notably Ohio and New York.

Through an arrangement with Mead Data Central, Butterworths Tele-publishing Ltd. began in the late 1970s to add English data bases to LEXIS. The main series of law reports (full text) since 1945 were the first to be made available. A major addition has been an annotated set of the Public General Acts and Statutory Instruments.[9]

(b) WESTLAW

WESTLAW began when, as a by-product of its publishing activities, West Publishing Company developed a machine-readable collection of key-numbered headnotes taken from its well-known National Reporter System. In doing so, it used a modified version of the QL retrieval system originally developed in Canada. Like LEXIS materials, WESTLAW documents are grouped into "libraries" – they correspond to the units in the National Reporter System from which they are taken – the *Supreme Court Reporter, Federal Reporter, Federal Supplement, Atlantic Reporter, Pacific Reporter, etc.* Consisting of headnotes, WESTLAW was not originally a full-text system, and its approach, compared with that of LEXIS, reflected a fundamental

---

7   James A. Sprowl, *A Manual for Computer-Assisted Legal Research* (Chicago: American Bar Foundation, 1976), p. 10.

8   The dates from which decisions are included are those given in Allan J. Onove, "A Comparison of the LEXIS and WESTLAW Databases," *Legal Economics,* March/April 1983, p. 27.

9   David Joseph, "Computers in Britain and America – The Way Ahead," *New Law Journal,* 133 (1983), 983 at 984.

difference in philosophies, which James A. Sprowl has summarized as follows: "The WESTLAW data base reflects the view that indexing and abstracting are essential to any search for legal concepts, while the LEXIS data base reflects the contrary view that formal indexing is not needed when the full-text of cases and statutes can be searched directly for words and phrases."[10] Undoubtedly there are advantages and disadvantages to both systems. Some content is lost when a decision is condensed into a summary, but some may be gained if the abstract is clear and concise. Moreover, the computer storage of headnotes is much less expensive than that of full text. In 1978, however, the WESTLAW data base was expanded to include the full text, in addition to the digest headnotes, of all decisions published by West. Gradually the full text of earlier decisions of both federal and state courts is being added. WESTLAW also offers specialized "libraries" in much the same areas as LEXIS; indeed, the coverage of the two systems is now very similar, although there are differences.

In an article published in March 1984, James A. Sprowl notes that "by the time you read this, enough new materials will have been added to both services [LEXIS and WESTLAW] to make it risky for you to rely on what you have just read."[11] I agree, and for this reason, I have not attempted to list everything offered by either service. For further information on WESTLAW and the American data bases in LEXIS, see the articles listed in footnotes 8 and 11.

(c) EUROLEX

A service of the Thomson Organisation, EUROLEX began in the United Kingdom about two years after Butterworths launched LEXIS there. EUROLEX's data bases, like those of LEXIS, contain many series of English law reports, but each of the two systems has developed its own areas of speciality. Only selected statutes and statutory instruments are available through EUROLEX, which instead has chosen to concentrate on developing a large European and Scottish data base. It has also added some secondary materials: included is *Current Law,* by arrangement with Sweet & Maxwell.[12]

2. AUTOMATED LEGAL RESEARCH IN CANADA

Although experimentation with computerized legal research has been going on in Canada since the 1960s, the acceptance of its use has been somewhat slower than in the United States. Within recent years, however, there has been growing interest in the field. Two main systems developed in Canada in the 1960s and 1970s, DATUM, dealing with Quebec law, and QL,

---

10   Sprowl, *Manual,* p. 56.
11   James A. Sprowl, "The Latest on Westlaw, Lexis and Dialog," *ABA Journal,* 70 (March 1984), 85.
12   Joseph, p. 984.

relating to that of the common law provinces of Canada. Because of the federal nature of Canadian government, there was some overlapping between the two; for instance, the *Supreme Court Reports* were included in both. DATUM is no longer operational, but other systems are being developed in the Province of Quebec. In the 1980s, QL is continuing to expand.

(a) DATUM and Other Quebec Services

The name DATUM is an acronym for "Documentation automatique des textes juridiques de l'Université de Montréal," a joint research project of the Faculty of Law and the Computing Centre of that university. The project, under the direction of Professor Ejan Mackaay of the Faculty of Law, began late in 1968 and was restricted to case law. Its aim was to provide the legal profession in the province with a bilingual computerized case retrieval system.

At first DATUM was offered to private lawyers, a total population of approximately 6,000 lawyers and notaries. The cost of the project could not, however, be covered in this way, and in July 1973 the services were made available to judges and lawyers within the public administration. In return, the government paid a fixed sum to the DATUM project. In September 1973 it was estimated that one-third of Quebec lawyers had become users of DATUM.[13]

In 1975, a Crown corporation called the Société québécoise d'information juridique (SOQUIJ) was created by the Quebec government to integrate the various legal information services in the province. As noted earlier, SOQUIJ now publishes the three series of *Recueils de jurisprudence du Québec*.[14] It also operated the DATUM system, which included in its data bases the full text of decisions of the Supreme Court of Canada published in the *Supreme Court Reports* (1950-79) and the reports of the Cour d'Appel (1950-79), Cour Supérieure (1945-79), and *Rapports de Pratique de Québec* (1966-79). During the last two years of DATUM's operation (1977-79) the updating of these collections was carried out by adding to the data bases only summaries of decisions. These summaries, prepared by the editors of SO-QUIJ and designed to facilitate computer research, were said by Claude Fabien to be excellent in quality.[15] They included those summaries published exclusively in *Jurisprudence Express,* a Quebec legal information service that aims to provide abstracts of decisions very soon after they are handed down.

The mode of access to DATUM, as chosen by SOQUIJ, was by way of a service centre; there were no terminals in law offices or libraries. Service was obtained by writing or telephoning the researchers at the centre. Based on experience, SOQUIJ created about 130 dossiers, which answered the most frequent requests for information.

---

13 Bing and Harvold, p. 118.
14 See p. 29, above.
15 Fabien, p. 3.

Legislation was not included in the DATUM data base. Another Quebec project at Laval University concentrated on this type of legal source material. Known as MODUL (Medium ordinateur et droit, Université Laval), it was an automated system for the permanent updating and retrieving of legislative texts. In 1979, the Quebec Official Publisher was preparing a machine-readable version of the Quebec statutes for incorporation into the DATUM data base unless the creation of a separate data base linked to the MODUL (by then the MODUL/DEPLOI) System was found to be preferable.[16] This did not materialize at the time because SOQUIJ, at the end of June 1979, interrupted its automated research services for an unspecified period. The reason was mainly financial, and DATUM has not been revived. However, at the time of writing in 1984, SOQUIJ was about to make available a data base containing the Quebec statutes. Quebec regulations were expected soon to be available in the same form.

(c) QL Systems

(i) *General*

A treaty project that began at Queen's University, Kingston, in 1961 may be regarded as the beginning of QL Systems. The purpose of the project was to collect and annotate all the treaties of the British Commonwealth. Since 1967 computerized text editing has been used to add information from these records.

In 1968, Professor Hugh Lawford, the moving force behind the treaty project, initiated another project that became known as QUIC/LAW – "Queen's University Investigation of Computing and Law". In that year IBM Canada and Queen's University launched a study of potential applications of computer-based systems for legal information retrieval. A production organization for converting legal sources into machine-readable form was established, and in 1971-72, the federal Department of Justice sponsored a test to measure its usage by lawyers and assess the feasibility of an expanded service.

At about the same time as the treaty project was developing in Kingston, an Alberta lawyer, Keith Latta, established in Edmonton a firm called Canadian Case Law Research Ltd. Its aim was to promote the use of the computer in case law research; its experiments concentrated on personal injury cases, as they seemed especially well adapted to the techniques of automated research. For instance, if one wanted to know the damages awarded in a particular type of accident, it was easy to retrieve all cases included in the data base relating to accidents of a similar type by using key words indicating the part of the body injured, the type of injury, *etc.* Canadian Case Law Research Ltd. offered a computer service to lawyers in the area. In 1968, Mr. Latta was appointed Professor of Law at Queen's University and from then until 1971 he worked with Professor Lawford on the QUIC/LAW project.

---

16   Fabien, p. 3.

Because of the rapid growth of QUIC/LAW and the prospect of commercial use of the system, Queen's University asked that it be incorporated as a separate entity outside the University. In 1973, QL Systems Limited was incorporated to carry forward the work begun by QUIC/LAW. It secured service contracts with various governments for the setting up of data bases of case law and legislation and for the use of its retrieval system. The federal Department of Justice is one of its most important clients.

In attempting to deal with nine provinces, a great variety of law report series, and federal and provincial statutes and regulations, QL has encountered problems that DATUM and other Quebec services did not have to face. Most significant is the copyright problem, there being a division of copyrights in the summaries of published decisions among several competing publishing firms, which have been reluctant to give up the rights.[17] Crown copyright in statutes at the provincial level has also led to difficulties. One encouraging development in the late 1970s was that Canada Law Book Company of Toronto acquired a minority share in the company and began adding its principal law report series to the data bases offered by QL Systems.[18]

QL has now added certain non-legal data bases: some of them may, on occasion, be useful to lawyers; others have no connection at all with law. The legal data bases available through QL at the time of writing fall within three categories: law reports and digests; constitutional Acts of Canada; statutes and regulations.

(ii) Law reports and Digests

Data Base	Abbreviation
All-Canada Weekly Summaries, beginning 1977	ACWS
Canadian Criminal Cases, beginning with 2d series, 1971	CCC
Dominion Law Reports, beginning with 2d series, 1955	DLR
Dominion Report Service, beginning 1968	DRS
Dominion Tax Cases, beginning 1971	DTC
Exchequer Court Reports, 1877-1971	ECR
Federal Court Reports, from 1971	FCR
	RCF (French)
National Reporter System	
This data base includes all	
Maritime Law Book report series	
as follows:	NRS
Alberta Reports, beginning with Vol. 35 (1982)	AR
Atlantic Provinces Reports, beginning with Vol. 1, (1975)	APR
Manitoba Reports, 2d series, beginning with Vol. 14 (1982)	MANR
National Reporter, beginning with Vol. 16 (1977)	NR

---

17   Fabien, p. 6.
18   Fabien, p. 6.

New Brunswick Reports, 2d series, beginning with Vol. 1
(1970)   NBR
Newfoundland & Prince Edward Island Reports, beginning
with Vol. 1 (1971)   NFL
Nova Scotia Reports, 2d series, beginning with Vol. 1 (1970) NSR
Ontario Appeal Cases, beginning with Vol. 1 (1984)   OAC
Saskatchewan Reports, beginning with Vol. 15 (1982)   SASK
Supreme Court Reports, from 1876   SCR

                                                               RCS (French)
Weekly Criminal Bulletin, beginning 1976   WCB
Western Legal Publications
   This data base contains B.C. Decisions   WLP for all
   and B.C. Labour Relations Board   series in this
   Decisions from 1979, also Supreme Court of   data base
   Canada, Alberta, Saskatchewan and Manitoba
   Decisions from 1980 and Federal Court
   of Appeal from 1981.
Western Weekly Reports, from 1968   WWR

At the time of publication, a data base containing the *Ontario Reports* from 1970 to date was in the process of being added.

Note that law reports in the QL data bases consist of headnotes only, not full text. However, the "headnotes" in the National Reporter System data base are very extensive, including all the material given at the beginning of each case in the Maritime Law Book report series. Thus, not only a summary of the report, but also detailed indexing under topic numbers and lists of cases and statutes noticed will be found. In some ways this is beneficial, but with the structure of the information in the NRS data base being different from that in other data bases, it is sometimes necessary to vary one's searching techniques; with the NRS data base a more specific type of query may be needed. Judicial considerations are also included in the headnotes to the cases in some of the other QL data bases.

Digests such as the *All-Canada Weekly Summaries* include the complete summary.

(iii) *Constitutional Acts of Canada*

This is the name given to a data base prepared by the federal Department of Justice that includes the full text of 42 constitutional documents, beginning with the Royal Proclamation of 1763 and ending with the Canada Act 1982. The English abbreviation for the data base is CAC; in French it is LCC. The documents are the same as those included in the appendices volume to the *Revised Statutes of Canada, 1970* with the addition of constitutional Acts passed since the publication of that revision. Although the text of each British North America Act is given separately, amendments made by these Acts are also incorporated into the original Act of 1867. However, the name "British North America Act" has been retained for pre-1982 Constitution Acts and amendments to the 1867 Act made by the Constitution Act, 1982, have not been incorporated into the former. Unfortunately, the manner of presentation leads to confusion between the Canada Act 1982 and its Schedule B, the Constitution Act, 1982. Sections of the latter appear on printouts as if they were sections of the former. If you ask for section 2 of the Canada Act 1982, section 2 of the Canada Act will be printed followed by s. 2 of the Constitution Act, 1982. Should you ask for a section of the Constitution Act, 1982, you will get nothing. It is unfortunate, too, that the schedule to the Constitution Act, 1982, has been omitted from the data base since it contains amendments to several of the earlier constitutional documents. At the time of writing, the proclamation of June 21, 1984, making the first amendments to the Constitution of Canada under the new procedures of 1982, had not been added to this data base.

(iv) *Statutes and Regulations*

Data Base	Abbreviation
Canada (federal)	
Statutes	RSC
	SRC (French)
Statutory Orders and Regulations	SOR
	DOR (French)
Alberta	
Statutes	SA
British Columbia	
Statutes	SBC
Regulations (Not all existing regulations are currently in the data base.)	RBC
Manitoba	
Statutes	SM
New Brunswick	
Statutes	SNB
Ontario	
Statutes	SO
Regulations	RO
Saskatchewan	
Statutes	SS

The names and abbreviations given to some of the data bases are rather confusing. For instance, there seems to be no logical reason why the federal statutes data base is called "Revised Statutes of Canada," whereas the provincial ones are called "Statutes". All the statutes and regulations contained in QL data bases are, in effect, full-text continuing consolidations.

To search a data base it is necessary to know the abbreviation used – *e.g.* RSC for federal statutes, SO for Ontario statutes.

When accessing QL data bases, it is possible to obtain without charge a list of all those currently available, along with their abbreviations. The data bases are listed in alphabetical order according to the abbreviations used. Thus, *Atlantic Provinces Reports* (APR) comes before *Alberta Reports* (AR). Legal, quasi-legal, and non-legal data bases are interfiled on the list.

In compiling the above lists of legal data bases I have arranged them so that a reader who wants to know only what law report series were available at the time of writing can find this out quickly. The same is true if only statutes and regulations are required. A list of quasi-legal data bases available from QL will be given later in this chapter.[19]

(c) The Canadian Law Information Council and QL Systems Limited

Interest in automated legal research increased in Canada during the late 1970s and early 1980s through the efforts of the Canadian Law Information Council (CLIC) to promote it. CLIC is a private, non-profit corporation formed in 1973 by a group representing the various components of the Canadian legal community – the federal and ten provincial Departments of Justice, the law societies of the provinces, and professional and university associations. Associate membership is open to law publishers. CLIC is concerned with all aspects of legal information as its varied publications show. The use of the computer for legal research is just one of CLIC's many interests, but it is an area in which CLIC is very active.

In the late 1970s, CLIC wanted to promote the establishment of a national automated retrieval system accessible to potential users through a network of terminals. To bring this about, it co-operated with QL Systems. Realizing that the data bases available through QL were not sufficiently comprehensive to satisfy the needs of Canadian lawyers, it took steps to increase the coverage. For instance, it acquired the right to convert to machine-readable form some of the publications of The Carswell Company Limited and, as part of this project, has added to the data bases offered by QL summaries of judgments in the *Western Weekly Reports* from 1968 to date.

To make computer-assisted legal research more readily accessible to law students and faculty, lawyers, and other researchers, CLIC set up service centres across Canada. A terminal was installed, usually in the Law Library, in each selected centre. One or two librarians were given training in its use, and they, in turn, were expected to give instruction to members of the institution and, within reasonable limits, research assistance to lawyers in the region. The thirteen service centres established by CLIC (eleven in university law libraries, one in the Law Society of Saskatchewan Library, and one in Newfoundland's Department of Justice) are no longer financially supported by it,

---

19   See p. 216, below.

but most of them continue to function. Other Canadian law school libraries, not selected as CLIC service centres, have in recent years acquired computer terminals and thus have access to QL data bases. Through various aspects of its work, CLIC continues to promote the development of automated legal research in Canada.

One question that arises in any discussion of automated legal research is whether it is better for lawyers to do their own research or for legal reference librarians to do it for them. There are advantages and disadvantages to both approaches. A skilled legal reference librarian, using the computer on a regular basis, is likely to become better equipped to formulate queries, having found, by experimentation, the best search words and commands to use in specific circumstances. On the other hand, a lawyer, specializing in a particular field, may have a better idea of the words and phrases likely to occur in statutes and reports in that specific area. The reference librarian, dealing with questions in all areas of the law, cannot be expected to be an expert in all of them. It seems probable that both approaches will have a place in the automated legal research of the future. The same situation exists with regard to manual legal research. Some lawyers prefer to do their own, whereas others prefer to have research assistants do it for them.

3. USE OF AUTOMATED RESEARCH TECHNIQUES IN SOLVING A LEGAL PROBLEM

If you are considering an automated search, the first thing to determine is whether it is appropriate in the particular circumstances. In some situations the answer will be obvious, in others less so. If you want to check statutory provisions relating to a particular subject in all Canadian provinces, automated searches will not now give you the information you need since the statutes of only six provinces are included in the QL data bases. If, on the other hand, what you want is a comparison of certain statutory provisions in the four western provinces, an automated search may give you the information more quickly than a manual one.

Some lawyers and librarians have the idea that they should go to the computer in only a few very complicated cases, or in those where all other methods have failed. Claude Fabien believes this to be a misconception. "In its present state of development," he wrote in 1979, "automated retrieval appears to be well-suited to the preliminary research, that which clears the way at the beginning of research. Library research should follow, rather than precede, automated retrieval."[20]

Some sample searches will give you an idea of when the use of the computer is appropriate and, if it is, how to formulate your queries.

In this chapter I want to keep technical information on using the computer terminal to a minimum, as there are manuals that deal with this in

---

20   Fabien, p. 26.

detail. However, to explain how to formulate queries, it is necessary to mention briefly the commands that are used. You ask the computer to retrieve all documents containing certain words by typing these words into the terminal. There is an "or" command represented by a space, an "and" command, represented by an ampersand, and a "but not" command represented by a percentage sign. An "or" command retrieves documents containing either of the words entered; an "and" command retrieves only those documents that contain both words. The command *discrimination % racial* is designed to retrieve documents on all types of discrimination except racial. The "but not" command should be used with caution as it may result in the omission of potentially relevant material. If you want a document retrieved only if it contains two or more words side by side you put them in quotation marks – for example, "Gross Negligence". You may also, by the use of an asterisk, truncate a word so that the search is performed on the stem rather than the full word. Thus a command to retrieve *discriminat** would retrieve words within the data base such as discriminate, discriminates, and discriminating. Truncation also retrieves documents with both singular and plural forms of a search word. All this sounds quite simple until you try it; the results are sometimes not what you would expect. For instance, in searching for cases involving the use of a breathalyzer to test the level of alcohol in the blood, it was found unwise to truncate test as not only documents containing the words *test* and *tests* were retrieved, but also a great many containing *testify,* which were not relevant to the query. However, before the main part of your search begins, you are told what terms have been generated by the root words. If you wish to omit any of them, you can modify your query before the main search begins. Here is a suggested query for a breathalyzer case search:

breath breathalyzer & test tests sampl*

This would retrieve all documents in the data base being searched containing the word *breath* or *breathalyzer* and *test* or *tests* or words beginning with the stem *sampl.* If a word has two spellings and you use only one of them in your query, a document that uses the other spelling will not be retrieved. "Breathalyzer" is a good example of a word with multiple spellings. The *Gage Canadian Dictionary* gives "breathalyzer" as the preferred spelling and "breathalyser" as an alternative, but at least two other spellings have been found in reports of some cases – "breathalizer" and "breathaliser". Thus, in the foregoing search, it really would be better to truncate the word thus: *breathal**.

Suppose the legal question dealt with in Chapter 4 had arisen in Alberta and you want to know whether a gratuitous passenger/gross negligence provision similar to that no longer in force in Ontario is law in this western province. You decide to try an automated search for the phrase "gross negligence" in the Statutes of Alberta data base. This query retrieves eight documents, one of which is the gross negligence section of Alberta's Highway Traffic Act (remember that the section rather than the complete Act is the unit in statute searching). The remaining seven documents retrieved were sections of other Alberta statutes such as the Municipal Government Act, the Emergency Medical Aid Act, and the Defamation Act. This illustrates the relevancy problem, which in this case was not great since only eight documents were retrieved and it was easy to identify the only one that was relevant. Section 182 of Alberta's Highway Traffic Act uses the term "guest without payment" rather than "gratuitous passenger," though the word "passenger" also occurs in this section. "Gross negligence" and *guest* or "Gross negligence" and *passenger* would probably have retrieved just one document.[21] It is not possible to combine "gross negligence" and "guest without payment" because only one phrase can be included in a query. It must be at the beginning and it may be immediately followed by an "and," but not an "or". However, you can combine two or more searches by using the save and combine feature. (Type *save* before proceeding to another search; saved searches will be numbered and can be combined in a query thus: #1 & #2. A saved search can be combined with a new one thus: #1 & guest*.) Saved searches cannot be transferred from one data base to another. A query has to be executed and saved separately for each data base being searched.

The relevancy problem is eased by the fact that the computer automatically ranks documents according to the frequency with which your search words occur, presenting first the one having the highest frequency. This increases the probability that the documents relevant to your query will appear early rather than later. If you prefer to have the documents presented in chronological order (the one of earliest date first) or in reverse chronological order (the one of most recent date first) you can enter a command to this effect. Chronological order may be preferred for some types of statutory research, especially if you want to see several sections of an Act in the order in which they appear. Reverse chronological order is often useful in case law research, where the most recent case on a point at issue may be of vital importance.

Finding the gross negligence/guest without payment section of Alberta's Highway Traffic Act was much easier using the computer than it would have been manually. To formulate your query and get the correct response, you did not need to know the name or date of the statute or the section number of the provision in which you were interested. Nor did you have to think up alternative subject headings under which the provision might be indexed. To find the same information manually, you would probably have gone to the index of Alberta statutes. Although it is a subject index rather than one arranged by the names of Acts, it contains no entry for "gross negligence," "negligence, gross," or "guest without payment". Under "negligence," there

---

21   In the chapter on automated legal research in the third edition of this book, it was assumed that the legal problem had arisen in New Brunswick (Banks, *Using a Law Library,* 3rd ed., pp. 185-89). A gross negligence/guest without payment provision was then in force in that province (Motor Vehicle Act, R.S.N.B. 1973, c. M 17, s. 26). This example is no longer suitable because the New Brunswick provision has been repealed (S.N.B. 1980, c. 34, s. 13). It seems to me that one shortcoming of automated research is that one finds no record of the repeal; the phrase being searched simply does not appear. (If you know the section number, you can check whether it has been repealed, but in this situation you can easily find the same information manually.)

is a subheading "motor vehicles, actions for damages," and a sub-subheading "passengers, standard of care", which directs you to s. 182 of c. H-7, which is the Highway Traffic Act. There are similar entries under "motor vehicles" and "passengers," but none of these entries tells you that a gross negligence/ guest without payment provision is contained in the section. You would probably have looked up this section to see what it contains. Alternatively, you might have approached the subject by going directly to the Highway Traffic Act (assuming that it was the correct statute to consult) and using its index to direct you to the provision.

When you begin to search in a data base you are told up to what date documents are included. It is important to note this date because if it is not current you may have to update your research manually. For instance, at the time of searching the Statutes of Alberta data base late in 1984, documents were included up to July 1 of that year; a manual search of *Provincial Pulse* indicated that no amendments to Alberta's Highway Traffic Act had since been passed or were pending. On the other hand, the Statutes of New Brunswick data base was up to date only to September 1, 1983 and that containing the Statutes of British Columbia to November 4, 1982. If you had been doing a search in one of these data bases, additional manual research, as for example in the latest Table of Public Statutes, as well as in the current volume of *Provincial Pulse,* would have been necessary.

Having confirmed that Alberta's gross negligence/guest without pay- ment provision is still in force, you will want to find cases that indicate what constitutes gross negligence. Of course, you will be especially interested in Alberta cases, but those from other jurisdictions may also be helpful if a gross negligence/guest without payment statutory provision was in force when the dispute arose. You decide to try an automated search in the *Dominion Law Reports* data base, formulating your query as follows:

"Gross negligence" & guest & without & payment

You retrieve ten cases, four from Nova Scotia (two are the same case at different levels), five from Alberta, and one from Newfoundland. In eight of the cases an important point at issue was whether the passenger in the car was a guest without payment within the meaning of the statute. This is not relevant to your problem, for it is clear that the hitchhiker who was injured was a guest without payment or gratuitous passenger. In one of the remaining cases, the driver apparently fell into a hypnoidal state; in the other he was very short of sleep, but was not under the influence of alcohol. What these cases show is that your query was in one way not broad enough and, in another, not sufficiently specific. By searching the words *guest & without & payment,* you retrieved cases which, in their headnotes, used the phrase "guest without payment," but not those that used the alternative phrase "gratuitous pas- senger". For instance, you did not retrieve any Ontario cases probably be- cause the Ontario statutory provision, when in force, used the phrase "gra- tuitous passenger" and most likely that term was used in cases decided under it. An important factor in your problem (remember that we are using the problem in Chapter 4 of this book, but assuming that the accident occurred in

Alberta instead of Ontario) is the extent to which the driver was under the influence of alcohol. By omitting any reference to this in your query, it was only by chance that one headnote containing the word "alcohol" was retrieved, and it was of little help since the driver was not under the influence of alcohol. It appears that there are not many gross negligence/guest without payment cases in the *Dominion Law Reports* data base in which alcohol was a factor. Had you added:

& alcohol

to your query, it seems reasonable to conclude that only one of the ten cases would have been retrieved. However, you may still want to search:

"Gross negligence" & guest & without & payment

in other data bases. For instance, I found that the only Alberta case retrieved from such a search in the WWR data base duplicated one already retrieved in the DLR search, whereas a search of the NRS data base retrieved a 1984 Alberta case not found in either of the previous searches. Note that even if you use the abbreviation of a single report series (*e.g.* AR) in the NRS data base, all series in that data base will be searched. If you want to limit your search to a single series, you can do so by segment or field searching, a technique that will be explained later in this chapter.[22]

You may now want to rephrase your query to include references to "gratuitous passenger". A search of three data bases using the following query:

"gross negligence" & gratuitous & passenger passengers
& intoxicat* drunk drinking alcohol liquor

brought the following results:

DLR – 14 documents retrieved
SCR – 1 document retrieved
WWR – 6 documents retrieved

The one *Supreme Court Reports* case duplicated one of the fourteen *Dominion Law Reports* cases; there was no other duplication. A study of the headnotes of all these cases showed a high degree of relevancy; all concerned accidents in which a gratuitous passenger (in some there was more than one passenger) was injured or killed and the question of the driver's intoxication arose. In many of the cases the amount of alcohol consumed by the driver appeared to be much greater than in the hypothetical case with which you are concerned; such cases are likely to be helpful to your client. The result of this search shows the importance of formulating queries with great care; it also indicates that with such care a high degree of relevancy can sometimes be attained. Various other related searches in the same or other data bases might retrieve additional useful cases. Remember, too, that you can combine searches by using the save and combine feature.

The foregoing illustration shows the value of using the computer at the beginning of your research. You have quickly found not only the names of many relevant cases, but also more information about them than a digest of cases contains. You will have to do some manual research because not all

---

22   See pp. 215-216, below.

report series are included in the QL data bases. Moreover, there is the possibility that you missed a case in the data base because it used a different word or phrase from those you had searched. The terminology used in the headnotes you found in your automated search will give you some guidance in continuing your research manually.

The advantages of beginning your research with the computer are even more apparent if the key words relating to your problem are ordinary English ones rather than legal terms. You expect to find words and phrases such as "negligence", "gross negligence", "gratuitous passenger", and "guest without payment" in the indexes and digests prepared with the needs of the lawyer in mind. Such indexes tend, however, to disregard ordinary words that may be part of a legal problem. Suppose, for instance, you have a client who has fallen down an escalator in a public building and been injured. He wants to sue the owner of the building for failing to provide stairs or an elevator for people like himself who for one reason or another find it difficult to use escalators. Your chances of finding, through manual research, cases involving falls down escalators are slight, for the word "escalator" is unlikely to appear in a legal index. An automated search, however, should retrieve such cases if there are any so long as the word "escalator" occurs in the headnote as one would expect it to. You might try the following query:

Escalator* & fall & injury injure injured

Truncation of *escalator* should retrieve headnotes containing both singular and plural forms – escalator and escalators; you might also have truncated *injur*.

A search of the DLR data base produced only one case involving an injury resulting from a fall down an escalator – *Kauffman v. Toronto Transit Commission* (1959), 18 D.L.R. (2d) 204. A different case, *McCormack v. T. Eaton Company Limited*, [1963] S.C.R. 180, was retrieved from the SCR data base. A more recent (1980) Quebec case, *Aubin v. Syndicat de Québec Ltée*, 3 A.C.W.S. (2d) 395, was retrieved from the ACWS data base. None of the three is very helpful since there is no suggestion that the person who fell down the escalator had objected to using it or had no choice in the matter. However, the searches do show that cases involving a very specific set of facts can be quickly retrieved through the use of the computer.

Seat and *belt* are ordinary English words that you might not expect to find in legal indexes. However, whether failure to use a seat belt (or seat-belt or seatbelt) constitutes contributory negligence when injuries are sustained in a motor vehicle accident has in recent years become a factor in many negligence cases. *Seatbelt* does appear in legal indexes; see, for instance, Illustration 11. Use of "seat belt" as a phrase or *seatbelt* as a word in an automated search is interesting partly because of the spelling differences and partly because a high degree of relevancy is generally achieved. In the course of manual research, I discovered that Maritime Law Book generally prints *seatbelt* as one word, whereas Carswell and some other publishers print it as two. I had not noticed that Canada Law Book uses a hyphen. In an automated search, the query "seat belt" will not retrieve cases in which the one-word spelling is used; the reverse is also true. I found, however, that the query "seat belt" will retrieve cases in which a hyphen is used. The reason for the high degree of relevancy in seat belt queries seems to relate to the issue of contributory negligence being involved. Moreover, all relate to injuries sustained in motor vehicle accidents. I have not yet come across a case relating to seat belts on airplanes.

4. OTHER EXAMPLES OF AUTOMATED SEARCHES

(a) Judicial Considerations

It is possible to use the computer to find citations to cases or to see if a case has been judicially considered. A couple of examples of the latter will be used as illustrations, though there are problems that have to be taken into account. You might treat the name of a case as a phrase and enter a phrase search thus:

"Lehnert v. Stein"

This, however, would not retrieve cases in which *Lehnert v. Stein* was referred to in the headnote by its original name *Stein v. Lehnert*. Nor would it retrieve cases in which the full name *Kurt Walter Lehnert v. Stephanie Stein* was used. It may, therefore, be better to enter the names separately, thus:

Lehnert & Stein

This will retrieve all headnotes in which the two names appear, whether as part of the name of a case or not. With relatively uncommon names, such as Lehnert and Stein, this may work quite well, but if the parties were called Smith and Jones you would encounter a further problem. Changing from a phrase to a name search means that you may retrieve irrelevant cases, as, for instance, those in which one of the parties was called Smith and the judge's name was Jones. If the names of the parties are very common, you would probably attempt to limit the search by adding another word, perhaps relating to the type of case you are seeking, as, for example, "negligence".

From experimentation in this area, I am inclined to conclude that, at least with older cases that have been judicially considered many times, it is better to begin with manual research. We have used *Lehnert v. Stein* as an example in searching for cases judicially considered in the *D.L.R. Annotation Service* (see Illustrations 9 and 10) and in the cases judicially considered tables in the *Canadian Abridgment* (2nd) (see Illustrations 86 and 88). To see whether any additional Supreme Court of Canada cases could be retrieved by an automated search, I entered the Lehnert & Stein query in the *Supreme Court Reports* data base. Seven cases were retrieved – the seventh was the original Supreme Court case *Lehnert v. Stein*. Of the other six, only three were listed in the cases judicially considered tables in the *Canadian Abridgment* (2nd) and three (two the same, one different) in the *D.L.R. Annotation Service*. Using Illustration 10, I also made a comparison of the *Dominion Law Reports* cases listed there with those retrieved from the DLR data base. Illustration 10 lists 49 cases in which *Lehnert v. Stein* was judicially considered, but only 28 of them are reported in the *Dominion Law Reports*. The same number of cases, 28 (omitting reports of the case itself) was retrieved from the DLR data base. However, on comparing the volume and page numbers, I discovered that one listed in the *D.L.R. Annotation Service* – 63 (2d) 450 – was not retrieved by automated research, whereas one case not listed in the *Service* – 54 (2d) 148 – was retrieved by the computer. On checking the reports of the two cases, I found that in the first, although *Lehnert v. Stein* was referred to in the text of the judgment, it was not listed in the headnote; therefore it could not be retrieved by an automated search of a data base not containing the full text. In the second case, *Lehnert v. Stein* was listed in the headnote as being judicially considered; it was therefore retrieved by an automated search. The second case's omission from the *D.L.R. Annotation Service* was presumably the result of human error.

One reason why I suggest that it is better to begin manually when searching for judicial considerations of a case such as *Lehnert v. Stein* is because much of the analysis has been done for you in the *Canadian Abridgment* (2nd) and the *D.L.R. Annotation Service* – you are there told in what way the case has been considered – has it been followed, distinguished, or what? Beginning with manual research will also make it easier to sort out the duplications that you are bound to encounter in your search for judicial considerations of *Lehnert v. Stein* in several data bases.

The situation may be different, however, if you want information on a recent case in which an earlier case in which you are interested has been judicially considered. Suppose, for instance, that you are looking for recent judicial considerations of *Toronto Railway Company v. King,* a Canadian case appealed to the Judicial Committee of the Privy Council and reported in [1908] A.C. 260. You have heard that it was considered in a recent case in one of the Atlantic provinces, but you do not know the name of the case nor are you sure of the jurisdiction. A search of the NRS data base for "Toronto Railway Company" & *King* retrieved six documents. In three of the cases, *Toronto Railway Company v. King* was judicially considered; in the other three it was not. (In the three irrelevant documents, a case in which Toronto Railway Company was one of the parties and another case in which The King was one of the parties were judicially considered.) It was easy to determine that the case you were looking for was *Shepherd v. Helm and Helm,* decided by the Nova Scotia Supreme Court Trial Division in November 1983 and reported in 60 N.S.R. (2d) 93 and in 128 A.P.R. 93. It would probably have taken you somewhat longer to find the same information manually in tables of cases judically considered. An index/digest volume covering Vol. 128 of the *Atlantic Provinces Reports* had not been published at the time of writing. However, the fact that *Toronto Railway Company v. King* had been judicially considered in *Shepherd v. Helm and Helm* was already recorded in the loose-leaf Appendix to the *Canadian Abridgment* (2nd).

(b) Finding Cases Decided by a Particular Judge

Most legal reference librarians have had the experience of being asked for all the cases decided by a particular judge or for all his judgments on a specific topic. There is no easy way to find this manually as cases are not indexed under the names of judges. This is an area where an automated search is likely to be especially helpful. There is some variation in the format of headnotes from one data base to another, but the DLR format may be given as an example:

1. Date 2. Style-of-Cause 3. Citation 4. Date/Judges/Court
5. Unused 6. Keywords 7. Summary 8. Counsel.

Each of the numbers is considered a field or segment and it is possible to limit a search to one or more of these fields. An example of a variation in format is that the SCR data base does not provide a field for counsel, but does have one that tells you from what court a case has been appealed to the Supreme Court of Canada.

Suppose you want to know what cases dealing with professional negligence have been decided by Mr. Justice Horace Krever of the Ontario High Court. A search of the DLR data base should give you some relevant cases. Here is a sample query:

Profession* & negligen* & @ 4 Krever

This requests the retrieval of documents containing words with the roots *profession* and *negligen* and containing headnotes of cases decided by a judge named Krever; @ 4 limits the search to field 4; thus if counsel's name were Krever or Krever were one of the parties, the headnote would not be retrieved. Only one document was retrieved by this query – the headnote of a 1983 case decided by Mr. Justice Krever in which the question of whether a surgeon had been negligent in the performance of his professional duties was an issue. The words "professions" and "negligence" occurred in the headnote. Being sure that Mr. Justice Krever had decided other cases dealing with professional negligence, I then checked to see how often his name occurred in the data base. For each data base there is an alphabetical listing of words contained in it. If you want to know whether and, if so, how often a word occurs you type *dict* followed by the word, thus:

dict Krever

This told me that the name Krever occurs 121 times in 119 documents in the DLR data base. No doubt the 119 documents dealt with a variety of subjects and I did not want all of them but I decided to try a more general search than my earlier one. Even though it might retrieve some irrelevant documents along with those I wanted, it seemed worthwhile to do so. I therefore typed in this query:

negligence & @ 4 Krever

Seven cases decided by Mr. Justice Krever were retrieved; five of them were relevant, dealing with professional negligence. One was the case already retrieved in the earlier search. The other four related to a physician, a lawyer, a surgeon, and an engineer. No word with the root *profession* occurred in either headnote; this explains why my earlier search had failed to retrieve them. The two irrelevant cases dealt with other types of negligence.

With practice, much useful information that would be difficult, if not impossible, to find manually can be obtained by segment searching. Segment printing is also useful. For instance, if you wanted a list of all 119 of Mr. Justice Krever's decisions contained in the DLR data base, but not the complete headnote of each, you could ask the computer to print only certain segments or fields. By typing in

$$F = 1,2,3$$

you would retrieve the date, style-of-cause, and citation of each case. You might want to include 4 to be sure that Mr. Justice Krever was the judge in each case, for the dictionary command gives the number of documents in which the name *Krever* is mentioned – all might not have been in field 4.

5. QUASI-LEGAL DATA BASES

Several of QL Systems' non-legal data bases may, on occasion, be useful to lawyers. I am inclined to call these data bases quasi-legal, rather than non-legal, for they do contain legal information. The following are the data bases that I would class as quasi-legal:

Data Base	Abbreviation
Business Information Wire, from September 1984 (The Canadian Press)	BIW
Canada News-Wire (English-language news releases) from May 1984	CNW
Canadian Business Index and Canadian News Index, from July 1974 (Micromedia Ltd.)	CNI
Canadian Press Newstex, from January 1981	CPN
Canadian Regulatory Reporter – Summaries of Decisions of Provincial and Federal Regulatory Boards, sponsored by CLIC	CRR
Hansard Oral Questions, from January 1973	HOQ HQO (French)
Hansard Written Questions, January 1973	HWQ HQE (French)
Tax Advance Rulings. Income Tax Rulings published by the Deputy Minister of National Revenue for Taxation of Canada. Sponsored by QL Systems	TAR
Tax Information Circulars from 1970 and Tax Interpretation Bulletins from 1971	TIC

Suppose you are interested in recent developments relating to the white paper on copyright entitled *From Gutenberg to Telidon,* published by Consumer and Corporate Affairs Canada in May 1984. You are aware that no bill to revise the Copyright Act has yet been introduced in Parliament, but you wonder whether questions have been asked on the subject. As noted above, QL offers data bases containing *Hansard Oral Questions* and *Hansard Written Questions* from January 1973. At the time of writing, both data bases were up to date to December 13, 1984.

The query *Copyright & Gutenberg* retrieved nothing from either data base, so you try the dictionary command to find out whether the word *copyright* occurs. The response from HOQ is that copyright occurs 63 times in 24 documents. The word after *copyright* in the alphabetical listing is *copyrighted;* it occurs five times in three documents. The word *copywright* (incorrectly spelled) occurs once in one document. Since the number of documents is not excessive you decide to have them all printed. This proves to be unwise because none of the documents retrieved from HOQ is recent enough to be relevant. In the HWQ data base, *copyright* occurs 13 times in 30 documents, *copyrighted* once in one document, and *copyrights* once in one document. One of the documents retrieved from HWQ is relevant. In view of the recent date of the white paper, a good move would have been to decide before beginning your search to have documents printed in reverse chronological order (type in GR after selecting the data base, but before entering search terms). The one relevant document in HWQ dated May 14, 1984 would then have been the first to appear and you could have stopped the printing by pressing the "break" key as soon as you saw that the other documents were of too early date to be relevant. Incidentally, the May 14th document referred to the "white paper on copyright" without mentioning its title *From Gutenberg to Telidon.* This explains why it was not retrieved by your earlier query, *Copyright & Gutenberg.* "White paper" & *copyright* would presumably have retrieved the one relevant document.

Your search of the HOQ and HWQ data bases has probably confirmed your impression that little action has been taken with regard to the white paper on copyright. You would, however, like to find in Canadian newspapers or periodicals recent articles on the need for copyright revision. Perhaps the CBI data base will help you. Using the dictionary command you learn that the word *copyright* occurs 260 times in 175 documents. It is unlikely that all relate to the need for revision of Canada's Copyright Act, so rather than looking at all 175 documents, you decide to try a phrase search on "Copyright Act". Only five documents are retrieved; and none of them is recent enough to meet your needs.

Since only five of 175 documents containing the word *copyright* also included the phrase "Copyright Act," you may have missed some relevant documents. You decide to try another search, entering the following query:
copyright & revision revisions law
This retrieves twenty documents. Most of them relate in some way to the need for revision of the copyright law, but only three are recent enough to have any connection with the white paper. Here again printing in reverse chronological order would be helpful.

There are some data bases offered by other systems that contain legal information. For instance, as noted in Chapter 5, *Legal Resource Index* is available online through DIALOG and the *Index to Legal Periodicals* is to be available through a new system called Wilsonline.[23] These indexes, though part of larger systems covering many disciplines, are themselves legal, rather than quasi-legal.

6. CONCLUSION

Though quasi-legal data bases include some information useful to lawyers, it is those that contain law reports and statutes that are most likely to help them in their day-to-day work. As QL's coverage of these primary sources of the law becomes more comprehensive, the system's usefulness increases. Its cost is moderate, considering the time it saves, and training data bases on which to gain practice are provided at less than the normal cost. Details are available from QL Systems Limited.

Automated legal research offers new challenges and opportunities. Do not avoid it through fear that you have to be a mathematician or a scientist in order to understand the computer. If you have the sort of mind that can cope successfully with legal studies and problems, you should, with practice, have no trouble formulating queries that will speedily give you information you need that would be difficult, if not impossible, to obtain through traditional methods of searching.

---

23   See pp. 187-188, 191, above.

Appendix 1
Suggestions for Further Reading

I make no attempt here to present a complete bibliography on legal research. My aim is simply to list a few books that I have found useful and that I think will assist others. Some of the books deal with matters that are closely related to legal research, but that are dealt with in this book only incidentally, if at all. Examples are legal writing, including the correct form of citation.

CANADIAN

Dykstra, Gail S., ed. *How to Update a Statute*
for all Canadian Jurisdictions. Ottawa: Canadian
Law Information Council, 1980.

The chapters in this booklet were first published in *CLIC's Legal Materials Letter,* 1979-1980. Each is written by a law librarian in the jurisdiction dealt with in the chapter. A new edition, to include information on regulations as well as statutes, is in preparation at the time of writing. Instead of having chapters by different authors, the new edition is being written by Mary Jane Sinclair, who is having each chapter reviewed by a law librarian in the appropriate jurisdiction.

Gall, Gerald L. *The Canadian Legal System.* 2nd ed.
Toronto: Carswell Legal Publications, 1983.

This book, the first edition of which was published in 1977, aims to provide the law student and general reader with a fundamental knowledge of the Canadian legal system. Its approach is philosophical, and, in addition to giving information on legislative and judicial authority, the courts, lawyers and judges, there are chapters on such topics as the nature, divisions, and sources of law, the doctrines of precedent and *stare decisis,* statutory interpretation, and fairness and natural justice in the administrative process. The general reader may have difficulty with some of the chapters, but Canadian law students should read this book before proceeding very far with their studies.

Le May, Denis. *La recherche documentarie juridique*
au Québec. Montréal: Wilson & Lafleur/SOREJ
Ltee, 1984.

For anyone doing research involving Quebec legal material this is a most useful book. In 1974, Denis Le May's earlier work, *Méthode de recherche en droit québécois et canadien* was published by the Presses de l'Université Laval. The later book is described by Judge Deschênes in the preface as not simply an updating, but rather a completely new and enriched work.

MacEllven, Douglass T. *Legal Research Handbook.* 2nd ed.
Toronto: Butterworths, 1983.

This book, based on lecture notes used by the author in teaching both manual and automated legal research, contains much useful information on a wide variety of topics. It deals mainly with legal materials relating to common law Canada, but there are also chapters on researching Quebec, English, American, and Australian and New Zealand law. Included as well are chapters on computerized legal research and on legal citation, helpful information for those administering law firm libraries, lists of publishers' addresses, and a table of report and digest abbreviations. Covering so many topics in less than 300 pages, the book's treatment of some is rather limited. Nevertheless, this is a very useful reference work.

Tang, Chin-Shih. *Guide to Legal Citation: A Canadian*
Perspective in Common Law Provinces. Toronto:
Richard De Boo Publishers, 1984.

This is the most comprehensive Canadian book published to date on legal citation. It deals with citing not only Canadian, English and American cases, statutes, and subordinate legislation, monographs, law journal articles, and loose-leaf services, but also government publications and international law materials. Some of the rules might be improved or clarified, but, on the whole, this is a useful guide to a difficult subject.

Turp, Daniel, et James Leavy. *Sources et méthodologie du droit*
· *québécois et canadien: notes et documents.* 2ᵉ ed. Montreal:
Les editions Thémis, Faculté du droit, Université de Montréal, 1983.

This is another useful Quebec book on sources and techniques of legal research. It appears to be primarily intended for use in a course rather than for private study. The many sample pages used as illustrations are presumably meant to be explained by an instructor, and the services of the Law Library at the Université de Montréal are outlined in an appendix.

Waddams, S.M. *Introduction to the Study of Law.* 2nd ed.
Toronto: The Carswell Company Limited, 1983.

This book, first published in 1979, should be read by everyone thinking of applying for admission to a Canadian law school. After introductory chapters on the meaning of law, legal education, the language of the law, and analysing legal problems, the author outlines the various divisions of public and private law and explains the difference between common law and equity and the place of legislation in our legal system. There is also a chapter on the structure of the courts and one on the legal profession. Additional useful information, such as words and phrases and common abbreviations, is given in appendices.

Yogis, John A., and Innis M. Christie. *Legal Writing and*
Research Manual. 2nd ed. Toronto: Butterworths, 1974.

The first edition of this book, by Innis M. Christie, was described in its preface as "a teaching book evolved for use in the Queen's Faculty of Law in connection with a programme of legal writing and research for first year law students." The second edition has the same purpose, but since it corrects many of the inaccuracies in the first edition, it is a greatly improved book, though now somewhat out of date.

ENGLISH

Dane, Jean, and Philip A. Thomas. *How to Use a Law
    Library.* London: Sweet & Maxwell, 1979.

This book aims to do for the English law student what mine tries to do for
the Canadian law student. It contains much well-presented and helpful information, including specialist contributions on community law by A.C. Page
and public international law by A.V. Lowe. Especially useful are several
algorithms showing the steps to take in doing various types of legal research.

Dane and Thomas have also prepared a tape slide set in five programmes
with the same title *How to Use a Law Library.* It was published by Sweet &
Maxwell in 1983.

Williams, Glanville. *Learning the Law.* 11th ed.
    London: Stevens, 1982.

This excellent little book introduces the reader to many aspects of the
study and practice of law. Though some of the chapters relate exclusively to
the situation in England, other parts of the book are as useful and interesting
to a Canadian law student as to an English one. The book deals not only with
the aspects of legal research with which mine is concerned, but also with such
matters as legal terminology, methods of study, case law technique, and the
interpretation of statutes. You may find that you want to read some parts of
this book (especially chapters 1-3) at the beginning of your legal studies, and
other parts later.

OTHER COMMONWEALTH

Campbell, Enid, E.J. Glasson, and Ann Lahore. *Legal
    Research Materials and Methods.* 2nd ed. Sydney:
    Law Book Company, 1979.

The first edition of this book, by Enid Campbell and Donald Mac-
Dougall, was published in 1967. The emphasis in both editions is on Australian and English materials, but information on New Zealand, Irish, Scottish, Canadian and American materials is also included. In addition to
describing the usual types of publications dealt with in books on legal research, the authors have included chapters on parliamentary publications,
government publications, and non-legal materials. Canadian law students
will find the book useful not only if they want to know something about the
sources of Australian law, but also for the general information and instructions given regarding legal research and writing.

Derham, D.P., F.K.H. Maher, and P.L. Waller. *An Introduction
    to Law.* 4th ed. Sydney: Law Book Company, 1983.

Its authors tell us that this book, originally published in 1966, "is written
for those who know no law." It is primarily for those who are contemplating
embarking on legal studies and will assist others to know something of what
the law is about. Though dealing to some extent specifically with Australian
law and legal institutions, its philosophical approach makes many parts of the

book as useful to Canadian as to Australian law students. The authors express the hope that the book "can be read and understood without need to refer to the contents of a law library." Nevertheless, they include at the end a useful appendix entitled "Using the Law Library," which has been completely revised and rewritten by Gretchen Kewley for the fourth edition.

A New Zealand edition of the book edited by H.R. Gray was published by Sweet and Maxwell (N.Z.) Ltd., Wellington, in 1968. Both the main part of the book and the appendix are adapted for use in New Zealand. A second New Zealand edition was published in 1972.

AMERICAN

Many detailed text books on legal research have been written in the United States. They deal mainly with American materials, but most include some information on English and a few on Canadian materials. Probably the best known and most widely used is:

Price, Miles O., Harry Bitner, and Shirley Raissi Bysiewicz.
Effective Legal Research. 4th ed. Boston: Little, Brown, 1979.

The fourth edition of this book, originally published in 1953, contains five new chapters. They deal with Australian, New Zealand, and South African materials, international law, and automated legal research. The former chapter on English and Canadian materials has been divided into two, one dealing with United Kingdom, the other with Canadian materials.

Other well known and useful books are:

Cohen, Morris L., and Robert C. Berring. *How to Find the Law.* 8th ed. St. Paul: West Publishing Company, 1983.

Earlier editions, up to and including the sixth, were by other authors. The seventh, published in 1976, was by Morris L. Cohen.

Cohen, Morris L. *Legal Research in a Nutshell.* 3rd ed.
St. Paul: West Publishing Company, 1978.
Jacobstein, J. Myron, and Roy M. Mersky. *Fundamentals of Legal Research.* New York: Foundation Press, 1977.

The first edition, published in 1977, was a successor to Pollock's *Fundamentals of Legal Research,* of which the fourth edition by Jacobstein and Mersky was published in 1973.

Canadian law students may use books such as those listed above for reference, but if they want to find out quickly how to look up information in American law reports, statutes, digests, or encyclopedias, they will probably find it more convenient to consult one or more of the instructional booklets issued by the publishers of major American sets. New editions and printings are issued at frequent intervals, so I am not listing dates of publication. The following are suggested.

West's Law Finder. A Research Manual for Lawyers.
St. Paul: West Publishing Company.

This booklet explains very clearly how to use several important sets, including the National Reporter System, West's Key Number Digest, *Corpus Juris Secundum,* and the *United States Code Annotated* (federal statutes in force). Canadian law students are likely to consult all these sets from time to time.

> *The Living Law. A Guide to Modern Legal Research Through the Pages of a Modern System.* Rochester: The Lawyer's Co-operative Publishing Company, San Francisco: Bancroft-Whitney Co.

Described here are the publications of the two companies that issue it, including *The American Law Reports, The Supreme Court Reports, Lawyers Edition,* and *American Jurisprudence,* 2d. The mode of presentation is through the use of a hypothetical legal problem. Though probably less frequently used by Canadian law students than the West sets, it is nevertheless useful to know something about them.

> *How to Use Shepard's Citations.* Colorado Springs: Shephard's Citations, Inc.

Shepard's Citations provide a detailed annotation service to federal and state cases and statutes. Because they are such an important aid to American legal research, most Canadian law school libraries subscribe to them, or at least to those volumes that annotate series that are in their library. The pamphlet, *How to Use Shepard's Citations,* is described on its title page as "A Detailed Presentation of the Scope and Functions of Shephard's Citation Books with Illustrative Examples and an Analysis of Their Relation to other Methods of Legal Research."

AUTOMATED LEGAL RESEARCH

For further information on automated legal research the following books are recommended.

> Bing, Jon, and Trygve Harvold. *Legal Decisions and Information Systems.* Oslo: Universitetsforlaget, 1977.
>
> *Computer-Assisted Legal Research: A Guide for Canadian Law Students.* Ottawa: Canadian Law Information Council, 1984. (An excellent instructional manual with illustrations and practice exercises.)
>
> Fabien, Claude. *Computerized Legal Research in Canada.* Ottawa: Canadian Law Information Council, 1979.
>
> Foster, Anne. *Automated Legal Research: a Manual for QL Users,* Ottawa: Canadian Law Information Council, 1981.
>
> Iosipescu, Michael and John Yogis. *A Comparison of Automated and Manual Legal Research: A Computer Study.* Ottawa: Canadian Law Information Council, 1981.
>
> Kling, Allan J. *Computer Assisted Legal Research Programmes at Canadian Law Schools.* Ottawa: Canadian Law Information

Council, 1983.

Slayton, Philip. *Electronic Legal Retrieval.* Ottawa:
Information Canada, 1974. (A Report prepared for the
Department of Communications of the Government of Canada.)

Sprowl, James A. *A Manual for Computer-Assisted Legal Research.*
Chicago: American Bar Foundation, 1976.

Tapper, Colin. *Computers and the Law.* London: Weidenfeld and
Nicolson, 1973.

Not to be confused with the same author's later book, *Computer Law,* which deals with such matters as computers and intellectual property, computer contracts, *etc.*

There are many articles on automated legal research. Examples are the following, referred to in Chapter 6 of this book.

Joseph, David. "Computers in Britain and America – The
Way Ahead." *New Law Journal,* 133 (1983), 983-84.

Onove, Allan J. "A Comparison of the LEXIS and WESTLAW
Databases." *Legal Economics,* March/April 1983, pp. 27-40.

Sprowl, James A. "The Latest on Westlaw, Lexis, and
Dialog." *ABA Journal,* 70 (March 1984), pp. 85-90.

Because this is a rapidly developing field in which it is important to keep current, consult the major periodical indexes described in Chapter 5 for the most recent articles relating to it.

Appendix 2

List of Preferred Citations –

Selected Canadian and English Law Reports and Related Publications

This is an amended version of a list used by Carswell. A series may be listed more than once if different citations are acceptable, especially if the publication has both English and French titles. Generally, square brackets are used on the list only where necessary to distinguish series of the same or similar names. Additional series may in fact include square brackets in their citation. To avoid duplication with the list of periodical abbreviations in Appendix 3, Canadian journals noted because they contain reports or digests of cases have been omitted from this list.

[ ] A.C.	Law Reports, Appeal Cases, 1891-
A.C.W.S.	All-Canada Weekly Summaries
A., N.W.T. & Y. Tax R.	Alberta, N.W.T. & Yukon Tax Reporter
A.P.R.	Atlantic Provinces Reports, 1975-
A.R.	Alberta Reports, 1977-
A.W.L.D.	Alberta Weekly Law Digest
Act.	Acton, Privy Council, 1809- 1811
Admin. L.R.	Administrative Law Reports, 1983-
All E.R.	All England Law Reports, 1936-
Alta. L.R.	Alberta Law Reports, 1908-1932
Alta. L.R. (2d)	Alberta Law Reports (Second Series), 1976-
App. Cas.	Law Reports, Appeal Cases, 1875-1890
Armour	Manitoba Reports, temp. Wood (Armour, ed.), 1875-1883
B.C. Corps. L.G.	British Columbia Corporation Law Guide, 1974-
B.C.L.R.	British Columbia Law Reports, 1977-
B.C.R.	British Columbia Reports, 1867- 1947
B.C.T.R.	British Columbia Tax Reporter
B.C.W.L.D.	British Columbia Weekly Law Digest
B.L.R.	Business Law Reports, 1977-
B.R.	Rapports judiciaires de Québec, Cour du Banc de la Reine (ou du Roi)/Quebec Official Reports, Queen's (or King's) Bench, 1892-1941
[ ] B.R.	Rapports judiciaires de Québec, Cour du Banc de la Reine (ou du Roi), 1942-1966
	Recueils de jurisprudence du Quebec, Cour du Banc de la Reine, 1967-1969

[ ] C.A.	Recueils de jurisprudence du Quebec, Cour d'appel, 1970-
C. & S.	Clarke & Scully's Drainage Cases (Ont.), 1898-1903
C.B.E.S.	Recueils de jurisprudence, Cour du bien-être social
C.B.R.	Canadian Bankruptcy Reports, 1920-1960
C.B.R. (N.S.)	Canadian Bankruptcy Reports, New Series, 1960-
C.C.C.	Canadian Criminal Cases, 1893-1962
[ ] C.C.C.	Canadian Criminal Cases, 1963-1970
C.C.C. (2d)	Canadian Criminal Cases (Second Series), 1971-1983
C.C.C. (3d)	Canadian Criminal Cases (Third Series), 1983-
C.C.E.L.	Canadian Cases on Employment Law, 1983-
C.C.L.	Canadian Current Law
C.C.L.I.	Canadian Cases on the Law of Insurance, 1983-
C.C.L.R.	Canadian Corporation Law Reporter
C.C.L.T.	Canadian Cases on the Law of Torts, 1976-
C.E.B. & P.G.R.	Canadian Employment Benefits and Pension Guide Reporter
C.E.L.R.	Canadian Environmental Law Reporter
C.E.P.A.R.	Canadian Estate Planning and Administration Reporter
C.E.R.	Canadian Customs and Excise Reports, 1980-
C.E.S.H.G.	Canadian Employment, Safety and Health Guide
C.H.F.L.G.	Canadian Health Facilities Law Guide
C.H.R.R.	Canadian Human Rights Reporter, 1980-
C.I.P.R.	Canadian Intellectual Property Reports, 1984-
C.L.L.C.	Canadian Labour Law Cases, 1944-
C.L.R.	Construction Law Reports, 1983-
C.L.R.B.R. (N.S.)	Canadian Labour Relations Boards Reports (New Series), 1983-
C.M.A.R.	Canadian Court Martial Appeal Reports, 1957-
C.M.P.R.	Canadian Mortgage Practice Reporter
C.N.L.R.	Canadian Native Law Reporter
C.P.	Recueils de jurisprudence, Cour provinciale
C.P.C.	Carswell's Practice Cases, 1976-
C.P.D.	Law Reports, Common Pleas Division, 1875-1880
C.P.R.	Canadian Patent Reporter, 1942-1971
C.P.R. (2d)	Canadian Patent Reporter (Second Series), 1971-
C.R.	Criminal Reports (Canada), 1946-1967
C.R. (3d)	Criminal Reports (Third Series), 1978-
C.R. [ ] A.C.	Canadian Reports, Appeal Cases, 1828-1913
C.R.C.	Canadian Railway Cases, v. 1-49, 1902-1939
C.R.D.	Charter of Rights Decisions, 1982-
C.R.N.S.	Criminal Reports, New Series, 1967-1978
C.R.R.	Canadian Rights Reporter, 1982-
C.R.T.C.	Canadian Railway and Transport Cases, v. 50-85, 1940-1966

C.S.	Rapports judiciaires de Québec, Cour supérieure/ Quebec Official Reports, Superior Court, 1892-1941
[ ] C.S.	Rapports judiciaires de Québec, Cour superieure, 1942-1966
[ ] C.S.	Recueils de jurisprudence du Québec, Cour supérieure, 1967-
[ ] C.S.P.	Recueils de jurisprudence, Cour des sessions de la paix
[ ] C.T.C.	Canadian Transport Cases, 1966-
[ ] C.T.C.	Canadian Tax Cases, 1917-1971
[ ] C.T.C. (N.S.)	Canada Tax Cases, 1971-
C.T.M.	Canada Tax Manual
Cam.	Cameron's Privy Council Decisions, 1867-1929
Cam. S.C.	Reports Hitherto Unpublished, Supreme Court of Canada, Cameron, 1880-1900
Can. C.L.G.	Canadian Commercial Law Guide
Can. Com. R.	Canadian Commercial Law Reports, 1901-1905
Can. F.L.G.	Canadian Family Law Guide
Can. I.T.G.R.	Canada Income Tax Guide Report
[ ] Can. L.R.B.R.	Canadian Labour Relations Boards Reports, 1974-1982
Can. S.L.R.	Canadian Securities Law Reporter
Can. S.T.R.	Canadian Sales Tax Reporter
Carey	Manitoba Reports, temp. Wood (Carey, ed.), 1875
Cart. B.N.A.	Cartwright's Constitutional Cases (Can.), 1868-1896
Cass. Prac. Cas.	Cassels' Practice Cases (Can.), 1899
Cas. S.C.	Cassels' Supreme Court Digest, 1875-1893
[ ] Ch.	Law Reports, Chancery, 1891-
Ch. D.	Law Reports, Chancery Division, 1875-1890
Ch. R.	Upper Canada Chambers Reports, 1846-1852
Chy. Chrs.	Upper Canada Chancery Chambers Reports, 1857-1872
Cook Adm.	Cook's Vice Admiralty Reports (Que.), 1873-1884
Cout. S.C.	Notes of Unreported Cases, Supreme Court of Canada (Coutlee), 1875-1907
Cox C.C.	Cox's Criminal Law Cases, 1843-1940
Cr. App. R.	Criminal Appeal Reports, 1908-
Cr. App. R. (S.)	Criminal Appeal Reports (Sentencing), 1979-
D.C.A.	Dorion, Decisions de la Cour d'Appel/Queen's Bench Reports, 1880-1884
D.L.R.	Dominion Law Reports, 1912-1922
[ ] D.L.R.	Dominion Law Reports, 1923-1955
D.L.R. (2d)	Dominion Law Reports (Second Series), 1956-1968
D.L.R. (3d)	Dominion Law Reports (Third Series), 1969-1984
D.L.R. (4th)	Dominion Law Reports (Fourth Series), 1984-
D.R.S.	Dominion Report Service
D.T.C.	Dominion Tax Cases, 1920-
di	Canadian Labour Relations Board Decisions/ Information

Draper	Draper King's Bench (Upper Canada), 1828-1831
E. & A.	Error & Appeal Reports (Grant) (Upper Canada), 1846-1866
E.L.R.	Eastern Law Reporter, 1906-1914
E.R.	English Reports (to 1865)
E.T.R.	Estates & Trusts Reports, 1977-
Ex. C.R.	Exchequer Court Reports of Canada, 1875-1922
[ ] Ex. C.R.	Canada Law Reports (Exchequer Court), 1923-1971
Ex. D.	Law Reports, Exchequer Division, 1875-1890
[ ] F.C.	Canada Federal Court Reports, 1971-/Recueil des arrets de la Cour federale du Canada, 1971-
F.L.R.A.C.	Family Law Reform Act Cases, 1980-
[ ] Fam.	Law Reports, Family Division, 1972- (previously [ ] P.)
Fox Pat. C.	Fox's Patent, Trade Mark, Design and Copyright Cases, 1940-1971
Godson	Godson, Mining Commissioner's Cases (Ont.), 1911-1917
Gr.	Upper Canada Chancery (Grant), 1849-1882
Harr. & Hodg.	Harrison & Hodgins' Municipal Reports (Upper Canada), 1845-1851
Hodg.	Hodgins, Elections (Ont.), 1871-1879
Hunt.	Hunter's Torrens Cases (Can.), 1865-1893
I.A.C.	Immigration Appeal Cases, 1970-1976
I.L.R.	Insurance Law Reporter (Can.)
Kn. P.C.	Knapp, Privy Council, 1829-1836
L.A.C.	Labour Arbitration Cases, 1948-1972
L.A.C. (2d)	Labour Arbitration Cases (Second Series), 1973-1981
L.A.C. (3d)	Labour Arbitration Cases (Third Series), 1982-
L. & C.	Lefroy & Cassels' Practice Cases (Ont.), 1881-1883
L.C. Jur.	Lower Canada Jurist, 1848-1891
L.C.R.	Lower Canada Reports/Decisions des Tribunaux du Bas-Canada, 1850-1867
L.C.R.	Land Compensation Reports, 1971-
L.N.	Legal News (Que.), 1878-1897
L.R.	All the Law Report Series from 1865-1875 (U.K.)
L.R. ... A. & E.	Law Reports, Admiralty and Ecclesiastical Cases, 1865-1875
L.R. ... C.C.R.	Law Reports, Crown Cases Reserved, 1865-1875
L.R. ... Ch.	Law Reports, Chancery Appeals, 1865-1875
L.R. ... C.P.	Law Reports, Common Pleas, 1865-1875
L.R. ... Eq.	Law Reports, Equity Cases, 1865-1875
L.R. ... Ex.	Law Reports, Exchequer, 1865-1875
L.R. ... H.L.	Law Reports, English and Irish Appeals, 1865-1875
L.R. ... P. & D.	Law Reports, Probate and Divorce, 1865-1875
L.R. ... P.C.	Law Reports, Privy Council Cases, 1865-1875
L.R. ... Q.B.	Law Reports, Queen's Bench, 1865-1875

L.R. ... Sc. & Div.	Law Reports, Scotch and Divorce Appeals to the House of Lords, 1865-1875
L.T.	Law Times Reports, 1843-1947
Law Repr.	The Law Reporter (Ramsay & Morin) (Que.), 1853-1854
Loc. Ct. Gaz.	Local Courts & Municipal Gazette (Ont.), 1865-1872
Low. Can. R.	Lower Canada Reports, 1851-1867
M.C.R.	Montreal Condensed Reports, 1853-1854
M.L. Dig. & R.	Monthly Law Digest & Reporter (Que.), 1892-1893
M.L.R. (Q.B.)	Montreal Law Reports (Queen's Bench), 1884-1891
M.L.R. (S.C.)	Montreal Law Reports (Superior Court), 1885-1891
M.M.C.	Martin's Mining Cases (B.C.), 1853-1908
M.P.L.R.	Municipal and Planning Law Reports, 1976-
M.P.R.	Maritime Provinces Reports, 1929-1968
M.T.R.	Maritime Tax Reporter
M.V.R.	Motor Vehicle Reports, 1979-
Man. L.R.	Manitoba Law Reports, v. 1-6, 1884-1890
Man. R.	Manitoba Reports, v. 7-67, 1891-1962
Man. R. (2d)	Manitoba Reports (Second Series), 1979-
Man. R. temp. Wood	Manitoba Reports, temp. Wood, 1875-1883
Man. & Sask. Tax R.	Manitoba & Saskatchewan Tax Reporter
Moo. P.C.	Moore, Privy Council, 1836-1862
Moo. P.C. (N.S.)	Moore (N.S.) Privy Council, 1862-1873
N.B. Eq.	New Brunswick Equity Reports, 1894-1912
N.B.R.	New Brunswick Reports, 1825-1929
N.B.R. (2d)	New Brunswick Reports (Second Series), 1979-
N.R.	National Reporter, 1974-
N.S.R.	Nova Scotia Reports, 1834- 1929
N.S.R. (2d)	Nova Scotia Reports (Second Series), 1970-
N.W.T.R.	Northwest Territories Supreme Court Reports, 1887-1898
[ ] N.W.T.R.	Northwest Territories Reports, 1983-
Nfld. & P.E.I.R.	Newfoundland and Prince Edward Island Reports, 1971-
Nfld. L.R.	Newfoundland Law Reports, 1817-1946
Nfld. Sel. Cas.	Tucker's Select Cases (Nfld.), 1817-1828
O.A.C.	Ontario Appeal Cases, 1984-
O.A.R.	Ontario Appeal Reports, 1876-1900
O.C.M.	Ontario Corporation Manual
O.L.R.	Ontario Law Reports, 1901-1931
[ ] O.L.R.B. Rep.	Ontario Labour Relations Board Reports, 1974-
O.M.B.R.	Ontario Municipal Board Reports, 1973-
Ont. Case Law Dig.	Ontario Case Law Digest

Ont. Corps. Law Guide	Ontario Corporations Law Guide
Ont. Elec.	Ontario Election Cases, 1884-1900
Ont. R.E.L.G.	Ontario Real Estate Law Guide
Ont. Tax R.	Ontario Tax Reporter
O.R.	Ontario Reports, 1882-1900
[ ] O.R.	Ontario Reports, 1931-1973
O.R. (2d)	Ontario Reports (Second Series), 1974-
O.W.N.	Ontario Weekly Notes, 1909-1932
[ ] O.W.N.	Ontario Weekly Notes, 1933-1962
O.W.R.	Ontario Weekly Reporter, 1902-1916
[ ] P.	Law Reports, Probate, 1891-1971
P.D.	Law Reports, Probate, Divorce and Admiralty Division, 1875-1890
P.E.I.	Haszard & Warburton's Reports, 1850-1882
P.P.S.A.C.	Personal Property Security Act Cases, 1980-
Patr. Elec. Cas.	Patrick, Contested Elections (Upper Canada), 1824-1849
Peters	Peters' Reports (P.E.I.), 1850-1872
P.R.	Practice Reports (Ont.), 1848-1900
Price	Price's Mining Commissioner's Cases (Ont.), 1906-1910
Pyke	Pyke's Reports, King's Bench (Lower Canada), 1809-1810
[ ] Q.B.	Law Reports, Queen's Bench, 1891-
Q.B.D.	Law Reports, Queen's Bench Division, 1875-1890
Q.L.R.	Quebec Law Reports/Rapports judiciaires de Quebec, 1874-1891
[ ] Que. C.A.	Quebec Official Reports (Court of Appeal), 1970-
Que. K.B. or Q.B.	Quebec Official Reports (King's or Queen's Bench), 1892-1941
[ ] Que. K.B. or Q.B.	Quebec Official Reports (King's or Queen's Bench), 1942-1969
Que. P.R.	Quebec Practice Reports/Rapports de Pratique de Québec, 1897-1944
[ ] Que. P.R.	Quebec Practice Reports/Rapports de Pratique de Québec, 1945-1982
Que. S.C.	Quebec Official Reports (Superior Court)/Rapports judiciaires de Québec, Cour Supérieure, 1892-1941
[ ] Que. S.C.	Quebec Official Reports (Superior Court)/Recueils de jurisprudence de Québec, Cour Supérieure, 1942-
Que. Tax R.	Quebec Tax Reporter
R.A.C.	Ramsay's Appeal Cases (Que.), 1873-1886
[ ] R.C.S.	Rapports judiciaires du Canada, Cour Suprême du Canada, 1963-1969
[ ] R.C.S.	Recueil des arrets de la Cour Supreme du Canada, 1970-

[ ] R.D.F.Q.	Recueil de droit fiscal Québecois, 1977-
R.D.J.	Revue de Droit Judiciaire, 1983-
[ ] R.D.T.	Revue de Droit du Travail, 1963-
R.F.L.	Reports of Family Law, 1971-1977
R.F.L. (2d)	Reports of Family Law (Second Series), 1978-
R.F.L. Rep.	Reports of Family Law, Reprint Series
R.J.Q.	Rapports judiciaires de Québec/Quebec Law Reports, 1874-1891
R.J.R.Q.	Rapports judiciaires revises de la province de Québec (Mathieu)/Quebec Revised Reports, 1726-1891
[ ] R.L.	La Revue Légale (Qué.), 1943-1979
( ) R.L.	La Revue Légale (Qué.), 1980-
R.L.N.S.	La Revue Légale (N.S.) (Que.), 1895-1942
R.L.O.S.	La Revue Légale (Qué.), 1869-1891
R.P.	Rapports de Pratique de Québec/Quebec Practice Reports, 1897-1944
[ ] R.P.	Rapports de Pratique de Québec/Quebec Practice Reports, 1945-1982
R.P.C.	Reports of Patent, Design, Trade Mark and Other Cases, 1884-1956
[ ] R.P.C.	Reports of Patent, Design, Trade Mark and Other Cases, 1957-
R.P.R.	Real Property Reports, 1977-
R. de Jur.	La Revue de Jurisprudence (Que.), 1895-1942
Ram. & Mor.	Ramsay & Morin, The Law Reporter/Journal de jurisprudence, 1853-1854
Ritch.	Ritchie's Equity Reports, by Russell (Nova Scotia), 1873-1882
Rus.	Russel's Election Cases (Nova Scotia), 1874
S.A.G.	Sentences arbitrales de griefs (Quebec), 1970-1981
S.C.R.	Reports of the Supreme Court of Canada, 1876-1922
[ ] S.C.R.	Canada Law Reports, Supreme Court of Canada, 1923-1962
[ ] S.C.R.	Canada Law Reports, Supreme Court of Canada/ Rapports judiciaires du Canada/Cour Suprême du Canada, 1963-1969
[ ] S.C.R.	Canada Supreme Court Reports/Recueil des arrets de la Cour Suprême du Canada, 1970-
Sask. L.R.	Saskatchewan Law Reports, 1907-1931
Sask. R., S.R.	Saskatchewan Reports, 1979-
Seign. Questions	Lower Canada Reports, Seignorial Questions/ Decisions des Tribunaux du Bas-Canada, vols. A & B
Sm. & S.	Smith & Sager's Drainage Cases (Ont.), 1904-1917
Stephens' Dig.	Stephens' Quebec Law Digest
Stevens' Dig.	Stevens' New Brunswick Digest

Stewart	Stewart's Vice-Admiralty Reports (Nova Scotia), 1803-1813
Stockton	Stockton's Vice-Admiralty Reports (N.B.), 1879-1891
Stu. K.B.	Stuart's Reports (Lower Canada), 1810-1835
Stuart	Stuart, Vice-Admiralty Reports (Que.), 1836-1874
T.B.R.	Tariff Board Reports, 1937-1962
T.B.R.	Tariff Board Reports/Rapports de la Commission du Tarif, 1963-
[ ] T.J.	Recueils de Jurisprudence: Tribunal de la Jeunesse
T.L.R.	Times Law Reports, 1884-1952
T.T.	Jurisprudence de droit du travail, Tribunal du Travail, 1970-1981
Tax A.B.C.	Tax Appeal Board Cases, 1949-1971
Taylor	Taylor's King's Bench Reports (U.C.), 1823-1827
Terr. L.R.	Territories Law Reports (N.W.T.), 1885-1907
Tru.	Trueman's Equity Cases (N.B.), 1876-1903
U.C.C.P.	Upper Canada Common Pleas Reports, 1850-1882
U.C. Ch.	Grant, Upper Canada Chancery, 1849-1882
U.C. Chamb.	Upper Canada Chambers Reports, 1846-1852
U.C. Jur.	Upper Canada Jurist, 1844-1848
U.C.E. & A.	Upper Canada Error & Appeal Reports, 1846-1866
U.C.K.B.	Upper Canada, King's Bench Reports (Old Series), 1831-1844
U.C.Q.B.	Upper Canada, Queen's Bench Reports, 1844-1881
U.C.Q.B.	Upper Canada, Queen's Bench Old Series, 1831-1844
W.C.B.	Weekly Criminal Bulletin
W.C.D.	Western Charter Digest
W.L.A.C.	Western Labour Arbitration Cases, 1966-
[ ] W.L.R.	Weekly Law Reports, 1953-
W.L.R.	Western Law Reporter, 1905-1916
W.L.T.	Western Law Times, 1890-1895
W.W.D.	Western Weekly Digests, 1975-1976
W.W.R.	Western Weekly Reports, 1912-1916
[ ] W.W.R.	Western Weekly Reports, 1917-1950 and 1971-
W.W.R. (N.S.)	Western Weekly Reports, New Series, 1951-1954 (Volumes 1-10 incl.)
W.W.R.	Western Weekly Reports, New Series, 1955-1970 (Volumes 11-75 incl.)
Y.A.D.	Young's Admiralty Decisions (Nova Scotia), 1865-1880

Appendix 3

Table of Periodical Abbreviations

This is an amended version of the Table of Periodical Abbreviations in the *Index to Canadian Legal Literature* (*Canadian Abridgment*). Included are not only Canadian legal periodicals, but also periodicals of other disciplines that sometimes contain articles on legal topics. Included as well are some volumes of essays and lectures. Journals may be listed more than once if different abbreviations are used or if there has been a name change. The original list notes law report series containing articles. These have been omitted from the amended list to avoid duplication between the Table of Periodical Abbreviations and the List of Preferred Citations in Appendix 2.

Acta Crim.	Acta Criminologica
Advocate	The Advocate (Vancouver Bar Association)
Advocate's Q.	Advocate's Quarterly: A Canadian Journal for Practitioners of Civil Litigation
Advocate (Toronto)	The Advocate (Students' Law Society, University of Toronto)
Alta. L.Q.	The Alberta Law Quarterly
Alta. L. Rev.	Alberta Law Review
Annals Air and Space	Annals of Air and Space Law
B.C. Branch Lectures	Program Reports, Canadian Bar Association, British Columbia Branch Meeting
B.C.L. Lectures	British Columbia Annual Law Lectures
Bull. Can. Welfare L.	Bulletin of Canadian Welfare Law
Bull. Que. Soc. Crim.	Bulletin of the Quebec Society of Criminology
Bus. Q.	The Business Quarterly: Canada's Management Journal
Can. Bank.	The Canadian Banker & ICB Review
Can. Bar A.J.	Journal: The Canadian Bar Association/L'Association du Barreau Canadien
Can. Bar J.	The Canadian Bar Journal
Can. Bar J. (N.S.)	The Canadian Bar Journal (New Series)
Can. Bar Papers	Papers Presented at the Annual Meeting ... Canadian Bar Association
Can. Bar Rev.	The Canadian Bar Review/La Revue du Barreau canadien
Can. Bar Year Book	Year Book, Canadian Bar Association
Can. Bus. L.J.	Canadian Business Law Journal/Revue canadienne du droit de commerce

Can. Chart. Acc.	The Canadian Chartered Accountant
Can. Com. L.J.	Canadian Community Law Journal/Revue canadienne de droit communautaire
Can. Com. L.R.	Canadian Communications Law Review/La Revue canadienne de droit des communications
Can. J. Corr.	Canadian Journal of Corrections/Revue Canadienne de Criminologie
Can. J. Crim.	Canadian Journal of Criminology/Revue Canadienne de Criminologie
Can. J. Crim. & Corr.	Canadian Journal of Criminology and Corrections/ Revue Canadienne de Criminologie
Can. J. Econ.	The Canadian Journal of Economics/Revue canadienne d'économique
Can. J. E.P.S.	The Canadian Journal of Economics and Political Science/Revue canadienne d'économique et de science politique
Can. J. Fam. L.	Canadian Journal of Family Law/Revue canadienne de droit familial
Can. J. Pol. Sc.	Canadian Journal of Political Science/Revue canadienne de science politique
Can. Lab.	Canadian Labour
Can. Lawyer	Canadian Lawyer
Can. Legal Aid Bul.	Canadian Legal Aid Bulletin/Bulletin Canadienne de l'aide juridique
Can. Leg. Studies	Canadian Legal Studies/Les etudes juridiques au Canada
Can. Pol. C.	Canadian Police Chief: Official Magazine of the Canadian Association of Chiefs of Police
Can. Pub. Admin.	Canadian Public Administration/Administration publique du Canada
Can. Soc. Forens. Sci. J.	Journal: Canadian Society of Forensic Science/La Societe canadienne des sciences judiciaires
Can. Taxation	Canadian Taxation: A Journal of Tax Policy
Can. Tax J.	Canadian Tax Journal
Can. Tax News	Canadian Tax News
Can. Wel.	Canadian Welfare
Can. Year Book Int. L.	The Canadian Yearbook of International Law/ Annuaire canadien de Droit international
C.C.F.	Canadian Criminology Forum
C.C.I.L.	Proceedings, Canadian Council on International Law
C. de D.	Les Cahiers de droit
C.E.L.A. Newsletter	Canadian Environmental Law Association Newsletter
Chitty's L.J.	Chitty's Law Journal
C.L.F.	Mémoires: congrès de la langue française au Canada
C.L.J.	The Canada Law Journal
C.L.R.	The Canadian Law Review and Corporation Legal Journal

C.L.T.	The Canadian Law Times
Coll. I. Dr. Comp.	Colloque international de droit comparé/International Symposium on Comparative Law
Conf. Comm. Uniformity Legis.	Proceedings of the ... Conference of Commissioners on Uniformity of Legislation in Canada
Corp. Bulletin	Bulletin, Bureau of Corporate Affairs
C.P. du N.	Cours de perfectionnement du notariat
C.P.P.	Canadian Public Policy
C.P.S.A.	Papers and Proceedings, Canadian Political Science Association
Crime and J.	Crime et/and Justice
Criminologie	Criminologie
Cr. L.Q.	The Criminal Law Quarterly
Current Law	Current Law and Social Problems
Dalhousie L.J.	Dalhousie Law Journal
Droit et Justice	Droit et Justice; Laurentian University Review
E.T.Q.	Estates and Trusts Quarterly
Etudes int.	Etudes internationales
Ext. Affairs	External Affairs: Monthly Bulletin of the Department of External Affairs
F.L.J.	The Fortnightly Law Journal
F.L.R.	Family Law Review
For. Investment Rev.	Foreign Investment Review
Gazette	Gazette: The Law Society of Upper Canada
Ind. Relations	Industrial Relations/Relations industrielles
Infor.	Canadian Journal of Operational Research and Information Processing
Interlex	Interlex: revue internationale de droit comparé général et special
Int. J.	International Journal
Int. Persp.	International Perspectives: A Journal of Opinion on World Affairs
Intramural L.J.	Intramural Law Journal (Queen's University)
Just.	Justinien: revue juridique publiée par la faculté de droit de l'Université d'Ottawa
Justice	Justice: le magazine du Ministère de la Justice du Québec
Lab. Gaz.	The Labour Gazette: A National Journal of Labour Affairs Devoted to a Better Work Environment
Lectures L.S.U.C.	Special Lectures of the Law Society of Upper Canada
Legis. Process	Legislative Process
L.E.S.A. Lect.	Alberta Law for the 80's
L.M.Q.	Legal Medical Quarterly
McGill Air and Space Conf.	McGill Air and Space Conference

McGill L.J.	McGill Law Journal/Revue de droit de McGill
Man. Bar News	Manitoba Bar News
Man. L.J.	Manitoba Law Journal
Man. L.S.J.	Manitoba Law School Journal
Meredith Lect.	W.C.J. Meredith Memorial Lectures
N.S.L. News	Nova Scotia Law News
O.D.	Obiter Dicta
Osgoode Hall L.J.	Osgoode Hall Law Journal
Ottawa L. Rev.	Ottawa Law Review
Philanthrop	The Philanthropist/Le Philanthrope
Pitblado Lect.	Isaac Pitblado Lectures on Continuing Legal Education
P.J.J.	Provincial Judges Journal
Plan Can.	Plan Canada
P.T.I.C.B.	Bulletin, Patent and Trademark Institute of Canada
Quaere	Quaere: The Saskatchewan Law Review Magazine Supplement
Queen's Intramural L.J.	Queen's Intramural Law Journal
Queen's L.J.	Queen's Law Journal
R.C.M.P. Q.	R.C.M.P. Quarterly
R.D.C.	Revue de droit comparé de l'Association québecoise pour l'étude comparative du droit
R. de D. McGill	Revue de droit de McGill/McGill Law Journal (cf. McGill L.J.)
R. de L. et de J.	La Revue de legislation et de jurisprudence
R. du B.	Revue du Barreau de la province de Québec
R. du B. can.	La Revue du Barreau canadien/The Canadian Bar Review (cf. Can. Bar Rev.)
R. du D.	La Revue du droit
R. du N.	La Revue du notariat
R.D.U.S.	Revue de droit (Université de Sherbrooke)
Rec. Laws	Recent Laws in Canada/Lois recentes du Canada
Rev. Can. D. Fam.	Revue canadienne de droit familial/Canadian Journal of Family Law (cf. Can. J. Fam. L.)
Rev. Can. Dr. Com.	Revue canadienne de droit communautaire/Canadian Community Law Journal (cf. Can. Com. L.J.)
Revue criminologie	Revue criminologie
R. Gen.	Revue générale de droit
R.J.T.	La Revue juridique Thémis
Sask. Bar Rev.	Saskatchewan Bar Review
Sask. Law Rev.	Saskatchewan Law Review
Studia Canonica	Studia Canonica
Symposium Jun. Bar	Symposium l'Association de jeune Barreau de Montréal
U.B.C.L.N.	University of British Columbia Legal Notes
U.B.C. L. Rev.	University of British Columbia Law Review

U.C.L.J.	The Upper Canada Law Journal
U.N.B.L.J.	University of New Brunswick Law Journal
Unif. L. Conf.	Proceedings, Uniform Law Conference of Canada
U.T. Fac. L. Rev.	University of Toronto Faculty of Law Review
U.T.L.J.	University of Toronto Law Journal
U.W.O. L. Rev.	University of Western Ontario Law Review
Western L. Rev.	Western Law Review
Western Ont. L. Rev.	Western Ontario Law Review

Index

This is a combined index and table of cases and statutes. Statutes mentioned in the text simply to illustrate the mode of arrangement or citation are not listed.